Global Directions: New Strategies for Hospitality and Tourism

Also published by Cassell

GLOBAL DIRECTIONS:
NEW STRATEGIES FOR
HOSPITALITY AND TOURISM

Edited by

RICHARD TEARE
BONNIE FARBER CANZIANI
AND
GRAHAM BROWN

CASSELL

Cassell
Wellington House
125 Strand
London WC2R 0BB

PO Box 605
Herndon
VA 20172

British Library Cataloguing-in-Publication Data

A catalogue record for this book is available from the British Library.

ISBN   0-304-33931-8   (hb)
　　　 0-304-33932-6   (pb)

Typeset by:
　　　The Bill Gregory Partnership, Polegate, East Sussex

Printed and Bound in Great Britain by:
　　　Redwood Books, Trowbridge, Wiltshire

CONTENTS

PREFACE

This book seeks to explore the interrelationships between the theory and practice of strategic planning and development in hospitality organizations and at tourist destinations by reviewing the literature and using case examples drawn from Europe, the USA and Australia. Specifically, the book contains thirteen chapters, divided into three self-contained Parts:

PART ONE: Strategic Planning
The aim is to provide a conceptual frame of reference for the book by means of a comprehensive review of the literature relating to the function, scope and realities of strategic planning. The purpose is to provide a concise, authoritative commentary on 'state of the art' developments as they relate to one aspect of strategic planning and its role in enabling hospitality firms to interpret trends and changes more accurately. This includes environmental scanning and trends analysis, the relationships between organizational structure, strategy and performance, the role of accounting and information systems in strategic planning and forecasting and the potential for enhancing team performance by widening the scope of involvement in planning. The five chapters in Part 1 concentrate on reviewing the concepts, systems and models applicable to strategy and development so as to provide a conceptual framework for applying topic principles to the process of strategic planning.

PART TWO: Organizational Development
The aim is to explain and illustrate the functional implications of change and development in hospitality firms by reviewing key concepts, models and systems relating to human resource management, environmental management, finance, marketing and service quality and information technology. Each of the five chapters in Part 2 focuses on one functional area for the purposes of (a) reviewing relevant literature and then (b) illustrating the implications for organizational design and development for a given function, using case examples drawn from North American hospitality firms. The purpose is to provide an account of how organizational development was or is being planned, developed and implemented in its commercial setting. Contributors have sought to illustrate the formation of strategies relating to the Part 2 organizational development theme and consider future initiatives that might be implemented.

PART THREE: Regional Development
The aim is to explain and illustrate the factors affecting tourism planning with particular reference to the debates relating to the development of tourism as viewed by developers and conservationists. Specifically each of the three chapters focuses on one aspect of regional development by (a) reviewing relevant literature; (b) illustrating key points using a case example drawn from an Australian tourism project; and (c) reviewing the implications for the

development of tourism in both specific and wider contexts. The purpose is to provide an account of how regional development was or is being planned, developed and implemented in its commercial setting and in so doing, illustrating the application of strategies related to the Part 3 regional development theme.

We are grateful to all the contributors and to the team led by Naomi Roth at Cassell for their support. We would also like to thank Sarah Beauchamp-Gregory the copy-editor.

RICHARD TEARE, BONNIE FARBER CANZIANI, GRAHAM BROWN
May 1997

CONTRIBUTORS

EDITORS

Richard Teare PhD FHCIMA is the Forte Professor of Hotel Management and Executive Director of CHART International, Department of Management Studies, University of Surrey, UK. A Non-Executive Director of the National Society for Quality through Teamwork, UK, he is Editor of the International Journal of Contemporary Hospitality Management and Research Director of the HCIMA's 'Worldwide Hospitality and Tourism Trends' CD-ROM. Dr Teare's publications include fourteen co-authored and co-edited books on aspects of strategic management and marketing in service industries.

Bonnie Farber Canziani PhD is an Associate Professor at the College of Business, San Jose State University, USA. She is a Regional Editor (Americas) of the International Journal of Contemporary Hospitality Management and works with service firms in the areas of: training and development and designing customer service systems. Dr Canziani is a west coast trainer in leadership and team management for the National Transit Institute, Rutgers University and has co-authored a book on training for hotels and restaurants. She is currently involved in multiple editing and research in services management and cross-cultural issues among others.

Graham Brown PhD is an Associate Professor, Centre for Tourism, Southern Cross University, Australia. He was a member of the Tourism Management Committee for Byron Shire for three years and currently serves as a member of the Cape Byron Headland Reserve Trust. Dr Brown was a Visiting Professor, Department of Management and Law, the University of Mauritius in 1993 and in the Department of Leisure and Recreation Studies, the University of Waterloo, Canada, in 1994. He was until recently, Regional Editor of the International Journal of Contemporary Hospitality Management in the Asia/Pacific region.

CONTRIBUTORS

Barbara A. Almanza PhD is Associate Professor, Department of Restaurant, Hotel, Institutional & Tourism Management, Purdue University USA. Prior to this, she taught at the Universities of Minnesota, South Dakota State and Illinois and worked as a Nutritionist and as a Consultant Dietician. Dr Almanza has served on the Editorial Review Boards of four journals and her research and publications span the study of how the health interests of foodservice customers influence their food choices, and aspects of waste management.

Jackie Brander-Brown is Senior Lecturer and Research Coordinator, Department of Accounting and Finance, Manchester Metropolitan University, UK. A chartered accountant, she has worked both in professional practice and as a financial controller for De Vere Hotels among others. She is currently undertaking a programme of part-time doctoral research at the School of Hotel & Catering Management, Oxford Brookes University specializing in the design of performance measurement and management accounting and control systems.

Kye-Sung (Kaye) Chon PhD CHE, is a Professor, Conrad N. Hilton College of Hotel and Restaurant Management, University of Houston, USA. A former hotel manager and tourism industry consultant, Dr Chon received his PhD in Hospitality and Tourism from Virginia Polytechnic Institute & State University. He is the founding Editor of the Journal of Travel and Tourism Marketing and is currently the Editor of the Hospitality Research Journal published by the Council on Hotel, Restaurant and Institutional Education.

Daniel J. Connolly is a Doctoral Candidate at Virginia Polytechnic Institute & State University, USA. A graduate of Cornell University, he received his MBA in Management Information Systems from The American University, Washington DC. He spent eight years working for the Marriott Corporation in the area of information systems where among many other projects, he created a competitive analysis and business intelligence programme to monitor key business and technology trends throughout the hospitality and foodservice industries.

Jorge Costa is a Research Associate, CHART International, Department of Management Studies, University of Surrey UK. A recipient of the Multi-Year Ambassadorial Scholarship from the Rotary Foundation, he has held several management appointments including the post of Head of the Marketing Department, Fernando Pessoa University, Porto, Portugal. He is a member of the WHATT-CD research team and has been a visiting lecturer at the IHTTI School of Hotel Management, Neuchatel, Switzerland and at several Portuguese universities.

Gavin Eccles is a Research Associate, CHART International, Department of Management Studies, University of Surrey, UK. A graduate of Sheffield Hallam University, he has travelled extensively and is the recipient of an Academic Scholarship Award sponsored by Cambells, UK Ltd. He is a member of the WHATT-CD research team and has been a visiting lecturer at the IHTTI School of Hotel Management, Neuchatel, Switzerland and the University of Algarve, Portugal.

Jonathan Edwards PhD is Reader in Land Based Studies, Department of Tourism and Retail Management, Bournemouth University, UK. He is also Course Leader of the School's BSc degree in Land Based Enterprise, with day-to-day responsibility for the operation of a Field Study Centre. His teaching and research responsibilities encompass aspects of tourism studies and European tourism management.

Livio R. Ferrone is a Senior Lecturer in Food and Beverage Operations, Department of Food and Hospitality Management, Bournemouth University, UK. He graduated from the Open University with a degree in Education and is currently engaged on a higher degree by research in the field of quality management. His research and professional interests lie in the areas of food production and service management.

Richard F. Ghiselli PhD is an Assistant Professor, Department of Restaurant, Hotel, Institutional & Tourism Management, Purdue University, USA. He has also taught at Northern Illinois University. A graduate of the University of Illinois and the Culinary Institute of America, Dr Ghiselli previously held a range of food and beverage and general management positions in clubs and restaurants. His research interests include solid waste management, employee deviance in food service and food service operations.

Peter Harris is Principal Lecturer in Accounting and Programme Director of the Master's degree in International Hotel Management at Oxford Brookes University, UK. His publications and research interests span the analysis of cost and revenue behaviour and the implementation of profit planning techniques in hotel organizations. He is Director, BAHA programme of Continuing Professional Education and a Visiting Professor at the Cornell University – ESSEC Institut de Management Hotelier International programme in France.

Hadyn Ingram is a Senior Associate, CHART International and Tutor, Department of Management Studies, University of Surrey, UK. He holds an MSc degree from Oxford Brookes University and is currently undertaking doctoral research in the area of teamworking and performance. He is a member of the UK WHATT-CD research team and a member of the HCIMA. He has extensive hotel general management experience and he owns a small town-centre hotel in Salisbury, Wiltshire.

Susan H. Ivancevich PhD, CPA is an Assistant Professor of Hospitality Accounting & Finance, Department of Tourism & Convention Administration, University of Nevada Las Vegas, USA. She received a BBA in Accounting from the University of Georgia and worked in public accounting for Arthur Andersen & Co. prior to taking a PhD in Accounting at Texas A&M University. The 1994–95 Hotel Association Professor of the Year, Dr Ivancevich is currently working on a textbook entitled Casino Accounting, Administration and Control.

William Y. Jiang PhD is an Associate Professor of Management, College of Business, San Jose State University, USA. He received his PhD and MPhil degrees in Industrial Relations and Human Resource Management from Columbia University and his research and teaching interests are executive compensation, incentive pay, and labour market analysis. A member of the Academy of Management, and the Association of Management, Dr Jiang has served as Chair of the Human Resource Group of the Association of Management.

Brian King PhD is an Associate Professor, Department of Hospitality & Tourism Management, Victoria University of Technology, Australia. Prior to entering academia, he worked in tour operations management and has held marketing positions in the airline and accommodation sectors. Dr King has also undertaken consultancy work for a number of organizations including UN-ESCAP and AUSAID. Author of three tourism marketing books and numerous articles, his research interests are in tourism marketing, planning and development.

Bob McKercher PhD is a Senior Lecturer and Course coordinator of the Tourism Management programme at Charles Sturt University, Australia. Prior to entering academia, he worked in the Canadian tourism industry where among other appointments, he served as Director of Canada's largest and oldest tourism trade association and developed tourism policies and strategic plans for the Canadian wilderness lodge industry. His research interests include tourism planning, sustainable tourism development and tourism marketing.

Michael D. Olsen PhD, is Professor of Strategic Management, Department of Hospitality & Tourism Management, Virginia Polytechnic Institute & State University, USA. Dr Olsen is Associate Editor of the International Journal of Hospitality Management and the Founding President of the International Academy of Hospitality Research. He has held visiting professorships in eight countries and his many publications include more than 150 articles and co-authorship/editorship of several books on strategic hospitality management.

Martin Oppermann PhD is a Senior Lecturer in Tourism at the Management Development Centre, Waiariki Polytechnic, New Zealand. Dr Oppermann received his PhD in Geography from Tubingen University, Germany and his main research interests lie in convention tourism and marketing. He currently serves as Editor-in-Chief of the recently launched Pacific Tourism Review, a quarterly refereed journal.

Paul A. Phillips PhD is a Lecturer at the Cardiff Business School, University of Wales, UK where he also received his MBA. He is a qualified accountant and marketer and has held senior line management positions in the UK as well as a senior consulting role for a leading multi-national consulting firm. His main research interests lie in the areas of strategic planning and performance, strategic management accounting, benchmarking and strategic control systems in hospitality organizations.

Gary Prosser is Professor & Head, Centre for Tourism, Southern Cross University, Australia. A sociologist, his current research examines the nature and extent of change in the social and economic characteristics of tourist destination areas. He has extensive experience of tourism planning throughout the Pacific Rim and maintains his involvement in industry affairs. He is an Associate Editor of the Journal of Tourism Studies and among other appointments, a Director of the Australian Tourism Research Institute.

Sarah Ridley is a Research Assistant, Centre for Culinary Research, Bournemouth University, UK. After graduating with a degree in Catering Systems she held a number of catering management positions prior to reading for an MSc degree in Marketing. She is currently undertaking a higher degree by research in the area of food service systems.

Alex M. Susskind is a Doctoral Candidate in the Department of Communication and an Instructor in the School of Hospitality Business at Michigan State University (MSU), USA. He holds an MBA from MSU, a degree in Culinary Arts from The Culinary Institute of America, and a Bachelor's degree from the Department of Restaurant, Hotel and Institutional Management at Purdue University. His industry work experience includes: food-service management, food production and hotel and restaurants consulting.

Roger Vaughan PhD is a Principal Lecturer in Tourism, Department of Tourism and Retail Management, Bournemouth University, UK. He has been an active researcher for many years and has conducted more than 40 studies relating to the evaluation of tourism and leisure provision in the community. He is a Fellow of the Tourism Society and was a member of the CNAA Register of Specialist Advisers (for Tourism).

Jannet Vreeland received her PhD from Texas A&M University and she is currently an Assistant Professor of Accounting at the University of Nevada, Reno, where she teaches financial, managerial and governmental accounting. Her research and publishing interests lie primarily in governmental accounting and reporting. Prior to pursuing an academic career, Dr Vreeland spent ten years working in Nevada's gaming industry.

PART ONE
STRATEGIC PLANNING

Richard Teare

INTRODUCTION AND OVERVIEW

In a business sense, hospitality and tourism organizations are no different from their counterparts in other service industries – they must compete for customers and use their resources wisely. The aim of Part 1 is to examine the planning dimensions relating to these tasks with reference to the external environment (chapter 1); the interrelationships between organizational structure and strategy (chapter 2); business performance (chapter 3); organizational culture and control (chapter 4) and competitiveness as determined by the interplay between structure, quality and teamworking (chapter 5). The approach throughout draws on a wide-ranging review of the literature and prior research so as to provide a conceptual frame of reference for the book. The purpose is to provide a concise, authoritative commentary on 'state of the art' developments as they relate to one aspect of strategic planning and its role in enabling hospitality firms to interpret trends and changes more accurately.

In order to make well-informed strategic decisions a wide array of information about the external environment is needed. The opening chapter reviews the concept of environmental scanning and, drawing on the evidence available from prior research studies and discusses the importance of external analysis to strategic planning. The chapter begins by considering the many ways in which external forces and events influence the organization and in view of this, contends that a systematic review of the external environment is the logical starting point for strategic planning. After this, scanning methods, models and applications are outlined. While as yet, there are few hospitality company examples of the integrated scanning-planning approach advocated here, there is little doubt that the benefits outweigh the costs associated with creating and building a linkage of this kind.

The relationships between the external environment and an organization's structures and strategies are dynamic ones and the extent to which adjustments can be manipulated or managed so as to achieve a desirable form of co-alignment is the central theme of chapter 2. In part, the degree of organizational flexibility and responsiveness to external change depends upon the features and characteristics of organizational design. A review of prior research reveals that hotel firms in particular have sought to monitor and balance the internal forces that more often than not, conflict with one another. The question of 'which way forward?' is not easily discerned when there are differing perceptions of the problem and these issues can be viewed more clearly by relating patterns of strategic behaviour to a typology. An empirically based structure and strategy effectiveness model is used to illustrate the main factors thought to affect co-alignment and this is reviewed with reference to hotel company examples. The chapter concludes by proposing ways in which the unit manager might play a more meaningful role in monitoring aspects of strategic fit, with particular reference to the customer interface.

It is widely assumed that strategic planning produces results in the sense that it assists the organization to perform better. While the planning-performance literature appears inconclusive, there are nonetheless indications that the two concepts are positively related and chapter 3 reviews empirical evidence drawn from strategic planning-performance studies published in the general and hospitality management literature. The chapter begins with a review of the various dimensions and phases of planning and compares and contrasts strategic planning with tactical and marketing planning so as to establish the context in which the planning-performance relationship can be critically examined. The analysis provides a basis for highlighting the key challenges for hospitality managers and the complexity arising from the contextual setting of organizations, in terms of enhancing performance through strategic planning.

It is increasingly recognized that organizational culture – the underlying values and beliefs that are shared by the members of an organization – has a significant influence on an organization's strategy. Chapter 4 explores this theme and the extent to which its influence should be formally recognized in the design of organizational control systems. Such control systems, which it has been argued are an inevitable characteristic of all forms of human organizations, are widely viewed as an essential element of the overall process of management, linking the processes of strategic planning and operational control. Given the importance of the international hospitality industry and the potentially serious consequences of imbalance or mismatch between organizational culture, strategic planning and management control, this topic merits closer scrutiny. Specifically, the chapter considers the variables that underlie an organization's culture and how they relate to planning and control and in a broader sense to organizational effectiveness.

Finally, chapter 5 considers the broad-ranging contribution that people make to the planning process, with particular reference to quality improvement and team-working in organizations. Starting from a structural perspective, the review considers the opportunities that can be derived from 'flatter' hierarchies in terms of releasing the human resource potential that exists inside organizations. A framework is used to draw out the links between organizational structure options, employee interaction and quality improvement strategies that might be used to maintain market-led, dynamic change in hospitality and tourism firms.

1

A Review of the Process of Environmental Scanning in the Context of Strategy Making

Jorge Costa, Richard Teare, Roger Vaughan and Jonathan Edwards

The main purpose of this chapter is to provide a conceptual framework for environmental scanning, to explain how the function is organized, how it is linked to strategic planning, and what strengths and weaknesses had been uncovered by organizations as they put the process into practice.

INTRODUCTION

Environmental scanning can be seen as the first step in the development of business strategies and the way by which organizations identify the main issues affecting them. By helping to detect opportunities and threats so that the organization may achieve a sustainable competitive advantage it fulfils two functions:

a)   informing strategy formulation; and
b)   monitoring for adjustments necessary as the environment changes.

In order to allow a better understanding of the main concepts used in the field of environmental scanning a review of the related key terms in this area of study will follow. (see Table 1.1).

Indicators	operational measures of environmental analysis
Trends	systematic variation of indicators over time
Patterns	meaningful clusters of trends
Segments	sections of the macroenvironment, such as social or political, created conceptually to facilitate analysis
Change	change in indicators, trends or patterns in one or more segments
Forces	the causes underlying changes or factors that cause such changes
Issues	environmental changes considered important in their implications for an organization
Projections/forecasts	future states of trends or patterns
Prediction	projections or forecasts accepted for strategic purposes
Analyst	an individual engaged in environmental analysis

Table 1.1: Key Terms in Environmental Analysis

THE CONCEPT OF ENVIRONMENT

Organizations are in constant interaction with their environment thus giving rise to a phenomenon termed in the literature as the 'environment-organizational interface' (Kefalas and Schoderbeck, 1973). The environment of an organization consists of the outside forces that directly or indirectly influence its goals, structure, size, plans, procedures, operations, input, output, and human relations (Segev, 1977; Preble, 1978). The importance of understanding the environment is demonstrated in research by Bourgeois (1985) where he shows that a firm which examines its environment accurately tends to achieve a higher than average level of economic performance.

The concept of environment and its effect on the organization (West, 1988) was introduced in the 'open systems' theory. The concept of an open system is based on the assumption that an organization's growth and survival is dependent on the nature of the environment that it faces (Fahey *et al.*, 1983). It has been recognized that different environments impose different demands and/or opportunities to organizations (Kefalas and Schoderbeck, 1973).

Thomas (1974) suggests that the application of systems theory to the corporate environment can be done by employing the concepts of 'resolution levels' or 'superordinate systems'. These can be grouped into two broad categories: 'operating environment' and 'general environment'. The operating environment[1] can be defined as the set of suppliers and other interest groups that the firm deals with, while general environment is defined as the national and global context of social, political, regulatory, economic and technological conditions (Thomas, 1974; Fahey and King, 1977; Daft, Sormunen and Parks, 1988). According to Daft *et al.* (1988), sectors[2] in the task and general environment are expected to influence scanning and other organizational activities because these sectors differ in uncertainty.

From the viewpoint of Thomas (1974) the analysis of the general environment is at least as important as the analysis of the operating environment for purposes of corporate planning. While sharing the same perspective, Fahey and King (1977) go further and look at the general environment as being more relevant to strategic planning and as requiring the greater degree of innovation in the information collection activities of businesses.

THE CONCEPT OF ENVIRONMENTAL SCANNING

The seminal work in this field was carried out by Aguilar (1967) and his purpose was to look at the ways in which top management gains relevant information about events occurring outside the company in order to guide the company's future course of action. In his study Aguilar (1967, vii) refers to environmental scanning as:

> scanning for information about events and relationships in a company's outside environment, the knowledge of which would assist top management in its task of charting the company's future course of action.

Presenting a similar perspective, Hambrick (1981) defines environmental scanning as the managerial activity of learning about events and trends in the organization's environment. Hambrick conceives it as the first step in the ongoing chain of perceptions and actions leading to an organization's adaptation to its environment.

The majority of authors (Kefalas and Schoderbeck, 1973; Keegan, 1974; Thomas, 1974; Fahey and King, 1977; Segev, 1977; Stubbart, 1982; Lenz and Engledow, 1986; Daft *et al.*, 1988) agree that the main functions of environmental scanning are:

- to learn about events and trends in the external environment;
- to establish relationships between them;
- to make sense of the data; and
- to extract the main implications for decision making and strategy development.

Despite being an established activity with well defined elements, environmental scanning is not in widespread use among business organizations (Jain,

1984; West and Olsen, 1989) and the scanning behaviour differs from one company to another (Hambrick, 1982; Farh *et al*., 1984; Lenz and Engledow, 1986; Daft *et al*., 1988; Preble *et al*., 1988; Olsen *et al*., 1994).

IMPORTANCE OF ENVIRONMENTAL SCANNING

Research shows that the degree of importance of environmental scanning in a company can be inferred by the way scanning activities are integrated into the overall planning process (Fahey and King, 1977). According to Jain (1984) as companies grow in size and complexity their need for formal strategic planning increases accordingly and with it the need for a systematic approach to environmental scanning. Thus, Jain adds that the effectiveness of strategic planning is directly related to the capacity for environmental scanning.

In this context Terry (1977) argues that the most obvious use for environmental scanning is gathering data for long range planning. Terry suggests that being such an important activity it can also be used for organizational development and design, development of agenda for executive boards or boards of management, and management education.

As organizations derive their existence from the environment they should scan and monitor their business environment and incorporate the impact of environmental trends on the organization by reviewing corporate strategy on a continuous basis (Jain, 1993). From Jain's standpoint scanning improves an organization's abilities to deal with a rapidly changing environment in various ways:

- It helps an organization capitalize early on opportunities;
- It provides an early signal of impending problems;
- It sensitizes an organization to the changing needs and wishes of its customers;
- It provides a base of objective qualitative information about the environment;
- It provides intellectual stimulation to strategists in their decision making;
- It improves the image of the organization with its public by showing that it is sensitive and responsive to its environment.

The information gathered by the environmental scanning process differs from industry or competitive analysis in two main aspects, it is broad in scope and it is future-directed (Stubbart, 1982). As such, environmental scanning should be conceptualized as a process of data collection about the business environment, which may help managers identify opportunities, detect and interpret problem areas and implement strategic or structural adaptations (Daft *et al*., 1988).

SCANNING CHARACTERISTICS AND PROCESSES

According to Murphy (1989) there are some characteristics of environmental scanning that can be seen as essential:

- It should be integrative – part of the planning and decision making system of the corporation;
- It should be relevant to strategic planning – focus on strategic issues and assistance in strategic decision making;
- It should take a holistic approach – so as not to miss any signals.

From Terry's (1977) viewpoint most environmental scanning will start in already existing organizations. Being so, much relevant data will be readily available like the company's mission and functional plans. These should be taken into account in setting up the process of environmental scanning, even though they may be radically altered after the scan has taken place. Drawing on this line of thought, the following considerations apply in designing an environmental scanning process (Terry, 1977):

- The scan needs to consider all possible influences in the company;
- The purpose of environmental scanning is not to foretell accurately the future, but to plot the issues which are likely to have impact on the company so it can be prepared to cope with them when they arise;
- The results of environmental scanning should be a proactive rather a reactive stance by the company towards its environment;
- It is not sufficient for managers to understand the plan that results from the environmental scan, it is crucial that they understand the thinking that has led to the development of strategic and tactical key issues;
- It should focus managers' attention on what lies outside the organization and allow them to create an organization that can adapt to and learn from that environment.

There are two distinct approaches within environmental scanning: the 'outside-in' or macro-approach, and the 'inside-out' or micro-approach (Fahey and Narayanan, 1986). The outside-in approach, adopts a broad view of the environment. It looks at all the existing elements in the outside environment facing the organization. Its main concerns are the longer-term trends, the development of alternative views or scenarios of the future environment and, the identification of the implications for the industry in which the firm operates and the implications for the firm itself. The inside-out approach takes a narrow view of the environment. It looks just for some elements in the outside environment as its view is constrained by the internal influences of the organization. For the main differences between these perspectives see Table 1.2.

THE CONTENT OF ENVIRONMENTAL SCANNING

The elements most commonly referred to as composing environmental scanning (Aaker, 1984; Fahey and Narayanan, 1986; Johnson and Scholes, 1993) are: political, economic, social, and technological elements, well known as 'PEST analysis'. The activity through which organizations collect data from these areas can be characterized as Irregular, Periodic, or Continuous, in increasing order of sophistication and complexity (Fahey *et al.*, 1981). According to these authors,

Irregular Systems are characterized by the reactive nature of planning as well as environmental scanning. On the other hand, they suggest that Periodic Systems are more sophisticated and complex, and, while the focus is still on problem solving, they exhibit greater proactive characteristics. Finally, they believe Continuous Systems are the ideal systems because attention is directed not only towards mere problem-solving but primarily towards opportunity-finding and the realization that planning systems contribute to the growth and survival of the organization in a proactive way.

	Outside-in	**Inside-out**
Focus and Scope	Unconstrained view of environment	View of environment constrained by conception of organization
Goal	Broad environmental analysis before considering the organization	Environmental analysis relevant to current organization
Time Horizon	Typically 1–5 years, sometimes 5–10 years	Typically 1–3 years
Frequency	Periodic/ad hoc	Continuous/periodic
Strengths	Avoids organizational blinders Identifies broader array of trends Identifies trends earlier	Efficient, well focused analysis Implications for organizational action

Source: Adapted from Fahey and Narayanan (1986)

Table 1.2: The Outside-in and Inside-out Perspectives

THE OUTCOME OF ENVIRONMENTAL SCANNING

The outcomes of environmental scanning, according to Fahey and Narayanan (1986), are:

- an understanding of current and potential changes taking place in the environment;
- the provision of important data for strategic decision makers; and
- the facilitation and development of strategic thinking in organizations.

Jain (1993) emphasizes that scanning serves as an early warning system for the environmental forces that may impact a company's products and markets in the future. As argued by Slattery and Olsen (1984) environmental scanning helps managers to foresee favourable and unfavourable influences and initiate strategies that will enable their organizations to adapt to the environment.

These outcomes can be divided into short-term and long-term outcomes. In the short term the outcome is to modify the company's actions in order to better explore opportunities and avoid threats. In the long-term the outcome is to inform the development of strategies.

However, while the outcomes of environmental scanning are very important the process of engaging in it is no less important (Fahey and Narayanan, 1986). Undertaking the process, according to these authors, leads to enhanced capacity and commitment in understanding, anticipating, and responding to external changes on the part of the firm's key strategic managers. Environmental scanning can be a powerful tool for strategic management if it has specific aims and objectives, and the commitment of the key players within the organization (Engledow and Lenz, 1989).

RESEARCH ON ENVIRONMENTAL SCANNING

Research on environmental scanning has followed different directions. Some studies focus their attention on the information-gathering activities of senior level executives (Aguilar, 1967; Kefalas and Schoderbeck, 1973; Keegan, 1974; Segev, 1977; Hambrick, 1982; Hoffman and Hegarty, 1983; Miller and Friesen, 1983). Other studies focus their attention on various analytical techniques and formal strategic planning systems (Post, 1973; Steiner, 1979; Lorange, 1982), while another approach (Narchal *et al.*, 1987) focuses attention on the social and psychological processes associated with organizational learning and executive decision making (Dill, 1962; Weick, 1979; McCaskey, 1982; Dutton and Duncan, 1983). Appendix 1 identifies the main research studies carried out in the field of environmental scanning, their research focus, research questions and/or hypotheses used.

THE RELATIONSHIP BETWEEN ENVIRONMENTAL SCANNING AND STRATEGIC PLANNING

As empirical research shows, any environmental scanning activity to be successful has to be linked to the formal planning process (Fahey and King, 1977; Jain, 1984; Engledow and Lenz, 1989). However, even though organizations realize and accept the need to relate environmental information to long-range plans, so far, most of them still perceive themselves as being primarily involved in relating environmental phenomena to short term choices (Fahey and King, 1977).

Jain (1993) proposes a seven step approach to explain the link between environmental scanning and corporate strategy in organizations:

1 Keep a tab on broad trends appearing in the environment;
2 Determine the relevance of an environmental trend;

3 Study the impact of an environmental trend on a product/
   market;
4 Forecast the direction of an environmental trend into the
   future;
5 Analyse the momentum of the product/market business in
   the face of the environmental trend;
6 Study the new opportunities that an environmental trend
   appears to provide;
7 Relate the outcome of an environmental trend to corporate
   strategy.

As Jain (1993) suggests, based on information about environmental trends and
their impacts, a company needs to review its strategy on two counts: changes
that may be introduced in current products/markets, and feasible opportunities
that the company may embrace for action. In fact, the identification of weak signals (Ansoff, 1990) in the business environment may provide the best opportunities in the long term for organizations.

SCANNING AND THE DEVELOPMENT OF STRATEGIES

The role of environmental scanning in organizations will vary according to the
concept of strategy applied. The concept of strategy varies according to the perspective of the author, and, as revealed by research, organizations also practice
different types of strategy. Glueck (1980) defines strategy as an:

> unified, comprehensive, and integrated plan . . . designed to ensure that the
> basic objectives of the enterprise are achieved.

There are other definitions of strategy which use the same approach. For
instance, from Quinn's (1980) viewpoint, strategy is the pattern or plan that
integrates an organization's major goals, policies, and action sequences into a
cohesive whole. According to this definition strategy can be seen as the framework that structures all the components needed to put the mission of the company into practice. A different perspective is the one developed by Mintzberg
(1994) where he defines strategy as a plan, or something equivalent – a direction, a guide or course of action into the future, a path to get from here to there,
and as a pattern, that is, consistency in behaviour over time. To better characterize these concepts, Mintzberg calls the former *intended strategy* and the latter *realized strategy*.

Strategy as a plan and strategy as a pattern, have different implications for
environmental scanning activities. According to research (Kefalas and
Schoderbeck, 1973; Fahey and King, 1977; Jain, 1984; Daft *et al.*, 1988), environmental scanning needs to be linked to strategic planning in order to be a successful activity. From this perspective, environmental scanning fits perfectly
into the planning process of the organization. However, in organizations where
strategies result from consistency in behaviour, the design of environmental
scanning activities for strategic decision making will have to follow a different
process.

As demonstrated by research (Kefalas and Schoderbeck, 1973; Fahey and King, 1977; Jain, 1984; Daft *et al.*, 1988), there is a strong link between environmental scanning and strategy making. While environmental scanning provides information for strategic decision making, the development of strategies justifies the need for environmental scanning by organizations. This justification is particularly important in periods of economic recession, when organizations try to cut down in costs, mainly in those departments where the importance of actions can only be assessed in the long term, as is the case with environmental scanning (Fahey *et al.*, 1981).

On the other hand, as Mintzberg (1994) argues, there are organizations where strategies are not made explicit, or simply do not exist formally. As strategies cannot be purely deliberate and a few can be purely emergent (Mintzberg, 1994), the most logical behaviour for an organization would be to develop some sort of formal planning process. However, considering that organizations will not formalize their strategies just to justify the creation of a scanning activity, the justification will have to originate from managers who must realize the importance of scanning the business environment for better decision making and planning, no matter what kind.

ENVIRONMENTAL SCANNING ACTIVITIES BY HOSPITALITY ORGANIZATIONS

In respect of hospitality organizations, despite the amount of empirical studies and the recommendations for them to undertake environmental scanning activities, research shows a different reality (Olsen *et al.*, 1994). In fact, according to Olsen *et al.* hospitality organizations are aware of the need to relate environmental information to long-range plans, but so far the majority are just relating this information to short-term decisions (Olsen *et al.*, 1994). According to the same study, managers are too concerned with the short term and, for this reason, their main goal is to get information about the economy, financing and customer needs and wants. This means that they are tempted to collect information through an informal process (Aguilar, 1967; Daft *et al.*, 1988). This being so, it is possible that one way to lead organizations to undertake environmental scanning activities, is to design the process in such a way as to fit the organization structures and needs and, as argued by Jain (1993), short-term scanning might be useful for programming various operational activities, as opposed to strategic planning activities.

ENVIRONMENTAL SCANNING MODELS AND THEIR APPLICATIONS

According to Gilbert (1993) a model can be defined as a theory or set of hypotheses which attempts to explain the connections and interrelationships between social phenomena. From his perspective, models are made up of concepts and relationships between concepts. As Gilbert proposes, a model can be used to make predictions about how the 'real world' will respond to changes, and the relationships specified in the model will also serve as an explanation of how the 'real world' works.

It can be said that corporate planning models are quiet recent when compared with other tools available in the business management field (Shim and McGlade, 1989). According to the same authors, the definition of a planning model varies with the scope of its application. In this context, the importance of an environmental scanning model resides in its potential to analyse more accurately the external environment and forecast business trends.

The need for a considerable amount of data about the external business environment is obvious when managers have to make certain business decisions. Information derived from within the company has little strategic value when it comes to the analysis of the task or general environment. In situations such as these, the collection of external data is a priority (Young, 1981). In order to better understand the application and use of environmental scanning models an analysis of the existing models will follow as a basis for identify their benefits and adequacy either for planning or non-planning companies.

Not all the authors writing on environmental scanning present models for scanning the environment. Some develop models either based on published information on the environmental scanning behaviour of organizations (Terry, 1977; Narchal, Kittappa and Bhattacharya, 1987; Ginter and Duncan, 1990; Camillus and Datta, 1991), or the findings of their empirical research (Aguilar, 1967; Fahey and King, 1977; Segev, 1977; West and Olsen, 1989), while others present frameworks or processes to follow when undertaking business environmental scanning (Kefalas and Schoderbeck, 1973; Keegan, 1974; Thomas, 1974; Aaker, 1983; Nanus and Lundberg, 1988; Murphy, 1989; Jain, 1993).

Some of these models provide a good illustration of the process of environmental scanning and the limitations to be overpassed when undertaking the activity. Five studies in particular (Aguilar, 1967; Fahey and King, 1977; Segev, 1977; Aaker, 1983; Jain, 1993) set up the context and highlight the steps to follow in order to develop an effective environmental scanning process. To better understand this process a detailed analysis of each of these studies will follow.

Aguilar (1967)

The first empirical study on the environmental scanning behaviour of organizations was carried out by Aguilar (1967). Aguilar's research concerns the kinds of external information that managers obtain and regard as important, the sources used by them to obtain this information and the ways by which this information was collected. It can be said that his work was essentially focused on recognition, search and internal communication of external information. As he states in his study, this was exploratory in the sense that it was more concerned with finding out what was happening than in 'proclaiming what should be happening'.

Modes of Scanning	Characteristics		
	Exposure to Information	**Purpose of Scanning**	**Recognition of relevance of data**
Undirected viewing	General	Not specific	Vague and tentative
Conditioned viewing	Direct	Signal a warning	Sensitive to prticular kinds of data
Informal search	Active	Looking for specific information	Act in a way that will improve the possibility of encountering the desired information
Formal search	Deliberate	To secure specific information or information relating to a specific issue	Follows a pre-established plan procedure or methodology

Table 1.3: Modes of Scanning and its Characteristics

In characterizing the scanning process Aguilar defines four different modes of scanning:

- undirected viewing;
- conditioned viewing;
- informal search; and
- formal search.

They differ between them in terms of their complexity of environmental scanning from the simplest form – undirected viewing – to the most sophisticated form – formal search. (See Table 1.3 for details.)

From Aguilar's viewpoint the real value of the concept of modes lies in the fact that it facilitates the understanding of not just what is happening, but why organizational scanning takes the various forms that it does.

This study by Aguilar gives us a first characterization of the different scanning behaviours of organizations and gives us the explanations for each particular mode of scanning. It has been the basis for the extensive research carried out in the field of business environmental scanning.

Fahey and King (1977)

Another important study is that by Fahey and King (1977) which consists of a descriptive analysis of a survey in which twelve large business organizations were questioned in depth about their environmental scanning activities. The objectives of the survey were the identification of environmental scanning processes and activities, and the assessment of the relationship of the activities to corporate planning. The study focused on the following aspects of environmental scanning (Fahey and King, 1977, p. 64):

> The scanning model used and any current changes occurring in the firm's scanning activities.
> The relative perceived importance of various environmental subsystems (social, political, regulatory, and so on) to the firm.
> The degree of integration of environmental scanning into the firm's planning process.

An important aspect of Fahey and King's study is the conceptual framework developed to characterize, evaluate and compare companies' scanning activities. Instead of four scanning modes, as developed by Aguilar, they present three scanning models (see Table 1.4) ranging from the less structured scanning activity, to the most complex one. The scanning models proposed are:

- the irregular model;
- the regular model; and
- the continuous model.

According to Fahey and King the irregular model can be seen as mainly a reaction to a 'crisis', while the regular model is more comprehensive and systematic than the previous and its approach is typically decision or issue oriented. The continuous model emphasizes the continuous monitoring of various environmental systems (political, regulatory, and competitive) and while the other models provide environmental information to support specific choices, the continuous model supports the variety of choices inherent in strategic planning.

Fahey and King's study provides an accurate analysis of the contemporary scanning activities by organizations and shows the range of different practices in use. As they demonstrate, despite the evidence shown by research towards the benefits of environmental scanning companies still face their business environment reactively and without any concern for its analysis and monitoring.

Characteristics	Scanning Models		
	Irregular	**Regular**	**Continuous**
Media for Scanning activity	Ad hoc studies	Periodically updated studies	Structured data collection and Processing systems
Scope of Scanning	Specific events	Selected events	Broad range of environmental systems
Motivation for activity	Crisis initiated	Decision and issue oriented	Planning process oriented
Temporal nature of activity	Reactive	Proactive	Proactive
Time frame for data	Retrospective	Primarily current and retrospective	Prospective
Time frame for decision impact	Current and near-term future	Near-term	Long-term
Organizational make-up	Various staff agencies	Various staff agencies	Environmental scanning unit

Source: Adapted from Fahey and King (1977)

Table 1.4: Scanning Model Framework

Segev (1977)

The process of environmental scanning faces other challenges in order to become an established organizational activity. Research conducted by Segev (1977) highlights some of these aspects. Segev's work is concerned with how formal scanning is actually used in strategy making and how the information is incorporated into strategic decision making. It is based on research conducted over a ten-year period in four organizations that had environmental analysis units (EAU) advising strategy-making teams (SMT). From the findings Segev developed a descriptive model of how environmental analysis[3] was being incorporated into strategic decision making. However, based on the analysis of this existing model he recommends another model to correct the 'malfunctions of the process'. This model (see Figure 1.1) focuses on deviations from the descriptive model and includes clarification of the participants' roles, changes in existing phases and their relationships, and recommendation of additional phases.

The descriptive model showed that scanning was performed by the SMT as an informal and unsystematic process (phase 1). To improve this activity Segev proposes a previous phase (1a) in order to transform environmental scanning into an 'on-going study of the environment' to be carried out by the EAU. This phase will also impact on the trigger (phase 3) and on the scanning behaviour of the SMT (phase 1).

Another proposed change occurs when moving from phase 2 to phase 5. The descriptive model showed the trigger (phase 3) as an event or set of events that initiated either strategy changes (phase 4) or a request for environmental data (phase 5). Segev proposes a different approach to this sequence which has to do with the creation of phase 11. The creation of this phase aims at facilitating the use of environmental analysis for changes in strategy (phase 4) which will lead to a request for environmental data.

The descriptive model presented phases 6 and 7 as separate phases. Phase 6 consisted in the assignment of environmental analysis project and definition of topic, carried out by the SMT and EAU and, phase 7 consisted in the operational definition of the environmental analysis topic, carried out by the EAU. From Segev's perspective, this two phase definition of a project instead of acting as a link between the strategy-making team and the environmental analysis unit served to 'magnify' the differences between the two groups. To solve this conflict he proposes the combination of the two separate phases so that the two groups can produce an assignment definition that can be used as an operational definition.

Finally, another change in the existing stages occurs in phase 10. The descriptive model showed an indirect impact of environmental data on strategy making affecting the SMT. Segev instead recommends more frequent exposure of the strategy makers to the data. He suggests that this additional exposure be achieved through periodical progress reports and, that this meeting between the two groups will also serve to familiarize analysts with the strategy makers' needs.

The so called 'malfunctions of the process' are due to a lack of interaction and clear communication between environmental scanners and strategy makers. The recommendations proposed by Segev are intended to bring the two groups into a closer relationship, so that the translation of environmental scanning into specific strategy changes can be performed co-operatively by analysts and strategy makers. This recommended model will allow environmental scanning to play a direct rather than indirect role in strategy making.

The conflicting relationship between scanners and planners is an important factor in the development of an environmental scanning process. This situation might explain the lack, or the improper use, of potentially useful information by companies, and also, the incorrect link between scanning and planning and consequent termination of scanning activities.

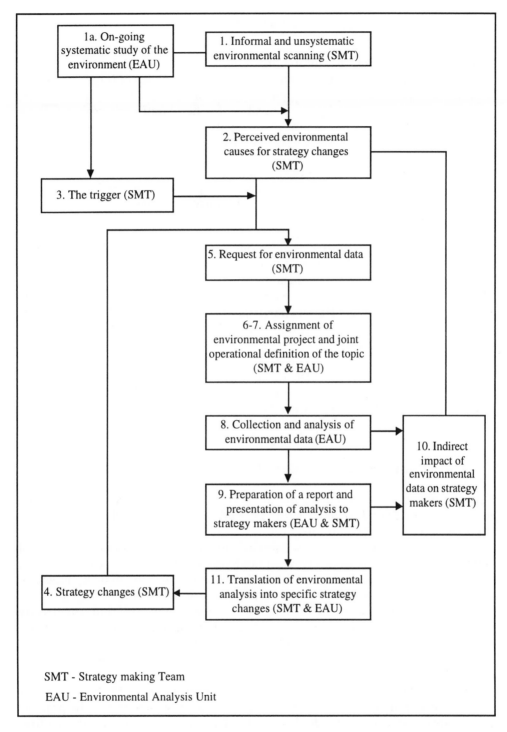

Figure 1.1: Recommended use of Environmental Analysis in Strategy Making

Aaker (1983)

Aaker (1983) proposes an interesting approach to environmental scanning. From his viewpoint, planning requires an external analysis of the environment and this analysis normally relies upon information that has been gathered in an *ad hoc* unsystematic way, by those involved in the planning process. From his perspective a considerable amount of information is exposed to managers but is lost, dissipated or unused. Aaker presents three reasons for this problem:

- The scanning effort tends to be undirected;
- The scanning effort is not partitioned among the participants;
- There is no vehicle to store and subsequently retrieve and disseminate the information.

To resolve this situation Aaker developed the 'Strategic Information Scanning System' (SISS), Figure 1.2, to enhance the effectiveness of the scanning effort and preserve much of the information now lost in the organizations. This system consists of six steps. Steps 1 and 2 specify information needs and sources, steps 3 and 4 identify the participants of the system and assign them to scanning tasks, finally steps 5 and 6 deal with the storage, processing, and dissemination of the information.

The information needs are often designed to identify emerging threats or opportunities, but they can also involve monitoring threats or opportunities already identified. As Aaker explains, information needs will be specific to a context, however, several general areas are often represented:

- competitors and potential competitors;
- market; and
- the environment that relates to the firm.

One important aspect is always to reduce the areas of information needed to a manageable number, by evaluating the actual or potential trends or events that are associated with such an area.

In regard to the information sources, the objective is to develop a list of sources that will comprise the core inputs to the strategic information scanning system. This list will consist of those information sources that organization members will be exposed to in the normal course of conducting business.

The participants of the SISS are those executives and staff that are directly involved in the planning process. Other members of the organization who are exposed to useful information sources should also be included. According to Aaker, *The purpose of the SISS is to capture and use that information that is available to the organization on a no-cost or low-cost basis.*

The assignment of scanning tasks is a core concept of the SISS. This 'partition' of the scanning task makes it manageable for those involved in the process. It consists of assigning individuals to scan information sources, considering first those regarded as highly useful. If several participants are assigned to the same information source it might be useful to divide it by information areas and, so explore the interests and backgrounds of the participants and at the same time reduce the scope of the task. On the other hand, the assignment task can also be organized by information need. According to Aaker, besides those with scanning assignments there will be others who will be exposed to useful information. In this case, if they are made aware of the strategic information scanning system and how to input information to it, they will be able to contribute.

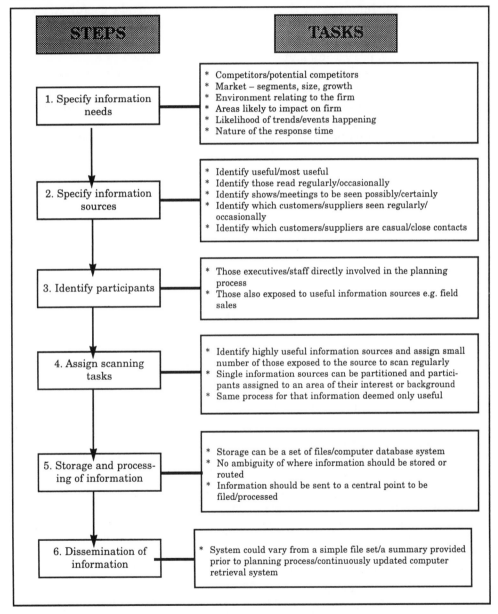

STEPS	TASKS
1. Specify information needs	* Competitors/potential competitors * Market – segments, size, growth * Environment relating to the firm * Areas likely to impact on firm * Likelihood of trends/events happening * Nature of the response time
2. Specify information sources	* Identify useful/most useful * Identify those read regularly/occasionally * Identify shows/meetings to be seen possibly/certainly * Identify which customers/suppliers seen regularly/occasionally * Identify which customers/suppliers are casual/close contacts
3. Identify participants	* Those executives/staff directly involved in the planning process * Those also exposed to useful information sources e.g. field sales
4. Assign scanning tasks	* Identify highly useful information sources and assign small number of those exposed to the source to scan regularly * Single information sources can be partitioned and participants assigned to an area of their interest or background * Same process for that information deemed only useful
5. Storage and processing of information	* Storage can be a set of files/computer database system * No ambiguity of where information should be stored or routed * Information should be sent to a central point to be filed/processed
6. Dissemination of information	* System could vary from a simple file set/a summary provided prior to planning process/continuously updated computer retrieval system

Source: Adapted from Aaker (1983)

Figure 1.2: Strategic Information Scanning System

Finally, Aaker argues that the storage and dissemination of information is crucial for the success of the system. He proposes a storage process that can be a simple set of files or a sophisticated computer-based information retrieval system. From his perspective the vital characteristic about the storage element is that organization members know where to send the information they have collected.

The Strategic Information Scanning System can provide useful strategic information which is achieved by focusing on target information needs, allocating effort among those exposed to relevant information and, having an effective system for storing, processing and disseminating information.

By following this simple and well organized process of environmental scanning, organizations are able to make full use of important available information, collected, processed and stored at a very low cost. This process proposed by Aaker is an interesting alternative to continuous scanning using an outside-in perspective, as looking at all sectors of the external environment is highly expensive and only large organizations will have the adequate resources to undertake such activity.

Jain (1993)

As mentioned before, an important aspect of environmental scanning is its relationship to strategy making. Jain presents an interesting perspective on the link between environmental scanning and corporate strategy. According to Jain, scanning serves as an early warning system for the environmental forces that may impact a company's products and markets in the future. However, despite its importance there is yet no accepted effective methodology for environmental scanning. From his perspective, the scanning activity in a company evolves over time, and there is 'no way to introduce a foolproof system from the beginning'. As he proposes, the level and type of scanning that a company undertakes should be custom designed, and a customized system takes time to develop into a viable system. Based on the above premises he presents the process by which environmental scanning is linked to corporate strategy (Figure 1.3).

According to the relationship presented in Figure 1.3 above, Jain recommends organizations to *Keep a tab on broad trends appearing in the environment*. As soon as the organizations have defined the scope of environmental scanning, they may periodically review broad trends in chosen areas.

The next step is to determine the relevance of an environmental trend as not everything occurring in the organization's environment may be relevant for it. Being so, there must be an effort to select those trends that are more likely to affect the organization.

The impact of environmental trends must be analysed as they can either pose a threat or an opportunity for the organization. The direction of these trends should also be examined because if an environmental trend appears to be significant for a certain product or market, it is important to determine the course it is likely to take.

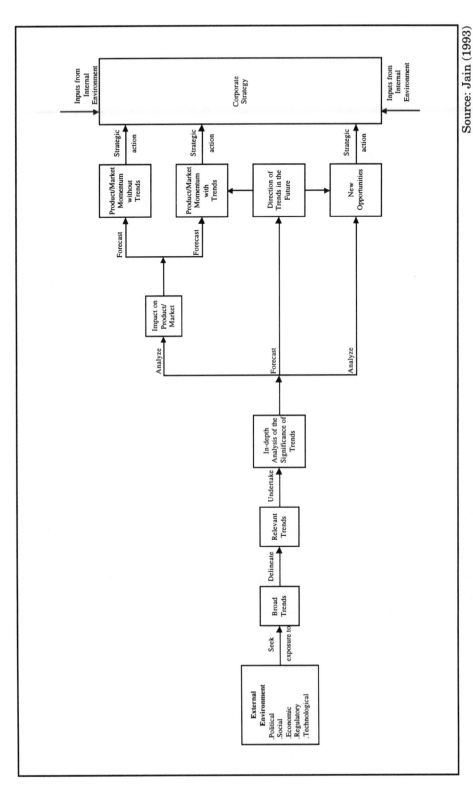

Source: Jain (1993)

Figure 1.3: Environmental Scanning Link to Corporate Strategy

At this stage organizations should analyse the 'momentum' of the product/market business with and without the impact of trends. It is important for organizations to develop two likely scenarios:

- what will happen if they do not take any measures to anticipate the trend; and
- what will the situation be if they plan to avoid or explore the threat or opportunity posed by the trend.

It is possible that the environmental trend will not be relevant for the near future of the organization, but it may indicate potential new opportunities in the medium- and long-term future. In this case, these opportunities should be monitored and analyzed for action.

Finally, Jain relates the outcome of environmental trends to corporate strategy. He proposes that, based on environmental trends and their likely impacts, organizations need to review their strategy on two counts:

- changes that may be introduced in current products/markets; and
- feasible opportunities that the company may embrace for action.

Jain's conclusion is rather important for the development of environmental scanning in organizations. As he states:

> Although procedural steps for scanning the environment exist, scanning is nevertheless an art in which creativity plays an important role. Thus, to adequately study the changing environment and relate it to corporate strategy, companies should inculcate a habit of creative thinking on the part of its managers.

Research clearly shows that companies should engage in environmental scanning in order to better explore opportunities and avoid threats. However, organizations are comprised of people, and ultimately the decision rests with the management whether or not to engage in environmental scanning. This activity is dependent upon the perspective and managerial approach of those in charge of the organization. According to this perspective and bearing in mind the existence of planning and non-planning companies, the scanning process has to be organized in such a way as to perform an important role in the company's strategy making, at a low cost and without absolute dependence of the formal strategic planning process.

RE-DESIGNING THE ENVIRONMENTAL SCANNING PROCESS

In order for companies to engage in environmental scanning the process has to match its needs and resources. One way to achieve this purpose is to take an inside-out perspective by selecting the areas where information is needed and the adequate sources to use. It is also important to choose the participants from those members of the organization exposed to relevant information and who possess the adequate background. They should be encouraged to develop a continuous process of environmental scanning, that explores the issues arising in the sources under analysis. According to the organizational structure, the information will be analysed, the importance to the organization will be inferred and storage/dissemination will be carried out by those members of staff playing vital roles in the strategy making process occurring, be it formal or informal. By following these steps the process of environmental scanning may be re-designed to perform the important role of information collection and analysis for strategic decision making, and at the same, time take into account the major limitations that normally affects the process, such as:

- too broad scope;
- lack of resources to undertake such a complex task; and
- the difficult justification for its existence if not linked to formal planning (see Figure 1.4).

CONCLUSION

As organizations exist in a certain environment, to survive they must carefully assess the state and changes occurring in this environment. Environmental scanning is a process through which organizations analyse the trends and patterns taking place in their business environment. Research shows that to be successful, scanning activities must normally be linked to strategic planning. However, business strategies are not just formally defined. They can be developed in advance of actions, or can be based on consistency in behaviour, which presents different settings for the implementation and development of scanning activities.

The literature review enables us to understand the environmental scanning process and its importance for the development of strategies. It also gives us the opportunity to analyse the limitations of the process when performed in certain circumstances. At this stage it is important to establish a link between the literature reviewed and the model proposed as an alternative to the existing models of scanning.

This establishment of such a link is possible thanks to important contributions in the field of strategy and environmental scanning (Aaker, 1983; Ansoff, 1990; Jain, 1993; Mintzberg, 1994; Olsen *et al.*, 1994) which allow us to critically evaluate the importance of scanning as practised by senior managers in the context of different modes of strategy making.

Working from this basis, the organization has to analyse its environment looking for those issues with the potential to affect its activity, which can be done by defining the strategic information need areas. This is achieved by adopting an inside-out perspective of environmental scanning. This approach will help the organization concentrate its attention in the most important areas of activity and scan them in order to detect, monitor and analyse, current and potential events and trends which may affect it in the medium- and long-term.

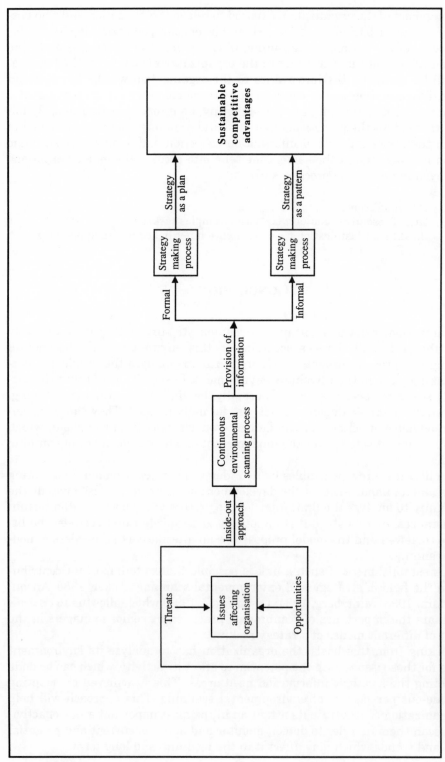

Figure 1.4: Environmental Scanning Process Re-designed

The principles underlying Aaker's (1983) Strategic Information Scanning System, are an important complement for the inside-out approach as they provide orientations for the selection of relevant sources and the assignment of scanning tasks. By following Aaker's system, the costs involved in setting up and running a continuous environmental scanning process will be minimal when compared to the advantages gained by developing the process.

By learning about events and trends in the external environment, the organization is able to establish relationships between them, make sense of the data and extract the main implications for decision and strategy making. Undertaking the process will allow an understanding of current and potential changes taking place in the environment, it will provide important data for strategic decision making, and facilitate and develop strategic thinking in organizations.

In order to achieve a sustainable competitive advantage organizations have to make their strategies taking into account their external environment, the main events and trends occurring in that environment, learn and adapt to the dynamics taking place and producing potential opportunities and threats.

APPENDIX 1. EMPIRICAL STUDIES ON ENVIRONMENTAL SCANNING

Authors	Research Questions and/or Hypotheses	Research Focus
Aguilar (1967)	What kinds of external information do managers obtain and regard as important? What sources do managers use to obtain this information? In which ways is this information collected?	Recognition, search, and internal communication of external information
Kefalas and Schoderbeck (1973)	Is the external environment of the companies in the study stable or dynamic? What is the average amount of time spent on acquisition of external information? What kinds of external information is acquired? What sources of external information are utilized by executives? What are the ways used by executives to acquire external information?	Examination of the relationship between external environmental characteristics and organization information-acquisition behaviour
Keegan (1974)	What are the main sources of external information used by executives? Are these sources internal or external to the organization?	Information sources utilized by headquarters executives in multinational companies
Fahey and King (1977)	What scanning model is used and what are the current changes occurring in the firm's scanning activities? What is the relative perceived importance of various environmental subsystems to the firm? What is the degree of integration of environmental scanning into the firm's planning processes?	Identification of environmental scanning processes and activities, and the assessment of the relationship of the activities to corporate planning

Authors	Research Questions and/or Hypotheses	Research Focus
Segev (1977)	How is formal analysis actually used in strategy making?	Incorporation of environmental analysis into strategic decision making
Hambrick (1981)	Is there an association between an executive's hierarchical level and scanning activity? Is there an association between an executive's functional area and scanning activity? Do these associations differ by industry?	Amount of scanning of different environmental sectors and amount of scanning overall
Fahey, King and Narayanan (1981)	What is the most sophisticated level of environmental scanning and forecasting that is in widespread current practice in various types of organizations? What is the average level of environmental scanning and forecasting that is in current practice? What are the future directions in which practice in the field should develop as viewed from various organizational perspectives?	Assessment of the most sophisticated and average levels of environmental forecasting and planning that are in widespread usage
Hambrick (1982)	The total amount of scanning conducted by executives in Prospectors is equal to the total amount conducted by executives in Defenders. Executives in Prospectors scan the entrepreneurial sector more than executives in Defenders. Executives in Defenders scan the engineering sector more than executives in Prospectors. The amount of administrative and regulatory scanning conducted by executives in Prospectors is equal to that conducted by executives in Defenders.	Relationships between the environmental scanning activities of upper-level executives and their organizations' strategies

Authors	Research Questions and/or Hypotheses	Research Focus
Stubbart (1982)	Information: How much? What kind? Where sought? Organization structure: Is there a unit? Number of persons and skills, reporting responsibility, relation to corporate planning department. Scanning process: Exchange of information with other units, contingency planning, variety and method of forecast, integration into corporate planning activities. Resources devoted to scanning: Money, man/months, types of personnel. Philosophy of scanning: What role does scanning have? Attitudes of top management, attitudes of other departments and divisions.	Use of greater resources and more formality in scanning and more continuous scanning methods
Culnan (1983)	Use of an information source will be positively related to perceptions of source accessibility. Use of information sources will be positively related to the perceived complexity of the task environment In a long-linked organization, staff employees will engage in more boundary-spanning activities and make greater use of external information sources than line employees.	Investigation of some of the variables that influence an individual's decision to use a particular information source for acquiring external information.
Jain (1984)	What leads companies to make a systematic effort to probe the future? What environments do they probe? What problems do they face in determining the corporate future? Does the evolution of strategic planning affect the scanning of the environment? If so, what lessons can be drawn from both the methods companies have pursued to connect strategic planning to environmental scanning and from the experience gained?	Evolution and state-of-the-art environmental scanning among corporations

Authors	Research Questions and/or Hypotheses	Research Focus
Farh, Hoffman, Hegarty (1984)	What are the important environmental traits (sectors, or segments) which the managers at the subunit level of analysis are likely to scan? What methods can be developed to assess the extent to which managers scan these environmental traits?	Study of environmental scanning as a source of decision influence to the subunit level of analysis among a sample of European executives.
Lenz and Engledow (1986)	How are environmental analysis units organized and staffed and where are they positioned within the hierarchies of corporations? What contingencies are of central importance when deciding on the organization and position of environmental analysis units? What conceptions of the organizational environment are used to guide environmental scanning and analysis activities? What are the advantages and disadvantages associated with various ways of organizing an environmental analysis unit?	Investigate corporations representing the most advanced administrative practice of environmental analysis
Daft, Sormunen and Parks (1988)	Sectors in the task environment create greater perceived strategic uncertainty for top executives than sectors in the general environment. Perceived strategic uncertainty across sectors will have a positive relationship with top executive scanning frequency. Perceived strategic uncertainty across environmental sectors will be positively associated with use of personal sources and negatively associated with use of impersonal sources of information about the environment. Perceived strategic uncertainty across environmental sectors will have a positive relationship with the use of	Introduction of evidence about the perceived uncertainty of external sectors, the means through which chief executives of manufacturing firms acquire information about those sectors, and chief executives' scanning patterns in

Authors	Research Questions and/or Hypotheses	Research Focus
Daft, Sormunen and Parks (1988) (Continued)	external sources and no relationship with the use of internal sources of scanning information. The relationships in hypotheses 2 through 5 will have higher correlations in high-performing organizations.	high- and low-per-forming companies.
Preble, Rau and Reichel (1988)	What is the nature of the scanning practices of Multinational Corporations? What are their environmental areas of concern? What is the nature and use of both internal and external sources of information? What are their forecasting techniques? How do they undertake risk evaluation?	Environmental assessment activities of US headquartered multinational firms
Engledow and Lenz (1989)	What is the structure of the analysis process in the organization? What are the links to planning? What models of the environment are in use? What are the problems in the process and implementation of the environmental analysis units? What is the history of the environmental analysis unit? What is the number and nature of personnel involved?	In-depth under-standing of advanced prac-tice of environ-mental analysis

Authors	Research Questions and/or Hypotheses	Research Focus
West and Anthony (1990)	What are the strategic orientations of the firms in the study? What are the performance differences between strategic clusters? What is the effect of environmental scanning (process) on strategic performance? Can performance differences within strategic groups be explained by individual firm scanning behaviour?	Identify and examine the performance differences between and among strategic groups in the industry and the assessment of the level of firm environmental scanning, to determine if it exerts a moderative effect upon the performance of individual firms within each strategic group
Kim and Olsen (1993)	What are the key issues in the political environment of NICs (Newly Industrialized Countries) considered important to hotel project development and business operation of the multinational hotel chain and its subsidiaries?	Identify key events in the political environment of NICs that impact the development and operation of hotels owned and managed by multinational hotel chains.

Authors	Research Questions and/or Hypotheses	Research Focus
Olsen, Murthy and Teare (1994)	Do CEOs (Chief Executive Officers) view various aspects of the environment of their operating domain as stable or volatile? How frequently do CEOs scan various categories of their environment? What level of interest do they have in scanning various events and trends occurring in their environment? Do they rely more on internal and personal than external and impersonal sources? Who is responsible for scanning activities in their firm? What types of decisions depend on the firm's scanning activities? What are the most important threats and opportunities for their firms in the next one- and five-year periods?	Assessment of environmental scanning practices in hotel firms and to learn how their executives view the uncertainty of the global business environment.

REFERENCES

Aaker, D. A. (1983). Organizing a Strategic Information Scanning System. *California Management Review,* 25 (2), 76–83.

Aaker, D. A. (1984). *Developing Business Strategy.* New York, John Wiley & Sons.

Aguilar, F. (1967). *Scanning the Business Environment.* New York, Macmillan.

Ansoff, I. and McDonnell, E. (1990). *Implanting Strategic Management.* 2nd Ed. London, Prentice Hall International.

Bourgeois III, L. J. (1985). Strategic Goals, Perceived Uncertainty, and Economic Performance in Volatile Environments. *Academy of Management Journal,* 28, 548–573.

Camillus, J. C. and Datta, D. K. (1991). Managing Strategic Issues in a Turbulent Environment. *Long Range Planning,* 24 (2), 67–74.

Culnan, M. J. (1983). Environmental Scanning: The Effects of Task Complexity and Source Accessibility on Information Gathering Behaviour. *Decision Sciences,* 14, 194–206.

Daft, R. L., Sormunen, J. and Parks, D. (1988). Chief Executive Scanning, Environmental Characteristics, and Company Performance: an Empirical Study. *Strategic Management Journal,* 9, 123–139.

Dill, W. (1962).The Impact of Environment on Organisational Development. *In:* Mailick, S. and Van Ness, E. (Eds.). *Concepts and Issues in Administrative Behavior.* Englewood Cliffs, NJ. Prentice-Hall.

Dutton, J. and Duncan, R. (1983). The Creation of Momentum for Change Through the Process of Organizational Sensemaking. *Working Paper,* J. L. Kellogg Graduate School of Management, Evanston, Northwestern University.

Engledow, J. L. and Lenz, R. T. (1989). Whatever Happened to Environmental Analysis? *In:* Asch, D. and Bowman, C. (Eds.) *Readings in Strategic Management.* London, Macmillan. 113–132.

Fahey, L. and King, W. (1977). Environmental Scanning in Corporate Planning. *Business Horizons,* August, 61–71.

Fahey, L., and Narayanan, V. K. (1986). *Macroenvironmental Analysis for Strategic Management.* St. Paul, MN, West Publishing.

Fahey, L., King, W. R. and Narayanan, V. K. (1981). Environmental Scanning and Forecasting in Strategic Planning – The State of the Art. *Long Range Planning,* 14 (1).

Farh, J. L., Hoffman, R. C. and Hegarty, W. H. (1984). Assessing Environmental Scanning at the Sub-Unit Level: A Multitrait-Multimethod Analysis. *Decision Sciences*, 14 (1), 197–220.

Gilbert, G. N. (1993). *Analyzing Tabular Data*. London, UCL Press.

Ginter, P. and Duncan, W. (1990). Macro-Environmental Analysis for Strategic Management. *Long Range Planning*, 23 (6).

Glueck, W.F. (1980). *Business Policy and Strategic Management*. New York, McGraw-Hill.

Hambrick, D. C. (1981). Specialization of Environmental Scanning Activities Among Upper Level Executives. *Journal of Management Studies*, 18, 299–320.

Hambrick, D. C. (1982). Environmental Scanning and Organizational Strategy. *Strategic Management Journal,* 3, 159–174.

Hoffman, R. C. and Hegarty, W. H. (1983). Cross-Cultural Research: A Model for Development of a Data Collection Instrument. *Proceedings of the Annual Meeting of the Academy of Management*. Dallas, Texas.

Jain, S. C. (1984). Environmental Scanning in US Corporations. *Long Range Planning*, 17 (2), 117–128.

Jain, S. C. (1993). *Marketing Planning and Strategy*. Ohio, South-Western Publishing.

Johnson, G. and Scholes, K. (1993). *Exploring Corporate Strategy: Text and Cases*. 3rd Ed. London, Prentice-Hall.

Keegan, W. J. (1974). Multinational Scanning: A Study of the Information Sources Utilized by Headquarters' Executives in Multinational Companies. *Administrative Science Quarterly*, 19, 411–421.

Kefalas, A. and Schoderbeck, P. P. (1973). Scanning the Business Environment. *Decision Sciences*, 4, 63–74.

Kim, C. Y. and Olsen, M. D. (1993). A Framework for the Identification of Political Environmental Issues Faced by Multinational Hotel Chains in Newly Industrialized Countries in Asia. *International Journal of Hospitality Management*, 12 (2), 163–174.

Lenz, R. T. and Engledow, J. L. (1986). Environmental Analysis and Strategic Decision Making: A Field Study of Selected 'Leading-Edge' Corporations. *Strategic Management Journal*, 7 (1), 69–89.

Lorange, P. (1982). *Implementation of Strategic Planning*. Englewood Cliffs, NJ. Prentice-Hall.

McCaskey, M. (1982). *The Executive Challenge*. Boston, MA. Pitman.

Miller, D. and Freisen, P. H. (1983). Strategy Making and Environment: The Third Link. *Strategic Management Journal*, 4, 221–235.

Mintzberg, H. (1994) The Fall and Rise of Strategic Planning. *Harvard Business Review*, January-February, 107–114.

Murphy, J. J. (1989). Identifying Strategic Issues. *Long Range Planning*, 22 (2), 101–105.

Nanus, B. and Lundburg, C. (1988). Strategic Planning. *Cornell Hotel and Restaurant Administration Quarterly*, 29 (2), 18–23.

Narchal, R., Kittappa, K. and Bhattacharya, P. (1987). An Environmental Scanning System for Business Planning. *Long Range Planning*, 20 (6).

Olsen, M. D., Murphy, B. and Teare, R. E. (1994) CEO Perspectives on Scanning the Global Hotel Business Environment. *International Journal of Contemporary Hospitality Management*, 6 (4), 3–9.

Post, J. (1973). Window to the World – A Methodology for Scanning the Social Environment. *Working Paper No. 175*, School of Management, Boston, MA. Boston University.

Preble, J. F. (1978). Corporate Use of Environmental Scanning. *Michigan Business Review*, 30 (5), 12–17.

Preble, J. F., Rau, P.A. and Reichel, A. (1988). The Environmental Scanning Practices of US Multinationals in the Late 1980's. *Management International Review*, 28, 4–14.

Quinn, J. B. (1980). *Strategies for Change: Logical Incrementalism*. Homewood, ILL, Irwin.

Segev, E. (1977). How to Use Environmental Analysis in Strategy Making. *Management Review*, 66, 4–13.

Shim, J. K. and McGlade, R. (1989). The Use of Corporate Planning Models: Past, Present and Future. *In:* Asch, D. and Bowman, C. (Eds.). *Readings in Strategic Management*. London, Macmillan.

Slattery, P. and Olsen, M. D. (1984). Hospitality Organizations and Their Environments. *International Journal of Hospitality Management*, 3 (2), 55–61.

Steiner, G. (1979). *Strategic Planning*, New York, Macmillan.

Stubbart, C. (1982). Are Environmental Scanning Units Effective? *Long Range Planning*, 15, 139–145.

Terry, P. T. (1977). Mechanisms for Environmental Scanning. *Long Range Planning*, 10, 2–9.

Thomas, P. S. (1974). Environmental Analysis For Corporate Planning. *Business Horizons*, 17, 27–38.

Weick, K. (1979). *The Social Psychology of Organising*. 2nd Ed. Reading, MA. Addison-Wesley.

West, J. J. (1988). *Strategy, Environmental Scanning and Their Effect Upon Performance: An Exploration Study of the Foodservice Industry*. Unpublished Doctoral Dissertation, Department of Hotel, Restaurant and Institutional Management, Blacksburg, VA, Virginia Polytechnic Institute and State University.

West, J. J. and Olsen M. D. (1989). Environmental Scanning, Industry Structure and Strategy Making: Concepts and Research in the Hospitality Industry. *International Journal of Hospitality Management*, 8 (4), 283–298.

West, J. J. and Anthony, W. P. (1990). Strategic Group Membership and Environmental Scanning: Their Relationship to Firm Performance in the Foodservice Industry. *International Journal of Hospitality Management*, 9 (3), 247–267.

Young, R. (1981). A Strategic Overview of Business Information Systems, *Managerial Planning*, 29, 28–37.

---

1   The operating environment is sometimes referred to as 'specific environment', 'immediate environment' and/or 'task environment'.
2   Sectors are the main elements comprising both task and general environment, i.e., competitors, suppliers, social, political, etc.
3   Some authors like Olsen *et al* (1993) use environmental scanning and environmental analysis interchangeably. As can be seen by Segev's definition of environmental analysis it comprehends the same elements and relationships as those described by Aguilar (1967) in his definition of environmental scanning.

2

The Relationship Between Organizational Structure and Strategy

Gavin Eccles, Richard Teare and Jorge Costa

Overview

This chapter addresses the alignment between structure and strategy at unit level and considers the changing role to be played by unit hotel managers. The match is becoming increasingly important for hotel firms in attempting to gain competitive advantage, be it in terms of the overall organization or more specifically, an attempt to increase customer satisfaction. Therefore, the structure of the organization has a significant influence upon business influence and success. This chapter is split into three parts: Part 1 – Structure and Strategy Co-Alignments; Part 2 – Structure and Strategy Co-Alignments in Hotel Management; and Part 3 – Implications Arising from Alignment Within Unit Hotel Management.

PART 1: STRUCTURE AND STRATEGY CO-ALIGNMENT

The hotel sector of the UK hospitality industry in the first half of the 1990s has faced an increasingly competitive and changing marketplace as well as a highly unpredictable external environment. (See Figure 2.1 below.) To a large extent both of these concerns have been outside the firm's control. Further, the 1990s may also see a movement towards individual hotel units becoming much more responsible for their own strategic decisions, where unit hotel managers may have to perform as strategic-thinkers, as well as practising their daily operations-oriented role. In order for this to be fulfilled, managers may need to consider their unit structure in the light of having to match or align their strategic decisions.

When considering the role that hotel managers play within their own unit, it can be noted that they exert little influence on the firms' overall long-term corporate policies. Rather, units become responsible for their business\tactical decisions, where action can be taken immediately to enable them to be more responsive to strategic decisions made by head office and be more pro-active to change occurring in markets and localized and regional environments. This chapter proposes a framework which managers might use to align their unit structure with the business decisions they make. Through appropriate alignment, the hotel is able to maintain a pro-active stance and remain responsive, in terms of satisfying customers, thus securing their competitive advantage.

Curtis (1993) notes that firms operating in the hotel sector are experiencing both competitive and changing times and suggests the reasons being :

- a biting recession which forces corporate hotel users to cut back on travel expenses and subsidiary hotel uses and, leisure tourists to actually reduce their expenditure;
- fluctuating exchange rates which are a powerful determinant of overseas demand;
- a dramatic growth in bedroom stock in the latter half of the 1980s, stimulated by the boom economy of 1986–1989;
- the spread of lodges and budget hotels has increased tension within the marketplace;
- hotels are faced with the stark reality of a fight to stay in business and are therefore:
  1 cutting costs and slimming staff numbers;
  2 frequently 'adding value' to services offered;
  3 engaging in tactical pricing – special offers, room only prices; resulting in:
- falling market demand, crippling debt and declining sales values that has led to an increase in the number of hotels placed in receivership;
- the increased use of franchizing and management contracts as a way of making profits with insubstantial risk.

Curtis concludes *that the state of market depression will not be relieved until demand returns and hotel revenues improve,* which is not foreseeable in the intermediate term. Contrary to this, Slattery (1995) notes that the hotel sector entered 1995 *on a trend of developing more effective supply, growing demand and improving operating practices.* His findings note that these next few years present better opportunities than at any other time in the 1990s.

Figure 2.1: A Changing and Competitive Marketplace

INTRODUCTION

Olsen (1993) explains that to increase performance levels in the hotel sector, firms may soon have to focus their development on co-aligning structure and strategy. Olsen summarizes his findings:

> without co-alignment between structure, strategy and the environment organizations may find difficulty in achieving long term success.

It is notable that much of the research relating to alignment in hotel firm settings originates in the United States and the intention in Part 1 is to review and interpret existing empirical work. Several of the key studies relating to this topic are summarized below :

Authors	Key Findings
Miles and Snow (1978)	Generation of four typologies to characterize organizations in terms of how they behave strategically. **Co-alignment** – organizations develop objectives, define strategies and then construct mechanisms to pursue their decisions.
Schaffer (1984)	The way organizations are structured can be influential in determining performance. **Co-alignment** – organizations conduct an external analysis, define strategies according to purpose, goals and objectives and then develop a structure that best fits their requirements
Schaffer (1986)	If organizations are to meet their objectives, they must seek to inter-link their competitive strategies and organizational structure. **Co-alignment** – after analysing the external environment, managers choose appropriate competitive strategies and then develop structures that properly support these decisions.
Miller (1989)	Successful strategies are dependent on more than just structure and need to take account of economic factors as well as international markets. **Co-alignment** – organizations first select their structure and then base their strategic decisions upon this. The strategic alternatives are drawn from Porter's generic strategies.

In relation to the above, co-alignment can be seen as the appropriate fit between an organizations' structure and its strategies. Defined more simply, organizational strategy tends to be more successful if implemented within a supportive, suitable structure. This process also requires an appreciation and understanding of the external environment, monitoring current trends and changes, enabling the three component parts (structure, strategy and environment) to work together in the best and most responsive way. The diagram below helps to explain this relationship:

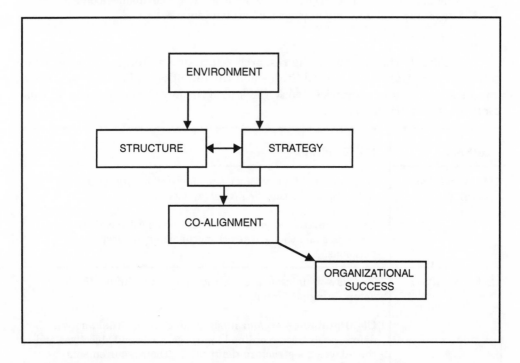

Figure 2.2: Relationship Between Structure, Strategy and Environment

Olsen (1989) observes that the hotel sector has been experiencing an accelerating pace of change and the way to respond is to contrive new situations, where: *the fittest will be those who are most successful in matching their strategy and structure* taking into consideration the dynamics of the external environment.

DEFINITIONS OF ORGANIZATIONAL STRUCTURE

Burns and Stalker (1961) and Chandler (1962) define structure as a process – a way of creating an organization to control their external environment. Organizations that operate in changing and uncertain environments tend to have *organic/flexible structures and processes*, allowing employees to react to changes in an attempt to generate tactical decisions. When operating in stable environments firms tend to have *mechanistic/highly bureaucratic structures*, where employees know their organizational role and thus work accordingly. It is through this bureaucracy that firms are able to gain a cost leadership form of competitive advantage. These findings imply that organizations can use their structure as a means of gauging the best ways of deploying resources to meet company objectives, noting the relationship as the *sequential pattern of environmental changes causes revisions of strategy and evolving organizational structures.*

Further studies have considered organizational structure, Thompson (1967), Pugh *et al.* (1968), Inkson *et al.* (1970), Child (1972), Reimann (1973), Bower (1982), Fredrickson (1986), Miller and Droge (1986) and Schaffer (1986), all note that structures within organizations provide:

- a formal allocation of work rules;
- channels of collaboration;
- clarification of the lines of authority and communication;
- an allocation of power and responsibility;
- prescriptive levels of formality and complexity.

ORGANIZATIONAL DESIGN

Ullrich (1976) explains that as businesses are dragged unwillingly into an era of unprecedented social and environmental change, the development of a firm's structure can influence business performance. Structure is therefore a crucial variable for firms trying to gain competitive advantage over their competitors, as structural changes influence the planning process and increase understanding of their environment. Likert (1967), notes the management value that organizations provide:

- support to employees;
- opportunities for group decision making;
- opportunities for group supervision;
- the establishment of goals.

Miles and Snow (1978) review organizational design, defining organizations by the strategic behaviour type that they adopt. Their research is based on the development of differing strategy types which can be used to interpret and solve problems – *analyser, defender and prospector*. Definitions of the strategic types are as follows:

1 Defender – Protect current market share
⇒ Retrenchment strategy;
2 Analyser – Protect current market share and locate new opportunities
⇒ Market penetration strategy;

3 Prospector –   Locate and exploit new product and market
                    opportunities
                    ⇒ Growth, product and market development strategy.

A fourth strategy type, *reactor*, referred to as strategic failure, is identified and arises when the fit between the two variables is inappropriate. Reactors are also characterized by differing degrees of instability. An adaptation of this work by Miles and Snow (1978) was undertaken by Webster and Hudson (1992), who conclude that:

> a model has been created which shows that the performance of an organization is largely the outcome of a series of choices made by the creators or top echelons of the organization

A different perspective is provided by Tannenbaum (1962) who explains that there is a relationship *between the type of influence processes found in an organization and the organization's effectiveness*. Further, Lawrence and Lorsch (1967) note that organizations that are most effective are characterized by differences within their departments, whilst those organizations that are least effective adopt a structure which is similar across all departments.

STRATEGY AND THE ENVIRONMENT

Before attempting to relate strategy to the environment, an understanding of strategy is required. Quinn (1980) defines strategy as *a pattern or plan that integrates an organization's major goals, policies and action sequences into a cohesive whole*. Contributions from Chandler (1962), Ansoff (1979) and Steiner *et al.* (1982) suggest that strategy is actually about integration, which needs to be based on good management practice. Their works explain that strategy is concerned with formulating objectives, defining a purpose and then setting rules and guidelines to carry out the proposals. A somewhat different explanation of strategy is proposed by Webster (1994), who refers to strategy *as being the building block of strategic management*. Therefore if the foundations are not laid down securely (strategy), the whole process, (strategic management), will not function properly within the organization. Webster finally adds that strategy can be seen as a linking process between where the organization is at present and where it would like to be in the future.

Strategy also considers both corporate and competitive strategic decisions. According to Johnson and Scholes (1993), corporate strategy refers to those decisions that cover the whole organization, i.e. the mission. This belief has arisen from prior work undertaken by Porter (1987), who explains that corporate strategy embodies both the overall plan of the organization and *brings together the diversified divisions of the company*. Therefore, organizations need to develop corporate strategies, as this enables employees to know exactly what their organization is concerned with and the part they must play. Further, both Porter (1987) and Johnson and Scholes (1993) recognize that organizations need a second level of strategy, 'competitive strategies'. These decisions take place at the business level and refer to the making of quick decisions when faced by sudden changes within their environment.

It can also be noted that the environment plays a key role in generating strategy and ultimately in achieving a successful match, as some decisions only function effectively within particular situations. As the environment becomes less predictable scanning needs to take place, helping organizations in their efforts to generate successful decision making theories (Thompson 1967).

	STABLE/CONTROLLED ENVIRONMENT	CHANGING/UNSTABLE ENVIRONMENT
STRUCTURE	Tight structure	Loose structure
STRATEGY	Cost leadership Bureaucracy	Differentiation Innovation

Adapted from Glass, M. (1991). *Pro-Active Management*. London, Cassell. 44–47.

Table 2.1: The Link Between Environmental Volatility/Stability and Structure and Strategy

Table 2.1 highlights the relationship between the environment and its impact upon structure and strategy. It proposes two types of environment, stable and changing and the appropriate structure and strategy linkages that organizations need to consider when attempting to take advantage of the external environment. Therefore, a tight organizational structure can be adopted when operating within a stable environment, aligned with a strategy of bureaucracy and cost leadership. The rigid structure allows employees to work productively to attain the goals of the organization.

Likewise, organizations also interact with environments that are constantly changing and unstable, thus effecting the most appropriate fit. Emery and Twist (1965) define this environment as a 'turbulent field', where change develops in the general environment and soon impacts upon the specific environment. According to Olsen (1989):

> the existing complexity of the environment is expected to increase, as will variability and uncertainty; the hospitality manager must be capable of knowing and understanding the events which occur in his/her business and general environment.

Given this scenario of environmental uncertainty it may be appropriate to explore the benefits of a loose structure, where differentiation and innovation can unfold. According to Glass (1991), Competitive times call for changes and by being innovative the organization can gain a competitive advantage. Without implementing a loose structure, a hierarchical firm is likely to experience difficulties in reacting to a change and therefore may ultimately lose business opportunities.

The relationship between strategy and the environment has been elaborated by a range of empirical studies as reflected by the contributions cited in Table 2.2:

Authors	Findings
Leontiades (1982)	Devising strategy in intensely competitive situations where strategy is used to respond to uncertainty.
Hofer and Schendel (1986)	A changing and competitive environment can play a major part in generating strategic decisions for organizations.
Peters (1987)	Faced by an upside-down world, those firms that develop strategies to take account of the environment have a better chance of remaining successful.
Schaffer (1987)	Organizational strategy is conceived as the means by which organizations attempt to link with and respond to their environment.

Table 2.2: Empirical Studies Concerning Strategy and the Environment

STRUCTURE AND STRATEGY ALIGNMENT

Due to the complex dynamics in any given market environment, the fit (alignment) between structure and strategy is not a one-time event. Hospitality organizations must continually re-orientate their business if they wish to match their competitive strategies with their organizational structure. Work undertaken by Schaffer (1986) considers this notion in US hospitality markets and notes:

> the mere choice of an appropriate competitive strategy will not ensure high performance levels unless organizational structure is appropriate and fits the strategy.

Miller (1989) observes that *the most effective combination of structure and strategy arises when the winner among competing organizations survives at the expense of its counterparts.*

Tse and Olsen (1990) observe that *success in strategy implementation depends partly on whether a firm's strategy is congruent and complementary with its structure* and they advocate the adoption of one of three generic structural types:

- Formalization;
- Complexity;
- Centralization.

A formal structure is characterized by rules, procedures, policies and instructions. Employees know their role within the organization and therefore work accordingly. Operational strategies relating to simple tasks may operate better within this structure, as there is little room for initiative to unfold. A complex structure is typified by a division of work both vertically and horizontally, allowing people to operate within different fields according to the amount of specialization and degree of personal expertize within the firm. Finally, a centralization approach can be adopted in helping to align the organization with its intended decisions. Here, decision-making authority is delegated to those performing significant functional tasks or related to hierarchical decision-making. This approach seems to work best when firms are operating in a stable environment, where the firm is forced to operate somewhat differently in order to differentiate its offerings. A cost leadership position will work best under this structural type, as power is controlled by a few people.

When considering alignment and the related performance impact, the literature in this area points to a link between organizational effectiveness and structure (Mintzberg, 1979, Schaffer, 1986, Miller, 1989 and Tse and Olsen, 1990). This then helps to explain the relevance of co-alignment to the planning process, as those organizations that devise structures to match strategy will be better placed to implement decisions. The key issue in this is the extent to which managers can create a more vibrant business climate, so that the staff catch this vision and adapt to become more responsive and pro-active. The outcome from alignment is that firms are able to increase sales and market performance, a vitally important consideration in today's environment. Olsen (1989) defines probable reasons for a failure to match structure and strategy:

- a high growth industry, ignoring weak markets in favour of new markets and opportunities;
- inexperienced management competing in a competitive and mature market;
- management has borrowed both ideas and theories from manufacturing firms and sought to apply them to a service industry setting;
- failure to ensure that structural change reflects prevailing conditions in dynamic markets;
- the inability of managers to adjust to new market conditions;
- Inability to relate structure and strategy to the operating environment.

Olsen's work suggests that is the main reason for alignment failure in hotel firms is inertia. The 1970s witnessed rapid industrial growth, characterized by the emergence of chains with highly structured and formal organizations creating a form of negative inertia that slows down decisions and according to Olsen (1989), . . . *can quickly bring a large multi-unit hotel chain to a halt.*

SUMMARY AND IMPLICATIONS

- Organizations need to be aware of their external environment through the implementation of an environmental scanning programme, in order to generate an understanding of the issues that they may face. Environmental concern is one of the most important issues in alignment, thus helping to develop future strategic decisions;
- Those markets which can be referred to as changing are best served by an organic or flexible structure. This allows the firm's employees to generate tactical decisions in an attempt to gain marketplace competitive advantage. A stable or predictable environment though requires a mechanistic or bureaucratic structure, where employees continue as normal, in a vain attempt to gain 'cost leadership' competitive advantage;
- Finally, the alignment process is not a one-time business event. Instead, organizations need to constantly engage themselves in attempting to establish the most appropriate fit. Once achieved, the process has to be continually monitored, taking into consideration any changes in the external environment that may influence their strategic decisions.

Part 2 aims to consider alignment and the unit hotel manager, an area that according to Olsen (1991) will see managers becoming much more responsible for the implementation of strategic decisions. This change can be referred to being a move from an operations-oriented managerial role to one which requires strategic-thinking, where success is realized through the greater involvement of people, so as to harness in full, the talents within the organization.

PART 2: STRUCTURE AND STRATEGY CO-ALIGNMENT IN HOTEL MANAGEMENT.

Arising from Part 1, this second part focuses upon co-alignment in hotel unit operations. The intention here is to establish a conceptual framework which illustrates the application of structure and strategy to the process of strategic planning, drawing upon examples selected from international hotel chains.

This match between structure and strategy is seen as an area that organizations do not always consider and a successful corporate fit is more likely to occur by chance than design. Therefore, the intention here is to explore the sources of competitive advantage that improved organizational performance can bring in the context of alignment. The adaptation of several models helps to explain the work undertaken in this field, backed-up by means of a descriptive model that offers a self-assessment perspective on the extent of structure and strategy relationships.

INTRODUCTION

According to Olsen (1989), during the last ten years the hotel sector has faced both industry maturity as well as the emergence of strategies based on defending current market and product positions. The rapid growth of the 1980s has passed and those firms doing well in the 1990s tend to be *the fittest and direct their strategies to reflect the conditions that exist in this type of environment* (Olsen, 1989).

In this sense, hotel firms need to consider:

- the evolving nature and characteristics of a mature marketplace;
- the relevance of strategies for protecting market share in the face of competition;
- the decentralization of organizational structures, to allow decisions to be taken at lower levels of the hierarchy;
- the recruitment and selection of managers who are sufficiently adaptable to interpret and respond to a competitive and dynamic environment;
- the development of a strategic-thinking unit managerial approach within the functional areas of the business (finance, human resources, marketing and administration).

Olsen notes that unit managers may need to change the way they think and act, evolving from a single-unit perspective to a broader multi-unit vision and professional style of management.

REVIEW OF EXISTING CO-ALIGNMENT MODELS

Schaffer (1986) explains that *for a hotel company to succeed, it must match up its competitive strategy and its organizational structure according to the realities of the market.* Writing at a time when the hotel sector faced an unpredictable/unstable marketplace, the author created a strategic choice model for organizations, that considers the problems organizations face in attempting to align structure and strategy within particular market environments:

The main implication arising from this model is that managers need to be constantly aware of the environment in which their product is to be positioned, allowing for the successful implementation of their plans. Further, organizations need to develop a structure that is supportive of these decisions. In terms of explaining Schaffer's strategic choice model (1986), it is noted that managers face three problems:

- entrepreneurial – consideration for the external environment;
- competitive   – selecting strategies that ensure success within their product and market domain;
- administrative – choosing an appropriate structure that ensures a strategic fit.

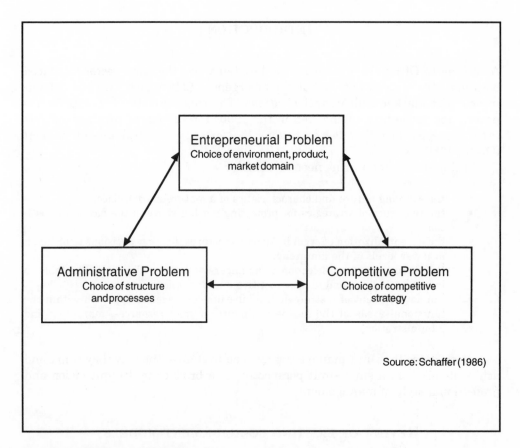

Figure 2.3: Strategic Choice Model

The outcome of Schaffer's model is that managers should have a thorough understanding of their business environment and the products and markets they seek to serve. Their strategic decisions will incorporate findings taken from the external analysis and thus implemented within an organization framework that is ready to accept these ideas.

Miles and Snow (1978) also considered ways of improving organizational performance in relation to strategy and structure. Their work, though not conducted in the hotel sector, revealed that organizations tend to select strategies, referred to as choosing a 'product-market domain' and then construct a mechanism, 'structure and process'.

Miles and Snow note that organizations should start from a business objective, typically protecting their current market share, or locating new opportunities. After deciding the strategy that they are to follow, an appropriate structure is defined, based on the premise that the firm either needs a less hierarchical approach or one that is highly centralized.

After completing these three stages, the organization will have adopted one of three generic positions – *defender, analyser or prospector*.

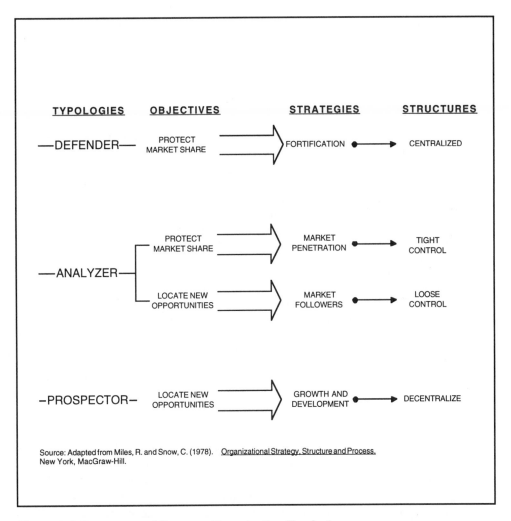

Figure 2.4: Structure and Strategy: Organization Typologies

Defender

The organization's objective is to protect its market share by concentrating on improving the efficiency of its existing operation. This is achieved through defensive strategies, including:

- narrowing the product/market domains;
- developing within existing target markets;
- attempting to reduce costs but improving quality;
- standardizing the firms service procedure.

This defender typology requires a centralized or bureaucratic organizational structure where employees concentrate solely on company policies and procedures. According to Schaffer (1986), Marriott Hotels have successfully followed a defender-strategy approach, as their mission focuses on being efficient, productive, controlled and profitable.

Prospector

If the organization adopts a prospector approach its aim is to find and locate new product and market opportunities by responding to emerging environmental trends. The strategies focus on growth and development and consider:

- responses to new market trends;
- product and market innovation;
- investment in infrastructure support such as its environmental scanning process;
- long-term capital investments;
- the development of prototype services/products.

If this approach is to be adopted, a decentralized and flexible structure is required, encouraging employees to express innovative ideas. All employees are encouraged to assist in locating new product and market opportunities, as well as discussing the relevant strategic decisions to be made.

Analyser

Within this typology, the firms objective is to either protect current market share (defender), or locate new opportunities (prospector). Defenders follow a strategy based on market penetration, attempting to get more people to use/purchase the product. A prospector on the other hand requires strategies based on market following, where competitors are analysed for the decisions they take. When attempting to penetrate markets the organization's structure needs to be of a controlled nature, as all those employed are encouraged to work towards the goal of extra sales. Market following on the other hand requires a loose structure as employees are encouraged to consider the nature of their competitor's work. Theoretically, this may help employees change their own way of operating and thereby generate new ideas and opportunities.

Peters (1987) argues that organizations that are seeking to sustain their success do not need to undertake detailed business planning, rather they should concentrate on ensuring that they remain responsive to change.

CO-ALIGNMENT WITHIN SELECTED HOTEL COMPANIES

As noted earlier little research appears to have been conducted on co-alignment issues in hotel firm settings. Most of the prior work has been undertaken in the United States, and Schaffer (1984) uses case illustrations from looking at Hyatt

Hotels and Best Western to identify the issues and actions needed. Schaffer was working on the assumption that structure plays a major part in organizational performance and conceptualized his findings through the *structure, strategy and effectiveness model.*

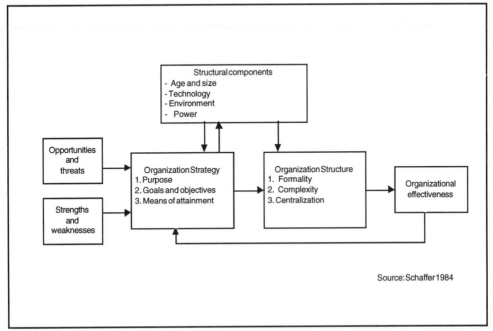

Figure 2.5: Structure and Strategy Effectiveness Model

After undertaking a business 'SWOT Analysis' (strengths, weaknesses, opportunities and threats), the organization is able to develop its strategy. This focuses upon:

- a purpose, what do we want to achieve;
- goals and objectives, what do we want to do; and
- means of attainment, how can we achieve.

After defining strategy, he advocates consideration of the most appropriate structure required to implement decisions. When developing a supportive structure, firms need to consider:

- formality – the degree to which rules and procedures influence the firm;
- complexity – the degree of specialization and task diversity;
- centralization – the distribution of authority within the firms hierarchy.

Structure is referred to as the means by which strategy implementation takes place and thus directly relates to the organization's effectiveness and performance (Schaffer 1984). When considering structure, a number of key variables need to be considered, referred to as 'structural components':

- age and size – larger organizations give rise to increasing responsibilities, thus widening the span of control of managers. In addition, older organizations tend to become more formalized, due to the presence of culture and resistance to change;
- technology – when an organization's technology is centralized and routine a mechanistic structure is most appropriate; whilst an organization's technology that becomes complex and non-routine will require a more decentralized, organic structure;
- environment – organizations that operate in stable environments tend to have a mechanistic nature, whilst those operating in a dynamic environment need to be flexible and pro-active;
- power – failure to consider the people with power within organizational structure may ultimately effect alignment.

In explaining the model, Schaffer notes that *the degree to which an organization is able to adapt not only its strategy, but also its structure to its situation will ultimately affect its performance.*

Schaffer used the structure and strategy effectiveness model to review Hyatt's US operations. Hyatt considers itself as operating within a business market for guest stays, a saturated marketplace which includes the following; Hilton International, Holiday Inn Crowne Plaza, Novotel Sofitel, Radisson International and Ramada Renaissance. In order to gain competitive advantage in this market, Hyatt implements a culture that is better suited to a decentralized structure, permitting unit-managers to be flexible and adaptable to their local environment. Each hotel therefore, functions as a semi-independent property under the Hyatt umbrella, where unit managers are given responsibility for implementing decisions within their unit. The benefit of this is that the unit manager is more aware of any changes within the external environment, thus is able to respond positively at the local level.

STRATEGY	STRUCTURE	ENVIRONMENT
Differentiate – Attract business person	Flexible and adaptable – Decentralization	Complete responsibility in adapting their unit

Table 2.3: Hyatt Hotels Success through Structure and Strategy Co-alignment

Schaffer's research also draws on work undertaken with the Best Western group, a firm set up as a non-profit association, to bring independent hotel operators together under one central reservation system. This is intended to improve an individual operators' competitive position, as their hotel is opened up to a global market. It can be noted that at present Best Western are not seeking to align structure and strategy, as seen recently in managerial changes which aim to establish a centralized and profitable organization.

STRUCTURE	Decentralization where power lies with individual members
STRATEGY	Enhanced competitive position. Non-profit association

Best Western– unsuccessful co-alignment after management change

STRUCTURE	A movement towards centralizing all operations
STRATEGY	To create an organization that is profitable

Table 2.4: Best Western – Co-alignment before Management Change

Schaffer's research helps to explain the importance of matching decisions within the context of the organization. Hyatt is experiencing greater success due in part to the strategic fit it has achieved. Best Western may suffer cultural and managerial problems.

To review the co-alignment challenge facing operators in the hotel, further exploration is needed. An indicative illustration follows in the form of a short profile of the Le Meridien acquisition of Forte.

Forte[1]

Forte, the largest hotel operator in the UK undertook major changes in their organizational structure in 1992, creating six individual hotel brands, 'strategic business units'. This enabled a focused strategy to develop, whereby each hotel was positioned within one of the brands. The relevance of this is being able to target the most appropriate consumer to a brand which will fulfil their requirements and not each individual hotel.

A more recent strategic decision taken by Forte was the acquisition of Meridien Hotels in the latter months of 1994, involving 54 upscale properties. According to Slattery (1995), one of the most important issues facing Forte is international expansion. The addition of eight Meridien hotels (as well as nine Forte Exclusive hotels) in Europe will allow Forte to participate more fully in this strong, dynamic, long-term growth market. In the United States, Forte had insufficient exposure to challenge the large companies, but the acquisition brings fifteen new properties into their portfolio. Slattery (1995) explains the reasons for the Meridien acquisition as:

> Strengthening Forte's position in continental Europe and North America, in addition the acquisition improves Forte's already strong position in the Middle East and via ten properties in the Asia-Pacific region gives Forte exposure there for the first time.

To align the acquisition, the following issues may need to be addressed:

- the creation of a new development team based in London, Paris, New York and Hong Kong to oversee the development of Meridien around the world;
- conversion of hotels located in Dallas, Amsterdam, Nassau Beach and Frankfurt to fit the now established Forte Meridien brand;
- integration of Meridien into Forte's central reservation system, Fortress 2, a world-wide reservation system, linked to 400,000 computer terminals in 90,000 travel agencies.

STRUCTURE AND STRATEGY CO-ALIGNMENT – A PROPOSAL FOR UNIT-MANAGERS

Research by Miles and Snow (1978) and Schaffer (1984, 1986) focuses on alignment between structure and strategy at the corporate level, but make no suggestions for units undertaking their own decisions. Olsen (1989) notes that as hotel companies decentralize their operations, a new emphasis will be placed upon strategic decisions at unit-level. Therefore, managers will have to go beyond implementing budgets and plans – the basics – and engage themselves in *strategy formulation, implementation and evaluation.*

During the 1980s, the unit manager was primarily concerned with implementing growth objectives as directed by their corporate head office. The head office was also responsible for setting guidelines and supporting the managers in their daily roles. However, as head office staff are reduced Olsen (1989) predicts that unit managers will have a different role to play, in essence being asked to compete effectively at the local level:

> where conditions are becoming extremely competitive, to scan the environment for threats and opportunities and to build a strategic plan for their units based on this type of analysis.

The following table sets out some of the issues that unit managers are likely to have to address in the future.

The table seeks to reflect the broader range of decisions that may have to be taken by unit-managers in the near future:

- a) Decisions within the hotel tradition – can be seen as an extension of current managerial work;
- b) Decisions with a business focus – consider the general business functions relating to a hotel;
- c) Decisions that cover ancillary and support – decisions outside the hotels' main areas requiring specialist inputs.

The distinction between corporate and competitive strategy is therefore changing and Tse and Olsen (1990) observe that the unit-manager is becoming more accountable for competitive strategies. Competitive (or business) strategy now focuses on how best to compete successfully within a particular industry/market segment, *by developing and maintaining sustainable competitive advantage.* In sum, the prospects are that unit managers will become more independent managers who are better placed to interpret and respond to the localized issues affecting their operation. In essence it means a sharper focus on generic business and finance issues as well as a more sophisticated response to customer needs. In this, the traditional autocratic style unit manager will give way to a more modern team-building and facilitation approach, where success is realized through the involvement of a greater number of people.

Hotel Tradition	Business Orientation	Ancillary Functions	Support Functions
Operations and line management	Accounting and finance	Buildings and maintenance	Stores and supplies – purchasing
Food and beverage management	Personnel and training	Computing	Fire and safety
Housekeeping	Audit and control	Public relations	Engineering

Source: Adapted from Slattery, P. and Clark, A. (1988)

Table 2.5: Typology of Unit-managers Activities

In support of the alignment process, a flatter, more fluid structure may be required, in which unit managers are encouraged to take greater responsibility for their personal development. This also suggests that they will be better equipped to exercise discretion, creativity and flair as they implement strategic decisions made by head office. A key issue therefore, is the extent to which unit managers can create and sustain a new, more vibrant business climate in their own units, so that management teams and staff can adapt to become more responsive and pro-active. This new vision for unit managers and the greater responsiveness to alignment, will need more than ever before, the support of cohesive and effective work teams. Managers will need support from their staff in both the generation of strategic ideas as well as the implementation of decisions, where staff need to be incorporated from all departments of the unit.

This will enable the unit manger to focus attention on the relationship between the internal organization and the strategies to be implemented, facilitated by concentrating internal efforts on the following:

- Control of processes – getting things right the first time;
- Customer focused culture – listening to customers;
- Continuous improvement – exceed the customers expectations;
- Communication – keeping in touch, upwards, downwards and horizontally.

Further, as well as fostering and developing an ethos of teamworking, unit managers may be required to give attention to testing and refining their structure. This will enable the hotel to maintain a pro-active stance and remain responsive, in terms of satisfying its customers. Units may also secure new forms of competitive advantage as decisions will be taken considering all aspects of the firm, as well as being implemented within a structure that is ready to accept these notions and ideas. According to Mintzberg (1989), the following variables are likely to be important in successfully matching the internal organization with strategy and decision making:

- flexibility– allowing employees to generate ideas and participate in decision making;
- adaptability – developing an organizational structure that is able to move as conditions within the marketplace change;
- empowerment – giving employees the power to be creative, in order to generate future ideas and help in the implementation of decisions;
- innovation – providing an environment where employees are allowed to express themselves, in a search for innovative findings;
- team support – the use of teams in helping managers to become 'strategic thinkers'.

To develop an organizational structure that enables the unit to be pro-active, unit managers will need to conduct brain-storming sessions involving staff from all departments, so as to generate ideas on how best to alter their structure to meet specified objectives. This will ensure that products are appropriately matched to the constantly changing perceptions of the customers that consume. Such initiatives will enable clear guidelines to be established on how best to satisfy needs, met through individual and work team effort. In all of this, management commitment is the key to ensuring that unit structures are ready to align with decisions from both within and above. In essence, Schaffer (1986) notes that in order for this to materialize, the following key improvements are necessary:

- Management led projects;
- Cross-department improvement teams;
- Workgroups;
- Individual action.

The following diagram reflects the key co-alignment issues facing unit managers and the benefits for the organization, its customers and employees:

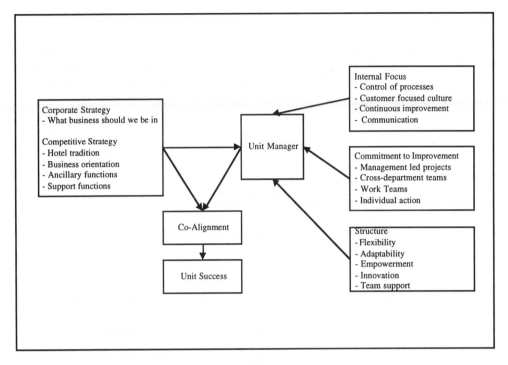

Figure 2.6: Unit Structure and Strategy Co-Alignment

PART 3: IMPLICATIONS ARISING FROM ALIGNMENT WITHIN UNIT HOTEL MANAGEMENT

INTRODUCTION

The first two parts of this chapter referred to alignment as being the actual process of matching structure and strategy. According to Schaffer the output from this is an improvement in the firm's overall performance. The final part seeks to explain in more detail the implications for unit managers working in multi-unit organizations.

The role of the unit manager in the alignment process, is one strand of management activity, and development can in fact focus on many variables that impinge on an optimal fit. Figure 2.7 illustrates this point:

UNIT MANAGERS AND THE PROCESS OF ALIGNMENT

As unit managers in the future are likely to be required to participate in a broader role, the process of co-alignment becomes potentially more important.

Through the process of matching structure and strategy, managers are able to ensure that their unit is both supportive of evolutionary change in the organization, as well as assuming a pro-active stance so that initiatives come from hotel units and not just central office. The implementation of a flatter structure in which managers are encouraged to take greater responsibility, suggests that they will be better equipped to exercise discretion, creativity and flair, as they implement strategic decisions made by head office.

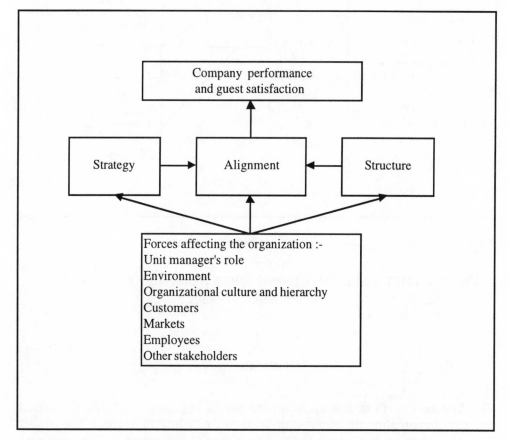

Figure 2.7: Issues and Forces that affect the most Appropriate Co-Alignment

LOOKING AHEAD – THE UNIT MANAGER'S ROLE

At present, alignment between structure and strategy is an area that many unit managers have yet to consider. A review conducted by Teare and Johns (1994) explains both job and roles that unit managers presently play. This is defined in terms of three broad areas:

- managing their operation on a day to day basis – the actual running of their unit hotel;

- managing specialist areas;
- manage any crisis that is brought upon their business.

The unit manager also needs to have an appreciation for managing people, i.e. staff. In the context of their role, this needs to consider managing both individuals as well as the established work-teams. The manager is also responsible for developing links outside the hotel, external contacts, which can help in the promotion of their business at both national and international levels.

In essence therefore, these above tasks are mainly operational, where the manager is in control of the unit as well as staff employed. In the latter part of the 1990s the new vision challenge is likely to include a rich array of managerial and entrepreneurial activity initiated and managed at unit level. A richer, more stimulating set of business and professional tasks will result in a broader scope of manager responsibility. Following corporate downsizing in the early 1990s, an appreciation for alignment between decisions and organizational structure is required, where the unit managers role may change.

These new opportunities to help generate the most appropriate strategic fit are likely to include a consideration for managing the business unit:

- business performance – through the implementation of an appropriate fit between structure, strategy and the environment;
- determining projects – which include the involvement of all unit staff;
- strategic decisions – generating and implementing decisions concerning the units future;
- legal complexity – understanding the laws of the business and their effects on unit performance.

There are several implications arising from alignment that are likely to impact on unit manager's work:

- Productivity and performance – As managers are likely to assume greater responsibility for leading initiatives that offer the prospect of improved unit level performance and productivity
- Customer satisfaction – Managers are likely to assume an enhanced role in improving overall customer satisfaction – accomplished by improving the quality of the product on offer and employee-customer interface.

REFERENCES

Ansoff, H. I. (1979). *Strategic Management*. New York, John Wiley and Sons.

Bower, J. L. (1970). *Managing the Resource Allocation Process: A Study of Corporate Planning and Investment*. Graduate School of Business Administration, Harvard University, Boston, MA.

Bower, J. L. (1982). Business Policy in the 1980's. *Academy of Management Review*, 7 (4), 630–638.

Burns, T. and Stalker, G. M. (1961). *The Management of Innovation*. London, Tavistock.

Chandler, A. D. (1962). *Strategy and Structure*. New York, Doubleday.

Child, J. (1972). Organizational Structure and Strategies of Control. A replication of the Aston Study. *Administrative Science Quarterly*, 17, 163–177.

Child, J. (1975). Managerial and Organizational factors associated with Company performance. A Contingency Analysis. *Journal of Management Studies*, 12, 12–27.

Drucker, P. F. (1969). *The Age of Discontinuity*. New York, Harper and Row.

Fredrickson, J. W. (1986). The Strategic Decision Process and Organizational Structure. *Academy of Management Review*, 11, 280–297.

Galbraith, J. R. and Nathanson, D. A. (1978). *Strategy Implementation: The Role of Structure and Process*. St. Paul, M.N., West Publishing.

Grinyer, P. H. and Yasai-Ardekani, M. (1980). Dimensions of Organizational Structure. A critical replication. *Academy of Management Journal*, 23, 405–421.

Hall, D. J. and Saias, M. A. (1980). Strategy follows Structure. *Strategic Management Journal*, 1, 149–163.

Hofer, C.W. and Schendel, D. (1986). *Strategy Formulation: Analytical Concepts* 11th reprint. St. Paul, MN, West Publishing.

Inkson, J. H. K., Pugh, D. S. and Hickson, D. J. (1970). Organization, Context and Structure: An Abbreviated Republication. *Administrative Science Quarterly*, 15, 318.

Johnson, G. and Scholes, K.(1993). *Exploring Corporate Strategy: Text and Cases*. 3rd ed. London, Prentice-Hall.

Lawrence, P. R. and Lorsch, J. W. (1967). *Organizations and Environment*. Homewood, IL, Irwin.

Leontaides, M. (1982). The Confusing Words of Business Policy. *Academy of Management Review* 7, 45.

Likert, R. (1967). *The Human Organization: Its Management and Value*. New York, MacGraw-Hill.

Miles, R. and Snow, C. (1978). *Organizational Strategy, Structure and Process*. New York, McGraw-Hill.

Miller, D. and Droge, C. (1986). Psychological and Traditional Determinants of Structure. *Administrative Science Quarterly,* 31, 539–560.

Miller, D. (1989). Configurations of Strategy and Structure: Towards a Synthesis. *In:* Asch, D. and Bowman, C. (eds.). *Readings in Strategic Management*. London, Macmillan.

Mintzberg, H. (1976). Planning on the left side, Managing on the right. *Harvard Business Review*, 54, 49–58.

Mintzberg, H. (1979). *The Structuring of Organizations: A Synthesis of the Research*. New Jersey, Prentice-Hall.

Mintzberg, H. (1989). The Structuring of Organizations. *In:* Asch, D. and Bowman, C. (eds.). *Readings in Strategic Management*. London, Macmillan.

Mintzberg, H. (1992). Five Ps for Strategy. *In:* Mintzberg, H. and Quinn, J.B. (eds.) *The Strategy Process: Concepts and Contexts*. London, Prentice-Hall. 12–19.

Olsen, M. D. (1989). Issues Facing Multi-Unit Hospitality Organizations in a Maturing Market. *International Journal of Contemporary Hospitality Management*, 1 (2), 3–6.

Olsen, M. D. (1991). Structural Changes: The International Hospitality Industry and Firm. *International Journal of Contemporary Hospitality Management*, 3 (4), 21–24.

Olsen, M. D., Tse, E. and West, J. (1992). *Strategic Management in the Hospitality Industry*. New York, Van Nostrand Reinhold.

Olsen, M. D. (1993). Accommodation: International Growth Strategies of Major US Hotel Companies. *Economic Intelligence Unit Travel and Tourism Analyst*, 3, 51–64.

Peters, T.(1987). *Thriving on Chaos*. London, Macmillan.

Porter, M. E. (1987). From Competitive Advantage to Corporate Strategy. *Harvard Business Review*, May/June 65, 43–59.

Pugh, D. S., Hickson, D. J., Hinings, C. R. and Turner, C. (1969). The Context of Organization Structures. *Administrative Science Quarterly*, 14, 91–114.

Quinn, J.B. (1980). *Strategies for Change: Logical Incrementalism*. Homewood, ILL, Irwin.

Radosevich, R. (1976). Strategic Implications for Organizational Design. *In:* Ansoff, H. I., Declerck, R. P. and Hayes, R. L. (eds.). *From Strategic Planning to Strategic Management*. London, John Wiley and Sons.

Reimann, B. C. (1973). On the Dimensions of Bureaucratic Structure: An Empirical Re-appraisal. *Administrative Science Quarterly*, 18, 462–476.

Schaffer, J. D. (1984). Strategy, Organization Structure and Success in the Lodging Industry. *International Journal of Hospitality Management*, 3 (4), 159–165.

Schaffer, J. D. (1986). Structure and Strategy: Two Sides of Success. *Cornell Hotel and Restaurant Association Quarterly*, February, 76–81.

Schaffer, J. D. (1987). Competitive Strategies in the Lodging Industry. *International Journal of Hospitality Management*, 6 (1), 33–42.

Slattery, P. and Clark, A. (1988). Major variables in the Corporate Structure of Hotel Groups. *International Journal of Hospitality Management*, 7 (2), 117–130.

Slattery, P. (1995). Quoted Hotel Companies: The World Markets 1995. *UK Research – Leisure and Hotels, Kleinwort Benson Securities*, March.

Steiner, G. A., Miner, J. B. and Gray, E. R. (1982). *Management Policy and Strategy*. New York, Macmillan.

Tannenbaum, A. S. (1962). Control in Organizations: Individual Adjustments and Organizational Performance. *Administrative Science Quarterly*, 7, 236.

Teare, R. and Johns, N. (1994). Structural Change and the Hospitality Management Curriculum. *International Journal of Contemporary Hospitality Management; Regional Forum*, 3–10.

Thompson, J. D. and Tuden, A. (1959). Strategies, Structures and Processes of Organizational Decision. *In:* Thompson, J. E. and Tuden, A. (eds.). *Comparative Studies in Administration*. Pittsburgh, University of Pittsburgh Press.

Thompson, J. D. (1967). *Organizations in Action*. New York, MacGraw-Hill.

Tse, E. (1991). An Empirical Analysis of Organizational Structure and Financial Performance in the Restaurant Industry. *International Journal of Hospitality Management*, 10 (1), 59–72.

Tse, E. and Olsen, M. D. (1990). Business Strategy and Organizational Structure: A Case of US Restaurant Firms. *International Journal of Contemporary Hospitality Management*, 2 (3), 17–23.

Ullrich, R. A. (1976). Organizational Design, Employee Motivation and the Support of Strategic Motivation. *In:* Ansoff, H. I., Declerck, R. P. and Hayes, R. L. (eds.). *From Strategic Planning to Strategic Management*. London, John Wiley and Sons.

Van de Ven, A. H. (1976). A Framework for Organization Assessment. *Academy of Management Review*, 1, 64–78.

Webster, M. (1994). *Strategic Hospitality Management. The Case of Swallow Hotels*. Leeds Metropolitan University, Unpublished Phil Thesis.

Webster, M. and Hudson, T. (1991). Strategic Management: A Theoretical Overview and its Application to the Hospitality Industry, *In:* Teare, R. and Boer, A. (eds.). *Strategic Hospitality Management*. London, Cassell. 9–31.

---

1   Forte plc were taken over by Granda plc in January 1996

3

A Review of Strategic Planning and Performance: Challenges for Hospitality Managers

Paul Phillips

INTRODUCTION

The aim of this chapter is three-fold. First to introduce the concept of strategic planning. This is achieved by considering the various dimensions of planning and the evolution of the process, in an attempt to get across the holistic vision necessary for effective strategic planning. The section concludes by defining the term *strategic planning* and comparing and contrasting strategic planning with tactical and marketing planning.

Second, to review the empirical evidence from previous strategic planning-performance studies published in the general and hospitality management literature. The overall aim is to establish if a relationship between strategic planning and performance has firmly been established. While it is certainly intuitively appealing to claim that the adoption of strategic planning should improve performance, it must be borne in mind that given the complexity of the contextual setting of organizations, it need not necessarily be the case.

A final objective is to identify some of the key challenges for hospitality managers in terms of enhancing performance through strategic planning.

THE STRATEGIC PLANNING PROCESS

Management scholars who believe in the open systems approach, are of the opinion that an organization's survival is dependent on its ability to adapt successfully in a changing environment. Strategic planning is a tool which can help management anticipate and monitor external shifts in the environment. Since its introduction into the business scene in the early 1970s, it has been on a roller coaster ride. To quote from Wilson (1994, p. 12):

it has been, successively, a fad, an anathema and just another management tool. It has bounced around the corporate hierarchy in search of a legitimate role and an appropriate home.

Nonetheless, from its origins in the USA, where it was used exclusively by manufacturing firms, strategic planning has now reached the stage where it is now practised in the UK, by several profit and non-profit making service organizations. However, when viewed from an academic perspective, the results of research, conducted to examine the performance consequences of formal strategic planning, has led to criticisms and has produced confusing and in some cases contradictory results. Nevertheless, it seems evident that the planning-performance relationships bears significantly on strategy research and practice and that strategy scholars should not forsake this line of enquiry altogether.

DIMENSIONS OF PLANNING

Steiner (1979) highlighted five key dimensions of business planning. These are shown in Figure 3.1, with the dimensions being:

- subject;
- elements;
- time;
- characteristics; and
- organization.

Steiner noted the following important observations.

First, the dimensions are not exhaustive, mutually exclusive or discrete. Other dimensions, such as organizational size, management style, experience curve, managerial ability and breadth of product line, could all have been included. Planning can be either short-range or long-range. The former typically pertains to a period of less than three years. Circumstances may vary from firm to firm and from industry to industry, which implies that the time-scale is actually situational specific. For example, long-range for oil companies can be in excess of a decade, whereas, in certain sections of the computer industry, long-range may be less than twelve months.

Second, business planning is such a complex subject, that each dimension (except characteristics) can be a plan in itself. A plan can be drawn up for a department or a product. Steiner in fact points out that the business planning is abstruse and can be viewed from several points.

Third, when defining or discussing business planning, it is important to consider what dimensions of planning and plans are under contemplation. For example, while it is advisable to have top management involved in acquisition studies, it is totally inappropriate to have them involved in decisions involving immaterial amounts of cash. Likewise, while the use of accounting techniques such as payback may be appropriate for minor capital expenditure, it might be dangerous if it was the sole technique used in acquisition analysis.

SUBJECT

Production

Research

New Product Dev.

Financial

Marketing

Acquisitions

Facility

Manpower

ORGANIZATION

Corporate

Subsidiaries

Functional Groups

Divisions

Departments

Product/Project/Concept

ELEMENTS

Charter

Creed

Purpose

Objective

Strategy

Policy

Programme

Budget

Procedure

Rule

Complex/Simple

Comprehensive Narrow Coverage

Major/Minor importance

Qualitative/Quantitative

Strategic/Tactical

Confidential/Public

Written/Unwritten

Prepared Formally/Informally

Ease of Implementation

Rational/Irrational

Flexibility/Inflexibility

Economical/Excessively Costly

Short Range

Medium Range

Long Range

Perpetual

CHARACTERISTICS

TIME

Source: Steiner, G.A., (1969), *Top Management Planning*

Figure 3.1: Five Key Dimensions of Business Planning

THE FOUR PHASES OF STRATEGIC MANAGEMENT

The development of strategic management has followed four discrete phases, Glueck *et al.* (1982). Strategic management (phase IV) is at one end of the continuum and budgetary control (phase I) at the other. This view was echoed by Phillips (1994), who observed four distinct phases in the hotel sector, Table 3.1.

Phase I: Budgetary Control

The origins of budgetary control dates back to the beginning of the twentieth century. Its primary aims are to compel planning, promote communication and co-ordination and to control deviations from planned targets. Nevertheless, although budgetary control methods result in better financial controls, their time horizon, typically a year, is inadequate for strategic decision-making.

Phase II: Long Range Planning (LRP)

The lack of emphasis on the future in budgeting, resulted in the use of LRP during the 1950s. As the term implies, its time frame can extend five, ten or more years into the future. While there are many merits in LRP, overall it is inadequate for strategy formulation. There are at least three significant reasons why LRP is not a strategic tool.

First, projections are usually based upon current operations, with recognition of micro and macro economic factors. Unfortunately, the external analysis is used to gauge how expansive or conservative the organization should be about current operations. This type of analysis is not suitable for determining a strategic direction, as LRP merely ends up becoming an extrapolation of the annual budget.

Second, instead of establishing up-front objectives as part of the LRP exercise, the past is used to predict the future. This results at worst in managers building plans on the foundations of historical analysis, rather than using the planning exercise to get the organization where it really wants to be.

Third, if the LRP becomes an extrapolation of the annual budget, it could become a numeric exercise, with managers tweaking the figures to satisfy the various financial objectives. While all LRP plans consist of figures, if figures lead the thinking process, then there is the danger that fundamental questions like 'what determines the future scope of the organizations activities'? remains unanswered. Put simply, 'doing things right' (efficiency), becomes more important than 'doing the right thing' (effectiveness). Failure to address this matter in a rapidly changing environment has led to the demise of several UK organizations during the last decade.

	Phase 1 Budgetary Control	Phase II Long-Range Planning	Phase III Strategic Planning	Phase IV Strategic Management
Effectiveness of formal business planning	Operational control Annual budget Functional focus	More effective planning for growth Environmental analysis Multi-year forecasts Static allocation resources	Increase market response to market and competition Thorough situation analysis and competitive assessment Evaluation of strategic alternatives Dynamic allocation of resources	Orchestration of all resources to create competitive advantage Strategically chosen planning framework Creative, flexible planning process Supportive value system and climate
Value System	Meet Budget	Predict the future	Think strategically	Create the future

Source: Adapted from, Gluck, Kaufman and Walleck, Strategic Management for Competitive Advantage, *Harvard Business Review*, July–August 1980, p. 157

Table 3.1: The Four Phases in the Evolution of Strategic Management

Phase III: Strategic Planning

Strategic planning originated in the USA in the 1960s and as the operating environments became hostile, was imported into European companies in the 1970s and early 1980s. Attention was placed upon developing a suitable direction for the organization. The more turbulent the environment, the greater the need for management to engage in 'strategic thinking'. Academics, practitioners and consultants fervently embraced the processes and tools of strategic planning. However, by the end of the 1980s strategic planning began to fall out of fashion for several reasons. Wilson (1994) termed these reasons the *seven deadly sins of strategic management*. These reasons are shown in Table 3.2.

- Staff took over the process

- Process dominated the staff

- Planning systems were virtually designed to produce no results

- Planning focused on the more exciting game of merger acquisition and divestitures at the expense of core business

- Planning process failed to develop true strategic choices

- Planning neglected the organizational and cultural requirements of strategy

- Single-point forecasting was an inappropriate basis for planning in era of restructuring and uncertainty

---

Source: Extracted from Wilson (1994), Strategic planning isn't dead it changed,
Long Range Planning, 27, 4, 12-24
Table 3.2: Wilson's Seven Deadly Sins of Strategic Management

It could also be argued that management were not obtaining the full benefits from strategic planning, due to the way that the technique is utilized. This has been observed by some writers. For example, to quote from Wilson, who in turn quoted Porter, who made the following point in a London Economist article on the *state of strategic thinking* May 1987:

> strategic planning in most companies has not contributed to strategic thinking. The answer, however, is not to abandon planning . . . Instead, strategic thinking needs to be rethought and recast . . . What has been under attack [is] the techniques and organizational processes which companies used . . .

Phase IV: Strategic Management

The thrust of strategic management is somewhat different from the other aspects of management. Although the terms strategic planning and strategic management are often used interchangeably by practitioners and consultants, there are subtle differences between the two terms. Ansoff (1987) explained these differences by stating:

1) Strategic planning is focused on making optimal strategy decisions, while strategic management is focused on producing strategic results, new markets, new products and/or new technologies;
2) Strategic planning is an analytical process, while strategic management is an organizational action process;
3) Strategic planning is focused on business, economic and technological variables. Strategic management broadens the focus to include psychological, sociological and political variables. Thus, strategic planning is about choosing things to do, while strategic management is about choosing things to do and also about the people who will do them.

This infers that not only is strategic management concerned with taking decisions about major issues facing the firm, but also with the actual implementation of the desired strategy. Phase IV therefore, signals the merging of strategic planning and strategic management into a single process.

We are now in a position to look at the relationship between strategic management, strategy and strategic planning. Figure 3.2 shows this relationship. Of particular importance is the fact that no attempt has been made to show a direct relationship between strategic planning and business performance.

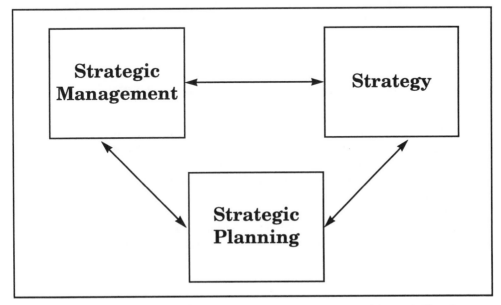

Figure 3.2: The Relationship Between Strategic Management, Strategy and Strategic Planning

DEFINITION OF STRATEGIC PLANNING

Prior to an evaluation of a definition of strategic planning, it is perhaps pertinent to comment briefly about what strategic planning is not. Steiner (1979)
made the following observations:

- Strategic planning does not attempt to make future decisions;
- Strategic planning is not forecasting product sales and then determining what
  should be done to assure the fulfilment of the forecasts with respect to items
  such as, material purchases, facilities, manpower, etc;
- Strategic planning is not an attempt to blueprint the future;
- Strategic planning is not necessarily the preparation of massive, detailed and
  interrelated sets of plans;
- Strategic planning is not an effort to replace managerial intuition and judge-
  ment;
- Strategic planning is not a simple aggregation of functional plans or an extrapolation of current budgets.

Therefore, if strategic planning within an organization becomes any of the
observations noted by Steiner, then it seems highly probable that maximum benefits will not accrue from the process.

Many empirical planning-performance studies have been more interested in
the classification of firms on a formal planning dimension, rather than a conceptualized definition of planning. Kudla (1980, p. 5), was one of the few studies
to make an attempt to define strategic planning, as:

> the systematic processes of determining the firm's goals and objectives for at
> least three years into the future and developing strategies that will govern the
> acquisition and use of resources to achieve these objectives.

STRATEGIC VERSUS TACTICAL PLANNING

To gain further insight into strategic planning it is important to understand the
differences between strategic and tactical planning. These differences are shown
in Table 3.3 and are based on the findings by Anthony (1964), Anthony (1965)
and Steiner and Cannon (1966). It can be seen that strategic planning is a cor-
porate/strategic business unit activity. Hence the frequent use of the term corporate planning. Tactical planning is more orientated towards day-to-day operational activities. Thus, it can be seen that strategic management requires planning at all management levels and the plans are used as a means of co-ordination and communication.

Element	Strategic planning	Tactical planning
Where conducted	Corporate/strategic business unit	Operational
Time horizon	Medium/long	Short/medium
Regularity	Continuous/irregular	Perioduc
Uncertainty	High	Medium
Nature of problem	Structured and one of a kind	Unstructured and repetitive
Performance indicator	Effectiveness	Efficiency
Breadth	Wide	Narrow
Information requirement	External	Internal
Vision	Holistic	Functional

Table 3.3: The Different Roles of Strategic and Tactical Planning

STRATEGIC VERSUS MARKETING PLANNING

The terms strategic and marketing planning are often used interchangeably by academics as well as practitioners, but again it is important to realize (Table 3.4) that they are quite different. Although the origins of strategic planning lay in marketing planning – the former becomes a prerequisite when in turbulent environments – a new direction is sought. The strategic plan provides boundaries and guidance for the marketing plan. When the strategic plan needs to be revised, the marketing plan can be used as an input into the revised strategic plan. Nevertheless, the time frame of the strategic plan makes it indicative that the strategic plan should be produced in the first instance before the marketing plan. Thus, although there is a cyclical relationship between the two, at a particular point in time, the strategic plan provides the framework for the next round of marketing planning, Greenley (1986a). The rule then is simple, develop the strategic plan first, as this entails scanning the external environment, assessing structural forces and developing suitable responses, involving all levels of management within the organization.

Strategic planning	Marketing planning
Concerned with overall long-range company direction.	Concerned with day-to-day performance and results.
Provides the long-range framework for the company.	Represents only one stage in the company's development.
Decisions made have an enduring effect.	Decisions can be changed or modified.
Corporate orientation is needed to match the company to its environment.	Functional and professional orientation tends to dominate.
Identification of new objectives and strategies.	Goals are derived from established objectives.
Objectives and strategies are evaluated with a corporate perspective.	Objectives are sub-divided into specific goals.
New areas and innovations can be investigated.	Continuance of current areas of business.
Relevance of objectives and strategies only available in the long-term.	Relevance of objectives and strategies is immediately evident.
Several issues may be abstract, deferrable and unfamiliar.	Issues are normally immediate, concrete and familiar.

Source: Greenley, G. E. (1986) The relationship of strategic and marketing plans.

Table 3.4: The Different Roles of Strategic and Marketing Planning

STRATEGIC PLANNING AND PERFORMANCE: LITERATURE REVIEW – GENERAL MANAGEMENT

Strategic Planning and Performance Studies

The management literature strongly advocates strategic planning as the key to superior performance. A review of the relevant literature has identified 32 relevant and published empirical studies. Table 3.5 provides a summary of the sample sizes, classifications of planning, performance measures and overall research findings. At first glance, it can be seen that 23 (72 per cent) of the studies identified a favourable link between strategic planning-performance. These results suggest that the conceptual literature is in agreement with empirical evidence.

This however, is a very tentative conclusion, as it is based upon mixed evidence. Moreover, a closer analysis of the methodologies used suggest that a 'Caveat' needs to be expressed when drawing conclusions from these research findings. This observation has been noted in several reviews, Kudla (1980); Armstrong (1982); Shrader, Taylor and Dalton (1984); Rhyne (1986); Greenley (1986b); Pearce, Freeman and Robinson (1987); and Greenley (1993).

From these reviews the consensus of opinion was that the studies were confusing and contradictory to reconcile. Armstrong (1982 p. 209) critiqued twelve studies and concluded that:

> serious research problems were found in these studies, so few conclusions could be drawn about how to plan and when to plan.

Pearce *et al.* (1987) critiqued eighteen studies and concluded at page 671 that empirical support for formal planning:

> has been inconsistent and contradictory

Greenley (1993, p. 10) concluded after a review of 29 studies, that:

> owing to the many differences found between the empirical studies, the overall conclusion is that their results cannot be legitimately combined to give a common result.

Greenley's review surprisingly ignored four important studies: Capon, Farley and Hulbert, (1987); Bracker, Keats and Pearson, (1988); Odom and Boxx (1988); and, Boyd (1991).

	Sample	Classification of Planning	Performance Measures	Findings
Ansoff *et al.* (1970)	93 manufacturing firms	High- and low-level planners	21 indicators	On virtually all relevant financial criteria, high-level planners significantly outperformed low-level planners
Eastlack and MacDonald (1970)	211 manufacturing firms	Managerial style only	Sales revenue only	Performance associated with strategic planning
Gershefski (1970)	323 mixed companies	Objectives and action plans	Sales revenue only	Planners out performed non-planners
Thune and House (1970)	36 mixed firms	Formal versus informal planners	Sales, stock prices, EPS, ROE, ROA	Formal planners' performance superior
Guth (1972)	More than 60 firms	Listing of policies and strategies	Growth and profitability	Planning improves performance
Herold (1972)	10 drug and chemical firms	Formal versus informal planners	Sales, Pretax profit, R&D expenditure	Planners outperformed non-planners
Rhenman (1973)	20 mixed companies	None given	Productivity	Planning and performance not related
Fulmer and Rue (1974)	386 mixed companies	Planners versus non-planners	Sales, earnings, ROS, rate of return	No difference between planners and non-planners
Grinyer and Norburn (1975)	21 mixed firms	Formal planners versus informal planners	Return of assets	No significant difference between formal and non-planners
Karger and Malik (1975)	90 industrial firms	Planners versus non-planners	13 indicators of effectiveness	Planners significantly out-performed non-planners

Table 3.5 – 3.8: Prior Strategic planning – Performance Studies

	Sample	Classification of Planning	Performance Measures	Findings
Burt (1978)	14 firms	Quality	13 indicators	High quality of planning is significantly associated with high levels of performances
Kallman and Shapiro (1978)	298 motor carriers	Five classes of planners. Based on commitment and sophistication	Revenue, profitability, ROC, ROE	No significant benefits from planning
Wood and LaForge (1979)	41 large banks	Comprehensive formal planners, partial planners, no formal planners	Growth in net income and ROI	Comprehensive long-range planners significantly outperformed those with no formal planning system
Kudla (1980)	129 mixed companies	Non-planners, incomplete, and complete planners	Stockholders' return	No significant difference between the returns earned by shareholders of planning and non-planning firms
Leontiades and Tezel (1980)	61 fortune 1000 firms	Importance of planning	ROE, ROA, PER, sales and EPS growth	No relationship
Klein (1981)	58 small banks	High, moderate, and low levels of planning	Deposit growth	No significant effects
Sapp and Seiler (1981)	301 banking institutions	Four levels. Completeness in terms of non-planners, beginning planners, intermediate planners and sophisticated	Deposit growth rate, ROE, capital-to-risk assets ratio, interest as a percentage of loans	Planners superior on three out of four measures
Robinson (1982)	101 small firms	Planners (with outside help) versus non planners	Profitability	Planners out-perform non-planners

Table 3.5 – 3.8: Prior Strategic planning – Performance Studies

	Sample	Classification of Planning	Performance Measures	Findings
Robinson and Pearce (1983)	50 small banks	Formal versus informal planners	Profit margin, loan growth, ROA and ROE	No relationship
Frederickson and Mitchell (1984)	27 forest product firms	Level of comprehensiveness	Average return on assets and sales growth	Comprehensiveness exhibited a consistently negative relationship with performance
Fredrickson (1984)	38 paint and coating manufacturers	Level of comprehensiveness	Average return on assets and sales growth	Comprehensiveness exhibited a positive relationship with ROA, but not sales growth
Robinson et al. (1984)	51 small firms	Stage of planning	Growth, profitability, productivity and employment	Planning and performance related
Ackelsberg and Arlow (1985)	135 small firms	Planners versus non-planners	Average of three years sales and profits	Planners superior
Whitehead and Gup (1985)	316 banks	Planners and non-planners	Deposit growth, ROA and ROE	No difference
Bracker and Pearson (1986)	188 small dry cleaning firms	Levels of sophistication	Growth in sales and profitability, ratio, ratio of costs to revenues	Planners superior on two measures
Rhyne (1986)	89 Fortune 1000 companies	Openness and length of planning horizon	Shareholder return	Strategic planners outperformed other types of planners

Table 3.5 – 3.8: Prior Strategic planning – Performance Studies

	Sample	Classification of Planning	Performance Measures	Findings
Capon *et al.* (1987)	113 Fortune manufacturing firms	Four levels. Corporate/Division strategic planners. Corporate/Division financial planners	5 year average of ROC	Strategic planning can improve performance, but it is not a necessary condition
Pearsc *et al.* (1987)	97 manufacturing firms	Planning formality	Sales growth, ROA and ROS	Formality significantly related to all indicators
Robinson and Pearce (1988)	97 manufacturing firms	Planning sophistication	Sales growth, ROA and ROS	Sophistication was found to significantly moderate the strategy-performance baseline
Bracker *et al.* (1988)	73 electronic firms	Planning sophistication	Growth in; revenue, net-income, present value and CEO compensation	Sophistication was found to support previous strategy-performance research
Odom and Boxx (1988)	179 churches	Planning sophistication	Growth in; attendance, offerings, total additions, baptisms	Planners superior on three out of four measures
Boyd (1991)	2,496 organizations	Formal planners versus informal planners	Meta-Analysis. 13 indicators	Modest correlation between planning and nine performance measures

Table 3.5 – 3.8: Prior Strategic planning – Performance Studies

Nonetheless given the paucity of empirical strategic planning-performance studies since 1988, it might seem that with the exception of Boyd (1991), researchers have abandoned this line of enquiry altogether. However, as strategic planning receives significant emphasis on MBA programmes and in books geared towards the academic and practitioner market, the planning-performance dichotomy remains an important issue for the 1990s. The thrust of future planning-performance research must therefore be geared towards overcoming some of the methodological deficiencies of previous research.

OVERVIEW OF THE STRATEGIC PLANNING-PERFORMANCE RELATIONSHIP

Empirical support for a favourable link between strategic planning-performance was found in the seminal studies by Ansoff, Arner, Brandenberg, Portner and Radosevich, (1970); Thune and House (1970); and Herold (1972).

The second wave of research sought to establish more rigorous methodologies for measuring formality. Fulmer and Rue (1974) sought to discriminate between four types of planners:

- primary;
- pro-forma;
- program-predictive; and
- impoverished.

This attempt proved unsuccessful, as did the following studies:

- Kudla (1980) – who classified planners as non-planner, incomplete planner and complete planner;
- Leontiades and Tezel (1980) – who experimented with the importance of planning; and
- Klein (1981) – who classified planners in terms of levels.

Recognizing the above negative findings led to a third wave of empirical research, which attempted to employ richer conceptualizations of planning. Wood and La Forge (1979, 1981) sought to classify organizations based on a seven-level Guttman-type of planning sophistication, Guttman, (1947). A score of zero on the scale implies a complete absence of planning, while a score of six indicates comprehensive planning. They concluded that comprehensive long-range planners significantly out-performed those with no formal planning system. Other multidimensional formality constructs were proposed by Fredrickson and Mitchell (1984) and Fredrickson (1984). Both studies defined comprehensiveness as a measure of rationality. The former study tested the relationship in an unstable environment and the latter in a stable environment. Comprehensiveness as defined by the authors was found to be positively related to performance in a stable environment and negatively related to performance in an industry with an unstable environment.

The rest of the 1980s saw researchers continuing to focus upon planning sophistication, Bracker and Pearson (1986); Robinson and Pearce (1988); Bracker *et al.* (1988); and Odom and Boxx (1988), all of which reported favourable results.

Significant progress in developing the planning-performance literature is reflected in the study by Capon *et al.* (1987). One of the major issues addressed was that of classification of planning. Capon and his team developed four categories of planning through a deductive approach:

   i. Corporate strategic planners;
   ii. Division strategic planners;
   iii. Corporate financial planners;
   iv. Division financial planners.

Their findings were encouraging, but they pointed out that although strategic planning can improve performance, it is not a necessary condition.

Boyd published a long and detailed meta-analytic review, which involved the aggregation of 29 samples on a total of 2,496 organizations. He surprisingly overlooked the contribution by Capon *et al.* (1987), who brought this to his attention in Capon, Farley and Hulbert, (1994). Boyd, concluded that the results of previous research were equivocal. He pointed out that existing research was subjected to a great deal of measurement errors, which underestimated the benefits of planning. Second, although the average effect size was small, many firms do not report significant, quantifiable benefits from participating in the strategic planning process. To advance the strategic planning-performance literature, he argued for more rigorous measures for formal planning, controls for industry effects and separate analysis for the various dimensions of organizational performance.

METHODOLOGICAL ISSUES

Performance

The first salient issue that needs to be considered is the definition of performance as used in empirical studies.

Improvement in business performance is at the heart of the strategic planning literature. Researchers frequently take financial performance, as a surrogate for business performance when investigating the planning-performance relationship. With the exception of studies involving Pearce, qualitative measures have largely been ignored. As financial performance is so widely used as an indicator of business performance, it may appear that there is nothing inherently wrong with the use of profitability as a determinant of strategic performance. The next section concentrates upon the advantages and disadvantages of using the sole performance measure, of profitability, then considers the other performance dimensions of effectiveness and adaptability.

Profitability is used as a benchmark for defining success in most studies and is used by leading professional journals such as, *Management Today* and *Business Week* in assessing performance. Performance has become an important component of empirical research in the field of corporate/business strategy. Return on investment (ROI) has become one of the most popular measures of profitability. However, despite its overwhelming popularity in business circles, it has been subjected to much consternation among academics, due to its practical, methodological and conceptual limitations.

ROI (Efficiency)

British companies are required by law to disclose specific financial information on an annual basis. The extent of disclosure depends on whether the company is public, private, listed or unlisted. These requirements produce quantifiable data which, when collated, provide a number of performance indicators. For public limited companies, for example, a profit and loss account, a balance sheet and cash flow statement must be produced. From these, various accounting ratios such as ROI and earnings per share (EPS) can be derived. These figures together with other financial indicators, paint a picture of the company's overall financial performance. Comparison then can be made with other company's reported figures, to establish if the company has performed well.

The use of ROI as a performance measure can be mainly attributed to the Du Pont company, who developed the Du Pont Model in the 1920s. By 1965, Ansoff asserted that ROI was a commonly and widely accepted yardstick for measuring business success. However, since these heights, the inadequacies of the model have been highlighted on several occasions.

Recent published accounts reporting the corporate performance of prominent companies such as BCCI; Polly Peck; Trafalgar House; Blue Arrow; and Maxwell Communications, all had something in common. The reported profits turned out to be misleading. The measure of profit derived from accrual based accounting have understandably come under a lot of criticism, the most vocal being by Smith (1993).

Market Share (Effectiveness)

Extreme caution needs to be exercised when using the sole measure of ROI. Other dimensions of business performance ought to be used. Failure to address the problem of say, falling market share, will eventually result in the financial collapse of an organization. As the indicator of ROI is used to assess efficiency, other facets of business performance need to be utilized, in an attempt to define good performance.

Several studies (notably in Japan) have shown how growth in market share can be ultimately more important than profitability, Morishima (1982); Tsuruni

(1984); Prestowitz (1988); and Van Wolferen (1989). There have been various explanations for this phenomena, but the most widely cited, appears to relate to the Japanese philosophy of having a job for life, which can only be achieved in a growing economy.

In most Western companies short-term profits drive corporate objectives. This results in market share (long-term objective) being in conflict with profitability (short-term objective). Thus, when earnings are under pressure, it is normal to see market share building investments reduce to boost profits. Moreover, in a declining market, some Western companies, take pleasure in boasting of their significantly better efficiencies in operating profits, compared to their foreign competitors. This suggests that Japanese companies see themselves as the providers of jobs, whereas Western counterparts see themselves as wealth generators for their shareholders.

Innovation (Adaptability)

The previous two performance dimensions has shown that although a business may be efficient, it may not necessarily be effective. Matters are further complicated if one considers that during turbulent times a business' success, may be largely dependent upon its ability to adapt to changing environmental conditions. This, third dimension of business performance, adaptability, is of primary importance to top corporate and business unit managers, Walker and Ruekert, (1987). One of the most common ways of measuring this variable is in terms of the number of new products/services, in relation to competitors.

It should also be noted that if performance is to be compared across the three performance dimensions of efficiency, effectiveness and adaptability, the user will have to make trade-offs. Thus, at a minimum, performance measures should ideally cover all the three performance dimensions.

Other Methodology Weaknesses

In an effort to complete the analysis and bring greater rigour and clarity to the strategic planning-performance relationship, it is imperative that some other major shortcomings be highlighted. The aim of future research should be to introduce some conceptual and methodological improvements to overcome some of the deficiencies of previous studies. While no one work, can fill the void, it is hoped that collectively researchers can stimulate a redirection of the strategic planning-performance literature. The weaknesses which need to be addressed include:

- characteristics of sample;
- research instrument;
- year of reporting; and
- duration of the study.

The following section summarizes the salient issues that need to be incorporated into future research.

Characteristics of Sample

The strategy concept and its application to business decisions is not a phenomenon found solely in manufacturing organizations. Yet, until quite recently research has not focused on the differences between the manufacturing and service sectors. The tendency has been to employ generalized findings in the manufacturing to the service sector. This appears surprising, given the unique elements of service delivery and findings of previous planning-performance studies.

For example, in our review of previous planning-performance studies only nine were conducted in the service sector. These sectors included banking, motor carriers, retailing, dry cleaning and churches. Of these studies five reported positive relationships. While three out of four studies conducted in the banking sector and the study in the motor carrier reported no relationships. On the other hand ten studies were conducted in a manufacturing setting and all the studies reported a positive planning-performance link. Whereas, eight out of the thirteen mixed studies reported a positive relationship. These observations therefore, indicate that the inherent characteristics of the sample would appear to be an important determinant of the planning-performance relationship.

Research Instrument

A mailed questionnaire is one of the most cost effective methods of obtaining information in a standardized form from different groups of people. Thus, it is hardly surprising that mailed questionnaires have been widely used by researchers. Unfortunately, most research studies do not disclose details pertaining to questionnaires used, which leads to little scope for replicating, or extending the literature.

Year of Reporting

The review of the strategic planning-performance literature has covered the period 1970 to the present. During this period there has been several economic cycles, which has meant that the knowledge of strategic planning would have increased. So it is probably fair to say that this would influence the strategic planning-performance relationship. The evidence would suggest that since the 1970s, strategic planning tools and techniques have permeated into the boardrooms of most large businesses within the leading industrial countries. Obviously, in some instances this dissemination has been impeded, through a lack of interest from senior management.

Duration of Study

Most questionnaires asked for performance data relating to a single point in time. This seems peculiar bearing in mind that some organizations may not see any strategic planning benefits until a couple of years after initial implementation. It therefore seems evident that researchers should adopt a longitudinal approach in future studies.

STRATEGIC MANAGEMENT IN THE HOSPITALITY INDUSTRY: A LITERATURE REVIEW

Olsen (1991) observed in his review of the hospitality strategic management literature that synergistic benefits will only be obtained if organizational leaders understood the concept. While there have been growth in the volume of prescriptive articles written about the strategy phenomena, hospitality managers are faced with a paucity of hard evidence about how different alternatives may effect performance. Put simply, it is one thing to be taught about the various strategy concepts, but it is another matter applying it outside the classroom and even more importantly, it is perhaps more pertinent to know which choices results in the highest pay-off in the long-term.

The objective of this section is to present a general overview of relevant hospitality strategy research conducted in the United States of America (USA). Then to form a structured view of the potpourri of empirical strategy research in the hospitality industry, by concentrating on the strategy-performance literature.

Overview

Although, Potetsionakis (1979) conducted a study of twelve leading hotel companies for the purpose of his MSc, at the University of Bath, all of the relevant empirical work emanates from the USA. Seminal works by Tse and Olsen (1988); West and Olsen (1988); and Schaffer and Spencer (1988), explored the strategy–performance relationship. These authors have been involved in subsequent research studies, many based at the Virginia Polytechnic Institute and State University, Virginia. It is interesting to note that American authors seem interested in both the food and lodging sectors. The food sector has been the focus of Tse and Olsen (1988); West and Olsen (1988); West (1990); West and Anthony (1990); and Tse (1991). Whereas, the USA lodging sector has been the focus of Schaffer and Spencer (1988); Dev (1989); Dev and Olsen (1989); Schaffer and Litschert (1990).

No empirical study has been performed in the UK which has looked at the strategy-performance link in the hospitality industry. Most UK research seem more interested in market analysis and pronouncing normative statements about various aspects of strategic management in the hospitality industry. However, although, the hospitality strategy literature is somewhat nascent, it still seems appropriate to examine the basic research thrust in the literature to date.

Basic Research Thrusts

Olsen (1991) identified three basic components making up the concept of strategy in the hospitality industry:

- strategy formulation;
- the content of strategy; and
- strategy implementation.

Viewing the hospitality literature from a conceptual angle, he categorized the basic thrusts in the following areas:

- environment;
- strategy formulation;
- strategy content; and
- strategy implementation.

The next section will briefly look at these research thrusts, prior to a more detailed analysis of the empirical strategy-performance studies.

The Environment

The notion of environmental scanning was the thrust of the early research in the hospitality industry, Olsen and Bellas (1980); Olsen and DeNoble (1981); DeNoble and Olsen (1982); Slattery and Olsen (1984); DeNoble and Olsen (1986); Kwansa *et al.* (1986); Pinto and Olsen (1987). The first empirical work in this area was not until West and Olsen (1988). From this work West and Olsen (1989) developed a normative model for environmental scanning. Nanus and Lundberg (1988) developed the 'QUEST' (quick environmental scanning technique) model and reported its use in a chain of restaurants. Subsequent work by Dev and Olsen (1989); West (1990); and West and Anthony (1990), have added to the environmental scanning-performance literature.

Modelling Strategy Formulation

With the exception of Tse (1988), all of the research in this area is conceptual. Various authors have proposed prescriptive models, Reid and Olsen (1981); Sirkis and Race (1982); Canas (1982); Gregg (1986); Fender (1990); Nebel and Schaffer (1992); and Fender and Litteljohn (1992).

The extent of the formalized strengths and weaknesses analysis among 150 restaurant firms, were the focus of an exploratory study by Tse (1988). Data collection was carried out by telephone interviews and mailed questionnaires to corporate planners of restaurant firms. Thirty six firms (24 per cent of the sample) replied and one-third of these respondents did not engage in strategic planning. Secondary data was used to augment the primary data. Incorporating work from King (1983); and Pearce and Robinson (1985), a framework of internal strengths and weaknesses assessment was proposed. Statistical analysis was conducted to determine the relationship of a formalized internal analysis process and financial performance. The results did not suggest that formalized internal analysis led to improved financial performance.

Strategy Content

The following statement by Olsen (1991, p. 228) succinctly summarizes the state of research in this area:

> ... it is evident from this review that research in the area of strategic content is in the early stages of development. It is less descriptive than the research in formulation. The thrust has been either to identify strategy typologies for the hospitality industry or to study relationships utilising typologies [Miles and Snow (1978); and Porter (1980)] developed in the manufacturing industry.

Strategy Implementation

Research in this area has only been reported once in the hospitality industry. Although DeNoble (1986) did not look at the fundamental concepts, he did look at the effect of merger and acquisition upon the implementation of strategy from a organizational structural perspective. Data collection was carried out by mailed questionnaires to 96 firms which had acquired a restaurant between 1976 and 1981. Forty seven firms (49 per cent of the sample) replied. The results indicated the following pattern of behaviour between parent firms and the acquired firm after merger and acquisition:

1) A high degree of executive involvement in matters related to the acquired firm;
1) A high degree of consolidation of the acquired firm's functional areas;
3) A low degree of autonomy for the acquired firm in making functional decisions;
4) A high degree of similarity between the two firms' personnel policies.

STRATEGY – PERFORMANCE LINK: A HOSPITALITY LITERATURE REVIEW

Strategic Planning and Performance Studies

Formal strategic planning, has been advocated by several hospitality researchers Reid and Olsen (1981); Reichel (1983); and Schaffer (1986), as a process that allows an organization to out-perform non-strategic planning firms. Nonetheless, there has been no study to date which has sought to test this relationship. As previously stated, empirical research has concentrated upon the environment, strategy formulation, strategy content and strategy implementation.

Overview of the Strategy–Performance Relationship

The first empirical studies tests of this relationship Tse and Olsen (1988); West and Olsen (1988); Schaffer and Spencer (1988) had mixed findings. However, since then researchers conducting similar studies have obtained encouraging results. An overview of the published studies is highlighted in Tables 3.9 – 3.11

The first empirical study to explore the relationships of strategy, organizational structure and financial performance, was conducted by Tse and Olsen (1988). Porter's (1980) framework was used to determine business strategy. Organization structure was evaluated using Dalton *et al.* (1980) attributes of complexity, formalization and centralization. The top management team in 296 American multi-unit restaurant firms were surveyed. The questionnaire used was based on previous work by Dess and Davis (1984) and Schaffer (1986). Ninety three firms out of the sample responded and two were unusable giving a 30.7 per cent response rate. Porter's (1980) generic strategies was used to categorize firms by their strategic orientation. The following hypotheses were developed to test the fit between strategy, structure and performance:

- H_1. There is no difference in return on sales, return on assets and growth in unit sales between different firm structural combinations for companies espousing a low cost strategy;
- H_2. There is no difference in return on sales, return on assets and growth in unit sales between different firm structural combinations for companies espousing a differentiation strategy.

T-tests and ANOVA statistical tests were conducted to test the above hypotheses. Results from both tests failed to reject both null hypotheses, which therefore indicated that there was no positive strategy-structure-performance link.

Study	Sample (number)	Methodology	Focus of study	Categorization on planning	Performance measures	Findings
Tse and Olsen (1988)	Restaurant (91)	Survey questionnaire	To explore the relationship of strategy, organizational structure and financial performance	Porter's generic strategies	Return on assets Return on sales and Growth in unit sales	Statistical analysis inconclusive to validate Porter's model
West and Olsen (1988)	Foodservice (65)	Survey questionnaire	To explore the effect of environmental scanning upon firm performance	Porter's generic strategies	Return on assets Return on sales and Growth in unit sales	Environmental scanning in support of intended strategy does relate in a positive fashion to firm performance
Schaffer and Spencer (1988)	Lodging (36)	Survey questionnaire	To explore the relationship between strategic consensus within top management teams and organizational performance	Porter's generic strategies	Percentage change in total revenues and Percentage of operating income to total revenue	Strategic consensus appears to have a curvilinear association with organizational performance
Dev (1989)	Lodging (204)	Survey questionnaire	To explore the relationship between strategy content, environmental uncertainty and financial performance	Miles and Snow	Income before fixed costs/total sales and Sales per available room	The strategy that will produce the best result is dependent on existing environmental circumstances

Tables 3.9 – 3.11: Prior Studies on Relationships between Planning and Performance in the Hospitality Sector

Study	Sample (number)	Methodology	Focus of study	Categorization on planning	Performance measures	Findings
Day and Olsen (1989)	Lodging (176)	Survey questionnaire	To explore the tenet that for firms in the lodging industry must find an optimal pattern of fit between the environment and the firm's business strategy	Miles and Snow	Income before fixed costs/total sales	A match between the state of the environment facing an organization and its business strategy is required for high performance
West (1990)	Foodservice (65)	Survey questionnaire	To explore the combined effect of both content (intended strategy) and process (environmental scanning) on financial performance	Porter's generic strategies	Average return on assets. Average return on sales and Average growth in unit sales	Firm's espousing low cost or differentiation perform significantly higher than focus firms; higher performing firms engage in significantly higher levels of environmental scanning; and the effects are additive
Schaffer and Litschert (1990)	Lodging (36)	Survey questionnaire	To explore the relationship between internal consistency (in strategy and structure) and performance	Miles and Snow	Percentage change in total revenue, over a four year period and, average change in operating profit as a percentage of total revenue	Marginal evidence that internal inconsistency as described by Miles and Snow contributes to higher performance over a four year period

Tables 3.9 – 3.11: Prior Studies on Relationships between Planning and Performance in the Hospitality Sector

Study	Sample (number)	Methodology	Focus of study	Categorization on planning	Performance measures	Findings
West and Anthony (1990)	Foodservice (65)	Survey questionnaire	To explore the performance differences between strategic groups and moderating effect of environmental scanning on individual firm performance within strategic groups	Porter's generic strategies	Average return on sales and Average return on assets	Strategic group membership is but one variable that has an impact upon performance
Tse (1991)	Restaurant (91) Lodging (36)	Survey questionnaire	To explore the relationship between strategy, structure and performance	Porter's generic strategies	Average return on assets Average return on sales and Average growth in unit sales	Generally speaking structure is found to have an impact on the performance in restaurant firms

Tables 3.9 – 3.11: Prior Studies on Relationships between Planning and Performance in the Hospitality Sector

The study by Schaffer and Spencer (1988) was the first to explore the relationship between strategic consensus within top management teams and organizational performance. Three identical questionnaires were mailed to the Chief Executive Officer (CEO), of 386 lodging organizations. The CEO was asked to complete one of the questions and distribute the other two to members of the top management team. Thirty six firms (9.3 per cent) returned three completed questionnaires and served as the sample. Strategy was measured through a self-typing method based on the work by Dess and Davis (1984). Cronbach's Alpha, Carmines and Zeller, (1979), was used to measure strategic consensus among members of the top management team. Data analysis consisted of a two step process. First zero-order correlations (Pearson's) was used to correlate strategic consensus and the four performance variables. Then the sample was divided into consensus levels of weak, moderate and strong. The results did not show a simple positive relationship. Strategic consensus was at first positively related to performance and then peaked at a certain point, but once it past this point, performance declined.

As previously stated environmental scanning was the thrust of the early research in the hospitality industry. Olsen and Bellas (1980), Olsen and DeNoble (1981), DeNoble and Olsen (1982), Slattery and Olsen (1984), DeNoble and Olsen (1986), Kwansa *et al.* (1986), Pinto and Olsen (1987). However, the first empirical study to look at the relationship between environmental scanning and firm performance was conducted by West and Olsen (1988).

In the West and Olsen study, multiple responses from three members of the executive committee, were requested from 310 multi-unit foodservice firms. Ninety two (30 per cent) fully satisfied the requirements of the researchers. Environmental scanning was assessed according to Hambrick's (1979) multi-method, multi-trait scale, which measures the level of a respondent's interest in and frequency of information search. Porter's (1980) model was used to define the areas involved in the scanning process. The performance measure (dependent variable) was regressed against the firm's total scanning (independent variable) to gauge the significance of the relationship. ANOVA statistical analysis was conducted to explore the differences between high and low performers. After removing outliers, both the power and the significance of the tests increase for return on assets (ROA) and resulted in both return on sales (ROS) and ROA becoming significantly correlated with scanning. In other words, high performing firms are involved in significantly greater amounts of scanning.

Dev (1989), Dev and Olsen (1989), West (1990), Schaffer and Litschert (1990), West and Anthony (1990) and Tse (1991) were the next wave of strategy-performance work published. All provided positive relationships, albeit marginal in some cases, Schaffer and Litschert (1990) and West and Anthony (1990). Studies by Dev (1989) and Dev and Olsen (1989) were based upon Dev's doctoral thesis which looked at environmental uncertainty, business strategy and financial performance. This took the early work by West and Oslen (1988) a stage further, as the thrust of the thesis was to investigate the notion that there exists an optimal pattern or fit between the environment and the firm's business strategy. Four thousand executives at 2,000 hotels with more than 150 rooms were sent questionnaires and 204 (10 per cent) hotels responded. This was the first time, that the Miles and Snow typology was used empirically in hospitality strategy–performance research. The Snow and Hrebiniak (1980) self-typing instrument was used to categorized participants. One-way and two-way ANOVA were used to test three hypotheses.

- H_1· No difference will be found in the performance of hotels classified according to their strategy type;
- H_2· In stable environments, there will be no difference in performance between hotels employing different strategies;
- H_3· In volatile environments, there will be no difference in performance between hotels employing different strategies.

The null hypothesis was accepted for the first hypothesis – that employing different strategies can result in equal performance. The results for the second hypothesis was rejected – that there is no performance implication when environment and strategy are matched. With regards to hypothesis three – the hypothesis was rejected but not for the same reasons as mentioned in the literature. Analysers were found to out-perform not only defenders, but also prospectors.

Robinson and Pearce (1988) observed in their review of the strategic management literature, that empirical research had moved from the traditional planning–performance relationship, to the study of the content–performance without any attempt to combine the two, in the study of organizational performance. The thrust of the study by West (1990) was to look at the additive effects (via hypothesis testing) of environmental scanning and performance, making use of data previously gathered by West and Olsen (1988). The results of the study suggested that strategic choice and environmental scanning are important and also additive to firm performance.

The Miles and Snow typology (1978) assumes a need for some form of internal consistency between strategy and structure. Any deviation from the suggested profile implies a weakness in the strategy/structure co-alignment, with a resulting negative effect on performance. Schaffer and Litschert (1990) were the first researchers to test this logic in the hospitality industry. They attempted to address the nature of the linkages among strategic content, organization structure and performance, making use of the work by Miles and Snow (1978). As Schaffer and Litschert had only identified the structural configuration for the defender and prospector, these were the only strategy types researched. These strategic types were measured using the 26-item structured questionnaire derived from the one employed by Dess and Davis (1984) and adapted to the lodging sector. The strategic characteristics observed by Miles and Snow (1978) were related to Dess and Davis (1984) making use of the work by Porter (1980). The dimensions of organization structure used was formalization, specialization and centralization. Data used in the previous study by Schaffer and Spencer (1988) was used to test the following hypotheses:

- H_1 Organizations that exhibit the same strategic type will also exhibit the same level of organization structure;

- H_2. Organizations that achieve internal consistency will out-perform those that do not achieve internal consistency.

To test the strength of hypothesis two, performance measured in terms of both total revenue and profitability is compared between prospectors and defenders:

- H_{2a}. Prospectors and defenders that achieve internal consistency will out-perform prospectors and defenders that do not when performance is measured by total revenue and profitability.

Then to further test the robustness of hypothesis two, the proposition that strategic types may differ in their performance was tested:

- H_{2b}. Prospectors that achieve internal consistency will out-perform prospectors that do not when performance is measured by total revenue;
- H_{2c}. Defenders that achieve internal consistency will out-perform defenders that do not when performance is measured by profitability.

Further hypotheses were tested to look at performance differences by type:

- H_{3a}. Prospectors that achieve internal consistency will out-perform defenders that also achieve internal consistency when performance is measured by total revenue;
- H_{3b}. Defenders that achieve internal consistency will out-perform prospectors that achieve internal consistency when performance is measured by profitability.

Principle component factor analysis Hair, Anderson, Tatham and Grablowsky (1979) was used to test the degree of importance associated with the strategic characteristics and methods employed in the lodging industry. A five factor solution which accounted for 47.5 per cent of the total variance, yielded clusters that compared favourably with Miles and Snow (1978). Three of the four strategic types as identified by Miles and Snow were also present (defender, prospector and analyser). In their concluding remarks Schaffer and Litschert (1990), stated that while the hypotheses testing was marginally favourable some were in the right direction and the results warrant further study.

Hunt (1972) in his study of the US home appliance industry during the 1960s observed that although concentration was high, industry profitability was dismal. In his conclusion, he noted that the concept of industry structure needed to be refined to include strategic groups. Thus, the concept of strategic groups provides an attractive middle ground between firm and industry analysis. However, it was not until the empirical work by West and Anthony (1990) that the concept of strategic groups was applied to the hospitality industry. The West and Anthony study examined performance differences between strategic groups in the foodservice industry and the moderating effect of environmental scanning on inter-group performance. Making use of data previously gathered in West

(1990) study, factor and cluster analysis were used to identify six strategic groups. While significant inter-group performance were observed, the authors stressed that group membership is but one variable that influences performance.

Tse's (1991) study was based extensively on Tse and Olsen (1988), with the most notable difference being the emphasis of the structure–performance link.

METHODOLOGICAL ISSUES

It is proper that a discipline, whether nascent or mature, should take stock of its progress once in a while and the strategic hospitality management literature is no exception. The two most striking features about the research performed to date is the fact that the studies have tended to focus on the strategy variables rather than planning variables. Second, most of the literature is rather normative and lack a rigorous empirical base, Olsen (1991) and Tse (1991).

Many authors who have reported findings from their empirical planning-performance work, used the same data more than once. Tse's (1991) paper is taken from data used in 1988. West managed to get two further papers from data gathered in West and Olsen (1988). Schaffer and Litschert's (1990) paper was based on data gathered in Schaffer and Spencer (1988) and Dev's (1989) paper bore a very similar resemblance to Dev and Olsen (1989).

Hospitality researchers have viewed the environment as a key contingency variable for strategy formulation. Thus, the initial finding that environmental scanning in support of intended strategy does relate in a positive fashion to firm performance has important implications for practitioners and academics. Subsequent environmental scanning–performances have increased the number of independent variables and have produced encouraging results. However, Prescott (1986) states that; research has not established whether environments are:

1) independently related to performance;
2) moderators of the relationship between strategy and performance; or
2) some combination of the two.

The strategy–structure-performance relationship is another area that is of interest to hospitality researchers. Although not all the tests conducted were found to be statistically significant, some of the results are of value to practitioners. Tse (1991, p. 70), pointed out the gaps in the hospitality literature:

> Results of this study suggest that room remains for both better measurement of the variables and for specification of additional explanatory variables. More research on other organizational attributes and how they could be used as substitutes for one another to effectively implement any given strategy, is necessary before a concrete conclusion can be reached. These attributes include different elements of structure, such as administration intensity, functional

co-ordination, interdependence and technology. Performance variables such as return on equity and return on investment can also be used to further determine the impact of strategy and structure on performance.

IMPLICATIONS FOR HOSPITALITY MANAGERS

After a synthesis of the strategic planning-performance relationship as reported in the general literature and strategy-performance relationship in the hospitality specific literature, it is now appropriate to highlight some of the key challenges for hospitality managers.

Strategic planning is often presented as some mysterious process, involving hard work with complex processes and being of benefit to large manufacturing type organizations. This chapter provides some evidence that strategic planning is an important managerial process for service firms and that thinking strategically makes good sense.

However, as succinctly stated by Greenley (1993, p. 3):

> . . . improved management effectiveness through strategic planning may lead to improved performance, but this will depend on the ability of managers to address the range of internal and external variables that impinge on performance.

Therefore the major challenge facing hospitality managers is to improve all aspects of their planning activities, so that they:

- Adopt a multi-functional approach to their decision-making;
- Make decisions based on a full analysis of facts;
- Have a realistic assessment of themselves *vis-à-vis* their competitors.

Already, some hospitality firms, are recognizing the value of strategic planning and the rewards it generates. This therefore, ought to represent a watershed for the industry and serve as a warning to those firms who have not fully considered the implications of strategic planning.

As a starting point, hospitality managers should determine the gap between their business unit and at least phase III (strategic planning) of Phillips' four phases (1994). Then attempt to close the gap, by making the necessary changes to their firm's value system and create the necessary structures and processes, that minimize implementation problems that are flexible to any rapid changes in the internal and external environment.

REFERENCES

Ackelsberg, R., and Arlow, P., (1985), Small businesses do plan and it pays off, *Long Range Planning*, 18, 5, 61–67.

Ansoff, H. I., (1965), *Corporate Strategy*, New York, McGraw-Hill.

Ansoff, H. I., (1987), The emerging paradigm of strategic behaviour, *Strategic Management Journal*, 8, pp. 501–515.

Ansoff, H. I., Arner, J., Brandenberg, R. G., Portner, F. E. and Radosevich, R., (1970), Does planning pay? The effect of planning on the success of acquisitions in American firms, *Long Range Planning*, 3, 2, 2–7.

Anthony, R., (1964), Framework for analysis in management planning, *Management Services*, March-April, 18–24.

Anthony, R., (1965), *Planning and Control Systems: A Framework for Analysis*, Boston, Harvard University.

Armstrong, J. S., (1982), The value of formal planning for strategic decisions: review of empirical research, *Strategic Management Journal*, 3, 197–211.

Boyd, B. K., (1991), Strategic planning and financial performance: A meta-analytic review, *Journal of Management Studies*, 28, 4, 353–374.

Bracker, J.S. and Pearson, J. N., (1986), Planning and financial performance of small, mature firms, *Strategic Management Journal*, 7, 503–522.

Bracker, J.S., Keats, B. W. and Pearson, J. N., (1988), Planning and financial performance among small firms in a growth industry, *Strategic Management Journal*, 9, 591–603.

Burt, D. N., (1978), Planning and performance in Australian retailing, *Long Range Planning*, 11, 3, 62–66.

Canas, J., (1982), 'Strategic corporate planning', in Robert C. Lewis, Thomas J. Beggs, Margaret Shaw and Stephen A. Croffoot (eds), *The Practice of Hospitality Management II*, AVI Publishing, Westport, Conn., pp. 229–236.

Capon, N., Farley, J. U. and Hulbert, J. M., (1987), *Corporate Strategic Planning*: New York, Columbia University Press.

Capon, N., Farley, J. U. and Hulbert, J. M., (1994), Strategic planning and financial performance: more evidence, *Journal of Management Studies*, 31, 1, 105–110.

Carmines, E. G. and Zeller, R. A., (1979), *Reliability and Validity Assessment*, Beverly Hills, Sage Publications.

Dalton, D. R., Todor, M. J., Spendolini, M. J., Fielding, G. J. and Porter, L. W., (1980), Organisation structure and performance: A critical review, *Academy of Management Review*, 5, 1, 49–64.

DeNoble, A., (1986), Restaurant acquisitions the post merger integration process in Robert C. Lewis, Thomas J. Beggs, Margaret Shaw and Stephen A. Croffoot (eds), *The Practice of Hospitality Management II*, AVI Publishing, Westport, Conn., pp. 91–101.

DeNoble, A. and Olsen, M. D., (1982), The relationship between the strategic planning process and the service delivery system, in Abraham Pizam, Robert C. Lewis and Peter Manning, (eds), *The Practice of Hospitality Management*, AVI Publishing, Westport, Conn., pp. 229–236.

DeNoble, A. and Olsen, M. D., (1986), The food service industry environment: market volatility analysis, *FIU Hospitality Review*, 4, 2, 89–100.

Dess, G. G. and Davis, P. S., (1984), Porter's (1980) generic strategies as determinants of strategic group membership and organizational performance, *Academy of Management Journal*, 27, 3, 467–488.

Dev, C. S., (1989), Operating environment and strategy: The profitable connection, *Cornell Hotel and Restaurant Administration Quarterly*, 30, 2, 9–14.

Dev, C. S. and Olsen, M. (1989), Environmental uncertainty, business strategy and financial performance: An empirical study of the US Lodging Industry, *Hospitality Education Research Journal*, 13, 2, 171–186.

Eastlack, J. O., and McDonald, P. R., (1970), CEOs role in corporate growth, *Harvard Business Review*, 48, 3, 150–160.

Fender, D. J., (1990), Getting started: The use of simple strategic frameworks, *International Journal of Contemporary Hospitality Management*, 2, 3, iv–vi.

Fender, D. J. and Litteljohn, D., (1992), Forward planning in uncertain times, *International Journal of Contemporary Hospitality Management*, 4, 3, i–iv.

Frederickson, J. W., (1984), The comprehensiveness of strategic decision process: extension, observations, future directions, *Academy of Management Journal*, 27, 445–446.

Frederickson, J. W. and Mitchell, T. R., (1984), Strategic decision process: comprehensiveness and performance in an industry with an unstable environment, *Academy of Management Journal*, 15, 91–101.

Fulmer, R.M. and Rue, L.W., (1974), The practice and profitability of long-range planning, *Managerial Planning*, 22, 1–7.

Gershefski, G. W., (1970), Corporate models – the state of the art, *Management Science*, 16, 6, 303–312.

Glueck, F., Kaufman, S. and Walleck, A. S., (1982), The four phases of strategic management, *Journal of Business Strategy*, 2, 3, 9–21.

Greenley, G.E., (1986a), The relationship of strategic and marketing plans *European Journal of Operational Research*, 27, 17–24.

Greenley, G.E., (1986b), Does strategic planning improve company performance? *Long Range Planning*, 19, 2, 101–109.

Greenley, G.E., (1993), *Research on Strategic Planning and Performance: A Synthesis*, University of Birmingham Working Paper, ISBN 0 7044 1273 X.

Gregg, Joseph B., (1986), 'Strategic planning: implications and applications for line managers', *FIU Hospitality Review*, 4, 1, 73–85.

Grinyer, P. H., and Norburn, D., (1975), Planning for existing markets: perceptions of executives and financial performance, *Journal of the Statistical Society*, 138, 1, 70–97.

Guth, W. D., (1972), The growth and profitability of the firm: a managerial explanation, *Journal of Business Policy*, 2, 3, 31–36.

Guttman, L., (1947), The Cornell technique for scale and intensity analysis, *Education Psychology Measurement*, 7, 247–279.

Hair, J. F., Anderson, R. E., Tatham, R. L. and Grablowsky, B. J., (1979), *Multivariate Data Analysis*, Tulsa, OK, Petroleum Publishing Company.

Hambrick, D. C., (1979), *Environmental; Scanning, Organisational Strategy and Executives Roles: A Study in Three Industries*, Unpublished doctoral dissertation, University Microfilm International. 7922294.

Herold, D.M., (1972), Long-range planning and organizational performance: a cross-validation study, *Academy of Management Journal*, 15, 91–101.

Hunt, M., (1972), *Competition in the Major Appliance Industry 1960–1970*, PhD dissertation. Harvard University.

Kallman, E. A., and Shapiro, H. J., (1978), The motor freight industry – a case against planning, *Long Range Planning*, 11, 1, 81–86.

Karger, D. W., and Malik, Z. A., (1975), Long range planning and organizational performance, *Long Range Planning*, 8, 6, 60–64.

King, W.R., (1983), Evaluating strategic planning systems, *Strategic Management Journal*, 4, 263–277.

Klein, H.E., (1981), The impact of planning on growth and profit, *Journal of Bank Research*, 33, 2, 4–9.

Kudla, R. J., (1980), The effects of strategic planning on common stock returns, *Academy of Management Journal*, 23, 1, 5–20.

Kwansa, Francis, Chekitan Dev, Nor Khomar Isak, Mary Kay Meyer, Michael D. Olsen, Regina Robichaud, Nazimudeen Saleem and Joseph J. West, (1986) 'An analysis of major trends and their impact potential affecting the hospitality industry as identified by the method of content analysis', *Proceedings of the Annual Conference of the Council on Hotel, Restaurant and Institutional Education*, pp 168–93.

Leontiades, M. and Tezel, A., (1980), Planning perceptions and planning results, *Strategic Management Journal*, 1, 65–75.

Miles, R. E. and Snow, C. C., (1978), *Organisational Strategy, Structure and Process*, New York, McGraw-Hill.

Morishima, M., (1982), *Why Has Japan Succeeded*, Cambridge University Press.

Nanus, B. and Lundberg, C., (1988), 'In QUEST of strategic planning', *Cornell Hotel and Restaurant Administration Quarterly*, 29, 2, 18–23.

Nebel, E. C. and Shaffer, J, D, (1992), Hotel Strategic planning at the business and unit level in the USA in Teare, R. and Olsen, M., (eds) *International Hospitality Management*, Pitman Publishing, pp. 228–252.

Odom, R.Y. and Boxx, W.R., (1988), Environment, planning processes and organizational performance of churches, *Strategic Management Journal*, 9, 197–205.

Olsen, M. D. and Bellas C. J., (1980), 'The importance of the environment to the food service and lodging manager', *The Journal of Hospitality Education*, 4, 2, 35–45.

Olsen, M. D. and DeNoble, A., (1981), 'Strategic planning in dynamic times', *Cornell Hotel and Restaurant Administration Quarterly*, 21(4): pp. 75–80.

Olsen, M. D., (1991), 'Strategic management in the hospitality industry: A literature review', *Progress in Tourism, Recreation and Hospitality Management*, 3, 215–31.

Pearce, J.A. and Robinson, R.B., (1985), *Strategy Formulation and Implementation*, Richard D. Irwin, Illinois.

Pearce, J.A., Freeman, E.B. and Robinson, R.B., (1987), The tenuous link between formal strategic planning and financial Performance, *Academy of Management Review*, 12, 4, 658–675.

Phillips, P.A., (1994), An Empirical Investigation of the Strategic Planning Practices of the Corporate Hotel sector in South Wales, *Conference Paper- Council for Hospitality Management Education*, 3rd Research Conference, Manchester Metropolitan University.

Pinto, E. and Olsen, M. D., (1987), 'The information needs of finance executives in the hospitality industry', *The Hospitality Education and Research Journal*, 11, 2, 181–90.

Porter, M., (1980), *Competitive Strategy: Techniques for Analysing Industries and Competitors*, The Free Press, New York.

Potetsianakis, E. E., (1979), *Corporate Planning of Established Firms in the Hotel Industry*, (Unpublished) MSc Dissertation, University of Bath.

Prescott, J. E., (1986), Environments as moderators of the relationship between strategy and performance, *Academy of Management Journal*, 29, 329–346.

Prestowitz, C. V., (1988), *Trading Places,* New York, Free Press.

Reichel, A., (1983), Strategic management: How to apply it to firms in the hospitality industry, *The Services Industry Journal*, 3, 3, 329–343.

Reid, R. and Olsen, M.D., (1981), A strategic planning model for independent food service operators, *The Journal of Hospitality Education*, 6,1, 11–24.

Rhenman, E., (1973), *Organisational Theory for Long Range Planning*, Wiley, London.

Rhyne, L.C., (1986), The relationship of strategic planning to company performance, *Strategic Management Journal*, 7, 423–436.

Robinson, R. B., (1982), The importance of outsiders in small firm strategic planning, *Academy of Management Journal*, 25, 1, 80–93.

Robinson, R.B. and Pearce, J.A., (1983), The impact of formalized strategic planning on financial performance in small organizations, *Strategic Management Journal*, 4, 197–207.

Robinson, R.B. and Pearce, J.A., (1988), Planned patterns of strategic behaviour and their relationship to business-unit performance, *Strategic Management Journal*, 9, 43–60.

Robinson, R. B., Pearce, J. A., Vozikis, G. S., and Mescon, T. S., (1984), The relationship between stages of development and small firm planning and performance, *Journal of Small Business Management*, 22, 2, 45–52.

Sapp, R. W., and Seiler, R. E., (1981), The relationship between long-range planning and financial performance in US commercial banks, *Managerial Planning*, 29, 32–36.

Schaffer, J.D., (1986), *Competitive Strategy Organisational Performance in the Lodging Industry: An Empirical Assessment of Miles and Snow's (1978) Perspective of Organisations*, Unpublished doctoral dissertation, Virginia Polytechnic Institute and State University.

Schaffer, J.D. and Litschert, R.J., (1990), Internal consistency between strategy and structure: Performance implications in the lodging industry, *Hospitality Education and Research Journal*, 14, 1, 35–3.

Schaffer, J.D. and Spencer, B.A., (1988), Strategic consensus and organizational performance in the lodging industry, *Hospitality Education and Research Journal*, 12, 3, 1–16.

Shrader, C. B., Taylor, L. and Dalton, D.R., (1984), Strategic planning and organizational performance: a critical appraisal, *Journal of Management*, 10, 2, 149–171.

Sirkis, R. L., Race, S. M., (1982), 'Strategic planning for the food service industry', in Abraham Pizam, Robert C. Lewis and Peter Manning (eds), *The Practice of Hospitality Management*, AVI Publishing, Westport, Conn., pp 37–47.

Slattery, P and Olsen, M. D., (1984), 'Hospitality organizations and their environments', *International Journal of Hospitality Management*, 3, 2, 55–61.

Smith, T., (1992), *Accounting for Growth: Stripping the Camouflage from Company Accounts*, Century Business.

Snow, C. C. and Hrebiniak, L. G., (1980), Strategy, distinctive competence and organizational performance, *Administrative Science Quarterly*, 25, pp. 317–336.

Steiner, G. A., (1979), *Strategic Planning: What Every Manager Must Know*, Free Press, New York.

Steiner, G. A., and Cannon, W., (1966), *Multinational Corporate Planning*, (eds), New York: Crowell-Collier and Macmillan Company.

Thune, S. S. and House, R.J., (1970), Where long range planning pays off, *Business Horizons*, 13, 82–87.

Tse, E. C., (1991), An empirical analysis of organizational structure and financial performance in the restaurant industry, *International Journal Of Hospitality Management*, 10, 1, 59–72.

Tse, E. C. and Olsen, M., (1988), The impact of strategy and structure on the organizational performance of restaurant firms, *Hospitality Education Research Journal*, 12, 2, 265–276.

Tsuruni, Y., (1984), *Multinational Management: Business Strategy and Government Policy*, Cambridge, MA, Ballinger Press.

Van Woiferen, K., (1989), *The Enigma of Japanese Power*, Cambridge, MA, MIT Press.

Walker, O. C., Jr and Ruekert, R. W., (July 1987), Marketing's role in the implementation of business strategies: A critical review and conceptual framework, *Journal of Marketing*, 51, 15–33.

West, J. J. and Anthony, W. P., (1990), Strategic group membership and environmental scanning their relationship to firm performance in the foodservice industry, *International Journal of Hospitality Management*, 9, 3, 247–267.

West, J. J. and Olsen, M. D., (1989), 'Environmental scanning, industry structure and strategy making: concepts and research in the hospitality industry', *International Journal of Hospitality Management*, 8, 4, 283–98.

West, J. J., (1990), Strategy, Environmental scanning and firm performance: An integration of content and process in the foodservice industry, *Hospitality Education and Research Journal*, 14, 1, 87–100.

West, J. J. and Olsen, M., (1988), Environmental scanning and its effects upon firm performance: An exploratory study of the foodservice industry, *Hospitality Education and Research Journal*, 12, 2, 127–136.

Whitehead, D. D., and Gup, B. E., (1985), Bank and thrift profitability: does strategic planning really pay? *Economic Review*, October, 14–25.

Wilson, I. (1994), Strategic Planning isn't Dead it Changed, *Long Range Planning*, 27, 4, 12–24.

Wood, D.R. and LaForge, R. L., (1979), The impact of comprehensive planning on financial performance, *Academy of Management Journal*, 23, 3, 516–526.

Wood, D.R. and LaForge, R. L., (1981), Towards the development of a planning scale: an example from the banking industry, *Strategic Management Journal*, 2, 209–216.

4

Organizational Culture and Control in a Strategic Planning Context: Implications for the International Hospitality Industry

Jackie Brander Brown and Peter Harris

There is now a growing understanding that the strategy of an enterprise, its structure, the sorts of people who hold power, its control systems and the way it operates, tend to reflect the culture of that organization.

Johnson and Scholes, 1993

INTRODUCTION

Organizational culture – that is the underlying values and beliefs shared by the members of an organization – is being increasingly recognized as having a significant influence on an organization's strategy as well as being a major contingent variable to be 'incorporated' in the design of effective organizational control systems. Such control systems, which it has been argued are an inevitable characteristic of all forms of human organizations, are widely viewed as an essential element of the overall process of management, linking the processes of strategic planning and operational control, while their potential power to positively assist organizations to achieve 'their' goals and objectives is well established.

However, it has also been claimed that failure by management to design control systems which are consistent with their organizations' culture and strategy will at best lead to organizational ineffectiveness, or may even result in active resistance to the control system – which could potentially result in the ultimate failure of the control system, seriously hindering the progression of an organization towards its goals and objectives.

Given the importance of the international hospitality industry in a global context and given the possible problematic implications that may arise from a 'mismatch' between organizational culture, strategic planning and management control, it would appear that this vital relationship deserves very serious consideration. More specifically then, this chapter will first consider the term 'organizational culture' including the influential variables that typically underlie an organization's culture and its significance and likely implications for the international hospitality industry. The chapter will then consider a number of significant areas concerning strategic planning and control, and in particular the 'essential' features of effective management control systems and evidence regarding management control systems in the international hospitality industry. Using these considerations as a base, the chapter will then develop a range of theoretical assertions concerning the relationship between organizational culture and management control in a strategic planning context and, its impact on overall organizational effectiveness for companies operating within the international hospitality industry.

ORGANIZATIONAL CULTURE

Culture refers to the underlying values, beliefs, and principles that serve as a foundation for an organizations management systems as well as a set of management practices and behaviours that both exemplify and reinforce those basic principles.

Denison, 1990

Although there have been many attempts to explain the term 'organizational culture' – Kroeber and Kluckhohn (1963) for instance identified no less than 164 meanings – it has been noted that there is still no absolute consensus regarding its definition, (Smircich, 1963; Mullins, 1992). There is, however, considerable agreement about – and overlap between – the key elements and dimensions of organizational culture (Reynolds, 1986), including those of shared meanings (Louis, 1985), central values (Ouchi, 1979; Barney, 1986) and beliefs (Lorsch, 1985; Schein, 1985; Gordon and DiTomaso, 1992). Similarly, while Johnson and Scholes (1993) note that 'sets' of such shared organizational meanings, central values and beliefs have been referred to by a number of other terms, including interpretative schemes (Bartunek, 1984), paradigms (Pfeffer, 1981) and recipes (Grinyer and Spender, 1979), it should also be noted that there is likewise considerable 'agreement' regarding the significance of organizational culture and its underlying influences and characteristics.

Significance of Organizational Culture

The significance of organizational culture for all forms of organizations has been recognized by a number of academic writers – see, for example, Pettigrew (1979); Ouchi (1979); Deal and Kennedy (1982) – and include both positive and negative viewpoints.

As well as Johnson and Scholes' recognition of the potential importance of organizational culture, noted previously, among other more positive implications associated with organizational culture is that noted by Mullins (1992):

> Organization culture will influence the pride that people have in their jobs and
> the appropriateness of the manager's methods of motivation. Culture is also a
> major determinant of organizational performance and effectiveness

Similar claims are made by Handy (1985) and Denison (1990), while both
Glover (1987) and van Donk and Sanders (1993) see organizational culture as an
effective management tool/control mechanism, especially with regard to daily
operational tasks, product quality and staff productivity. In this context, and
with regard to the specific nature of the hospitality industry, Mullins (1992) also
suggests that organizational culture is likely to prove a vital component in the
standards of delivery of service to customers.

A number of researchers have also considered the relevance and importance
of the 'strength' of an organization's culture, with Peters and Waterman (1982)
finding it to be an essential quality of excellent companies while both Denison
(1990) and Gordon and DiTomaso (1991) suggest that a strong culture can be a
predictor of good short-term performance.

However, more cautionary viewpoints of organizational culture have also
been expressed, including the concern, already noted, that any failure by management to design control systems that are consistent with their organization's
culture may lead to active resistance to the control system, (Flamholtz, 1983;
Markus and Pfeffer, 1983; Gordon, 1991). Flamholtz (1983), for instance, provides an example of managers in an organization – where the culture strongly
emphasized sales – virtually ignoring the organization's budgetary control and
administration systems. Handy (1985) meanwhile goes further in suggesting:

> Many of the ills of organizations stem from imposing an inappropriate struc-
> ture on a particular culture, or from expecting a particular culture to thrive in
> an inappropriate climate.

While both Glover (1987) and Schein (1992) highlight the problem of managers
being insufficiently aware of, or misunderstanding, the effects of corporate culture. Glover (1987), for example, claims that in the context of hospitality operations, if management misunderstand the impact of organizational culture the
quality of products and services may suffer through a 'cult of ineffectiveness' – a
'cult' arising from such organizational characteristics as a lack of agreed standards of performance, a lack of balanced controls and poor communication.

This apparent positive/negative, 'double-edged' nature of organizational culture is particularly relevant in the context of strategic planning: both Schwartz
and Davis (1981) and Shrivastava (1985) note that organizations may find –
with regard to their strategic decision making – their cultures may be a source
of strength, grounded as they are in experience, or they may be a source of weakness – this particularly where culture acts to 'restrict' decision alternatives.

Influences on Organizational Culture

An organization's culture will emerge and develop over time, and it is likely to be affected by a complex combination of influential variables – many reflecting the industry in which the organization operates (Gordon, 1985 and 1991; Reynolds, 1986). A number of important general factors that are likely to play a critical role in the development of organizational culture are illustrated in Figure 4.1, and considered below:

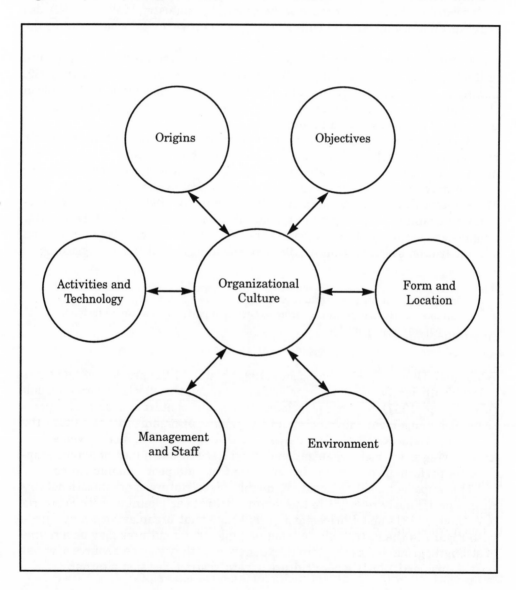

Figure 4.1: Influences on Organizational Culture

Origins

The reason and manner in which an organization was originally founded, the particular era in which it was founded and the philosophy and values of its owners and first senior managers are all likely to have a significant impact on an organization's culture (Handy, 1985; Mullins, 1992; Johnson and Scholes, 1993). Moreover, Mullins (1992) also notes that significant events in an organization's history – such as merger or take-over, or a new generation of managers – may result in 'changes' in that culture.

Activities and Technology

Mullins (1992) notes that the nature of organizations' key activities will also have an important effect on its culture and, in particular, states that relevant contributory factors include the range and quality of products and services provided by the organization, the importance of its reputation and the typical type of customer – and with regard to the hospitality industry poses the following illustrative comparison of such factors:

> . . . a traditional, high-class hotel, particularly noted for its cuisine, with a popular mass-production fast-food chain store.

Key activities though will not only affect how an organization undertakes its main functions, but is also likely to affect the nature and extent of an organization's technology, including its methods of undertaking work. Studies such as those of Woodward (1958), Perrow (1967), Daft and Macintosh (1978) and Merchant (1984) all serve to indicate that an organization's technology is an important influencing factor on organizational culture: Woodward (1958), for example, demonstrated that the form of an organization's technology can be a major determinant in the effectiveness of organizations through an appropriate 'matching' with the organization's culture and structure. Handy (1985) meanwhile confirms that an organization's culture should appropriately match the underlying technology, as no one culture can be preferable in all circumstances.

Objectives

Handy (1985) also proposes that the objectives of an organization are seldom 'clear-cut' – for instance, although many business organizations may cite profitability as their primary objective, in reality organizations must give attention to much wider considerations, including long-term survival, growth and development, product/service quality and social responsibilities (Handy, 1985; Mullins, 1992). Both Handy (1985) and Mullins (1992) further contend that these objectives will not only influence an organization's culture, but may themselves be influenced by changes in the culture.

Form and Location

An organization's size and structure has often proved to be a significant influence on an organization's culture, (Handy, 1985): for instance, Mullins (1992) notes that larger organizations tend to have relatively formalized cultures. Additionally, increased size has also been found to lead to the formation of separate regions, divisions and departments and potentially the development of multi-site operations, with significant implications for co-ordination and communication. Mullins (1992) also notes that rapid expansions or contractions in the size or rate of growth of an organization will also significantly influence culture.

Meanwhile, the geographical location and associated physical characteristics of an organization will also have an important influence on an organization's culture – for instance, compare a luxurious resort hotel in an out-of-the way location with a busy city-centre business hotel. This impact of underlying locational factors, such as on the range of services provided and on opportunities for development, is likely to be even more pronounced in an international context.

Management and Staff

Mullins (1992) notes that executives will almost certainly have a considerable effect on the nature of an organization's culture: Peters and Waterman (1982) suggest that 'excellent' companies begin with strong leaders. However, it should also be noted that 'ordinary' members of staff, throughout all levels and areas of an organization will also help shape the dominant culture of an organization. Indeed, Handy (1985) claims that when selecting employees, organizations are essentially determining their culture.

Environment

The nature of an organization's environment – that is the economic environment, the market, the competitive scene as well as the geographical and societal environment – can be crucially important in determining its culture, (Handy, 1985). For instance, it may be suggested that if an organization is operating in an environment which is diverse and changing, an 'organic' rather than a 'mechanistic' organizational culture is more likely to be more responsive to the new choices and challenges, risks and restrictions presented by the external environment (Burns and Stalker, 1961; Handy, 1985; Mullins, 1992).

The evidence presented here suggests that organizational culture is an intricate and subtle phenomenon which has far reaching implications for the management control of an undertaking. As indicated, it is influenced by numerous economic, business and operational factors and yet it in turn it also influences these factors – indeed Weick (1985) has suggested that culture and strategy at times may even be substitutable for each other. Thus, is organizational culture the 'driving force' of an organization, or is it 'driven by' the organization? Whilst such an understanding involves circular reasoning – the 'chicken or egg argument' – it is nevertheless apparent that organizational culture is a prominent and integral component in the management control of an organization. In fact, its presence and influence suggests that it is fundamental to the underpinning of an organization.

ORGANIZATIONAL CULTURE AND THE INTERNATIONAL HOSPITALITY INDUSTRY

In order to apply the knowledge of organizational culture to the design of effective management control systems, it is important to understand the composition of the particular business involved. Whilst the international hospitality industry can be said to include hotels, restaurants, catering and tourism facilities, its major components comprise the provision and service of accommodation, food and beverages. As hotels usually incorporate all these activities it is useful to understand the complexity of hospitality services within the context of a hotel.

The main services offered by a hotel are organized through rooms, bar and restaurant facilities. The room letting activity represents a near pure, intangible 'service' product comparable to an airline flight or car rental, where the facility is hired (borrowed) for a predetermined period. The bar activity represents a 'retail' product which comprises buying, displaying, merchandizing and selling various drinks – similar in principle to department stores and shops. The restaurant activity contains a 'manufacturing' or 'production' function that includes the purchase and conversion of raw materials into finished products (meals) and their distribution and sale to customers in a manner similar in principle to car manufacturers and domestic appliance producers. Thus, the co-ordination of significant services, retail and production functions is required to provide an integrated hotel product. Although the knowledge of the hotel business alone does not identify or attempt to assess the influence of organizational culture present, it does highlight the degree of complexity within which the organizational culture issues are required to be explored with regard to the international hospitality industry.

Investigations carried out thus far into the cultural orientation of the many various sectors of the international hospitality industry have particularly concentrated on an 'external versus internal' emphasis – that is essentially on the relative degrees of organizations' outward/market or inward/cost orientation – and its likely implications, for instance, for 'effective' strategies and controls.

A number of important factors which it is argued may have a significant impact on the cultural orientation of international hospitality organizations are considered here, including:

Cost Structure

It has been suggested that, in general, the higher the proportion of fixed costs in a hospitality organization, the greater should be the degree of that organization's market orientation – and the greater in consequence the dependence of the business on market demand (Kotas, 1975; Harris, 1992). Moreover, both Kotas and Harris also consider that the higher the relative proportion of an organization's variable costs, the greater should be the degree of cost orientation and the lesser the degree of dependence on market factors. The likely effect of an organization's cost structure on its profitability and profit stability can be usefully portrayed by means of the comparative CVP charts, as in Figure 4.2.

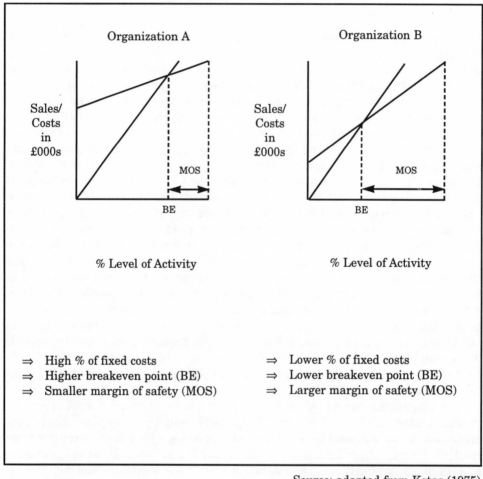

Source: adapted from Kotas (1975)

Figure 4.2: Effect of Cost Structure on Profit Stability

As many hospitality organizations typically experience a high percentage of fixed costs – due, for example, to such factors as their form and location, their activities and technology – while with regard to their variable costs, may find it difficult to benefit from economies of scale (Harris, 1992), their ultimate profitability is dependent to a considerable extent on their turnover. Hence, it is suggested that managers when considering strategic planning and control in such situations should particularly concern themselves with the revenue side of the business – for instance with food and beverage quality standards, acceptability of services, pricing decisions and sales mix analyses.

Capital Intensity

High capital intensity has been linked to a relatively high level of fixed costs, for example due to the effects of related depreciation and maintenance charges. The result of this combination on the balance of costs, as has been noted previously, is likely to affect the degree of market orientation of a business. Hospitality organizations – again as a result largely of their activities and technology – are not only capital intensive but also capital specific and are typically located where their 'output' is consumed, which again suggests a relative emphasis on consumer demand by management would be most appropriate.

Labour Intensity

The production and delivery of hospitality services is mainly carried out by people rather than by machines, with considerable implications for an organization's culture. Although in recent years considerable resources have been expended by hospitality organizations in an effort to reduce dependence upon the human factor, the main advances have been made through increased productivity attained from improved working arrangements, de-skilling and training, as opposed to any significant introduction of mechanization. Consumer demand and requirements in the provision of rooms, food and beverage services are such that machines have, so far, been unable to replace human beings to any appreciable extent.

Demand for Products and Services

Many hospitality organizations operate in complex environments and typically experience considerable fluctuations in demand levels, with many establishments experiencing peaks of intensive activity as well as slack periods (Harris, 1992). A particular factor that can aggravate this problem of sales instability, is that of fixed capacity – for instance in terms of seats or beds – which may mean that an organization may not be able to accommodate all potential customers when demand is 'heavy', while when business is 'slack' substantial fixed costs still have to be met. The combination of relative sales instability with fixed capacity can therefore present many serious problems for hospitality managers who, Kotas (1975) suggests, *must* take a more market oriented approach if they are to solve them.

Nature of Products and Services

One of the key factors which particularly distinguishes hospitality operations is the nature of their products and services. It is claimed that hospitality organizations are characterized by the relatively low volume but wide choice of their products and services, which also tend to be intangible and highly perishable: a bed-night unsold, for example, represents an irretrievable loss of revenue (Jones and Lockwood, 1989; Harris, 1992). Also another significant characteristic of hospitality operations is the immediacy of their activities: a customer requesting a meal or drink, for instance, cannot realistically be asked to wait until a later date. Given such characteristics, it may be suggested that the greater will be an organization's 'dependence' on consumer demand. Moreover, where these characteristics are associated with sales instability, Kotas (1975) again suggests that a market oriented approach must exist.

Note: in order to determine the orientation of hospitality organizations, Kotas [(1975); (1986)] developed a 'business orientation chart', an example of which is shown in Figure 4.3.

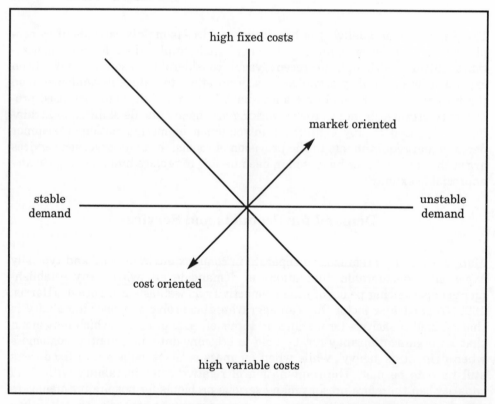

Source: adapted from Kotas (1986)

Figure 4.3 The Business Orientation Chart

The chart, by reflecting the relative proportions of an organization's fixed and variable costs alongside the stability of its consumer demand, enables the assessment of the extent to which an organization may be said to be cost or market oriented – the most market oriented being positioned in the upper right-hand quadrant, the most cost-oriented in the lower left-hand quadrant. Although the chart does not explicitly take account of either the capital intensity of an organization, nor the perishability of its products or services, Kotas (1975) contends that these factors are reflected by the relative cost structure and stability of demand.

MANAGEMENT CONTROL

> . . . control is an inevitable feature of all human organizations . . .
>
> *Flamholtz, 1983*

Like 'organizational culture', the term 'management control' has been interpreted in a wide variety of ways, both by practising managers as well as academic writers: Rathe (1960) for instance lists 57 meanings, ranging from 'prohibition' to 'manipulation'. Other 'negative' interpretations, such as those of Fayol (1949) and Tannenbaum (1968), have linked the process of control with notions of domination, conformance, regulation and exploitation, while more positive views have suggested that management control is concerned with integration, motivation, communication, improvement and mediation (Collins, 1982; Jones, 1985; Cunningham, 1992; Mullins, 1993). A more 'positive' point of view has been expressed by Anthony (1965), who defines management control as:

> . . . the process by which managers assure that resources are obtained and used effectively and efficiently in the accomplishment of the organization's objectives.

Significantly, as shown in Figure 4.4, Anthony saw management control as linking the processes of strategic planning and operational control by ensuring that the everyday operational tasks of an organization form a co-ordinated set of actions directed at assisting the achievement of an organization's overall goals (Anthony, 1965; Otley, 1995). A similar opinion is expressed by Ward (1992) who views control as a positive tool, acting as a 'learning process' within the task of strategic planning.

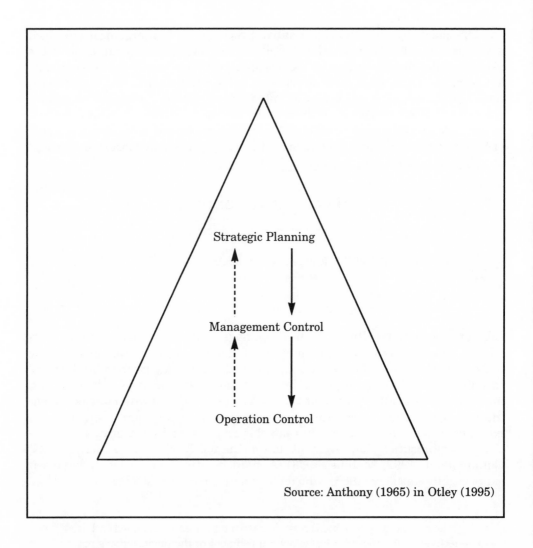

Source: Anthony (1965) in Otley (1995)

Figure 4.4: The Position of Management Control

One important implication of such considerations is that the exercise of control methods and techniques should not only be in the hands of those employees holding managerial positions. Rather, it should involve every employee from the customer interface right through to the boardroom, as everyone in the organization is involved in activities aimed at achieving organizational objectives, (Otley, 1987).

A second important implication is that effective management control systems will incorporate a wide variety of control methods and techniques – including, for instance, standardized procedures and operating manuals, job descriptions, supervision and personnel appraisals, staff meetings and training courses, budgets and forecasts, performance measures and reports, (Flamholtz, 1983; Otley, 1987; Otley and Wilkinson, 1988). The all too common concentration by many researchers on accounting (financial) controls and in particular on the use of budgets, can reflect only a partial consideration of the 'real' impact of management control.

Elements of Management Control

Whatever the combination of management control methods and techniques utilized by an organization to link strategic planning and operational control, a number of essential elements in a control system have been recognized, as illustrated in Figure 4.5.

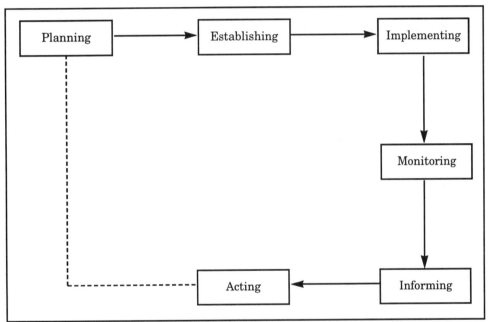

Source: adapted from Brander Brown (1995)

Figure 4.5 The Process of Management Control

Planning

The first stage in a control process is typically that of planning – including strategic planning – involving the specification of the primary goals and objectives of the organization. Hall (1975) describes such goals as:

> . . . the desired ends or states of affairs for whose achievement system policies are committed and resources allocated.

Mullins (1993) notes that planning is a vital step in a system of management control, as it is essential for both the organization's management and employees to fully understand and appreciate what is being asked of them and why, while both Peters and Waterman (1982) and Goldsmith and Clutterbuck (1985) found that successful companies that demonstrated a very clear understanding of organizational objectives were able to keep central controls to a minimum.

Establishing

Having determined the organization's plans, the second stage in the management control process is the setting of realistic, verifiable and clear standards of performance which are relevant to the organization's stated goals and objectives and reflect the level of aspiration sought to be attained for such goals and objectives (Flamholtz, 1983). Among others, Cole (1993) and Mullins (1993) suggest that these performance standards can be utilized at a later stage in the control process as a base from which to establish the direction and extent of the organization's success in achieving its objectives.

Implementing

Having established appropriate standards of performance, an organization can then implement its plans involving the ongoing utilization of a range of appropriate control tools and techniques (Flamholtz, 1983). Hopwood (1976) identifies three categories of such controls: administrative, social and self-control while Mullins (1993) suggests that such controls can focus on the measurement of inputs, outputs and processes or the behaviour of people; they can be concerned with general results or with specific actions; they can involve the evaluation of the overall performance of the organization as a whole or with individual sections of it.

Monitoring

The monitoring stage in a typical management control process involves the measurement, by means of a detector or sensor (Anthony and Govindarajan, 1995), of the resulting actual performance in terms of objective attainment and the comparison of these results with the standards set previously. For such measurements and comparisons to be worthwhile, however, it is firstly important that they fully reflect the standard of performance achieved. Eder and Umbreit (1989) suggest that this implies that a variety of measures must be used: accounting and non-accounting, quantifiable and non-quantifiable. It is also important that the assessment of variances between actual and planned performance takes account of both positive as well as negative deviations.

Informing

The results determined at the monitoring stage of the control process must be relayed – for example via management reports, presentations, review meetings and by formal or informal discussions – on a timely basis to management and employees (Cole, 1993; Mullins, 1993). The provision of effective feedback information can assist with the confirmation and acceptance of deviations between desired and actual performance achieved by the organization. More importantly it should also assist with the identification of the likely causes and implications of such deviations.

Acting

Based on the feedback information provided, management can then decide whether they need to take any corrective action and what sort of action they may need to take, in order to keep their organization moving towards the achievement of its goals and objectives. Cole (1993) notes that most organizations only require action to be taken when the deviation against standard is significant – the principle of 'management by exception'. Typically the choices facing management in this respect will involve actions, either to improve actual performance, or to modify the plans and standards set.

It should be noted though that even if an organization has all of these components in place in its control system, these elements alone would not be sufficient to 'ensure' the organization will achieve its objectives. For that to be the case the management control system would both need to reflect the specific contextual circumstances in which the organization finds itself and also demonstrate a number of characteristics that have been found to be specifically associated with effective control.

Organizational Context

The idea that the design of control systems should reflect the specific contextual circumstances in which an organization operates, has been recognized by practising managers for some considerable time and has been subject to investigation and development by academic theorists since the mid-1970s. Emmanuel, Otley and Merchant (1990) note that this approach, generally termed 'contingency theory', is based on the notion that there is no one management control system which can be suitable for all organizations in all circumstances. Instead, contingency theorists have sought to identify those features of an organization's context to which an organization's management control system should be 'matched' if it is to attain an acceptable degree of effectiveness. Such features have been found to include environment (Otley, 1978; Rusth, 1990); organization size and structure (Hopwood, 1976; Otley, 1980; Merchant, 1981); technology (Woodward, 1958; Perrow, 1967; Daft and Macintosh, 1978; Merchant, 1984) and, of particular relevance here, both an organization's culture and strategy.

As already discussed, an organization's culture typically comprises the underlying values, beliefs and principles shared by its members and which consequently tend to influence their ideas, behaviour and actions, (see for example Ouchi, 1979; Denison, 1990; Gordon and DiTomaso, 1992). Although research into cultures can be traced back to anthropological studies in the 1920s, it is only recently that academic researchers have begun to investigate the significance of culture for organizational control systems, (Langfield-Smith, 1995). For instance, as noted previously, it has been claimed – by such researchers as Flamholtz (1983) and Markus and Pfeffer (1983) – that a failure by management to design control systems that are consistent with their organization's culture, can lead to active resistance to the control system with potentially damaging consequences. Meanwhile, it has been argued, for instance by Dermer (1977), that different corporate strategies should logically result in different forms of management control systems. Thus far though, empirical research into the relationship between strategy and effective forms of control has been somewhat limited and the resulting implications unclear. However, Govindarajan and Gupta (1985) and Merchant (1985) established that a relative emphasis on long-run criteria enhanced effectiveness for organizations with a 'build' strategy, while short-run criteria represented a more restricting influence. Also Omar (1993), found that (accounting) control systems were very significant in guiding management to set appropriate strategic organizational objectives.

An important overall conclusion reached by Abernethy and Stoelwinder (1991) with regard to the possible 'overall' impact of contingent contextual variables is:

. . . the better the match, the more effectively the organization will perform

Characteristics of Effective Control

Irrespective of how well 'matched' a control system is to its particular contingent factors, in order for a system of management control to attain even a basic level of effectiveness it will also need to demonstrate a number of other significant features. For instance, Otley and Berry (1980) claim that for a management control system to be effective it must satisfy the four necessary conditions outlined in Table 4.1.

Otley and Berry (1980) also suggest that if any of these conditions are not met then a management control system could be said to be 'out of control'.

In addition to these 'required' conditions identified by Otley and Berry (1980), a number of other important features associated with effective management control systems have also been identified:

Understandable

If an organization's control system is to be fully effective, it must be clearly understood by all managers and employees involved with it. This has very serious implications – as noted by Mullins (1993) – for instance, for the level of detail and technical sophistication of any reports utilized in the system and also for the style of report used.

Condition One:	The organization's goals and objectives must be clearly identified – for without a clear aim the process of control has no meaning
Condition Two:	The organization's performance must be measurable on the basis which is consistent with the goals and objectives specified – thus enabling a useful comparison to be made
Condition Three:	A predictive model of those activities of the organization which are to be controlled must be determined – this is needed to assist with the identification of causes of deviations and in the assessment of any proposed corrective actions
Condition Four:	There must be the capability of taking corrective action – such that the degree of deviation between desired and actual performance may be effectively reduced

Source: adapted from Otley (1987)

Table 4.1 Conditions for Effective Control

Timely

For a management control system to be effective it is important that feedback information is produced on a timely basis: Cole (1993) for instance has suggested that timeliness is vital for effective control, particularly when unexpected deviations have occurred. Indeed, it may even be considered desirable that anticipatory indications of deviations – that is the exercise of feed-forward controls – should be reported even before they occur.

Directed

Management control systems should concentrate on those activities vital to the success of the organization (Mullins, 1993) and to significant deviations from the standards set (Cole, 1993). 'Unnecessary' controls can be both time-consuming and demotivating, as well as diverting attention from the essential matters.

Flexible

Control system methods and techniques must maintain their relevance by adapting to changing circumstances. It is particularly important that they should not reflect the often-used response, *'but this is the way we've always done things . . .'* Indeed, Mullins (1993) contends it is essential that management control methods and techniques are reviewed on an ongoing and regular basis to help in 'ensuring' they remain appropriate and relevant.

MANAGEMENT CONTROL IN THE INTERNATIONAL HOSPITALITY INDUSTRY

Although as Cullen and Rhodes (1983) suggest that management in hospitality organizations need a wide range of control mechanisms, empirical research concerning management control in the hospitality industry is, to date, somewhat limited. Moreover, what evidence there is, is concentrated in four main areas: budgetary control systems, the use of internal controls, quality control and human resource management.

Budgetary Control Systems

According to the Chartered Institute of Management Accountants (1991), the process of budgetary control involves:

> . . . the establishment of budgets relating the responsibilities of executives to the requirements of a policy, and the continuous comparison of actual with budgeted results, either to secure by individual action the objectives of that policy or to provide a basis for its revision.

It is perhaps worth re-emphasizing at this stage that budgetary control is only one of a wide range of control tools available to management and consequently, studies that concentrate only on budgetary control, can only ever give a partial view of an organization's approach to management control.

With regard to the international hospitality industry, research indicates that there is a considerable degree of consensus among managers and academic writers alike that the budgetary control process is a very valuable and worthy control tool. Schmidgall (1990) has suggested that an important underlying reason for this apparent support is the perception that budgets can encourage hospitality managers to set positive targets for themselves and other employees. Moreover, it is felt that such targets, when properly used, can provide a positive motivating influence, supporting the achievement of the organization's aims.

Schmidgall and Ninemeier (1987) have noted the utilization of increasingly sophisticated budgetary control techniques, particularly in multi-unit hospitality operations, while in order for such control systems to be applied effectively they recognized a need for high levels of properly controlled and co-ordinated information. Interestingly though, Schmidgall and Ninemeier (1987) also established that simplified budgeting systems are felt to be more suitable for small or single-unit organizations and, as Rusth (1990) noted, where perceptions of environmental uncertainty are high.

Significantly, the hospitality industry is clearly recognizing that the process of budgetary control should not be viewed solely as a technical process – indeed, it is perceived to involve many potential behavioural considerations (Ferguson and Berger, 1986). O'Dea (1985) has claimed that the success of budgetary control systems in hospitality organizations can be 'measured' by the extent to which they provide the necessary motivation for individuals to maximize their contribution to the achievement of the goals of the organization. Moreover, O'Dea (1985) also notes that in situations where management do not participate in the budgeting process, or where budget targets are perceived as being unattainable, it is likely that the control process may be 'disrupted' as a result of a range of possible dysfunctional behavioural consequences, including feelings of tension and mistrust. This is supported by Harris and Hazzard (1992) who suggest that if the budget process is mishandled and targets are totally imposed from above, then the budget will usually be regarded as a threat rather than a challenge – and as a result will be resisted. Further evidence of potential negative aspects of budgetary control in the hospitality industry have been identified by Pickup (1985), who considers that the typical industry budgetary systems tend to demonstrate an adversarial nature, often resulting in serious dysfunctional implications for those organizations. As an example, Pickup (1985) notes that such control processes may 'encourage' management to 'play a budget game' – which, it is suggested, can prove to be a very expensive game indeed!

Umbreit and Eder (1987) interestingly consider that the form of budgetary control systems currently being used in hospitality companies are not sufficiently comprehensive. They suggest that to be fully effective such systems should not only include quantifiable outcomes, but must also provide indicators of such key dimensions of managerial behaviour as the ability to motivate and to communicate with employees.

Internal Control Systems

The term 'internal control system' has been comprehensively defined by the Audit Practices Committee (1980) as:

> ... the whole system of controls, financial or otherwise, established by the management in order to carry on the business of the enterprise in an orderly and efficient manner, ensure adherence to management's policies, safeguard the assets and secure as far as possible the completeness and accuracy of records.

As such, then, internal control systems tend to concentrate on the more day-to-day, operational aspects of an organization – and like budgets represent only one of the range of control methods and techniques at management's disposal.

While it is for the organization's management to determine the exact nature of the internal controls to be applied, the need for strong internal controls in hospitality organizations is well established given that a key result area for such organizations is the protection of their assets (Jones and Lockwood, 1989) and that most hospitality operations will undertake, on a daily basis, a substantial volume of transactions – many of which will be for immediate settlement – usually involving a considerable number of staff1989). Particularly common examples of internal controls used in hospitality organizations include:

Records and Documents

Given the volume of transactions normally undertaken by most hospitality organizations, it is vital that proper and effective records and documents are maintained. Typically such documentation will include guest registration cards, meal and bar dockets, authorizations for allowances and approved time-sheets. Additionally, in order to enhance their effectiveness, Schmidgall (1990) suggests that such documents may be sequentially numbered or in multi-part form as appropriate.

Segregation of Duties

The primary objective underlying the use of segregation of duties as an internal control is the prevention and detection of both errors and fraud. Given the particular nature of hospitality organizations, as already noted, it is especially important that no one member of staff can fully process and record a transactioninternal control can be established by ensuring that the actions involved in initiating requisitions, in authorizing orders, in receiving and storing goods and ultimately in executing payments are kept separate.

Surveillance

Active surveillance by managers involves 'catching things as they happen' rather than analysing them 'after the event'. Venison (1983) further suggests that such surveillance is a particularly essential part of revenue control, and suggest that:

> ... the same traits which help the manager keep observation on guest standards will help him control the business.

Physical

Cote (1988) notes that hospitality organizations specifically use physical controls to assist in the safekeeping of their assets and records. Common examples of physical controls include keeping locks on cellars and storerooms, holding currency and important records and documents in fire-proof safes and restricting access to computers by the means of passwords.

Quality Control

The need for effective quality management in hospitality organizations has been widely accepted for some considerable time by both academic researchers and practising hospitality managers alike. Recent research in the area though suggests that if hospitality organizations are to have effective quality management and control they need to develop an integrated and structured approach to quality, that may involve such key components as:

Quality Culture

If an organization's quality management is to achieve any degree of effectiveness it must establish a culture of quality, which embraces everyone in the organization – and where everyone is encouraged to contribute. However, what organizations must never underestimate is that the creation of a quality culture should not be a 'once only' activity (van Donk and Sanders, 1993). Rather, it requires innovation, participation, sharing and commitment on an ongoing basis.

Teamwork

The concept of taking a team approach to quality management is not a new one – see Deming (1986) – but it is particularly vital in hospitality organizations, where the potential for friction over matters of quality is considerable, especially as employees in the industry are typically highly specialized and departmentalized. It has been found, for instance by Heymann (1992), that where teams work together to overcome difficult situations, especially when these often produce quality problems, they can focus on ultimate guest satisfaction from the perspective of the overall organization and thus assume a collective responsibility.

Customer Perspective

It has been claimed that all too often the policies and procedures hospitality organizations follow with regard to quality management are concerned with what management believe their customers should want, rather than reflecting input from the actual customers and from those front-line employees who are in daily contact with them. A more effective approach, Heymann (1992) suggests, is for such policies and procedures to be developed for the benefit of the customer rather than for the benefit of the organization's system.

Even where hospitality organizations have successfully combined such factors into an integrated approach to quality, they must also take on board that effective quality management and control is an on-going process, with continuous improvement – a recognized major determinant in 'successful' organizations – as its goal.

Human Resource Management

Probably more than any other industry international hospitality organizations operate in a 'people industry', (Keiser, 1989). Personnel are a vital component in the quality of service provided by hospitality organizations. Consequently, it is firstly essential for the effective functioning of a hospitality organization's control system that the personnel employed are motivated, competent and trustworthy, (Cote, 1988; Keiser, 1989). A significant implication of this for hospitality organizations is that both management and employees must be carefully selected and trained and also, that they must be appropriately encouraged, supervised and rewarded for their efforts.

Also, it is likely that effective control systems in hospitality organizations will be supported by effective human resource development, including the investment by organizations in training and skills programmes – including both social and technical skills. However, the all too common incidence of such organizations claiming that they cannot afford the costs of such programmes can be met by the following conclusion from Heymann (1992):

> Managers who don't have time for training don't have time for quality.

THEORETICAL ASSERTIONS

While the complex nature of the range of activities undertaken by organizations operating in international hospitality industry has already been referred to, it should be noted that this chapter has only 'scratched the surface' with regard to the true extent of the complexity of the industry. Keeping this in mind and considering forecasts concerning the future of the industry (see for example EIU, 1991) and the previous sections regarding relevant aspects of organizational culture and control in a strategic planning context, a number of suggestions can be made in respect of some significant theoretical implications and assertions for organizations within the industry.

Firstly, it may be suggested that employees must improve their awareness of cultural differences within their organizations, perhaps by 'measuring' culture, (Hofstede *et al.*, 1990; van Donk and Sanders, 1993). Such 'measurements' may indicate whether the organizations should be treated as having a single culture, or a collection of sub-cultures, which in turn may provide useful information with regard to decisions about the organization's strategy, structure and control systems – for example with regard to the potential 'outcomes' of possible mergers or take-overs.

Secondly, evidence produced by the EIU (1991) suggests that not only is the hospitality industry becoming both more concentrated and more international, but also that significant organizations within the industry are both increasing in size and spread. Such 'forecasts' have serious implications for the appropriateness of organizational strategic planning and control – indications are that plans and control systems involving a flexible but administrative approach, which can reflect the interdependencies between individual responsibility centres as well as incorporating an emphasis on longer-run criteria, will prove most effective.

A third key area of concern identified by the EIU (1991) is a strong expectation that the international hospitality industry will continue to experience tremendous advances in its support technologies – in particular in such areas as guest intelligence, teleconferencing, in-room check-out and computer reservation systems. This potentially has serious implications for the interaction of culture, strategy and control: in those parts of the industry where it is anticipated that these technological advances will lead to increased degrees of automation, and less direct involvement between different departments and between guests and staff – for instance especially in reservations and reception – it is likely, based on past research, that more 'formal' plans and controls will prove most effective. However, it is important that managers in the hospitality industry also keep in mind that such advances in technology will not lead to increased levels of automation in all areas of their organization – for instance, food and beverage service and housekeeping are likely to be less affected – such that their plans and control systems will need to incorporate a range of levels of formality.

Finally, the apparent external market culture associated with many hospitality organizations will need to develop in order to embody the anticipated changes in the environment they face. The EIU (1991) suggests that such changes are likely to involve 'shifts' in customers particular 'wants and needs' – the most significant of these changes will probably be a move towards shorter business trips and holidays, an increasing demand for quality products and services together with a concern for 'value for money'. Such developments, which although being considered of less importance for the industry in the 1990s than the developments in technology noted above, it is suggested will require even greater degrees of 'customer orientation' – with implications for greater 'openness', for ongoing two-way communication, for a more organic structure and for a more flexible approach. It is also suggested that if hospitality management are to be able to assess the degree of their organization's 'customer orientation' they will again need to establish ways of measuring organizational culture on a regular basis. Such measurements should assist management to assess cultural changes and differences within their own organizations and so reflect on the likely implications for the effectiveness of their organizations strategic plans and controls.

REFERENCES

Abernethy, M.A. and Stoelwinder, J.U. (1991) Budget use and task uncertainty, system goal orientation and subunit performance: a test of the 'fit' hypothesis in not-for-profit hospitals. *Accounting, Organizations and Society*, 16: 2, 105–120

Anthony, R.N. (1965) *Planning and Control Systems: A Framework for Analysis*. Boston: Division of Research, Harvard Graduate School of Business.

Anthony, R.N. and Govindarajan, V. (1995) *Management Control Systems*. Chicago: Irwin.

Audit Practices Committee (1980) *Operational Guideline 3.204 Internal Controls*

Barney, J.B. (1986) Organizational culture: can it be a source of sustained competitive advantage. *Academy of Management Review*, 11, 656–65

Bartunek, J.M. (1984) Changing interpretative schemes and organizational restructuring: the examples of a religious order, *Administrative Science Quarterly*, 29, 355–372

Brander Brown, J. (1995) Management control in the hospitality industry: behavioural implications, in Harris, P.J. (Ed.) *Accounting and Finance for the International Hospitality Industry*. Oxford: Butterworth Heinemann.

Burns, T. and Stalker, G.M. (1961) *The Management of Innovation*. London: Tavistock Institute.

Chartered Institute of Management Accountants (1991) *Management Accounting Official Terminology*. London: CIMA.

Cole, G. (1993) *Management Theory and Practice*. London: DP Publications.

Collins, F. (1982) Managerial accounting systems and organizational control: a role perspective. *Accounting, Organizations and Society*, 2:7, 107–122

Coltman, M.M. (1987) *Hospitality Management Accounting*. New York: Van Nostrand Reinhold.

Cote, R. (1988) *Understanding Hospitality Accounting II*. East Lansing, Michigan: Educational Institute of the American Hotel & Motel Association.

Cullen, H.V. and Rhodes, G.E. (1983) *Management in the Hotel and Catering Industry*. London: Batsford Academic and Educational Ltd.

Cunningham, G.M. (1992) Management control and accounting systems under a competitive strategy. *Accounting, Auditing and Accountability Journal*, 5:2, 85–102

Daft, R.L. and MacIntosh, N.B. (1978) A new approach to design and use of management information. *California Management Review*, 2, 82–92

Deal, T.E. and Kennedy, A.A. (1982) *Corporate Cultures: The Rites and Rituals of Corporate Life*. Reading, MA: Addison-Wesley.

Deming, W.E. (1986) *Out of Crises: Quality, Productivity and Competitive Position*. Cambridge: Cambridge University Press.

Denison, D.R. (1990) *Corporate Culture and Organizational Effectiveness*. New York: John Wiley & Sons.

Dermer, J. (1977) *Management Planning and Control Systems: Advanced Topics and Cases*. Chicago: Irwin.

Economist Intelligence Unit (1991) *Competitive Strategies for the International Hotel Industry*. London: Business International

Eder, R.W. and Umbreit, W.T. (1989) Measures of managerial effectiveness in the hotel industry. *Hospitality Education and Research Journal*, 333–341

Emmanuel, C., Otley, D. and Merchant, K. (1990) *Accounting for Management Control*. London: Chapman & Hall.

Fayol, H. (1949) *General and Industrial Management*. London: Pitman.

Fenton, L.S., Fowler, N.A. and Parkinson, G.S. (1989) *Hotel Accounts and their Audit*. Oxford: ICAEW/Alden Press.

Ferguson, D.H. and Berger, F. (1986) The human side of budgeting. *Cornell HRA Quarterly*, August, 87–90

Flamholtz, E.G. (1983) Accounting, budgeting and control systems in their organizational context: theoretical and empirical perspectives. *Accounting, Organizations and Society*, 8, 153–169

Glover, W.G. (1987) The cult of ineffectiveness. *Cornell HRA Quarterly*, February, reprinted in Rutherford, D.G. (1990) *Hotel Management and Operations*. New York: Van Nostrand Reinhold.

Goldsmith, W. and Clutterbuck, D. (1984) *The Winning Streak*. London: Weidenfeld & Nicolson.

Gordon, G.G. (1985) The relationship of corporate culture to industry sector and corporate performance, in Kilmann, R.H., Saxton, M.J., Serpa, R. and associates (Eds.) *Gaining Control of the Corporate Culture*. San Francisco: Jossey-Bass.

Gordon, G.G. (1991) Industry determinants of organizational culture. *Academy of Management Review*, 16, 396–415

Gordon, G.G. and DiTomaso, N. (1992) Predicting corporate performance from organizational culture. *Journal of Management Studies*, 29, 783–798

Govindarajan, V. and Gupta, A.K. (1985) Linking control systems to business unit strategy: impact on performance. *Accounting, Organizations and Society*, 9, 125–135

Grinyer, P. and Spender, J-C. (1979) Recipes, crises and adaptation in mature businesses. *International Studies of Management and Organization*, 9, 113–123

Hall, F.S. (1975) Organization goals: the status of theory and research, in Livingstone, J.L. (Ed.) *Managerial Accounting: The Behavioural Foundations*, Columbus, Ohio: Grid Publishing.

Handy, C.B. (1985) *Understanding Organizations*. Harmondsworth: Penguin.

Harris, P.J. (1992) *Profit Planning*. Oxford: Butterworth-Heinemann.

Harris, P.J. and Hazzard, P.A. (1992) *Managerial Accounting in the Hospitality Industry*. Cheltenham: Stanley Thornes.

Heymann, K. (1992) Quality management: a ten-point model. *Cornell HRA Quarterly*, October, 51–60

Hofstede, G., Neuijen, B., Daval Ohayv, D. and Sanders, G. (1990) Measuring organizational cultures: a qualitative and quantitative study across twenty cases. *Administrative Science Quarterly*, 35, 286–316

Hopwood, A.G. (1976) *Accounting and Human Behaviour*. Englewood Cliffs, NJ: Prentice Hall.

Johnson, G. and Scholes, K. (1993) *Exploring Corporate Strategy: Text and Cases*. Englewood Cliffs, NJ: Prentice-Hall.

Jones, C.S. (1985) An empirical study of the role of management accounting systems following take-over or merger. *Accounting, Organizations and Society*, 10: 2, 177–200

Jones, P. and Lockwood, A. (1989) *The Management of Hotel Operations*. London: Cassell.

Keiser, J.R. (1989) *Principles and Practices of Management in the Hospitality Industry*. New York: Van Nostrand Reinhold.

Kotas, R. (1975) *Market Orientation in the Hotel and Catering Industry*. Leighton Buzzard: Surrey University Press.

Kotas, R. (1986) *Management Accounting for Hotels and Restaurants*. Glasgow: Surrey University Press.

Kroeber, A.L. and Kluckhohn, C. (1963) *Culture: A Critical Review of Concepts and Definitions*. New York: Vintage Books.

Langfield-Smith, K. (1995) Organizational culture and control, in Berry, A.J., Broadbent, J. and Otley, D.T. (Eds.) *Management Control: Theories, Issues and Practices*. London: Macmillan.

Lorsch, J.W. (1985) Strategic myopia: culture as an invisible barrier to change, in Kilmann, R.H., Saxton, M.J., Serpa, R. and associates (Eds.) *Gaining Control of the Corporate Culture*, San Francisco: Jossey-Bass.

Louis, M.R. (1985) An investigator's guide to workplace culture, in Frost, P.J., Moore, L.F., Louis, M.R., Lindberg, C.C. and Martin, J. (Eds.) *Organizational Culture*. Beverly Hills, CA: Sage.

Markus, M.L. and Pfeffer, J. (1983) Power and the design and implementation of accounting and control systems. *Accounting, Organizations and Society*, 8: 2, 205–218

Merchant, K.A. (1981) The design of the corporate budgeting system: influences on managerial behaviour and performance. *The Accounting Review*, LVI: 4, 813–829

Merchant, K.A. (1984) Influences on departmental budgeting: an empirical examination of a contingency model. *Accounting, Organizations and Society*, 9: 3/4, 291–307

Merchant, K.A. (1985) Budgeting and the propensity to create budget slack. *Accounting, Organizations and Society*, 10: 2, 201–210

Mullins, L.J. (1992) *Hospitality Management: A Human Resources Approach*. London: Pitman Publishing.

Mullins, L.J. (1993) *Management and Organizational Behaviour*. London: Pitman Publishing.

O'Dea, W. (1985) Budgetary control – a behavioural perspective. *International Journal of Hospitality Management*, 4: 4, 179–180

Omar, N.H. (1993) *Study of Accounting Control Systems, Strategy and Business Performance in the UK Electronics Industry*, unpublished Ph.D. thesis, Department of Accounting and Finance, The Manchester Metropolitan University

Otley, D.T. (1978) Budget use and managerial performance. *Journal of Accounting Research*, 16, 122–149

Otley, D.T. (1980) The contingency theory of management accounting: achievement and prognosis. *Accounting, Organizations and Society*, 5: 4, 413–428

Otley, D.T. (1987) *Accounting Control and Organizational Behaviour*. Oxford: Heinemann.

Otley, D.T. (1995) Management control, organizational design and accounting information systems, in Ashton, D., Hopper, T. and Scapens, R.W. (Eds.) *Issues in Management Accounting*. Englewood Cliffs, NJ: Prentice Hall.

Otley, D.T. and Berry, A.J. (1980) Control, organization and accounting. *Accounting, Organizations and Society*, 5, 231–246

Otley, D.T. and Wilkinson, C. (1988) Organizational behaviour: strategy, structure, environment and technology, in Ferris, K.R. (Ed.) *Behavioural Accounting Research: A Critical Analysis*. Columbus, Ohio: Century VII Publishing Co..

Ouchi, W. (1979) A conceptual framework for the design of organizational control mechanisms. *Management Science*, 25: 9, 833–847

Perrow, C. (1967) A framework for the comparative analysis of organizations. *American Sociological Review*, 194–208

Peters, T.J. and Waterman, R.H. (1982) *In Search of Excellence: Lessons from America's Best-Run Companies*. New York: Harper and Row.

Pettigrew, A.M. (1979) On studying organizational cultures. *Administrative Science Quarterly*, 24, 570–581

Pfeffer, J. (1981) Management as symbolic action: the creation and maintenance of organization paradigms, in Cummings, L.L. and Staw, B.M. (Eds.) *Research in Organizational Behaviour*, 3, 1–5

Pickup, I. (1985) Budgetary control within the hotel industry. *International Journal of Hospitality Management*, 4: 4, 149–155

Rathe, A.W. (1960) Management controls in business, in Malcolm, D.G. and Rowe, A.J. (Eds.) *Management Control Systems*. New York: Wiley.

Reynolds, P.D. (1986) Organizational culture as related to industry, position and performance. *Journal of Management Studies*, 23, 333–345

Rusth, D.B. (1990) Hotel budgeting in a multinational environment: results of a pilot study. *Hospitality Research Journal*, 14: 2, 217–222

Schein, E.H. (1985) How culture forms, develops and changes, in Kilmann, R.H., Saxton, M.J., Serpa, R. and associates (Eds.) *Gaining Control of the Corporate Culture*. San Francisco: Jossey-Bass.

Schein, E.H. (1992) *Organizational Culture and Leadership*. San Francisco: Jossey-Bass.

Schmidgall, R.S. (1990) *Hospitality Industry Managerial Accounting*. East Lansing, Michigan: Educational Institute of the American Hotel & Motel Association.

Schmidgall, R.S. and Ninemeier, J.D. (1987) Budgeting in hotel chains: co-ordination and control. *Cornell HRA Quarterly*, May, 79–84

Schwartz, H.M. and Davis, S.M. (1981) Matching corporate culture and business strategy. *Organizational Dynamics*, 10: 1, 30–48

Shrivastava, P. (1985) Integrating strategy formulation with organizational culture. *Journal of Business Strategy*, 5, 103–111

Smircich, L. (1963) Concepts of culture and organizational analysis. *Administrative Science Quarterly*, 28, 339–358

Tannenbaum, A.S. (1968) *Control in Organizations*. London: McGraw-Hill.

Umbreit, W.T. and Eder, R.W. (1987) Linking hotel manager behaviour with outcome measures of effectiveness. *International Journal of Hospitality Management*, 6, 139–147

van Donk, D.P. and Sanders, G. (1993) Organizational culture as a missing link in quality management, *International Journal of Quality and Reliability Management*, 10: 5, 5–15

Venison, P. (1983) *Managing Hotels*. London: Heinemann.

Ward, K. (1992) *Strategic Management Accounting*. Oxford: Butterworth-Heinemann.

Weick, K.E. (1985) The significance of corporate culture, in Frost, P.J., Moore, L.F., Louis, M.R., Lindberg, C.C. and Martin, J. (Eds.) *Organizational Culture*. Beverley Hills, CA: Sage.

Woodward, J. (1958) *Management and Technology*. London: HMSO.

5

Strategic Competitive Advantage Through Structure, Quality and Teamwork

Hadyn Ingram, Richard Teare, Sarah Ridley and Livio Ferrone

INTRODUCTION

Drucker (1994) suggests that central focus for organizations is how best to manage the business so as to ensure that profits are made and that the enterprise is successful over time. Conventionally, profitability in business organizations can be improved in one or more of three ways:

- by cost reduction;
- by increasing selling prices; and
- by improving market share.

Reducing costs, however, may lead to a decline in standards, thereby weakening market share and putting pressure on the selling price. In the 1990s, however, greater buyer power has made cost reduction and premium pricing strategies less effective at a time when many firms are changing from production to consumer orientation. In a climate of greater competition, firms can gain greater market share by differentiating their products or services from those of their competitors (Porter, 1980). In the past, the sole source of competitive advantage for many hospitality units was their favourable location (such as on a major route or by the sea), but changing travelling and leisure patterns have demanded that operators use customer-focused differentiation strategies in order to survive and grow.

The aim of this chapter is to devise an effective strategic framework that can be used by hospitality and tourism firms in the future. The first part reviews the existing literature concerning structure, quality and people so that the key ideas in these areas may be identified. Part two considers some frameworks and approaches which will facilitate the introduction and continuation of the new strategy, leading to the synthesis of a new model with its interrelationships and implications for the future.

STRUCTURE

The Relationship Between Strategy and Organizational Structure

Organizational structures reflect the strategy identified by management which is to attain the organization's objectives. Structure in an organization is influenced by its strategy, culture, management style and attitudes, employee involvement and satisfaction and channels of communication. Chandler (1962) demonstrates that a change in strategy is likely to result in administrative problems, because the existing organizational structure is not adapted to cope with the new strategy and structural changes may need to occur. Different strategic directions, such as cost leadership and differentiation generally, tend to give rise to different forms of organization. An organization following a cost leadership strategy, with an emphasis on cost efficiency and control, will of necessity be more structured, with clear job responsibilities, frequent and detailed reports on organizational efficiency and cost and tight control over budgets. In contrast, the structure for an organization following a differentiation strategy will need to be more flexible, more informal with a decentralized structure, but strong co-ordination between functions to encourage group work and creativity.

This section reviews some definitions of the concept of structure and contrasts historical configurations in organizational structure with recent trends and especially the relationship between structure and quality.

Organizational Structure

Mintzberg (1983) defines structure as *the sum total of the ways in which its labour is divided into distinct tasks* and then its co-ordination is achieved among these tasks. The elements of structure should be selected to achieve an internal consistency or harmony, as well as a basic consistency with the organization's situation.

An organizational structure, typically represented by the organization chart, normally reflects the strategy identified by management to reach the organization's objectives. Structures are organized to achieve the goals of the company. Organizational structure shows how internal efficiency and overall effectiveness have been balanced through the identification and use of key activities, such as chain of command, level of bureaucracy and technology, to achieve the company's goals.

Historical Overview

Many organizational structures within companies today have developed from structures originating in the mid 1950s. They are based on structural typologies suggested by Taylor, (1911) Fayol, (1916) and Weber (1964). Their objectives were to increase output and employee efficiency through standardization and the breaking down of the manufacturing process into tasks. This is now known as the Classical Theory of Management and from it developed the Bureaucratic Model, described by Max Weber as the most efficient instrument in large scale administration, which is characterized by rules and regulations, a pyramidal, hierarchical organizational form, limited span of control, delegation of responsibility, specific jobs and positions. 'Classical theory', according to Robey (1991) *is the most rational of all approaches to organization design, it offers principles of structure that, if followed, will ensure effective performance.*

Nevertheless, there is no 'right' structure for every organization. The Contingency theory holds that the effectiveness of an organization depends on the fit between an organization's structure and the contingencies it faces. Structures vary with size, employee characteristics, dependence on external forces, the volatility of the environment and technology. The bureaucratic, mechanistic approach seems appropriate for structuring an organization in a stable environment where routine activities are common and where the strategy aims to increase productivity to keep up with demand. A more flexible, organic approach, is necessary for an organization in a dynamic environment with non-routine activities, such as those activities which provide customer service. In this situation, the strategy should focus upon a continual review of changes occurring within consumer expectations.

Recent Trends

The business environment has radically changed in the last decade. Increased competition, globalization, privatization, deregulation and new technologies have forced companies to re-examine their operations. The majority of organizations have to pay close attention to their environment, which is constantly changing and exerting pressure on the companies to alter their strategies in order to remain in the market. Customers are becoming more sophisticated, looking for higher standards in quality, innovation, responsiveness and convenience. As a result, service organizations must gain a stronger commitment to customer satisfaction and focus closely on real customer needs and expectations.

Strategic changes are often achieved through, or accompanied by, restructuring in organizations. Organizations are moving towards flatter, more flexible and responsive structures as the hospitality industry evolves from being highly fragmented to becoming more consolidated (Olsen, 1991). The middle management layer is being removed in many organizations in order to cut costs and to obtain a faster response to competitive and market changes. Worthy (1950) believes that, *flatter, less complex structures . . . tend to create a potential for improved attitudes, more effective supervision and greater individual responsibility and initiatives among employees.* Management style, attitudes and behaviour patterns are evolving in order to accommodate organizational structural changes. Employees are being empowered, middle managers have become guides and coaches rather than commanders and checkers. Decisions are made at the customer-staff interface instead of being referred up the chain of command. There is a trend towards teamwork and project management, which is integral to all work, rather than applied to a few special tasks. Many technical or support activities are being 'outsourced' on a contractual or consultancy basis.

Some outcomes of these organizational changes are improved communications, reduced red tape and increased responsiveness to customer demand, resulting in enhanced employee and customer satisfaction. Communication is becoming horizontal rather than vertical and managers are concerned with releasing potential from those around them.

McGregor's Theory Y – the belief that employees accept work as natural, seek responsibility and exercise self-direction and self-control to achieve company objectives – will dominate the way employees are managed, as organizations attempt to motivate people by involvement, encouraging 'reflective self-management'. The values of the American telecommunications company AT&T reflect those of companies in the 1990s *respect for individuals, dedication to helping customers, adhering to the highest standards of integrity, innovation and teamwork* (Heller, 1994). These changes in working practices and job descriptions require an investment in education and training, in order for employees to understand their new roles within the organization and to develop new skills.

The advantages of flatter organizational structures, teamwork and empowerment include:

- customer-oriented companies;
- improved response to customer enquiries/complaints;
- faster response to competitive and market changes;
- reduced time lag between decision and action;
- more fluid, team-based approach;
- greater job enrichment, employee involvement and satisfaction;
- reduced absenteeism and turnover of staff;
- increased employee innovation and creativity through a team approach;
- improved communications, through the breaking down of barriers and a cross-functional approach;
- enhanced efficiency and standards.

There are disadvantages, however, to this new organizational approach, which must be faced and overcome if success is to be achieved. There may be resistance from middle management, for example, due to their changing roles and uncertainty about their future. Major cultural changes are required throughout the whole company, which must be understood and implemented by all employees.

Organizational Structure and Quality

Interest in quality is not new, but companies that are unable to provide excellence in quality may not survive the 1990s. As such, it is becoming a new competitive tool, since it is important as a determinant of choice. Jan Hubrecht, formerly Managing Director of Scott's Hotels (now part of the Whitbread Hotel Group), sees quality as a differentiating strategy, *we decided to find a way to satisfy customer needs that was superior to the competition and would differentiate us from them. We chose the TQM route*. Quality improvement programmes at Scott's now stress customer focus, employee training and empowerment, top management support and commitment (Fender, 1990).

Quality, however, cannot be pursued in isolation, it must be enmeshed in the overall strategy of the organization. A strategy to gain competitive advantage through quality improvement, will require devolving authority to the employees, making them responsible for the quality within their section of the value chain. As Bertram (1993) suggests *it is important to remember that success is dependent not only on a few key people, but on the efforts of every individual who accepts they are a link in the chain*. Every employee in the chain is able to influence the degree to which the requirements and expectations of the customer are met. Employee involvement is essential, as is the removal of barriers, so that employees can contribute freely. The creation of teams, the empowering of employees and the devolvement of authority, are methods for increasing employee involvement and hence improving customer communication and response time.

Summary

Organizations achieve their objectives through evolving an effective structure which matches external forces and internal characteristics. More powerful external changes have forced many organizations to react by restructuring into flatter and more flexible patterns, so that they may respond more rapidly to future competitive and market changes. Restructuring can improve communication and delegate decision-making to operational levels so that employees at the customer interface are empowered to make customer-centred decisions. This structural freedom is inextricably linked to effective quality strategies in hospitality and tourism industries.

STRATEGIES FOR QUALITY

Darwent (1990) suggests that performance of hospitality firms has been affected by the political and economic turbulence of the 1980s and more recently by the uncertainty of the 1990s. In the intensifying struggle for market share, many hospitality firms are recognizing the validity of Porter's theory, that strategy should be shaped by reference to prevailing competitive forces. Of particular interest are Porter's (1980) generic strategies of product differentiation, by brand identification and adding value through the improvement of customer service. Following the example of the USA, hotel chains in the UK such as Forte have branded their products so as to offer an easily distinguishable choice of hotels to customers. Connell (1992) suggests that branding strategies may also assist management to focus upon the specification and improvement of service, thereby deriving competitive advantage through consistency of quality delivery. In this section, the concept of quality is explored. First, a range of definitions from the literature will suggest a spectrum of dimensions of quality which assists in the analysis of the nature of the hospitality product. This is followed by a review of current frameworks for achieving, improving and assuring quality and their relevance to hospitality firms.

Definitions of Quality

What exactly is quality? The following table offers a selection of suggested definitions and their implications:

Table 5.1 suggests that quality represents the standard of an organization's output as ultimately judged by the consumer of that output. Also highlighted is the complexity and subjectivity of quality, especially when related to non-physical products like services, which cannot be so easily standardized or replicated.

Table 5.2 contrasts the features of physical and non-physical products: The differences shown in Table 5.2 emphasize the difficulty of ensuring the consistent quality of personal service. Service delivery is affected by such factors as the skills and motivations of the service provider and is subjectively judged by the consumer's previous experiences, preferences and moods. For the hospitality industry, these factors are important in understanding the nature of the product offering.

What is the Hospitality Product?

Hospitality firms mainly offer products, like a restaurant meal, that comprise tangible and intangible elements. Lockwood (1994) suggests that while fascinated with quality, the hospitality industry finds difficulty in implementing it because of the unique combination of product and service. Mullins (1992) agrees that the actual delivery of hospitality services differs widely and that the benefits derived are associated with feelings or emotions. This implies that consumers use subjective and inconsistent frames of reference to judge the quality of services, presenting difficulties for the hospitality operator in satisfying the customer.

SOURCE	DEFINITION	IMPLICATIONS
The Oxford Minidictionary [17]	*Degree or level of excellence; characteristic, something that is special about in a person or thing*	Quality has two components (1) its inherent characteristics and (2) a standard of excellence
The British Standards Institute [18]	*The totality of features and characteristics of a product or service that bear on its ability to satisfy stated or implied needs.*	Quality must resolve the user's actual or perceived needs
Juran [19]	*Fitness for purpose or use*	Quality is judged by its ability to meet those needs
Ernst and Young [20]	*Conformance to specifications . . . the relative absence of defects*	Quality is judged positively and negatively by comparison to the expectation.
Feigenbaum [21]	*The total composite product and service characteristics of marketing, engineering, manufacture, and maintenance through which the product and service in use will meet the expectation by the customer*	Quality is derived through a range of processes which transform the end product
Oakland [22]	*Simply meeting the requirements*	Quality must be equal to the demands place upon it
Deming [23]	*A predictable degree of uniformity and dependability, at low cost and suited to the market*	Quality is also measured on a cost/benefit basis
Dodwell and Simmons [24]	*Concerned with 'delighting the customer'*	The ultimate test of quality is a subjective one
Day and Peters [25]	*Quality is rather like pornography in this respect. We may not be able to define it easily, but we know it when we see it*	Quality is difficult to pinpoint, but, rather like beauty, it is in the eye of the beholder.

Table 5.1: Quality Definitions and Implications

Day and Peters (1994) suggest that quality in service industries has both static and dynamic dimensions. Static quality represents the expectation of the customer that the wing of the aeroplane will stay on, or that the hotel bed is free of cockroaches. Customer expectation itself changes over time as extra facilities such as in-flight meals become the rule rather than the exception. Dynamic quality occurs during service delivery and offers opportunities for the customer to be 'delighted' by the extra efforts of staff to, for example, address the customer by name. Static quality can and should be systemized, because defects in the tangible product are a primary cause of customer dissatisfaction, but dynamic quality is not as easily achieved. By definition, spontaneous acts of dynamic quality, cannot be pre-arranged or scripted, but are nevertheless an important means of customer satisfaction.

GOODS	SERVICES
* **tangible:** physical properties, can be touched and inspected before purchase	* **intangible:** cannot be seen and may be paid for after consumption
* **standard:** can be produced to a standard template by which its quality can be verified	* **variable:** they depend upon who provides them, when they are provided and the individual needs of the customer
* **storage:** goods are put into stock pending distribution to agents or consumer	* **perishable:** cannot be stored in the same way and incur an opportunity cost if not consumed
* **distribution:** distributed by the manufacturers and resold to the consumer	* **inseparability:** produced and consumed at the same time. If the service is delivered by a person, then that person is part of the service

Source: P Kotler, *Marketing Management*, Prentice-Hall International. 1991, pp. 456–459

Table 5.2: Comparison of Goods and Services

Quality Outcomes

Singleton-Gree (1993) argues that, in order to succeed in a highly competitive environment, a business has to make sure it is producing the goods or services that the customer wants; it gets its quality right; and that it delivers on time. There is a growing body of evidence that suggests there are direct links with the satisfaction of the server and customer, repeat sales and profits (Partington and Schneider, 1979; Shostach, 1985; Schneider and Bowen, 1985). Heskett *et al.* (1990) suggest that quality, repeat usage, profits and investment form a self-reinforcing cycle as shown in Figure 5.1.

Quality in service delivery can lead to more repeat custom and greater sales revenue. This can enable serving staff on performance-related pay to earn more and enhance the quality of their service to the customer. In addition, the extra profit generated can enable service firms to invest in upgrading facilities to the customer and in training schemes for service improvement.

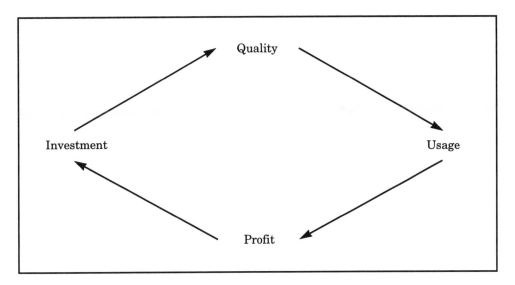

Figure 5.1: The Self-Reinforcing Service Cycle

Frameworks for Quality

The background to the current understanding of the use of quality as a means of competitive advantage originated with the Japanese who adopted the concept of 'total quality control' in the 1950s. Manufacturing industry in the USA lost market share to the Japanese, whose focus changed from the manufacture of cheap, second-rate goods to being seen as leaders in quality products, in what western organizations viewed as 'mature' markets (Glass, 1991). In the early 1980s the erosion of market share was so great that western industry took greater notice of the way in which the Japanese dealt with quality.

Quality Circles

Quality circles have their origins in Japan and comprise groups of workers who meet regularly with supervisors to discuss work-based problems and recommend solutions. Faulkener (1983) argues that the uptake of quality circles in the hospitality industry is somewhat limited, perhaps owing to cultural differences inherent in non-Japanese companies (Johns and Wheeler, 1991). Lawler and Mohrman (1988) acknowledge the inherent weaknesses of quality circles and suggest that considerable organizational effort is required to sustain them over a period of years.

Controlling Quality

Total Quality Control is attributed to Armand Feigenbaum (1983) who argues that responsibility for quality should be spread through the organization and the emphasis should be upon a *right first time* philosophy. Having observed quality frameworks in Japan, Phillip Crosby developed the first zero defects programme in the USA. The programme challenged the premise that errors in production are inevitable and that, by aiming for zero defects, improvement could replace detection (Crosby, 1979). Deming extended this concept, arguing that the eradication of the causes of variability would mean greater consistency in output and thus enhance a product's reputation (Flood, 1993). Juran (1989) concurs and notes that management is responsible for quality, suggesting that over 80 per cent of all problems at work result from systems that people work under and only 20 per cent are due to the workers themselves. He developed a three stage approach to the management of quality:

- quality planning;
- quality control; and
- quality improvement.

The first stage, quality planning, is concerned with the determination of quality goals; the development of plans to meet those goals; the identification of the resources to meet those goals; and the translation of the goals into quality. After the planning stage, comes control achieved by evaluating performance, comparing the performance with set goals and taking action to resolve the differences. Only after product quality is controlled, can the final stage be brought to bear in improving quality, as an ongoing and continuous process.

Crosby, Deming and Juran all agree that the implementation of quality programmes necessitates full commitment and support from the top as well as extensive training and the participation of all employees (Oakland, 1989). These ideas have developed into systematic quality assurance systems such as BS 5750 (ISO 9000) which require validation by an outside body such as the British Standards Institution (BSI). Registration for these certificates is increasingly seen as a desirable overt standard of quality and is sometimes demanded by larger organizations of their suppliers.

Quality in Service Industries

The production-oriented approaches to quality outlined above have been criticized as being inappropriate to the hospitality product. Johns (1992) suggests that such BSI terms such as *packaging and storing* and *installation and operation* do not apply even to the tangible aspect of the hospitality product. Even specialist systems for food quality management like the Hazard Analysis Critical Control Point (HACCP) approach are production-oriented, requiring detailed specification and standardization (Johns and Wheeler, 1991). Research by Witt and Witt (1989) confirms the view that managers in the hospitality industry tend to be unfamiliar with manufacturing control systems, to the detriment of productivity. Senge (1990) suggests that defensiveness, inherent in operational systems prevents organizations from learning and improvement, despite the importance of such learning as a source of competitive advantage in the 1990s. Berry *et al.* (1993) have produced a model in which the ten components of service quality are listed and described in Table 5.3.

This typology of service attributes was found to be a useful way of combining the technical and functional components of service quality. It was further developed by Brogowicz *et al.* (1990) into a questionnaire and scale called SERVQUAL for measuring the gap between customers' expectations and the perception of the delivery of service quality. Fick and Ritchie (1991) studied SERVQUAL in tourism services (airlines, hotels and restaurants) and suggest that it is useful in comparing service quality across various sectors. They concluded, however, that SERVQUAL may not be the most valid approach to defining service quality. Teare (1991) also used gap analysis to measure the difference between customer expectations and satisfaction in both experienced and inexperienced hotel users. His research reinforces the link between brand loyalty and positive prior experience and suggests that ineffective services are an especially potent source of consumer dissatisfaction especially in inexperienced hotel users. While branding may provide a useful means of ensuring static quality through an explicit framework for product specification, dynamic quality is not so easily originated and replicated.

ATTRIBUTE	DESCRIPTION
Reliability	Consistent in performance and dependability
Responsiveness	Willingness or readiness of employees to provide service
Competence	Knowledge and capability of contact personnel
Access	Approachability and ease of contact
Courtesy	Politeness, friendliness and consideration of service staff
Communication	Informing customers and listening to them
Credibility	Trustworthiness and honesty
Security	Freedom from danger, risk or doubt
Rapport	Understanding the customer's individual needs
Appearance	Physical look of facilities and personnel

Source: Adapted from Berry, Zeithaml and Parasuraman (1993)

Table 5.3: Service Attributes

Experiences from Hospitality Firms

A study by Walker and Salameh in 1990, suggests that few hotels in the USA have adopted quality assurance systems, but found that those who did so performed better in the tangible quality of food and drink. This reinforces the view that quality systems are important, but it may be too rigid to be applicable to the service element of the hospitality product. Flexibility in hospitality operations is emphasized by Litteljohn (1990) so as to respond appropriately to changes in the needs of customers and the wider environment. A human resource strategy offering potential for quality improvement is the Investors in People (IIP) programme, which is generally considered by hospitality operations as an alternative to BS 5750. The Moat House in Glasgow, for example, found the IIP programme to be more customer friendly and less costly than BS 5750 and has benefited from reduced labour turnover and absenteeism as a result (MacVicar and Brown, 1994). Page (1994) reports that the effect of a quality management programme at Sutcliffe Catering was to move the focus from *crisis management* to a more strategic approach, characterized by systematic corrective action. Sutcliffe recognized the spurious nature of *quick-fix* methods and assert that continuous improvement programmes must be sustained in the long term.

Summary

It has been suggested that definitions of quality demonstrate the complexity and multi-dimensional nature of the quality concept. Complexity is compounded by the fact that its effect is judged by the consumer in a subjective and erratic way which, in turn, affects repeat purchase behaviour. For their part, organizations recognize that they must differentiate themselves from the competition by means of a quality strategy which ensures a consistent product. Service industries experience particular difficulty in specifying and therefore replicating, the intangible nature of their products. Quality assurance frameworks based on manufacturing goods before distribution are not wholly applicable to the hospitality product, especially the service element. While research using gap analysis methods is a useful retrogressive tool to audit and analyse service breakdown, proactive frameworks to ensure quality before delivery do not appear to be widely used. Nonetheless, the experience of some firms in the sector suggests that proactive approaches to quality can provide a form of competitive advantage, but they should be based around human resources and should form a sustained, long-term strategy for customer satisfaction.

TEAMWORK: QUALITY THROUGH PEOPLE

It has been shown that strategy, structure and quality need to be continually reviewed so that organizations serve their environments in a flexible way. Zeffane (1992) suggests that *the key to business success in the 1990s will also revolve around how well business uses and involves its workers.* This implies that a new style of leadership and management will be needed, that place more focus both on developing and coordinating workers' skills and delegating authority down the organizational hierarchy. Leavitt (1975) suggests that more attention is being devoted to groups as organizational building blocks, so instead of work being done by individuals, it is assigned to autonomous groups responsible for specific tasks. Schein (1988) reports higher quality and greater performance from such work teams in some industries. This section reviews the ways in which thinking has developed in this area and considers its relevance to hospitality and tourism industries as a means of improving work practices.

Group Dynamics

In western society, there is evidence to suggest that superior organizational performance may be directly attributable to effective teamwork (Varney, 1989; Katzenbach and Smith, 1993). Perhaps the father of group work and research is Emile Durkheim, who attempted to show that society is based on fundamental solidarity among people. He suggests that this solidarity derives from interpersonal relationships among members of primary groups and he defines the primary group as a small group of people characterized by face-to-face interactions, interdependency and strong group identification (Spendolini, 1992). These groups include families, peer groups and groups of co-workers. Research in this area began in earnest in 1928 in the USA with the Hawthorne Studies, from which Elton Mayo (1933) derived several critical factors in building productive work teams, the most important of which is the central role played by the group leader in facilitating the conditions in which members will feel comfortable and motivated. This work was continued by the social psychologist Kurt Lewin in the 1930s, who coined the phrase *Group Dynamics* to explain the conscious and unconscious interacting forces within a small human group that cause it to behave in a particular way. Studies in this field also revealed the complexity and wide range of the forces at work (Forsyth, 1983).

As a training method for large numbers of leaders, the group dynamics approach was found to be too time-consuming; moreover, it was viewed as being flawed by hidden assumptions of various kinds, especially concerning leadership. Adair (1986) suggests that, as a system of philosophy, this movement reflected the culture of American society of the 1950s and especially of contemporary humanistic psychologists. Group Dynamics was replaced by T-group methodology, which was pioneered in the 1950s and 1960s and was successful with groups of strangers, but had mixed results with established work groups. Dyer (1987) comments that the T-group approach was unstructured and what was needed was a more focused process for work groups.

Human Relations Approaches

After the Second World War, motivation in the workplace was re-examined. Whyte's research in 1955 suggested that money is not the prime motivator for employees and that led the way to the human relations theories of self actualization. Maslow (1954) and McGregor (1960) argue that employees feel alienated because they are unable either to find self-fulfilment, or to link their work with overall organizational goals. These assumptions which McGregor termed *Theory Y* challenge classical management methods and suggest that employees should not be controlled, but should be given opportunities to integrate their personal goals with those of the organization. Schein (1988) contends that if workers do not actively seek self-actualization at work, then either they may not have been given opportunities to express it, or have not yet fulfilled lower order needs.

Work Groups

The social value of the group, in both manufacturing and service industries, is much more valued in the human relations approach to management and Likert (1961) suggests this is because of the recognition that group forces affect the behaviour of entire organizations. Bass (1960) defines a group as a *collection of individuals whose existence as a collection is rewarding to the individuals*. Schein (1988) defines a group as any number of people who:

  a)   interact with one another;
  b)   are psychologically aware of one another; and
  c)   perceive themselves to be a group.

Formal groups form part of the structure that is created by managers with the aim of implementing plans and achieving objectives. Often such formal groups are disposed by work function or task, for example housekeeping or food production departments. Spencer and Pruss (1992) suggest that they may also be set up on a permanent or temporary basis as committees, task forces, strategy teams and so on. Festinger, Schachter and Back's research (1950) reveals that proximity to others during the course of work contributes to friendship and association, but, in hospitality firms, informal groups arise from social needs that are not necessarily associated with the work done. Gullen and Rhodes (1983) suggest that these informal groups generate their own culture and values that may conflict with those of the organization, causing resistances to the changes which managers are trying to bring about.

Work Teams

What is the difference, if any, between work groups and work teams? Some authors suggest that teams are more focused groups which exhibit a unitary perspective. Larson and LaFasto (1989) suggest that *a team has two or more people; it has a specific performance objective or recognizable goal to be attained and that co-ordination of activity among the members is required for the attainment of the team goal or objective.* Adair (1986) contends that teams must possess a definable membership, group consciousness, a sense of shared purpose and interact in a unitary manner. Mayo (1933) holds that teams may then be portrayed as 'effective work groups' whose effectiveness rests upon the degree of motivation, co-ordination and purpose and whose synergy produces an energy and creativity which is beyond them as individuals. This unitary and focused energy can be harnessed by organizations to address increasingly complex problems and is a primary strategy for continuous improvement (Kinlaw, 1992; Magjuka, 1993). Building teams is, therefore, a potentially rewarding task for management that must be approached with knowledge and sensitivity. Schutz (1958) derived the notion of compatibility between the members of a group that led to the work of Belbin. Schutz further argues that it is possible to predict how well a group will come together by looking at the compatibility of the group members. He suggests there must be some measure of implicit agreement on the degree of closeness within teams as to the personal feelings of the members of the group. Brindle (1992) concludes that effective grouping depends upon matching personality types and balancing levels of skill, knowledge and expertise so that potential conflict can be minimized. Meredith Belbin's research at the Henley Administrative Staff College (1993) offers a typology of team roles and behaviour in the group situation which is useful for planning team development.

The eight roles are:

Role name	Typical features
Completer-Finisher	painstaking, orderly, conscientious
Company Worker	conservative, dutiful, predictable
Team Worker	socially-orientated, mild, sensitive.
Shaper	highly strung, outgoing, dynamic
Monitor-Evaluator	sober, unemotional, prudent
Chairman	calm, self-confident, controlled
Resource Investigator	extroverted, enthusiastic, communicative
Plant	individualistic, serious-minded, unorthodox

Table 5.4: Belbin Team Roles

Team Development

Tuckman (1965) suggests that groups, like organizations, develop in four main stages from formation to maturity when they are most effective, but cautions that the team-building process may be an emotional and stormy one involving conflict and disagreements. While Tuckman advocates team-building as a desirable strategy, some commentators suggests that, under certain circumstances, it may be inappropriate, ineffective or unnecessary. Schein (1988), for example, comments that no definitive answer is yet available to the question of whether problems may be best solved by individuals or groups. He asserts that groups tend to make riskier decisions than individuals, but that the process takes longer. Dyer (1987) indicates that team programme should not begin *unless there is clear evidence that a lack of effective teamwork is the problem*. Zaltman and Duncan (1977) suggest that teams can frustrate the change process by rejecting and resisting changes that do not conform to group norms and culture. This *parochial* thinking is a feature of cohesive task groups that are common in hospitality firms where work is often allocated by function or department. Whyte's classic study in 1955 of the American restaurant industry clearly demonstrated the perceived difference in status between chefs and waitresses and the effects upon performance. The comments of Mullins (1992) that work in hospitality operations is so group-based, suggests that knowledge of team processes is important to quality improvement. Staw (1986) observes that inter-group rivalry is also important as a means of promoting internal group unity, but needs to be carefully managed. Dann and Hornsey (1986) hold that interdepartmental conflict is a major characteristic of hotels that occurs because the framework in which activities take place gives rise to interdependence between departments. Conflicting perceptions of priorities and goals, such as the speed versus quality dilemma will affect the quality of the product offering to the customer.

Successful Teams

The link with the environment is seen by Ansoff *et al.* (1976) as a key consideration for management which suggests that organizations need to be open to learning. Argyris (1991) argues that defensive 'single-loop' reasoning among managers often prevents them from the kind of critical reflection that is necessary for continuous improvement. Professionals studied by Argyris exhibited a high aspiration for success and an equally high fear of failure, especially when asked to measure performance against some formal standard.

Nonaka (1991) reports that Japanese firms like Honda, Canon and Sharp have become successful due to rapid and adaptive organizational responsiveness facilitated by continuous innovation and self-renewal. Goss (1994) suggests that the success of these firms is also due to their philosophy that *people were indeed the key asset of the business and that the management of people was a central strategic issue, rather than a necessary inconvenience*. Glass (1991) postulates that in many Japanese companies, there is great emphasis placed upon the work group and teamwork as a means of benefiting both individuals and organizations. Ansoff *et al.* (1976) argue that the Japanese are better able to overcome human and organizational inertia through *a parallel planning-implementation process*. While western problem-solving is serial in character, Japanese processes tend to use involvement to assure *cultural and political acceptance* and thereby optimal decision-making can occur.

Summary

It has been suggested that although teamwork can be of benefit to both organizations and employees, implementing a programme of team-building is far from easy and a mutually supportive environment cannot simply be wished into existence. Implementing team practices involves support from top management in structuring the team effectively and reviewing team processes regularly. Despite the difficulties, Kinlaw (1992) suggests that:

> improved organizational outcomes in areas of satisfied external customers, reputation, competitiveness, market share, profitability and mission success are created through the many projects of continuous improvement undertaken by teams.

A replication of the experiences of manufacturing-based teams may not be appropriate to service operations so, more flexible and appropriate approaches should be considered for hospitality and tourism sectors. Service quality is a desirable outcome for hospitality and tourism firms that can only be delivered by people, whose efforts must be coordinated through the use of effective teamwork and supportive structures.

APPROACHES

Summarizing, section one addressed the three issues of structure, quality and teamwork as a source of competitive advantage. Section two seeks to explore relevant approaches for tourism and hospitality organizations and will address five key questions:

- What scale of change should be sought; global or incremental?
- What role can teams play in improving quality?
- What organizational attitudes might best support effective change?
- What are desirable outputs of performance and how can they be measured?
- How should actual performance be compared to best practice?

Frameworks for Change

The central problem in evolving strategy is to assess how an organization might change and Johnson and Scholes (1989) suggest that this can be done by comparing the gap between required and actual performance. The strategic approach taken by individual organizations will vary as well as their attitudes towards risk and decision-making. Some may seek the potential rewards accompanying organizational change, while others may favour evolutionary change by means of a more gradual approach which enables greater flexibility in dynamic environments.

These approaches are characterized by two contrasting frameworks:

- Business Process Re-engineering (BPR); and
- Continuous Improvement (CI).

Business Process Re-engineering (BPR)

Business Process Reengineering is a term which is attributed to Michael Hammer, a mathematician from the Massachusetts Institute of Technology (Kennedy, 1994). Hammer defines reengineering as the fundamental re-thinking and radical redesign of business processes to achieve dramatic improvements on critical measures of performance. Klein (1993) defines BPR as:

> the rapid and radical redesign of strategic, value-added business processes – and the systems, policies and organizational structures that support them – to optimize the work flows and productivity in an organization.

He suggests that BPR differs from more traditional improvement programmes in that it seeks performance breakthroughs – radical and discontinuous improvements – rather than incremental improvements. Mullin (1994) describes BPR as a company-wide shift in values and styles of behaviour whose common elements include:

- courageous leadership from the top;
- company-wide understanding of the need for radical change;
- an obsession with customer needs;
- employee participation and feedback;
- an effective system for measuring performance against goals.

Continuous Improvement (CI)

Bessant *et al.* (1994) define Continuous Improvement as *a company-wide process of enabling a continuing stream of focused incremental innovation*. Small, independent businesses which are typical of the hospitality industry may find that CI offers a more credible alternative than branding or accredited quality assurance schemes. Continuous Improvement is internally conceived and implemented and can compare favourably in cost with externally validated criteria-led schemes like BS 5750, which may be viewed as intrusive and inflexible. Evidence cited by Bessant *et al.* (1994) suggests that CI is often unsuccessful, frequently failing to take root in organizations that try to implement it because of design and management faults. Despite its apparent simplicity, making CI work is a complex, organization-wide task that requires a high level of commitment and a supportive organizational context.

Which Approach?

Raynor (1993) offers a middle-ground approach by suggesting that BPR offers the potential for radical change that requires bold thinking and courageous action, but that continuous improvement is the integrating philosophy that gives BPR its true power. By taking a longer-term strategic view, firms may mitigate the potentially negative effects of dramatic change upon the organization and its workforce and obtain lasting benefit. An ideal approach would draw upon the best qualities from both BPR and CI and includes the following characteristics:

- instigated from the top but develops participation at the operational level;
- engenders long-term commitment aimed at customer satisfaction;
- sustains support for the approach.

The Role of Teamwork

The aim of enabling quality improvement in service industries can only be achieved through members of organizations who work together in a collaborative relationship and who focus upon customer satisfaction. The National Society for Quality through Teamwork (NSQT) is an organization which is dedicated to enabling the goals of continuous improvement, people involvement and customer service. Their Executive Director, Cyril Atkinson, offers a framework which he refers to as the *Total Teamwork Way* in which both *reactive* and *proactive* teams operate. Self-managed *reactive* teams seek workplace improvement and corrective action to identified problems using techniques such as brainstorming, customer feedback, or management statistical analysis. Equally important are the *proactive* process improvement teams, who are appointed by management to find generic ways of further developing and enhancing work systems and processes. Atkinson (1994) suggests that the key is *a complete understanding of the customer's needs and expectations which is funnelled into the business as its reason for existence, simply called the company mission.* This statement of company objectives creates a climate of continuous change by utilizing a *mix of six* ingredients:

•	*management commitment*	support from top management;
•	*education*	ensuring that everyone knows the language and uses the techniques;
•	*recognition*	appreciation of the efforts of individuals and teams;
•	*implementation*	delegation of responsibility to empowered teams;
•	*measurement*	self-set goals which are benchmarked against high performers;

- *regeneration*   ensuring that the programmes continues and
                                          evolves.

The NSQT suggest that these six factors help to create a climate and a structure
which facilitates the introduction and maintenance of continuous change.

Organizational Attitudes

Continuous change therefore requires an initial and sustained willingness to
change by people in organizations and an atmosphere in which change processes are kept under constant review. This implies an approach in which organizations look for improvement by learning from internal and external experiences.
Jashapara (1993) suggests that *the only source of sustainable competitive advantage may lie in its ability to learn faster than its competitors* and this involves
competitive learning organizations. Further, this flexible responsiveness to
change should be viewed as a continuous process rather than a one-time event,
especially in view of the accelerating rate of change in business environments.
Accordingly, in order to avoid the confusion and helpless paranoia, which Handy
(1990) has observed among many firms, management should continuously seek
to improve business processes and products by adopting an approach which
rejects complacency. This approach implies a willingness to learn and improve
and it may be facilitated by the use of theoretical frameworks which assist in
structuring and managing the change process.

Measuring Outputs

Organizations can be seen as *systems* which interact with their environment by
taking in inputs in the form of raw materials, resources and people and transforming them into outputs, such as finished goods and services. Outputs also
represent desirable performance outcomes for organizations such as satisfied
customers, quality standards and financial returns. In order to measure the
effectiveness of their strategy, organizations need to find ways of measuring
actual performance against the desired system outputs.

   Performance measurement can provide information through which organizations set targets and measure progress towards achieving them, but how
should performance be measured? Johns and Edwards remark that economic or
'hard' concepts like productivity can be used to measure the relationship
between the inputs and outputs of an operation, but desirable service outputs
are less easy to quantify. Employee attitude, for example, was ranked in Geller's
research (1985) as the most important critical success factor to hotel companies,
but is difficult to measure accurately. The *soft systems* approach developed by
Checkland and Scholes (1990) may be more appropriate to service encounters
that are complex and in which each feature of the system must be seen in a holistic way. Johns and Edwards (1994) suggest that measures of productivity and
performance aim at short-term operational (often financial) objectives, rather

than the strategic goals of the business. Unfortunately, Heap (1992) suggests that *many organizations concentrate upon those factors which are measurable, rather than those that have a major contribution to organizational effectiveness.*

One approach which offers a more even spread of hard and soft performance measures is the balanced scorecard. Kaplan and Norton (1992) offer a set of financial measures which report the results of actions already taken as well as operational measures that drive future performance. These may be viewed in four perspectives as shown in Figure 5.2:

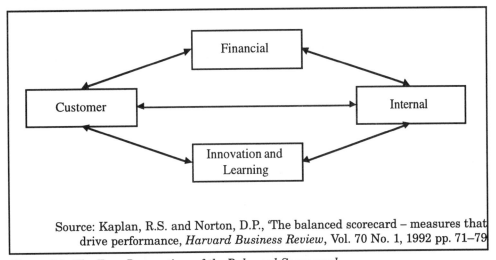

Source: Kaplan, R.S. and Norton, D.P., 'The balanced scorecard – measures that drive performance, *Harvard Business Review*, Vol. 70 No. 1, 1992 pp. 71–79

Figure 5.2: The Four Perspectives of the Balanced Score-card

- customer perspective: a key area of concern which seeks to measure customer satisfaction by formal and informal methods;
- financial perspective: 'bottom line' measures such as sales, profits and return on investment;
- innovation and learning perspective: activities such as the identification of new markets, staff development and improvements to facilities;
- internal processes: relate to those operations, processes and skills which have the greatest impact upon customer satisfaction, such as teamwork and employee development, as well as internal measures of efficiency such as gross profit percentages.

Preliminary research by Brander Brown and McDonnell (1995) in applying the balanced score-card approach to hotels suggests that the internal business perspective is the most challenging sphere to measure. Measures of cost and efficiency are absolute, but how could, or should the degree of teamwork and co-ordination be accurately measured? The number of team meetings or training, for example, may show the level of management time and resource commitment to these important activities, but may not accurately reflect their effectiveness.

Measuring Standards

Part 1 suggested that the specification of quality outcomes was an essential component for assuring quality to the customer, but that the service component of the hospitality product was intangible and difficult to define. While research continues to find more relevant generic frameworks for the industry, individual firms should continue to seek answers within their own organizations through internal analysis. Mintzberg's *soft analysis* approach (1994) may be appropriate to this situation because, in the absence of sharply defined goals, it *is more important to pose the right question than to find the right answer, to incorporate an appreciation for soft data alongside the necessary analysis of hard data*. Such an approach may be a useful consideration in future research for measuring standards in hospitality and tourism industries.

Comparing Performance

The final aspect to be considered is the way in which organizations might relate their business practices to those of others to ensure that their strategies are optimized. Spendolini (1992) suggests that benchmarking is a potentially beneficial learning strategy which enables companies to compare their products, services and work processes to those of other organizations. Yasin and Zimmerer (1995) propose a two-stage benchmarking system in which performance is investigated internally and then compared with best practice, demonstrated by both rival firms and those from unrelated industries. The practice of benchmarking may be compared to systematic strategic planning frameworks in which internal and external environments are scanned in order to match internal capabilities with external requirements.

Summary

As a preparatory step before the proposal of a new framework for effective quality improvement, it may be valuable to summarize the key points that have been reviewed in this section:

- An effective framework for strategic competitive advantage through customer satisfaction should initially be driven from the top, but would constantly develop through the participation of every member of the organization;
- Organizational structure should enable teams at all levels of the organization to play a major part in making effective decisions so as to improve product and service quality;
- The organization and its members should be always willing to learn from internal and external sources;
- Although performance is difficult to measure and standards difficult to define in service industries, the articulation process is a worthwhile and illuminating activity;

- Actual performance and standards should be regularly benchmarked against comparable best practices both inside and outside the organization.

A THEORETICAL MODEL AND ITS IMPLICATION

The final section proposes a theoretical framework for quality improvement which integrates and synthesizes the key components summarized in section two by means of a descriptive model. The implications for hospitality and tourism industries are then to be discussed.

A Model for Quality Improvement Through People

Within the framework of strategic planning, opportunities exist to re-align organizational structure with its environment using a customer-driven quality and teamwork approach as shown in Figure 5.3.

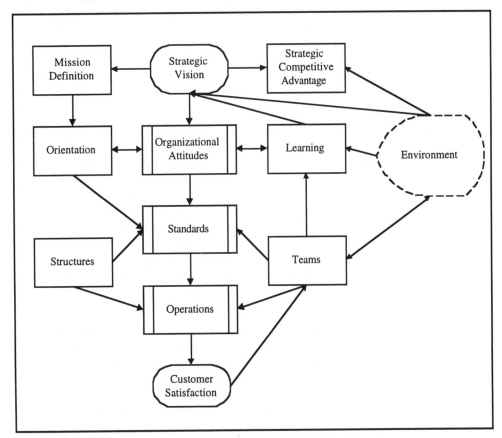

Figure 5.3: A Framework for Continuous Improvement through People

The framework is aimed squarely at satisfying the customer by harnessing the latent creative energy of teams at every level in the organization. This energy should be driven by top-level teams who need to manage the process of change so as to channel the efforts of teams at lower levels who are closest to the customer. Those organizations who succeed will be those who harmonize the efforts of their employees in a unitary way:

- **Vision** A necessary starting point for an effective quality improvement programme is the conception of a clear vision of satisfactory outcomes as measured by customer satisfaction. This vision is conceived by management as a means of achieving strategic competitive advantage and is defined and articulated through a company mission statement which reflects the organization's orientation.

- **Attitudes** Organizational orientation is also be shaped by an organization's attitudes towards change and learning. An inquisitive and open approach towards the external environment will ensure that its structure and strategy is co-aligned with both its market and its customers. A flexible orientation maximizes the scope for such co-alignment.

- **Standards** It is necessary for standards to be defined so that prouct and service quality can be effectively communicated to staff who deliver them, so that the final offering is consistent. It has been suggested that the definition of standards offers the greatest challenge to service providers, which may be assisted by techniques such as benchmarking and balanced score-card approaches to performance measurement. Further, the re-definition of standards should not solely be a function of top management; self-regulating teams at operational level have an important part to play in this process.

- **Operations** Operations represent organizational activities which produce and deliver goods and services to the customer. In hospitality and tourism industries, these operational activities are often complex and offer scope for human or system errors, thus resulting in periodic quality failure and customer dissatisfaction. Once again, operational teams should have an input to continuously re-shaping operational systems and structures which meet the changing needs of the business and its customers.

Implications for Hospitality and Tourism Organizations

Processes

This framework provides a structure which can be of assistance to hospitality and tourism organizations in providing a holistic perspective on the key issues and their potential implications. The process should not, however, be seen as an end in itself, but as an enabling management tool which is flexibly interpreted by management. Organizational ambition and attitudes towards risk, for example, will determine the rate at which change is pursued; incrementally or radically. Whichever approach is espoused, it should offer a long-term and not 'quick-fix' methodology for customer satisfaction. Consistency of approach provides as great a challenge as consistency of service.

Two areas have been identified as both essential and challenging for service industries:

- standards; and
- operations.

Existing frameworks of quality specification have their origins in manufacturing industries and are not wholly appropriate to service industries, thus more research is required to develop more relevant methodologies. Meanwhile, this should not prevent organizations from analysing quality, because they may learn much from the search. As Woodside (1991) suggests *Quality should be measured because what gets measured gets done.* The restructuring of the organization using the quality through teamwork approach can overcome many of the problems inherent in service delivery. A more consistent service quality can be offered to the customer, leading to greater customer satisfaction and improved profits. Such strategies are not easy to accomplish, but their successful implementation brings rewards for organizations and the people within them.

Similarly, operational processes offer scope for improving the speed and consistency of service delivery, especially if they are continuously and objectively reviewed by operational teams who are given full resource support by top management. In this way, operational frustrations such as user-unfriendly cash handling systems or badly designed service areas may be avoided.

People

Organizations within the hospitality and tourism industries can benefit from this customer-driven and team-facilitated approach. From the employee viewpoint, this approach may be seen as a manipulative way of increasing productivity during periods of stagnant economic growth. If that is the case, it will be doomed to failure because employee attitudes, which are critical to success, will not be fully engaged. It is, therefore, essential, that the management vision is a genuine and long-term one which takes full account of both extrinsic and intrinsic motivators. Accordingly, due regard should be given to what Herzberg (1959) terms *hygiene* factors such as reward systems, job security and working conditions that should be regarded by the workforce as equitable. This can enable intrinsically motivating factors such as responsibility, a sense of achievement and personal growth to stimulate motivation and consequent job satisfaction in employees.

In this way, if the management vision is genuine and sensitive, it will elicit a genuine response from employees resulting in a mutually-beneficial arrangement in which both the organization and its people stand to improve their performance. It has been argued here that frameworks for quality improvements in hospitality and tourism services need further research if they are to become effective methodologies for satisfying ever more discerning customers. Further research is required to develop understanding of the true nature of performance in their industrial context.

REFERENCES

Adair, J. (1986) *Effective Teambuilding*, Aldershot, Hants: Gower.

Ansoff, H.I., Declerk, R.P. and Hayes, R.L. (1976) From strategic planning to strategic management. In Ansoff, H.I., Declerk, R.P. and Hayes, R.L. (Eds.) *From Strategic Planning to Strategic Management*, pp. 39–78. London: John Wiley.

Argyris, C. (May-June 1991) Teaching smart people how to learn. *Harvard Business Review*, 99–109.

Atkinson, C. (1994) Continuous improvement the total teamwork way. *International Journal of Contemporary Hospitality Management*, 6, 3, i–iii.

Bass, B.M. (1960) *Leadership, Psychology and Organizational Behaviour*, New York: Harper and Row.

Belbin, M. (1993) *Team Roles at Work*, Oxford: Butterworth-Heinemann.

Berry, L.L., Zeithaml, V.A. and Parasuraman, A. (1993) Quality counts in services too. *Business Horizons*, 3, 44–54.

Bertram, D. (1993) *The Role of Junior and Middle Level Management in TQM*, TQM Practitioner Series, Technical Communications (Publishing) Ltd.

Bessant, S., Caffyn, S., Gilbert, R, Harding, R. and Webb, S. (1994) Rediscovering continuous improvement. *Technovation*, 14, 1, 17–29.

Blau, P.M. (1970) *On the Nature of Organizations*, New York: Wiley, pp. 80–84.

Brander Brown, J. and McDonnell, B. (1995) The balanced score-card: short term guest or long term resident? *International Journal of Contemporary Hospitality Management,*7, 2/3, 7–11.

Brindle, L. (Summer 1992) Handing out the oscars: a new look at team building. *Human Resources,* 92–96.

Brogowicz, V., Delene, L.M and Lyth, D.M. (1990) A synthesised service quality model and its implications for future research. *International Journal of Service Industry Management*, 1, 27–45.

Chandler, A.D. (1962) *Strategy and Structure*, MIT Press.

Checkland, P. and Scholes, J. (1990) *Soft Systems Methodology in Action*, New York: Wiley.

Connell, J. (1992) Branding hotel portfolios. *International Journal of Contemporary Hospitality Management*, 1, 26–32.

Crosby, P.B. (1979) *Quality is Free*, New York: McGraw-Hill.

Dann, D.T. and Horney, T. (1986) Towards a theory of interdepartmental conflict in hotels. *International Journal of Hospitality Management*, 5, 23–28.

Darwent, C. (December 1989) Room at the inn. *Management Today*, 99–107.

Day, A. and Peters, J. (1994) Rediscovering standards: static and dynamic quality. *International Journal of Contemporary Hospitality Management*, 1/2, 1994,. 81–84.

Deming, W.E. (1982) *Quality, Productivity and Competitive Position*, Cambridge, MASS: MIT Center for Advanced Engineering Study.

Dodwell, S. and Simmons, P. (1994) Trials and tribulations in the pursuit of quality improvement. *International Journal of Contemporary Hospitality Management*, 1/2, 14–18.

Drucker, P.F. (1964) *Managing for Results*, New York: Harper and Row.

Dyer, W.G. (1987) *Team Building: Issues and Alternatives* 2nd. edn. Reading, MASS: Addison-Wesley.

Faulkener, E. (September, 1983) Will quality circles work in American foodservice operations?. *Restaurant and Institutions*, 149–156.

Fayol, H., (1916) *Administration Industrielle et Generale*, London: Pitman.

Feigenbaum, A.V. (1983) *Total Quality Control* 3rd. edn., New York: McGraw Hill.

Fender, D. (1990) Getting started – the use of simple strategic frameworks. *International Journal of Contemporary Hospitality Management*, 2, 3, iv–vi.

Festinger, L, Schachter, S. and Back, K. (1950) *Social Pressures in Informal groups: A Study of a Housing Project,* New York: Harper and Row.

Fick, G.R. and Ritchie, J.R.B. (1991) Measuring service quality in travel and tourism industry. *Journal of Travel Research* 2, 2–9.

Flood, R.L.(1993) *Beyond TQM*, Chichester: John Wiley and Sons.

Forsyth, D.R. (1983) *An Introduction to Group Dynamics*, p. 14. Monterey, CA: Brookes-Cole.

Geller, A.N (February 1985) Tracking the critical success factors for hotel companies. *Cornell H.R.A. Quarterly*, 76–81.

Glass, N.M. (1991) *Pro-Active Management: How to Improve your Management Performance*, pp. 183–188. London: Cassell.

Goss, D. (1994) *Principles of Human Resource Management,* p. 4. London: Routledge.

Gullen, H.V. and Rhodes, G.E. (1983) *Management in the Hotel and Catering Industry*, Batsford.

Handy, C. (1990) *The Age of Unreason*, Harmondsworth: Penguin.

Hawkins, J.M. (1988) *The Oxford Minidictionary*, p. 411. Oxford: Oxford University Press.

Heap, J. (1992) *Productivity Management: A Fresh Approach*, p. 39. London: Cassell.

Heller, R. (January 1994) The manager's dilemma. *Management Today*, 42.

Herzberg, F., Mausner, B. and Synderman, B.B. (1959) *The Motivation to Work*, 2nd. edn., Chapman and Hall.

Heskett J.L., Sasser, W.E.Jr. and Hart, C.W.L. (1990) *Service Breakthroughs: Changing the Rules of the Game*, pp. 2–5. New York: The Free Press.

Jashapara, J. (1993) The competitive learning organization: a quest for the Holy Grail. *Management Decision,* 31, 8, 52–62.

Johns, N. (1992) Quality management in the hospitality industry. *International Journal of Contemporary Hospitality Management,* 4, 3–7.

Johns, N. and Wheeler, K. (1991) Productivity and performance measurement and monitoring, in Teare, R. and Boer, A. (Eds.), *Strategic Hospitality Management,* pp. 45–71. London: Cassell.

Johns, N. and Edwards, J.S. (1994) *Operations Management for the Hospitality Industry,* pp. 2–3. London: Cassell.

Johnson, J. and Scholes, K. (1989) *Exploring Corporate Strategy: Text and Cases,* pp. 204–206. London: Prentice-Hall.

Juran, J.M. (1980) *Quality Planning and Analysis,* New York: McGraw-Hill.

Juran, J.M. (1989) *Juran on Leadership for Quality,* New York: The Free Press.

Kaplan, R.S. and Norton, D.P. (1992) The balanced scorecard – measures that drive performance. *Harvard Business Review,* 70, 1, 71–79.

Katzenbach, J.R. and Smith, D.R. (March–April 1993) The discipline of teams. *Harvard Business Review,* 111–120.

Keiser, J.R. (1989) *Principles and Practices of Management in the Hospitality Industry,* 2nd. edn. New York: Van Nostrand Reinhold.

Kennedy, C. (1994) Re-engineering: a day with Mike Hammer. *Director,* 47, 9, 13–14.

Kinlaw, D.C. (1992) *Continuous Improvement and Measurement for Total Quality: A Team-Based Approach,* Homewood, ILL: Business One Irwin.

Klein, M.M. (1993) IEs fill facilitators role in benchmarking operations to improve performance. *Industrial Engineering,* 25, 9, 40–42.

Kotler, P. (1991) *Marketing Management,* pp. 456–459. Englewood Cliffs, NJ: Prentice-Hall International.

Larson, C.E. and Lafasto, F.M.J. (1989) *Teamwork: What Must Go Right / What Can Go Wrong,* Newbury Park, CA: Sage.

Lawler, E. and Mohrman, S. (Spring 1988) Quality circles: After the honeymoon. *Organizational Dynamics,* 42–54.

Leavitt, H.J. (1975) Suppose we took groups seriously? In Cass, E.L. and Zimmer, F.G. (Eds.) *Man and Work in Society,* New York: Van Nostrold Reinold.

Likert, R. (1961) *New Patterns of Management,* New York: McGraw-Hill.

Litteljohn, D. (1990) Hospitality research: philosophies and progress, in Teare, R.(Ed.), *Managing and Marketing Services in the 1990s,* pp. 209–232. London: Cassell.

Lockwood, A. (1994) Using service incidents to identify quality improvement points. *International Journal of Contemporary Hospitality Management,* 1/2, 75–80.

MacVicar, A. and Brown, G. (1994) Investors in People at the Moat House International, Glasgow. *International Journal of Contemporary Hospitality Management,* 1/2, 53–60.

Magjuka, R.J. (April 1993) The 10 dimensions of employee involvement. *Training and Development,* pp. 61–67.

Maslow, A. (1954) *Motivation and Personality,* New York: Harper and Row.

Mayo, E. (1933) *The Human Problems of an Industrial Civilization,* Boston: Division of Research, Graduate School of Business Administration, Harvard University.

McGregor, D. (1960) *The Human Side of Enterprise,* New York: McGraw Hill.

Mintzberg, H. (1983) *Structure in Fives: Designing Effective Organizations,* p. 3. London: Prentice-Hall.

Mintzberg, H. (1994) *The Rise and Fall of Strategic Planning,* p. 332. Hemel Hempstead: Prentice-Hall.

Mullin, R. (1994) Reengineering as an art, not a science. *Chemical Week,* 155, 2, 32–33.

Mullins, L.J. (1992) *Hospitality Management: A Human Resources Approach,* pp. 183–184. London: Pitman.

Nonaka, I. (November–December 1991) The knowledge-creating company. *Harvard Business Review,* 96–104.

Oakland, J.S. (1989) *Total Quality Management,* Oxford: Butterworth-Heinemann.

Oakland, J.S. (1989) *Total Quality Management,* p. 281. Oxford: Butterworth-Heinemann.

Olsen, M.D. (1991) Structural changes: The international hospitality industry and firm. *International Journal of Contemporary Hospitality Management,* 4, 21–24.

Olsen, M.D., Murthy, B. and Teare, R. (1994) CEO perspectives on scanning the global business environment. *International Journal of Contemporary Hospitality Management,* 4, 3–9.

Page, C. (1994) Sutcliffe Catering's approach to continuous improvement. *International Journal of Contemporary Hospitality Management,* 1/2, 75–80.

Parkington, J.J. and Schneider, B. (1979) Some correlates of experienced job stress: a boundary role study. *Academy of Management Journal,* 22, 270–181.

Porter, M.E. (1980) *Competitive Strategy: Techniques for Analyzing Industries and Competitors,* New York: Free Press.

Raynor, M.E. (1993) Reengineering: a powerful addition to the arsenal of continuous improvement. *CMA Magazine,* 67, 9, p. 26.

Robey, D. (1991) *Designing Organizations,* pp. 484–486. Boston: Richard D. Irwin.

Schein, E. (1988) *Organizational Psychology,* 3rd. edn. Englewood Cliffs: Prentice-Hall International.

Schneider, B. and Bowen, D.E. (1985) New services design, development and implementation and the employee, in George, W.R. and Marshall, C.E. (Eds.), *Developing New Services,* pp. 82–10. Chicago: American Marketing Association.

Schutz,W. (1958) *FIRO: A Three Dimension Theory of Interpersonal Behaviour,* New York: Rinehart and Co.

Senge, P.M. (1990) *The Fifth Discipline: The Art and Practice of The Learning Organization*, p. 102. London: Bantam.

Sherif, M. (1936) *The Psychology of Social Norms*, pp. 219–232. New York: Harper and Row.

Shostack, G.L. (1985) Planning the service encounter, in Czepiel, J.A., Soloman, M.R. and Surprenant, C.F., (Eds.), *The Service Encounter*, pp. 243–253. Lexington, Mass: D.C.Heath.

Singleton-Gree, B. (May 1993) If it matters, measure it!. *Accountancy*, 1197, 52–53.

Spencer, J. and Pruss, A. (1992) *Managing Your Team*, London: Piatkus.

Spendolini, M.J. (1992) *The Benchmarking Book*, New York: AMACOM.

Staw, B.M. (Summer 1986) Organizational psychology and the pursuit of the happy/productive worker. *California Management Review*, 40–53.

Taylor, F.W. (1911) *Principles of Scientific Management*, New York: Harper Brothers.

Teare, R. (1991) Consumer strategies for assessing and evaluating hotels, in Teare, R. and Boer, A. (Eds). *Strategic Hospitality Management: Theory and Practice for the 1990s*, pp. 120–144. London: Cassell.

The British Standards Institution (1987) *BS 4778, Quality Vocabulary: Part 1 International Terms, Part 2 National Terms* (ISO 8402, 1986), London: The British Standards Institution.

The Ernst and Young Quality Improvement Consulting Group (1990) *Total Quality: An Executive's Guide for the 1990s*, pp. 4–5. Homewood: Business One Irwin.

Tuckman, B.W. (1965) Developmental sequence in small groups. *Psychological Bulletin*, 63, 384–399.

Varney, G.H. (1989) *Building Productive Teams: An Action Guide and Resource Book* 1st. edn. San Francisco: Jossy-Bass.

Walker, J.R. and Salameh. (February 1990) The QA payoff. *Cornell Restaurant Administration Quarterly*, 57–59.

Weber, M. (1964) *The Theory of Social and Economic Organizations*,translated by Henderson, A.M. and Parsons, T. Parsons, T. (Ed.), New York: The Free Press of Glencoe.

Whyte, W.F. (1955) *Money and Motivation: An Analysis of Incentives in Industry*, New York: Harper and Row.

Witt, C.A. and Witt, S. (1989) Why productivity in the hotel sector is low. *International Journal of Contemporary Hospitality Management*, 2, 28–34.

Woodside, A.G. (1991) What is quality and how much does it really matter? *Journal of Health Care Marketing*, 11, 4, 61–67.

Worthy, J.C. (April 1950) Organizational structure and employee morale. *American Sociological Review*, 179.

Yasin, M. and Zimmerer, T.W. (1995) The role of benchmarking in achieving continuous quality performance, Unpublished Thesis.

Zaltman, G. and Duncan, R. (1977) *Strategies for Planned Change* New York: Wiley.

Zeffane, R. (1992) Organizational structures: design in the nineties. *Leadership and Organization Development Journal* No. 6, 18–23.

PART TWO
ORGANIZATIONAL DEVELOPMENT

Bonnie Farber Canziani

Introduction and Overview

Each of the chapters in the following section makes a unique contribution to our understanding of how multiple environmental forces impact the strategic development of hospitality organizations. The reader is invited to explore five different areas of the hospitality organization:

- human resources,
- operations;
- finance;
- marketing; and
- information technology,

from a focused vantage point. Each chapter leads the reader from a general overview of forces impacting these five areas to pertinent case study examples of individual hospitality companies' responses to those forces and finishes with a set of recommendations for hospitality practitioners. It is apparent from the many examples set forth in this set of readings that the hospitality industry is proactive in its response to changes in its external environment and, at times leads other industries in terms of their initiatives, e.g., in finding solutions to environmental challenges and in meeting the needs of customers through quality programs and the use of information technology.

Chapter 6 on human resource management, provides detail on the redefined and expanded human resource management practices developed to meet ever-changing labour market, the intensifying domestic and global competition and the need for continuous improvement of products and services. Human resource management is defined as a series of integrated decisions about the employment relationship that influences the satisfaction of employees and the effectiveness of organizations. Jiang and Susskind call for specific practices to be incorporated into various human resource functions, both strategically and operationally, such as:

1) the need to value and properly manage workforce diversity;
2) the need to accommodate the highly heterogeneous workforce in terms of work arrangements, dependent care, job sharing, dual-careers, disabilities and other individual- and family-related needs;
3) the need to offer alternative work schedules, employee assistance programmes and various other employee service programs;
4) the need to balance employee rights and business requirements;
5) the need to comply with an increasing number of government regulations in human resources;
6) the need for increased training and human capital investment; and
7) the need to link human resource management and its contributions to the bottom line of the organization.

The chapter concludes with the thought that the late 1990s and the coming century promise more changes and challenges. Hospitality organizations will have more success in maintaining their competitive advantage, if they constantly identify their human resource needs and opportunities and engage proactively in human resource planning in conformity with their overall business strategy.

Unique responses to environmental forces in the area of operations are well exemplified in chapter 7 on environmentalism and the hospitality industry by Almanza and Ghiselli. They document clearly that environmentalism is a critical issue for the hospitality industry and impacts many areas of operation. It demonstrate that, because of its importance, changes in the way the industry has done business are imminent. Ultimately, the hospitality industry will be required to reduce/control the operational activities – in particular the by-products – that adversely affect the health or well being of others. Examples of the environmental efforts of industry leaders like Disney, McDonald's, the Culinary Institute of America and school district U-46 in Legion, Illinois demonstrate the groundwork that will make it easier in the future for other hospitality companies to develop a responsible environmental strategy.

Ivancevich and Vreeland present another facet of the hospitality industry – gaming – and discuss the implications of changes in gaming legislation and financing structures for the development of this unique industry. Specifically, chapter 8 presents these issues in terms of the Las Vegas gaming market, a market which has undergone rapid growth and significant market changes in recent years. In the first section of this chapter, they discuss the history of gaming in Nevada, as well as provide a review of investing and financing trends in the gaming industry. Next, they discuss the organizational development implications of these trends, providing examples from Mirage Resorts Incorporated, a major casino hotel corporation engaged in business in the Las Vegas market. Lastly, conclusions and recommendations for firms evaluating financing and expansion alternatives in the gaming industry are presented.

Chapter 9 examines the critical marketing concept of customer satisfaction and service quality. With the advent of relationship marketing strategies in many hospitality organizations, the longevity of the customer-service provider relationship becomes a crucial objective. Delivering quality service has become a key strategy for hospitality firms as they recognize that enhanced customer service can differentiate their offerings from competitors. Many industries, including hospitality, are turning to quality management practices that focus on the needs of the customer and that support the achievement of product and service quality. Management of service quality is the application of quantitative methods and human resources to control and improve materials and services supplied to a service firm – work processes or technology used to create services – and organizational focus on meeting customer needs. Examples of companies' efforts in this domain include those of Ritz-Carlton, Marriott and, Singapore Airlines. Conclusions are drawn in order to enable the reader to extract useful practices for their own operations.

In chapter 10 Connolly and Olsen discuss how, by taking advantage of technology, hotels can access new markets, develop new services and enhance existing services. These authors suggest that the increased power of the personal computer, the creativity of software developers and the declining costs of computers and technology, have made it possible to automate business processes and services within hotels and restaurants that were never before considered.

For the hospitality industry, the application of computers and information systems are important as a competitive method, for they play a crucial role in service delivery, product differentiation and organizational economics. Information systems planning is defined in this chapter as a methodical process that looks at an organization's goals and objectives, studies the business plan and, develops a strategy to apply information technology or computer-based systems to support the organization in executing its business plan. The chapter outlines a comprehensive information systems architecture upon which hospitality information systems should be built and provides the reader with an excellent overview of progress in this important field.

Part 2 provides a place where past and future meet to inform the reader of challenges and opportunities facing hospitality organizations as they strive to grow and develop under the continual influence of external forces. Organizational development is looked at from five specific vantage points: human resource management:

- operations;
- finance;
- marketing; and
- information technology.

Conclusions are drawn that provide hospitality managers with detailed information for their own pursuit of excellence.

6

Human Resource Management: Challenges for the Hospitality and Tourism Industries

William Y. Jiang and Alex M. Susskind

INTRODUCTION

The hospitality and tourism industry is often considered a people enterprise because of its labour-intensive and service-oriented nature. For a people enterprise, human resource management undoubtedly constitutes one of the most important management areas. Starting from the idea that one of the major two inputs in an economic enterprise consists of people – the other being capital – this chapter first discusses the importance of human resource management and its role in hospitality organizations, with an overview of the human resource management field. It then examines the changing human resource landscape, in terms of the numerous trends and challenges confronting human resource managers, such as changes in workforce demographics, work patterns, cultural diversity and international competition. Against the backdrop of these new challenges, the chapter discusses theories and practices in several functional aspects of human resource management, including human resource planning, employee recruitment and employee training and development. The chapter then shifts its emphasis to compensating human resources and reviews some innovative reward systems. The latter part of the chapter presents a case study of the effects of downswing in an hospitality organization.

THE IMPORTANCE OF HUMAN RESOURCE MANAGEMENT

Economic theory posits that in any economic enterprise, there are only two inputs: capital and labour. Capital represents physical and financial resources, such as buildings, machinery, equipment and other material assets; labour represents human resources. Schultz (1971) and Becker (1975) further defined the productive part of labour as human capital, which is the stock of productive knowledge, skills, abilities and similar attributes embodied in human beings. Although buildings, equipment and financial assets are necessary resources required by hospitality organizations, employees, with their inherent human capital, are particularly important, for it is they who design and produce the goods and services, control the quality, market the products and services, allocate and utilize the financial assets and, set overall strategies and objectives for the organization. Without effective people, it is simply impossible for any organizations to achieve their objectives. Without human resources, physical and financial capital would simply have no use. This is particularly true of the service sector of the economy and particularly true of the hospitality and tourism industry, because employees are an integral part of the service delivery system.

The success of hospitality organizations depends on the effective management of human resources. Previous generations of managers often focused their attention on managing financial and physical resources as indicators of an organization's success. The human factor was considered an expense rather than an investment. Extensive research in human capital theory suggests that the investment and proper utilization of human capital is one of the major reasons for economic development (Kiker, 1971; Schultz, 1981). Modern managers have discovered that an organization's human resources hold the key to attaining the organization's goals of productivity, quality and services.

People management is an absolute imperative for the organization's short-term and long-term success and survival. Whether companies effectively manage their human resources has become a primary business criterion in judging the success and reputation of a company. For example, *Fortune* magazine rates America's most admired corporations by considering, among other criteria, the ability to attract, develop and keep talented people (*Fortune*, various years). Good management of human resources can increase organizational commitment, job satisfaction and employees' enthusiasm at work. This will in turn be felt by customers. As Schneider and Bowen (1992) observe, extensive training, performance feedback and fair compensation have a strong impact on the quality of customer service. Numerous studies have shown that organizations with effective human resource management tend to have higher levels of productivity (Bartel, 1989; Dravetz, 1988; Fitz-enz, 1990; Huselid, 1995), greater organizational commitment and higher level of employee trust (Ferris and Buckley, 1995; Ichniowski, 1990) and greater likelihood of achieving organizational strategic goals (Butler, 1988; Schuler and MacMillan, 1984; Smith-Cook and Ferris, 1986).

Human resource management is particularly important if we consider the ever intensifying international competition that is part of the corporate life today and is bound to remain so in the next century. As Lester Thurow (1992) points out, one reason organizations have to value human resource management is that they need human talent to compete in the twenty-first century. Indeed, training and developing employees to compete in a global environment and attracting and retaining valued employees to enhance productivity have become an absolute business necessity. The last two decades witnessed increasing trends of business globalization. The realization that organizations are no longer operating in a closed local or domestic system, but in an open and international system, caused managers to look beyond traditional ways of controlling costs and achieving production goals. Survival in today's world economy requires managers who recognize that employee efforts determine the degree of product quality and services released into the global market place.

Human resource management also plays an important role in reinforcing and enhancing the overall strategies of the organization. Galbraith and Nathanson (1978) were among the first organizational theorists who recognized the need to fit human resources into organizations' strategy implementation process. Subsequent research on human resource management and organizational strategy has three major thrusts, as reviewed by Baird and Meshoulam (1988) and Lengnick-Hall and Lengnick-Hall (1988):

1) matching managerial style or human resource activities with organization strategies;
2) forecasting human resource requirements, given certain organizational strategic objectives and environmental conditions; and
3) presenting means for integrating human resource management into the overall organizational strategy.

Extant literature on all three approaches testifies to the important role that human resource management plays in achieving and strengthening organizations' strategic objectives (Anthony, Perrewe and Kacmar, 1993; Baird and Meshoulam, 1984, 1988; Buller, 1989; Buller and Napier, 1993; Burack, 1988; Butler, 1988; Butler, Ferris and Smith-Cook, 1988; Fombrun, Tichy and DeVanna, 1984; Schuler and Jackson, 1987).

The strategic role of human resource management emphasizes that people in an organization are valuable resources representing a source of competitive strength if they are managed properly and effectively. The strategic role of human resource management usually assumes a long-term and strategic focus. Typical strategic human resource activities include, but are not limited to, human resource planning, monitoring workforce trends and issues, organizational restructuring and downsizing, compensation planning and strategies and compliance with evolving legal regulations (Desatnick, 1979; Mathis and Jackson, 1994).

In addition to its strategic role, human resource management has a heavy operational role with its focus on the administrative side of human resources. Typical functions include: (Desatnick, 1979; Mathis and Jackson, 1994)

- recruiting and selecting;
- employee training and development;
- reviewing workplace health and safety issues;
- resolving employee complaints/grievances; and
- administering employee payroll and benefits programmes.

Human resource management is truly a dynamic management function. Since every manager is, to a certain extent, a human resource manager, it is crucial that all managers in an hospitality organization have an accurate view of human resource management and its role in organizations.

CHANGES AND CHALLENGES IN HUMAN RESOURCE MANAGEMENT

As an ever-changing and evolving field, today's human resource management offers a host of challenges and opportunities for those who see the importance of effective use of human resources in their organizations. Today's and tomorrow's employers are faced with a variety of issues that must be resolved in order to create the conditions necessary to obtain and retain an effective work force. Some of the most important changes affecting human resource management stem from shifts in the economy, from a manufacturing-oriented economy to a service-oriented economy and shifts in demographics in the labour force. For example, the United States has been witnessing an ever-increasing diversity in its work force. This diversity movement is causing a shift away from the classic 'melting pot' metaphor to the multiculturalist 'salad bowl' metaphor – every ingredient in the salad bowl retains its distinctive quality (Bhawuk and Triandis, 1995). Extensive literature has discussed the current and anticipated workforce changes and what impact these changes will have on human resource management (e.g., Baron, Dobbin and Jennings, 1986; Beer and Spector, 1985; Carnevale, 1991; Dravetz, 1988; Johnston, 1991; Johnston and Packer, 1987). Specifically, these changes can be classified into the following five categories listed below. These changes promise to constantly pose challenges and opportunities to today's human resource managers:

A. Economic and Business Changes:

- shifts of manufacturing to service industries;
- increasing number of business mergers and strategic alliances;
- an increasingly global economic and business environment;
- intensifying domestic and international competition;
- the constant need for organizational restructuring and its attendant downsizing.

B. Demographic Changes Within the Workforce:

- women's entrance into the workforce;
- increase of racial/ethnic minorities in the workforce;
- increasing number of dual-career families;
- increasing number of labour force entrants with inadequate skills;
- increasing variety of family structures/patterns;
- changing composition of the workforce with respect to gender, age, ethnicity, family status, life-style, physical ability/qualities, sexual/affectional orientation, or any combination of these.

C. Changes in Work Patterns:

- changing work schedules (flexitime, compressed week and other alternative work schedules);
- growth of contingent workers (part-timers, temporary employees, subcontractors, etc.);
- telecommuting (working at home or at telecommuting centres);
- expatriation and repatriation of foreign assignees.

D. Technological Developments:

- electronic work places;
- increasing reliance on automation and technology;
- more sophisticated information and communication technology;
- the rapid development of the information superhighway, such as the Internet.

E. Social Changes:

- increasing diversity, multi-ethnicity and multiculturalism;
- increasing social/government legislation;
- greater concern for employee rights and privacy and confidentiality of personal information;
- greater awareness of legal and ethical issues in the workplace.

These economic, social, labour market and technological changes offer a host of implications to human resource management. In order to survive these changes and meet these challenges, organizations need to be capable of rapid response, adaptable and flexible, lean and concerned about costs, conscious of quality, focused on customers and able to innovate (Schuler and Jackson, 1996). These organizational characteristics can be obtained and maintained only with a good workforce. An organization can only be as good as its employees. New policies and practices in human resource management must be developed to support the organization to meet the business challenge.

SELECTED FUNCTIONS OF HUMAN RESOURCE MANAGEMENT

Human Resource Planning

Strategic planning is the process of identifying organizational objectives and the actions needed to achieve those objectives. Strategic planning must be organization-wide to insure that each component of the organization is included in the planning analysis. An organization's strategic planning would be incomplete without the development of an effective human resource strategy. Therefore, in human resource planning, two levels of planning are involved: first, strategic planning that affects all components of an organization and second, planning for the human resources necessary to achieve the organization's goals.

Strategic planning involves:

1) a clear statement of the organizational philosophy and mission that includes purposes, goals, corporate identity and organizational values;
2) an evaluation of organizational culture and various means of measuring organizational culture; and
3) measures and steps of achieving the objectives identified.

Human resource planning mainly involves forecasting the organization's future needs for human resources, forecasting the internal and external supply of human resources and, the balancing of the demand and supply of human resources. The importance of human resource planning can be seen in at least three respects:

1) the function provides a basis for establishing and maintaining an effective workforce in the organization;
2) the function contributes to productivity in controlling labour costs and enhancing efficiency; and
3) the function also contributes to achieving the short-term and long-term strategic objectives of the organization.

For these reasons, organizations should always integrate human resource planning with their strategic planning (Walker, 1995; Ulrich, 1988; Dyer, 1986; Burack, 1988; Manis and Leibman, 1988).

The classic definition of human resource planning was given by Vetter (1967) as:

> . . . the process by which management determines how the organization should move from its current manpower position to its desired position. Through planning, management strives to have the *right* number and the *right* kinds of people, at the *right* places, at the *right* time, doing things which result in both the organization and the individual receiving maximum long-run benefits. (p. 15, emphasis added)

Factors such as projected turnover, changing needs in terms of quantity and quality of employees, product upgrading and expansion and technological advances, need to be considered in forecasting human resource demands. Assessing the internal supply of human resources involves evaluating internal strengths and weaknesses, auditing internal jobs and developing skill and talent inventories. For the external human resource supply, assessing the various relevant external factors, or environmental scanning, is very important. That includes assessing such factors as workforce composition, governmental influences, general economic conditions, business competitive conditions and changing occupational patterns.

In balancing the demand and supply of human resources, organizations may find themselves in a paradoxical situation. On the one hand, organizations often find a labour shortage, that is, a shortage of workers with adequate skills. On the other hand, they are faced with the need to trim their existing workforce as part of the organizations' re-engineering process. As a result, more and more organizations are engaged in remedial training and educational programs to bring up the skill levels of their employees or their potential employees. In some cases, hospitality corporations are joining forces with different levels of governments, or with educational institutions, to invest heavily in general education, training and development of skill standards. Yet at the same time, these organizations are scrambling to learn the proper ways of trimming human resource surpluses. A variety of methods have been used to manage human resource surpluses as part of the strategic human resource planning process, including attrition, early retirement inducement and, outright layoffs. The latter part of this chapter will exemplify the practice of downsizing in an hospitality organization.

Human Resource Recruitment

Recruiting is the process of cultivating a representative pool of qualified job candidates so that qualified employees can be selected. The process involves identifying sources of candidates and generating job applicants from the available sources. Recruiting constitutes an important time dimension for organizations since human resources need to be on the job when they are needed.

Before hospitality organizations go out to find job candidates, they should realize that the most valuable candidates might be already with the organization. Through the auditing of internal skills and talents and internal job-posting, employers can often find the most qualified candidates for their opening positions. The advantages of recruiting or promoting from within are numerous, which include sound information about each other in terms of mutual expectations, corporate cultural fit, previous skill and performance assessment, positive impact on employee morale, opportunity to integrate organizational objectives with individual career goals, recruitment and selection cost savings, maximal return on training and hiring investment in current employees and positive impact on employee loyalty and organizational commitment (Doeringer and Piore, 1971; Mathis and Jackson, 1994).

Most of the time, however, organizations find it necessary to seek candidates from outside sources for the advantage of a larger talent pool and candidates' bringing in new ideas and new perspectives from outside, although external recruitment will be more costly and require greater need for orientation and adjustments. External recruitment sources are numerous and vary in terms of their costs and effectiveness. Advertising, employment agencies, college recruiting, referrals, walk-ins, mail-ins and professional organizations' placement services, are some of the common methods.

In recent years, many innovative recruiting methods have been developed and new sources of candidates have been tapped into to serve organizations' special staffing needs, especially for the hospitality and tourism industry. Some innovative recruiting sources include such non-traditional labour pools as part-timers, temporaries, retirees and, staff leasing firms. Organizations are making increased use of temporary or contingent personnel for a variety of reasons. For one thing, temporary help may be used to staff vacancies before a formal employment relationship is entertained. The individual can be observed in a *try before you buy* relationship. For another, organizations can flexibly increase and decrease their employment levels with little notification to the affected people (Caudron, 1994; Fierman, 1994). Because of these advantages, there seems to be a growing employer reluctance to hire full-time regular employees. The cost of keeping a full-time workforce has become excessive, according to some employers and the excess is growing because of various governmentally mandated costs. The employer reluctance seems also to stem from the increasing number of regulations that define the employment relationship.

The effectiveness of an organization's recruitment is affected by recruiting methods, the communications and administrative procedures. It is important to realize that the job and organizational information conveyed to candidates and the way to convey it will affect not only the effectiveness of the recruitment process, but also the image and reputation of the organization (Gatewood, Gowan and Lautenschlager, 1993).

Human Resource Training and Development

Training and development represent an organization's intentional efforts to provide employees with specific skills, knowledge, behaviour or attitude in order to improve current or future job performance (Schuler and Jackson, 1996). Training and development seek to bring about a relatively permanent change on the part of employees with regard to their work performance capabilities. Training and development involve the same learning activities. However, a distinction between training and development is sometimes made: training provides employees with specific knowledge and skills for use on present jobs, development, on the other hand, is usually broader in scope and focuses more on individuals gaining new knowledge and skills useful for both the present and future jobs (Gomez-Mejia, Balkin and Cardy, 1995). Development focuses on enhancing an employee's capacity to handle additional responsibilities successfully and on increasing capabilities of employees for their continued growth and advancement in the organization. Extensive literature exists on human resource training and development (e.g.: Becker, 1975; Carnevale, Gainer and Meltzer, 1990; Carnevale, Gainer and Schultz, 1990; Carnevale, Gainer and Villet, 1990; Ferman, Hoyman, Cutcher-Gershenfeld and Savoie, 1990; Goldstein, 1993; London, 1989; Sims, 1990).

A recent estimate indicates that US companies spend over $200 billion annually on employee training and development (McKenna, 1990). The size of the investment underscores the importance of training activities. Even in such an economically developed country as the United States, more than 20 million people cannot read, write, figure, or communicate well enough to perform most jobs. Over half of the Fortune 500 corporations report that they have to conduct remedial training for their employees (Mathis and Jackson, 1994). Smaller firms share this training problem and also offer remedial education to many employees.

Organizations that invest heavily in training and developing their employees, understand that having a better qualified workforce can give them a competitive advantage over their competitors. Today's businesses will not be able to compete in global markets unless their employees possess the level of skills and education necessary to perform tomorrow's jobs. In addition, according to human capital theory, training and development constitute one of the major forms of human capital investment, which is vitally important to the survival and success of an economic enterprise (Jiang, 1996a). So the question for every business is not whether to train and develop, but how best to accomplish the necessary employee training and development. There are four basic phases in a typical training or development programme:

- assessing the training needs;
- setting the training objectives;
- selecting the training methods; and
- evaluating the training process and the training programme.

The needs assessment phase involves such steps as organizational analysis, task analysis, employee analysis and succession analysis to determine the future human resource needs of the organization. The objective-setting phase requires a clear articulation of the desirable skill-based outcomes or affective outcomes resulting from the training program. The objectives should be specific and quantifiable with objective measures.

A number of training and development methods exist, each one suited to a set of specialized training needs. The focus of such programmes can be people-oriented, job-specific, or oriented towards conceptual learning. Training methods fit into two categories:

1) on-the-job techniques; and
2) off-the-job techniques.

Some of the popular methods include:

1) on the job: coaching/mentoring, understudy, job rotation, internship and apprenticeship; and
2) off the job: classroom training, simulations, programmed instruction, conference/group discussion, case studies, role-playing, in-basket techniques and business games.

Evaluation of training, like other activities of an organization, compares results to the stated set of objectives. Kirkpatrick (1987) specifies four levels of training evaluation criteria:

1) ***reactions:*** refers to trainees' judgements of the usefulness of the training program and the quality of its delivery;
2) ***learning:*** refers to the extent to which principles, facts and techniques are understood and retained by the trainees;
3) ***behaviour:*** relates to changes in job-related behaviours or performance that can be attributed to training; and
4) ***results:*** refers to the extent to which the organization realizes tangible outcomes that can be attributed to training, such as enhanced productivity, lower labour costs, or higher product or service quality and higher customer satisfaction level.

The rapidly changing business environment, changes in technology and the increasing business competition, will put constant pressure on organizations to train and develop their employees. The need for better efficiency and higher productivity requires every organization to undertake the responsibility for systematically training and developing its employees.

Compensation Strategies in Human Resource Management

The compensation system is an essential integrating mechanism through which the efforts of individuals are directed towards an organization's strategic objectives. When properly designed, an organization's compensation system can be a key contributor to the effectiveness of the organization and the satisfaction of employees (Gomez-Mejia and Welbourne, 1988). In the last two decades, compensation management as a function of human resource management has been elevated to great strategic importance. The function has been undergoing a transformation from being a micro-oriented, bureaucratically-based, applied discipline that emphasizes tools and techniques, to a broader field focusing on such concepts as 'congruency,' strategic fit and linkages that involve close articulation between the compensation system and other organizational functions and overall corporate business strategy (Gomez-Mejia and Balkin, 1992; Gomez-Mejia and Welbourne, 1988; Lawler, 1990).

The organizational strategy and the compensation strategy are closely related. While the organizational strategy usually refers to the overarching, long-term directions of an organization that are critical to the effectiveness, survival and success of the organization, the compensation strategy focuses on the patterns of compensation decisions that are critical to employees' work performance and to the implementation of the organizational strategy. The compensation strategy consists of tailoring compensation objectives to organizational strategic goals and tailoring compensation policies to the strategic environment of the organization. Strategic compensation policy decisions should always be in conformity with the strategies and objectives of the organization (Gerhart and Milkovich, 1990; Gomez-Mejia and Balkin, 1992; Lawler, 1990; Milkovich, 1988; Milkovich and Newman, 1996). Compensation strategies are set, among other things, to accomplish such goals as minimizing turnover, controlling labour costs, rewarding productive employees and maintaining pay levels within those of the prevailing market (Milkovich and Newman, 1996).

Two overarching objectives of the compensation system are efficiency and equity. Under these general objectives, a compensation system should have the following basic purposes in five dimensions:

1) attracting potential job candidates;
2) retaining current valued employees;
3) enhancing productivity;
4) increasing satisfaction; and
5) maintaining proper control of labour costs.

These five basic purposes of compensation will shape the design of the compensation system, determine the pay policies and serve as standards to evaluate the effectiveness of the pay system.

In designing a compensation system, many strategic choices need to be made. First of all, the competitiveness of the compensation system needs to be determined *vis-à-vis* the external labour market. Market competitiveness reflects the degree to which an organization feels the need to **lead, match**, or **lag** behind wages paid in the external labour market. Adopting a **lead** policy can help attract employees in a tight labour market and retain the current valued employees. A **match** policy is the common approach of paying the 'prevailing wage,' while keeping your cost compatible with the industry standards. A **lag** policy sometimes is called for because of the organization's poor financial circumstance, or an excess supply of labour with some employees willing to accept a wage lower than the prevailing rate. Other strategic choices include issues concerning the number of pay levels, the criteria of pay differentials among the different levels, the size of the differentials, basis of pay such as performance v membership, individual performance v group performance, short-term v long-term orientation, types of pay forms to offer and the mix among forms of pay and the relative weight of each form in the pay package.

Factors that may affect these strategic choices in compensation include the overall organizational strategy, the external environment, the labour market and product market circumstances and, the organization's employee characteristics, including their needs and preferences. In order to have an effective pay system, pay strategies can be tailored to individual employees' characteristics. Flexible compensation, in which employees can allocate their total compensation between cash and benefits and among different benefit items, is an example of this strategic choice.

Traditionally, an organization's reward system has been dominated by the job-based system, in which different jobs within an organization are analysed and evaluated and a relative hierarchy of jobs is derived from the job evaluation results for the purposes of pay (Gerhart and Milkovich, 1993). The system is characterized by paying the job rather than paying the person who performs the job. As compensation systems evolved, the need became obvious to distinguish job performers' contributions and base compensation, at least partially, on these contributions rather than on the jobs.

In the past few decades, there have been many innovative compensation practices that depart from the traditional job-based pay system. Supported by developments in economic and psychological theories, a variety of pay-for-performance plans have been developed, all with two built-in factors: a set of performance criteria and a link between performance and rewards. The main purpose of all pay-for-performance plans, or incentive plans, is to align employees' interests with those of the organizations (Jiang, 1996b). Among the numerous advantages of having incentive plans, are increased pay equity (to each according to his/her contributions), increased productivity, increased employees' earnings and reduced supervisory and monitoring costs. The most common pay-for-performance plans include piece rate plans and standard hour plans based on individuals' performance and gainsharing and profit sharing plans based on group performance. Extensive literature exists on these various incentive plans (e.g., Berger and Tice, 1986; Baker, Jensen and Murphy, 1988; Balkin and Gomez-Mejia, 1987; Graham-Moore and Ross, 1983; Kanter, 1987).

Another major development in incentive pay is the emerging popularity of equity-based compensation plans. Equity-based pay plans give employees an equity stake in the organization. They usually have a long-term focus of three, five or ten years. This type of incentive plan can help align the interest between employees and the organization on a long-term basis, thus increasing employees' organizational commitment and giving employees a sense of identity with the organization (Wilson, 1994). The most common types of equity-based compensation include stock options, stock appreciation rights, restricted stocks and various stock discount purchase plans (Ellig, 1982; Wilson, 1994).

Another major innovation towards paying the person *v.* paying the job is the development of the skill-based pay system. This is a fundamentally different approach to compensation from either the traditional job-based pay system or the incentive pay-for-performance system. Unlike the traditional job-based pay system, which allocates pay on the basis of the value of the jobs and the pay-for-performance system, which allocates pay according to performance or contributions, the skill-based pay system allocates pay for the level of knowledge, skills, or competencies of the employees. The system assumes that rewards should be given for acquired skills, not necessarily for the performance of such skills. A survey of firms with these programmes found that approximately three-quarters of them had higher employee job satisfaction and better product quality and productivity than under the former systems (Lawler 1990; Ledford, 1991).

To be effective, the skill-based pay system requires a managerial commitment to these forms of pay. Employees must spend considerable time in identifying and learning the required knowledge and skills required for their various jobs. In addition, a process must exist for verifying that employees maintain their competencies. One advantage of this pay system is the greater flexibility of the workforce, because it encourages employees to acquire multiple skills. The system emphasizes the organization's concern for employees, rather than for jobs and is very conducive to employee career development. It promises development of a leaner and better workforce as corporations strive to enhance their competitiveness in the new global business environment.

At this point a sample case is offered to highlight some of the human resource planning issues described earlier in this chapter. The case emphasizes the issue of organizational restructuring in the form of downsizing and discusses the implications of this practice for managers confronting this type of organizational change.

HUMAN RESOURCES IN PRACTICE: A CASE STUDY ON DOWNSIZING

Downsizing can occur as a result of internal reorganization. Management within an organization can decide that decreases in the number of workers employed in their organization must be made to survive. The company can merely reduce its workforce or restructure it as well. Whether a reduction and/or a restructuring is implemented, those who survive the layoff will be subjected to many changes. These changes may require the workers to redefine their jobs, work roles and their communication relationships which, in turn, may affect their perceptions and attitudes pertaining to their new work environment.

As a result of a changing business climate and a desire to streamline corporate office operations, a large international hotel company decided to implement an organizational restructuring in the form of downsizing. The company's central office employed approximately 140 workers in seven departments or functional units. The functional units represented were:

a) finance;
b) accounting;
c) marketing;
d) rooms;
e) engineering;
f) administration; and
g) personnel.

The average age of the workforce under study was 30, with an approximately even mix of male and female workers.

Upper management was interested in looking at the effects that a restructuring would have on those employees who remain in the organization following a downsizing. As such they desired to collect details concerning the effects of the downsizing. They were particularly interested in examining changes that occur in workers' levels of job satisfaction, attitudinal organizational commitment and perceptions of job-related stress. Management believed that they could use these data to monitor the progress of workers in the changed environment, smooth over any rough spots, restore any lost satisfaction and commitment with employees' jobs and the organization respectively and reduce perceived stress which resulted from the planned organizational change. The information gathered from the downsizing in the central office was intended to provide insight into the effects of the process of restructuring to guide additional restructuring at the unit level of the company.

The Planned Restructuring

Prior to the downsizing, management agreed that 23 per cent of the workforce would be dismissed. The layoffs would be accomplished in several ways:

a) some workers would be given an opportunity for early retirement (if they met specific qualifications);
b) some workers would given the option of transfer from the corporate office to an operational unit; and
c) some workers would be given one month notice of their dismissal and no other alternatives.

This plan was devised entirely by top management, was non-negotiable and was to be implemented within four months of its creation.

Data Collection

Based on management's decision for the restructuring, a research design was formulated to gather information from the workers to be used in the analyses. It was decided that survey instruments would be anonymously administered to employees 60 days before the restructuring (pre-test) and 60 days following the restructuring (post-test). These extended time periods were selected to help control for any possible effects of priming employees prior to the announcement of the downsizing and to allow for a reasonable amount of adjustment time following the downsizing. The actual downsizing was announced 30 days prior to the layoffs.

Subjects were assured that their participation in the survey was voluntary, that strict confidentiality in their responses would be maintained and guaranteed that their name would not appear on any report generated from the survey. Additionally the workers were assured that an outside agent would be responsible for the collection and analysis of the surveys and that completing (or not completing) the surveys would have no impact on their status or position in the company.

Measurement

Survey measures were used to evaluate worker perceptions of job-related stress and attitudes (job satisfaction and organizational commitment). Stress was measured using a nine-item scale adapted from Kahn, Wolfe, Quinn and Snoek (1964). Items from this scale were combined to yield an overall measure of stress. Organizational commitment was measured using the Organizational Commitment Questionnaire (OCQ) devised by Mowday, Steers and Porter (1979). The OCQ yields an affective commitment score by averaging responses on thirteen items. General job satisfaction was measured using a five-item instrument developed by Hackman and Oldman (1973). All of the preceding scales required the respondents to indicate their level of agreement with each question on a five-choice metric (strongly agree = 1; agree = 2; neutral = 3; disagree = 4; and, strongly disagree = 5). Subjects provided basic demographic information during the pre-test only.

Results

As an outcome of the restructuring, two workers opted for early retirement, eight workers opted for transfers and an additional 23 workers were dismissed, for a total of thirty-five layoffs. These layoffs were distributed in the following manner:

1) three from the finance department;
2) two from the accounting department;
3) four from the marketing department;
4) three from the rooms division;
5) three from the engineering department;
6) four from the administration unit; and
7) four from the personnel department.

The average age of the surviving workforce remained at 30, with a mix of male and female workers similar to the original workforce.

Pre-test Results

Pre-test results were compiled from the employee survey responses to the three attitude scales measured in the manner described above. For each construct (organizational commitment, stress and job satisfaction) a mean, standard deviation and sample size were calculated (see Table 6.1). Additionally, correlations among the three constructs were calculated and are reported in Table 6.2.

Variable	N	Mean	Standard Deviation
Stress	140	3.78	0.807
Organizational Commitment	136	2.30	0.621
Job Satisfaction	137	2.10	0.742

Table 6.1 Descriptive Statistics of Pre-test Scale Items

Variable	(1)	(2)	(3)
Organizational Commitment (1)	1.0000	−0.7834**	0.8618**
Stress (2)	−0.7834**	1.0000	−0.7585**
Job Satisfaction (3)	0.8618**	−0.7585**	1.0000

N of cases: 137   2-tailed significance**, $p < 0.001$

Table 6.2: Correlation of Pre-test Combined Variable Scales

Results indicate that employees during the time of the pre-test had high levels of job satisfaction (x = 2.10), a high level of organizational commitment (x = 2.30) and a low to neutral level of stress (x = 3.78). It is important to note that the organizational commitment and job satisfaction scales were coded designating a low numerical response as a high level of the variable. Stress, on the other hand, was coded to denote high levels of stress from low numerical responses.

These responses could be interpreted to show that the organizational environment was pleasing to the workers. They generally enjoyed their work and the work environment did not appear to be overwhelming or stressful to them. It is interesting to note that correlations among the variables reported in Table 6.2 were consistent with the proposed relationships found in the academic literature. Organizational commitment was shown to be positively and strongly correlated to job satisfaction, with a strong negative relationship to stress. Furthermore, stress was negatively related to job satisfaction (Brockner, 1988; Davy, Kinicki and Scheck, 1991; Kahn and Byosiere, 1992). In sum, the pre-test data provided a good cross-sectional snapshot of the workers' attitudes concerning their work prior to the restructuring.

Post Test Results

Results were compiled from the employee post-test survey responses to the three attitude scales measured in the same manner described for the pre-test. For each construct (organizational commitment, stress and job satisfaction) a mean, standard deviation and sample size were calculated (see Table 6.3.) Additionally, correlations were calculated among the three constructs and are reported in Table 6.4.

Results indicate that employees during the time of the post-test had a lower level of job satisfaction (x = 4.23), a lower level of organizational commitment (x = 3.37) and an increased level of reported stress (x = 2.13). These responses could be interpreted to show that the changes which occurred as a result of the organizational restructuring modified workers' perceptions and attitudes of their organizational environment, their general satisfaction with their work and, the amount of stress they perceive in their work environment. It is interesting to note that the directions of correlation among the variables reported in Table 6.4 were consistent with the relationships reported above in the pre-test. As before, organizational commitment was shown to be positively and strongly correlated to job satisfaction, with a strong negative relationship to stress and stress was negatively related to job satisfaction.

Variable	N	Mean	Standard Deviation
Stress	101	2.13	1.08
Organizational Commitment	102	3.57	1.93
Job Satisfaction	100	4.23	1.63

Table 6.3: Descriptive Statistics of Post-test Scale Items

Variable	(1)	(2)	(3)
Organizational Commitment (1)	1.0000	−0.6745**	0.7798**
Stress (2)	−0.6745**	1.0000	−0.7585**
Job Satisfaction (3)	0.7798**	−0.7585**	1.0000

N of cases: 100   2-tailed significance**, p<.01

Table 6.4: Correlation of Post-test Combined Variable Scale

Comparison of Pre-test and Post-test Data

There was a noticeable change in the survey responses between the pre-test and post-test surveys. These changes suggest that the restructuring of the organization affected workers' attitudes and perceptions over time. Table 6.5 displays the change scores for each measured variable. Organizational commitment decreased by 55 per cent. A large change such as this, indicates that workers' sense of belonging to the organization shifted, in part, as a result of restructuring. Prior to the downsizing workers appeared to be fairly committed to the organization. Following the downsizing, their level of commitment could be described as neutral to weak. Job satisfaction was impacted greatly. In the pre-test, workers reported a moderately high level of job satisfaction. In the post-test, however, this level shifted dramatically to moderately low. Stress increased by 56 per cent, indicating that the new work environment created additional work related tension. In sum, there were notable changes in employees' attitudes and perceptions uncovered by comparing the pre-test and post-test measures.

Variable	Pre-test	Post-test	% Change
Organizational Commitment	230	3.57	−55%
Stress	3.78	2.13	56%
Job Satisfaction	2.10	4.23	−101%

Table 6.5: Comparison of Pre-test and Post-test Data

Implications for Hospitality Managers

The examination of workers' attitudes and perceptions in organizational settings is an import issue for researchers and practitioners alike. Having the ability to understand how changes in work environments impact the affected workers is of great use in managing concerns which emerge during organizational change programmes.

These results suggest that layoff survivors experience great negative shifts in organizational commitment and job satisfaction and an increase in work-related stress. To counter-balance these effects, it would be wise to intentionally provide surviving workers with support and a strong sense of belonging to maintain their levels of existing commitment following organizational change. Furthermore, changes in the nature of work (such as job design and work role changes), should be carefully monitored to keep the workers' level of job satisfaction high and minimize levels of stress. While most restructuring occurs for financial reasons, the resulting changes should be closely observed to protect the well-being of the human resources which remain in the workforce following the restructuring.

These findings have great practical significance and provide some insight into how management should handle organizational change. It is important to note that the changes reported in the survey results could be impacted by several other moderating or mediating variables. It would be valuable to further explore this topic by examining other variables which could impact these reported results.

CHAPTER CONCLUSIONS

The ever-changing labour market, the intensifying domestic and global competition and the need for continuous improvement of products and services, all call for redefined and expanded human resource management practices. Human resource management is defined as, a series of integrated decisions about the employment relationship that influences the satisfaction of employees and the effectiveness of organizations (Milkovich and Boudreau, 1994). In other words, human resource management has for its purpose employee satisfaction and organizational effectiveness. As a result, human resource managers find a lengthening list of needs to be satisfied and incorporated into various human resource functions, both strategically and operationally:

- the need to value and properly manage workforce diversity;
- the need to accommodate the highly heterogeneous workforce in terms of work arrangements, dependent care, job sharing, dual-careers, disabilities and other individual- and family-related needs;
- the need to offer alternative work schedules, employee assistance programmes and various other employee service programmes;
- the need to balance employee rights and business requirements;
- the need to comply with an increasing number of government regulations in human resources;
- the need for increased training and human capital investment;
- the need to better select, train, evaluate and compensate human resources;
- the need to link human resource management and its contributions to the bottom line of the organization;
- the need to link more closely human resource management activities to organizational strategic management process;
- the need to engage in more progressive and proactive human resource management practices;
- the need to manage human resources within an ethical framework, such as more emphasis on fairness, eliminating favouritism, sexual harassment and other forms of discrimination and the building of human dignity in the workplace;
- the need to adapt all and any human resource policies and practices to these changes.

The late 1990s and the coming century, promise more changes and challenges. Hospitality organizations will have more success in maintaining their competitive advantage if they constantly identify their human resource needs and opportunities and engage proactively in human resource planning, in conformity with their overall business strategy.

REFERENCES

Anthony, W.P., Perrewe, P.L. and Kacmar, K.M. (1993) *Strategic Human Resource Management*. Orlando, FL: Harcourt Brace Jovanovich.

Baird, L. and Meshoulam, I. (1988) Managing the two fits of strategic human resource management. *Academy of Management Review* 13, 116–28.

Baird, L and Meshoulam, I. (1984) Strategic human resource management: Implications for training and human resource professionals. *Training and Development Journal*, 38, 76–78.

Baker, G.P., Jensen, M.C. and Murphy, K.J. (1988) Compensation and incentives: Practice vs. theory. *Journal of Finance* 43, 305–350.

Balkin, D.B. and, L.R. (1987) Toward a contingent theory of compensation strategy. *Strategic Management Journal* 8, 169–182.

Baron, J.N., Dobbin, F.R. and Kennings, P.D. (1986) War and peace: The evolution of modern personnel administration in US industry. *American Journal of Sociology* 92, 350–83.

Bartel, A.P. (1989) Formal employee training programs and their impact on labour productivity: Evidence from a human resources survey. *Washington, DC: National Bureau of Economic Research Working Paper No. 3026.*

Becker, G.S. (1975) *Human Capital*, 2nd Ed., New York: Columbia University Press.

Beer, M. and Spector, B. (1985) Corporate wide transformations in human resource management. In Walton, R.E. and Lawrence, P.R. (Eds.), *HRM Trends and Challenges*, pp. 219–253, Boston: Harvard University Press.

Berger, L.A. and Tice, T.E. (May–June, 1986) Incentives: The strategic side of compensation planning, *Journal of Compensation and Benefits*, 325–329.

Bhawuk, D.P.S. and Triandis, H.C. (1995) Diversity in the workplace: Emerging corporate strategies. In Ferris, G.R. and Buckley, M.R. (1995) *Human Resource Management: Perspectives, Context, Functions and Outcomes.* (3rd Ed.), pp. 84–96, Englewood Cliffs, NJ: Prentice-Hall,.

Brockner, J. (1988). The effects of work layoffs on survivors: research, theory and practice. *Research in Organizational Behaviour*, 10, 213–255.

Buller, P.F. (1989) Successful partnerships: HR and strategic planning at eight top firms. *Organizational Dynamics* 17, 27–43.

Buller, P.F. and Napier, N.K. (1993) Strategy and human resource management integration in fast-growth versus other mid-size firms. *British Journal of Management* 4, 77–90.

Burack, E.H. (1988) Linking corporate business and human resource planning: Strategic issues and concerns. *Human Resource Planning* 8, 133–146.

Butler, J.E. (1988) Human resource management as a driving force in business strategy. *Journal of General Management* 13(4), 88–102.

Butler, J.E., Ferris, G.R. and Smith-Cook, D.S. (1988) Exploring some critical dimensions of strategic human resource management. In Schuler, R.S., Youngblood, S.A. and Huber, V.L. (Eds.), *Readings in Personnel/Human Resource Management*, pp. 3–13, St. Paul, MN: West.

Carnevale, A.P. (1991) *America and the New Economy: How New Competitive Standards Are Radically Changing American Workplaces*. San Francisco: Jossey-Bass.

Carnevale, A.P., Gainer, L.J. and Meltzer, A.S. (1990) *Workplace basics: The Essential Skills Employers Want*. San Francisco: Jossey-Bass.

Carnevale, A.P., Gainer, L.J. and Schulz, E. (1990) *Training the Technical Work Force*. San Francisco: Jossey-Bass.

Carnevale, A.P., Gainer, L.J. and Villet, J. (1990) *Training in America: the organization and strategic role of training*. San Francisco: Jossey-Bass.

Caudron, S. (July 1994) Contingent work force spurs HR planning. *Personnel Journal*, 52–60.

Davy, J.A., Kinicki, A.J. and Scheck, C.L. (1991). Developing and testing a model of survivor responses to layoffs, *Journal of Vocational Behaviour,* 38 (3), 302–317.

Desatnick, R.L. (1979) *The Expanding Role of the Human Resources Manager*. New York: AMACOM.

Doeringer, P. and Piore, M. (1971) *Internal Labour Markets and Manpower Analysis*. Lexington, MA: Heath.

Dravetz, D. (1988) *The Human Resources Revolution*. San Francisco: Jossey-Bass.

Dyer, L. (Ed.) (1986) *Human Resource Planning: Tested Practices in Five US. and Canadian Companies*. New York: Random House.

Ellig, B.R. (1982) *Executive Compensation: A Total Pay Perspective*. New York: McGraw-Hill.

Ferman, L.A., Hoyman, M., Cutcher-Gershenfeld, J. and Savoie, E.J., Eds., (1990) *New Developments in Worker Training: A Legacy for 1990s*. Madison, WI: Industrial Relations Research Association.

Ferris, G.R. and Buckley, M.R. (1995*) Human Resource Management: Perspectives, Context, Functions and Outcomes*. Englewood Cliffs, NJ: Prentice-Hall.

Fierman, J.(January 1994) The contingent workforce. *Fortune*, 30–40.

Fitz-enz, J. (1990) *Human Value Management: The Value-adding Human Resource Management Strategy for the 1990s*. San Francisco: Jossey-Bass.

Fombrun, C.J., Tichy, N.M. and DeVanna, M.A. (Eds.) (1984) *Strategic Human Resource Management*, New York: Wiley.

Galbraith, J.R. and Nathanson, D.A. (1978) *Strategy Implementation: The Role of Structure and Process*. St. Paul, MN: West.

Gatewood, R.D., Gowan, M.A. and Lautenschlager, G.J. (1993) Corporate image, recruitment image and initial job choice decisions. *Academy of Management Journal* 36, 414–427.

Gerhart, B. and Milkovich, G.T. (1990) Organizational differences in managerial compensation and financial performance. *Academy of Management Journal* 33, 663–91.

Gerhart, B. and Milkovich, G.T. (1993) Employee compensation: Research and practice. In Dunnette, M.D. and Hough, L.M. (Eds.), *Handbook of Industrial and Organizational Psychology*, Vol. 3. Palo Alto, CA: Consulting Psychological Press.

Goldstein, I.L. (1993) *Training in Organizations*. 3rd Ed. Pacific Grove, CA: Brooks/Cole.

Gomez-Mejia, L.R. and Balkin D.B. (1992) *Compensation, Organization Strategy and Firm Performance*. Cincinnati, OH: South-Western.

Gomez-Mejia, L.R., Balkin D.B. and Cardy, R.L. (1995) *Managing Human Resources*. Englewood Cliffs, NJ: Prentice-Hall.

Gomez-Mejia, L.R. and Welbourne, T.M. (1988) Compensation strategy: An overview and future steps. *Human Resource Planning* 11(3), 51–70.

Graham-Moore, B. and Ross, T.(Eds.) (1983) *Productivity Gainsharing*, Englewood Cliffs, NJ: Prentice-Hall.

Hackman, J.R. and Oldmam, G.R., (1980). *Work redesign*. Reading, MA: Addison-Wesley.

Huselid, M. (1995) The Impact of Human Resource Management Practices on Turnover, Productivity and Corporate Financial Performance. *Academy of Management Journal* 38, 635–72.

Ichniowski, C. (1990) Human resource management systems and the performance of US manufacturing businesses. *NBER Working Paper No. 3449*.

Jiang, W.Y. (1996) Human capital, forthcoming in *International Encyclopedia of Public Policy and Administration*, New York: Henry Holt.

Jiang, W.Y. (1996) Executive compensation structure and firm characteristics, forthcoming in *Journal of Pay and Reward Management*.

Johnston, W.B. (March-April, 1991) Global workforce 2000: The new world labour market. *Harvard Business Review* 69 115–27.

Johnston, W.B. and Packer, A.H. (1987) *Workforce 2000*. Indianapolis, IN: Hudson Institute.

Kahn, R.L., Wolfe, D.M., Quinn, R.P. and Snoek, J.D. (1964). *Organizational Stress: Studies in role Conflict and Ambiguity*, New York: Wiley.

Kahn, R.L. and Byosiere, P. (1992). Stress in organizations. In M.D. Dunnette and L.M. Hough (Eds.) *The Handbook of Industrial and Organizational Psychology, Second Edition, 3*, pp. 571–649, Palo Alto, CA: Consulting Psychologists Press.

Kanter, R.M. (January 1987) From status to contribution: some organization implications of the changing basis for pay. *Personnel*, 64(1), 12–37.

Kirpatrick, D.L. (1987) Evaluation. In Craig, R.L. (Ed.) *Training and Development Handbook: A Guide to Human Resource Development* (3rd Ed.,) pp. 301–310, New York: McGraw-Hill.

Kiker, B.F. (1971) *Investment in Human Capital.* Columbia, SC: University of South Carolina Press.

Lawler, E.E., III (1990) *Strategic Pay*. San Francisco: Jossey-Bass.

Ledford, G.E., Jr. (1991) The design of skill-based pay plans. In Rock, M.L. and Berger, L.A. (Eds.), *The Compensation Handbook*. New York: McGraw-Hill.

Lengnick-Hall, C.A. and Lengnick-Hall, M.L. (1988) Strategic human resources management: a review of the literature and a proposed topology. *Academy of Management Review* 13, 454–70.

London, M. (1989) *Managing the Training Enterprise: High-Quality, Cost-Effective Employee Training in Organizations*. San Francisco: Jossey-Bass.

Mannis, G.L. and Leibman, M.S. (March 1988) Integrating human resource and business planning. *Personnel Administrator*, 32–38.

Mathis, R.L. and Jackson, J.H. (1994) *Human Resource Management*, St. Paul, MN: West.

McKenna, J.F. (1990) Take the 'A' training. *Industry Week* 239, 22–29.

Milkovich, G.T. (1988) A strategic perspective on compensation management. In Rowland, K and Ferris, G (Eds.) *Research in Personnel and Human Resource Management* 6, 263–288.

Milkovich G.T. and Boudreau, J.W. (1994) *Human Resource Management*, Burr Ridge, IL: Irwin.

Milkovich G.T. and Newman, J.M. (1996) *Compensation*, (5th Ed) Chicago: Irwin.

Mowday R.T., Steers, R.M., and Porter, L.W., (1979). The measurement of organizational commitment. *Journal of Vocational Behaviour*, 14, 224–247.

Schneider, B. and Bowen, D.E. (Fall 1992) The service organization: human resources management is crucial. *Organizational Dynamics*, 39–52.

Schuler, R.S. and Jackson, S.E. (1987) Linking competitive strategy and human resource management practices. *Academy of Management Executive* 3, 207–19.

Schuler, R.S. and Jackson, S.E. (1996) *Human Resource Management* (3rd Ed.). New York: West.

Schuler, R.S. and MacMillan, I.C. (Fall 1984) Gaining a competitive advantage through human resource management practices, *Human Resource Management* 23, 241–56.

Schultz, T.W. (1971) *Investment in Human Capital*. New York: The Free Press.

Schultz, T.W. (1981) *Investment in People: The Economics of Population Quality*. Berkeley, CA: University of California Press.

Sims, R.R. (1990) *An Experimental Learning Approach to Employee Training Systems*. Westport, CT: Quorum Books.

Smith-Cook, D. and Ferris, G.R. (1986) Strategic human resource management and firm effectiveness in industries experiencing decline. *Human Resource Management* 25, 441–458.

Thurow, L.C. (1992) *Head to Head*. New York: William Morrow.

Ulrich, D. (1987) Organizational capability as a competitive advantage: human resource professionals as strategic partners, *Human Resource Planning*, 69–84

Ulrich, D. (1988) Strategic human resource planning. In Schuler, R.S., Youngblood, S.A. and Huber, V.L. (Eds.) *Readings in Personnel and Human Resource Management*, 3rd Ed., pp. 57–71, St. Paul, MN: West.

Vetter, E.W. (1967) Manpower Planning for High Talent Personnel. Ann Arbor, MI: University of Michigan, Graduate School of Business, Bureau of Industrial Relations.

Walker, J.W. (1995) The ultimate human resource planning: Integrating the human resource function with the business. In Ferris, G.R. (Ed.) *Handbook of Human Resource Management*. Oxford, England: Blackwell.

Wilson, T.B. (1994) *Innovative Reward Systems for the Changing Workplace*. New York: McGraw-Hill.

7

Environmentalism and the Hospitality Industry

Barbara A. Almanza and Richard F. Ghiselli

BACKGROUND ON ENVIRONMENTAL CHALLENGES

In recent years the hospitality industry has faced a number of challenges. Some of these, such as high labour turnover, may prove to be chronic, others such as decreases in productivity, may prove cyclical or be relatively short-lived. In all likelihood many of the challenges have developed in conjunction with the industry's unprecedented growth. During the last two decades food service sales in the US have grown from $42.8 billion in 1970 to over $276 billion in 1994 (National Restaurant Association, 12/94); on average food away from home accounted for 38.2 per cent of all food expenditures in 1992 (US Bureau of the Census, 1994). Hotel sales have also been increasing: in 1994 they exceeded $75.4 billion (Staff, 1994).

While not every issue challenges each segment of the hospitality industry alike, some are a concern for all. The interaction between the industry and the environment is clearly one of these. For example, the industry utilizes important resources such as energy and water to bring its goods to market. The imminent question is how these resources can be used in a responsible manner. Along with managing inputs judiciously, the industry must also limit the impact of its activities – specifically, the effect on the environment. In many instances, air quality has become a concern to customers and employees. The largest environmental concern, however, has been the quantity and type of waste generated by hotels and food service operations.

Energy Usage

Considerable amounts of energy are used by food service operations to safely store many highly perishable products, to prepare them in a variety of ways, to serve them in a climate-comfortable environment and to keep the facilities and equipment clean and sanitary. Hotels may have similar demands, but this depends on the services offered; where services are limited, energy usage depends primarily on occupancy. This situation is reflected, perhaps, in the amount spent on energy: for food service the average cost in 1989 was $2.81/sq. ft.; for lodging facilities it was $1.15 (US Dept. of Energy, 1992). While both were larger than the average energy expenditure for all commercial buildings in the US – which was $1.12/square foot (US Bureau of the Census, 1994) – food service was more than 2.5 times the amount. Energy expenditures for other types of industries are shown in Figure 7.1.

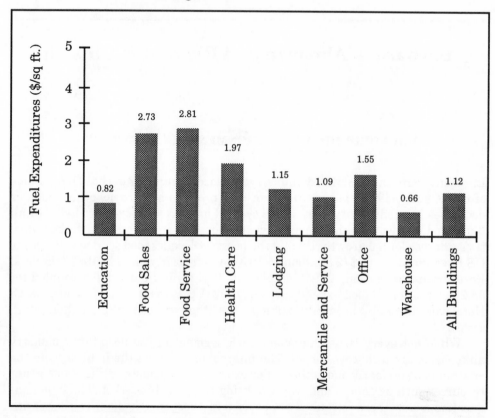

Adapted from: *Commercial Buildings Energy Consumption and Expenditures 1989,* (p. 19), by the US Dept of Energy, Energy Information Administration

Figure 7.1: Fuel Expenditure for Various Types of Commercial Buildings, 1989

Since many hotels and food service operations are in use and/or open for business much of the day, higher energy consumption and expenditures should be expected. Therefore, a better indicator of demand may be the Gross Intensity per hour of operation. This ratio reflects the average amount of energy used (in BTUs) per square foot per hour of operation. In comparison to other industries, food service is particularly demanding. Figure 7.2 shows the Gross Intensity for various commercial buildings.

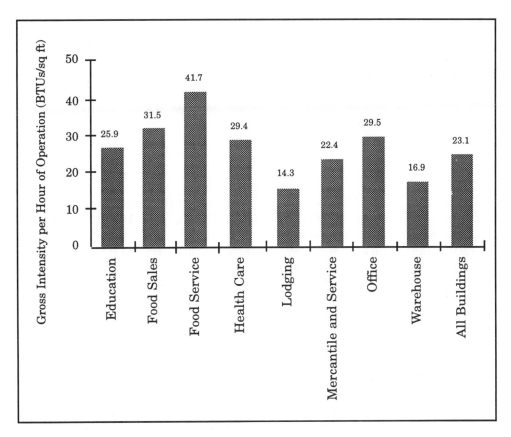

Adapted from: *Commercial Buildings Energy Consumption and Expenditures 1989*,
(p. 19), by the US Dept of Energy, Energy Information Administration,
April 1992, Washington DC

Figure 7.2: Gross Intensity for Various Types of Commercial Buildings, 1989

The median utility cost for restaurants in 1993 varied by segment; it ranged between $6.13 and $8.36 per square foot (NRA, 10/94). This cost included not only the amounts spent on electricity and gas (energy), but also expenditures for water, ice, refrigeration supplies and waste removal. As such it is not directly comparable to the Department of Energy figure. Subtracting the two, however, gives some indication of the amount spent for these other needs.

Limited-menu, no-table-service restaurants spent more on utilities per square foot than other restaurant types; the median utility cost in this segment was $8.36/square foot. The higher cost may be due to the high volume of business many of these restaurants enjoy, the limited amount of floor space they occupy and inherent operating procedures. That is, limited-menu, no-table-service restaurants are often high volume operations, that make extensive use of disposable service-ware (sometimes exclusively) and have limited kitchen space and seating. Given the high volume, limited space and that waste removal costs are included, the energy/square foot ratio is bound to be higher – especially in those areas with hefty waste removal charges.

The greatest incentive to reduce or control energy consumption in food service is its cost. Since 1990, energy costs have hovered around 3 per cent of sales, but have been as much as 4.6 per cent. While this may not seem like much, it is considerable in light of the rather low profit margins in the industry; over the same period, net income before taxes ranged between 2.9 per cent and 9.0 per cent of sales – depending on the (food service) segment.

Air Quality

A number of states and local communities have recently banned smoking in the workplace (McLaughlin, 1/20/95; McLaughlin, 3/1/95; Allen, 1995). Restaurants, bars and hotels are within the purview of many of these laws and regulations. Moreover, the Occupational Safety and Health Administration (OSHA) has proposed *national* air quality standards designed to protect employees from air contaminants – in particular second hand smoke (Allen, 1994; Sanger, 1994). Under these rules, collectively known as the *Indoor Air Quality* Standards, smoking would be permitted only in areas that are completely enclosed and that are exhausted directly to the outside (MacDonald, 1994). Also, the areas would have to be maintained under negative air pressure to contain the smoke.

The effect of food service equipment on air quality has recently been recognized also. Major concerns include refrigerated equipment, charbroilers, deep-fat fryers and large-scale baking equipment (Sellers and Ward, 1991).

Although chlorofluorocarbons have been used in refrigerated equipment since the 1930s, their potential effect on the ozone layer was not recognized until the 1980s (Sellers and Ward, 1991). Because of the concern with ozone depleting chemicals, the use of CFC-based refrigerants is being phased out in several countries, including the US and Canada. Among the implications for food service are the use of new interim refrigerants, decreased energy efficiency, higher unit costs, increased service demands for equipment and major recapitalization requirements on the part of manufacturers and suppliers for R and D.

Cooking equipment also faces emissions control standards in some areas. Los Angeles, California (with the worst air quality in the US) requires charbroilers to meet emissions standards. All such equipment must be registered and tested to reduce reactive organic gases (ROG). This is done by means of a smoke opacity test – the degree to which emissions block light. Measured at the exhaust outlet, the opacity cannot exceed 20 per cent for any three minute period per hour. To decrease emissions, operators may have to clean the extractor systems and duct surfaces. Carl's Jr. restaurant chain has gone a step further and has begun installing electrostatic precipitators, which electrically charge smoke and grease particles and magnetically pull them out of the exhaust flow. Precipitators are not always effective, in that the exhaust air needs to be dry. If grease hits the grids in the precipitators, arcing and burn out results. Other systems include afterburners and several 'scrubber' water-wash systems. Both of these last alternatives have disadvantages in that afterburners result in additional fuel consumption and water-wash systems use another valuable commodity – water.

Deep-fat fryers are also likely to face regulation in California because of airborne grease. Regulations for deep-fat fryers are controversial however, because the alternative solutions are expected to be ten times more expensive than for charbroilers.

Although California's standards may not be implemented elsewhere, they do point out the possible environmental impacts that food service equipment may have. It seems likely that food service equipment designers will be called on to develop equipment that better addresses a variety of environmental concerns, including air quality.

Water Usage

In a recent study of *hot water* consumption at a full-service restaurant in the US, daily usage over a one year period averaged 10.5 gallons (39.8 L)/meal (Thrasher and DeWerth, 1994). This was considerably more than the amounts previously reported for *overall* usage: depending on the type of food service/restaurant, the total average demand ranged between 0.7 gal (2.6 L) water/meal and 2.4 gal (9.1 L)/meal (ASHRAE, 1987).

At an institutional setting in Denmark, researchers found the food service department consumed approximately 0.8 gal (3 L) of water/meal (Mikkelsen, 1993); of this amount, dishwashing-related activities accounted for close to 89 per cent of the total and food preparation approximately 5 per cent. Interestingly, the study also found that water consumption was significantly higher when the dish machine was operated by unskilled personnel. Possible reasons for differences between the American and Danish studies include the availability of water, preparation methods, equipment differences, style of service and/or cultural differences.

Water usage at a full-service hotel averaged, over a year's time, 70.7 gallons (276.9 L) of *hot water*/occupied room; of this amount 27.2 gallons (103.1 L) were used for kitchen and laundry services and 42.5 gallons (161.1 L) were used in the (occupied) guest rooms (Thrasher and DeWerth, 1994). The American Hotel and Motel Association has indicated that *overall* water usage varies with hotel size; the average is 218 gallons (828.4 L) per occupied room, or approximately 145 gallons (551 L)/per guest/day (Aulbach, 1988).

Regardless of hospitality type, where fresh water is scarce, use restrictions and/or higher rates will force managers to conserve. Occasionally, cost and volume factors have made it economically practical for large operations to process their waste water and re-utilize it elsewhere in the operation. For example, Disney World reclaims 4 million gallons (15.2 million L) of waste water each day (Hayward, 1994). After 'initial' usage the water is treated and used for horticultural purposes such as golf courses and lawns. In another case, water consumption at a resort in Thailand was reduced approximately 45 per cent by reclaiming and treating used water (Goodno, 1994). Besides horticultural purposes, the reclaimed water was used to clean floors and to flush toilets. Because of the tremendous demand to maintain their landscapes, clubs and resorts with golf courses are ideal settings for this practice. In fact, in the South-Western US, many golf courses already use reclaimed water (Trager, 1994).

For most operations this approach would be too expensive since a treatment plant is needed to process the waste water. Yet because of the sizeable demand for water in the hospitality industry, food service operations and hotels and motels will have to find ways to limit its use while maintaining a clean and/or sanitary environment and ensuring customer satisfaction. A number of large hotels have agreed to participate in the Environmental Protection Agency's Water Alliances for Voluntary Efficiency (WAVE) programme. This programme encourages hotels and motels to install equipment that uses water more efficiently. To help implement the programme, the EPA has offered technical support including training sessions and computer software (Hasek, 1994). Among the hotels that have decided to participate are Westin, Hyatt, Marriot, Sheraton and Hilton.

Solid Waste Management

Over the last thirty years both the total amount and the average amount of solid waste generated per person per day have steadily increased (US Environmental Protection Agency (EPA), 1994). Although EPA (1990) estimates and archaeological studies by Rathje (1991) have not found hotels and food service operations to be primary sources of solid waste, the public has a negative perception of the type and quantity of waste generated (Cummings and Cummings, 1991; Liddle, 1990a; Rathje, 1991; Scarpa, 1989). As a result, legislators, those concerned with the environment and, the public have implicated them and the food service sector in particular, as major contributors to landfill waste. Furthermore, these groups have looked – and will continue to look – for initiatives and efforts to reduce the total amount of waste. Since the services offered by hotels and food service operations are often prepared, provided and consumed on site, the effect of which concentrates much of the waste and then collected there as well, hospitality managers may be in the best position to manage and reduce the amount waste being sent to landfills.

The US Environmental Protection Agency has set overall goals for reducing the total amount of solid waste being landfilled. To this end an integrated approach to waste management has been suggested and a hierarchy of waste management practices identified. In order of priority they are:

- source reduction (including re-use);
- recycling;
- composting;
- combustion; and
- landfilling. (US EPA, 1989).

According to the EPA:

> As we approach the twenty-first century, integrated waste management is
> clearly the solution to our growing waste needs. Through source reduction and
> recycling, we can reduce generation and increase recovery and, in turn, reduce
> our reliance on combustors and landfills. (EPA 1990, ES–15).

By the year 2000 the EPA would like to see 50 per cent of the solid waste
stream recycled (US EPA, 1989). This approach provides the context within
which the hospitality industry should endeavour to manage its waste.

Concerns with Landfilling

In a nation-wide public opinion survey, the Wall Street Journal/NBC News
(1990) found that 80 per cent of those surveyed believed it was more important
to protect the environment than to keep prices down.[1] Nonetheless, the general
public has been reluctant to embrace the use of polystyrene, even though fabri-
cators (voluntarily) removed fully halogenated chlorofluorocarbons (CFCs) from
the manufacturing process and it is recyclable. While the link between the use
of CFCs and the depletion of the ozone layer may explain a large part of the dissatisfaction with foam packaging, some of the animosity towards this (refash-
ioned) material may be due to lingering perceptions and the general uncertainty that exists in determining the best method of disposal for increasing amounts
of waste.

Most Americans are opposed to continued landfilling if it means locating a
new landfill near their community (Byers, 1990). They are also against incineration; hostility to incineration has spawned NIMBYism (Not In My Back Yard)
and blocked many proposed incinerators (Commoner, 1990; Landers, 1989).
Perhaps as a result, over a thousand mayors and council members cited solid
waste management as the second largest problem facing government
(Cummings and Cummings, 1991).[2]

The major concern with the continued use of landfilling as a means of waste
disposal is the fear of ground water contamination (O'Leary and Walsh, 1991a
and 1991b; Cummings and Cummings, 1991). Other concerns with landfilling
include gas generation through the decomposition of solid waste (particularly
methane gas), pests and rats, air quality around the landfill and the uncertainty with the long term impacts of landfilling (O'Leary and Walsh, 1991a and
1991b).

Waste Generation and Disposal

The appellations 'disposable society' and 'throw-away society' aptly characterize
the striking increase in the amount of waste generated over the last thirty years.
During this period the total amount of waste has more than doubled and the per
capita amount is more than 1 √ times what it was in 1960. Increases of this magnitude suggest a tremendous upsurge in consumption and may reflect the

(seemingly) hectic pace of modern life. Moreover, the changing composition of the waste stream illustrates the increasing disposition towards convenience and disposability and mirrors advances in technology. Table 7.1 shows the total and per capita amounts of waste generated in the US since 1960.

	Total Materials Generated (in millions of tons)						
	1960	1970	1980	1988	1990	1991	1993
Total Municipal Solid Waste[1]	87.8	121.9	149.6	179.6	195.7		207[3]
Total Municipal Solid Waste II[2]					293.0	280.7	
	Per Capita (pounds per person per day)						
Total Municipal Solid Waste[1]	2.66	3.27	3.61	4.00	4.3		
Total Municipal Solid Waste II[2]					6.4	6.1	

Notes:
1. Adapted from *Characterization of Municipal Solid Waste in the United States: 1990 Update*. (pp. 10, 79) by United States Environmental Protection Agency, 1990. Source: Franklin Associates, Ltd., and *The EPA Municipal Solid Waste Factbook*, version 1.2, 27 May, 1994, Washington, DC. Source: Franklin Associates, Ltd.
2. Glenn and Riggle (1991) and Glenn (1992). According to Glenn and Riggle, the rather large differences are due to the way the EPA defines Municipal Solid Waste. See Glenn and Riggle (1991). The per capita amounts are based on resident population fig-ures as estimated by the Bureau of the Census (US Department of Commerce, 1992).
3. Popkin, R. (1995). Good News For Waste Watchers. *EPA Journal*, 21(1), p. 18.

Table 7.1: US Total and Per Capita Waste Generation, 1960–1991

Over the next fifteen years, further increases are expected. Waste from plastics and paper are expected to continue increasing at a faster rate than the waste from most other materials. EPA projections for total and per capita generation of municipal solid waste are given in Table 7.2.

While per capita output is highest in the US, at the global level, waste quantities are also growing. Daily per capita outputs are estimated to be 3 lb. in Tokyo, 2.4 lb. in Paris and 1.5 lb. in Rome (Cummings, 1992).

The predominant method of disposal in the US has been landfilling, however, more waste is gradually being diverted. In 1990 recycling and composting efforts recovered almost six times the amount that was recovered in 1960. Despite this fact, considerably more waste has been generated overall and the increase in recovery, as a per cent of the total, has been just over 10 per cent. The end result is that more waste has needed disposal: after recovery by these two methods, 1.06 more pounds per person per day were generated in 1990 than in 1960. Table 3 shows the amounts of waste generated, the amounts recovered, the amounts disposed of through combustion and discards to landfills.

	Total Materials Generated (in millions of tons)		
	1995	2000	2010
Total Municipal Solid Waste	199.8	216.0	250.6
	Per Capita (pounds per person per day)		
Total Municipal Solid Waste	4.21	4.41	4.86

Note: Adapted from *Characterization of Municipal Solid Waste in the United States: 1990* Update. (pp. 59, 61) by United States Environmental Protection Agency, 1990. Source: Franklin Associates, Ltd.

Table 7.2: US Total and Per Capita Waste Generation Projections, 1995–2010

	Total Municipal Solid Waste (in millions of tons)[1]				
	1960[1]	1970[1]	1980[2]	1990[2]	1993[2]
Generation	87.8	121.9	151.9	195.7	207
Recovery through recycling and composting	5.9	8.6	14.5	33.4	45
Combustion	27.0	24.9[2]	13.7	31.9	33.1
Discards to landfill	54.9	88.2	123.3	129.9	128.9

Notes.
1. Adapted from *Characterization of Municipal Solid Waste in the United States: 1990* Update. (pp. 74-79) by United States Environmental Protection Agency, 1990. Source: Franklin Associates, Ltd., and *The EPA Municipal Solid Waste Factbook*, version 1.2, 27 May, 1994, Washington, DC. Source: Franklin Associates, Ltd.
2. Popkin, R. (1995). Good News For Waste Watchers. *EPA Journal*, 21(1), p. 18.

Table 7.3: Generation and Disposal of Municipal Solid Waste in US, 1960–1990

Organizational development

While the US does not burn as large a percentage of its waste as many other industrialized countries, it is second only to Japan in the total amount incinerated (millions of tons). The reason for this is because of the tremendous quantity of waste generated. Perhaps the availability of space in both the US and Canada have made these countries more willing to bury their trash. For comparative purposes, Table 7.4 shows the total amount of municipal waste generated in a number of industrialized countries and the waste management practices that are being used to control it.

	Canada[4]	Germany[4]	Netherlands[4]	Japan[4]	Switzerland[4]	US[5]
Generation (millions of tons)[3]	16	27.9	7.4	49.3	3	195.7
Recovery through recycling	10%	na	4%	3.4%	na	17.4%[6]
Recovery through composting	<1%	2.9%	3.9%	<1%	8.3%	
Incineration	8.6%	16.9%	33.5%	74.4%	76.6%%	16.3%
Discards to landfill	82%	77.2%	43%	na	15%	66.3%

Notes:
1. According to the OECD, definitions associated with waste and waste disposal vary by country. As a result, amounts may not be directly comparable.
2. Percents may not total to 100% because of rounding.
3. The U.S. amount is in U.S. tons; all other countries are in metric tons.
4. Adapted from *OECD Environmental Data Compendium 1993*, 1993, Paris. Source: OECD/OCDE.
5. From *The EPA Municipal Solid Waste Factbook*, version 1.2, May 27, 1994, Washington, DC. Source: Franklin Assoc., 1992.
6. Recycling and composting together.

Table 7.4: Generation and Disposal of Municipal Solid Waste in Selected Industrialized Countries, 1990[1,2]

Although there has been an increase in the number of recycling programmes, an increase in the number of materials recovery facilities and an increase in the use of incineration (Glenn and Riggle, 1991a; Glenn, 1992), the total amount of waste that has had to be landfilled has increased. As a result concerns remain that landfill capacity will continue to decline more rapidly than discards requiring landfilling (US EPA, 1990).[3]

Amounts of Food Service-Related Waste

Modern technology, along with strict sanitary (packaging) requirements, a desire for convenience and a need to keep costs low, have led to the widespread use of disposable packaging and service-ware in food service. Because of the concerns with current waste disposal methods, legislators, environmentalists and the public have insisted that solid waste be reduced. Accordingly, managing solid waste has become a critical issue in this industry.

Rathje (1991), founder of the Garbage Project at the University of Arizona, has indicated that most people mistakenly believe landfills are 20–30 per cent fast-food packaging, 30–40 per cent polystyrene foam and 25–45 per cent disposable diapers. Through his excavations he has found, however, that fast-food packaging makes up only a quarter of a per cent of the average landfill.

The EPA has not measured food service waste *per se*, but has estimated total amounts for many of the products/materials that might be found in food service waste. The total amounts from all sources, not just food service, for these products are listed in Table 7.5; they are presented as a percentage of the total municipal waste stream.

	Percent of Total Municipal Solid Waste			
	1960	1970	1980	1988
Paper plates and cups	0.3%	0.3%	0.4%	0.4%
Milk cartons (paper/paperboard)			0.4	0.3
Corrugated boxes	8.3	10.4	11.4	12.9
Plastic plates and cups			0.1	0.2
Soft drink bottles (plastic)			0.2	0.2
Plastic wraps			0.5	0.6
Total plastics packaging	0.2	1.7	2.3	3.1
Food/other bottles/jars	4.2	3.6	3.2	2.2
Food/other cans (steel)	4.3	2.9	1.9	1.4
Beer/soft drinks cans (aluminium)	0.1	0.2	0.6	0.8

Note: Adapted from *Characterization of Municipal Solid Waste in the United States: 1990 Update*, (pp. 38, 43) by United States Environmental Protection Agency, 1990. Source: Franklin Associates, Ltd.

Table 7.5: Selected Items Generated in Municipal Waste Systems, as a per cent of Total Municipal Solid Waste, 1960–1988

Except for plastics and corrugated boxes, the relative amounts of these items have changed little over the last 30 years. Moreover, the figures do not support the contention that food service has been a major producer of landfill waste. Rather, the figures suggest that food service has been a 'scapegoat' (Cummings and Cummings, 1991; Scarpa, 1989). The correct view may be that a 'garbage information crisis' has been created through the 'garishly visible packaging' that is used (Scarpa, 1989).

Operational analyses have produced more detailed information about the type and quantities of the waste products generated in food service. One study found paper to be the largest component (by volume) of the total amount of waste generated in various food service operations (Scarpa, 1990). Specifically, paper accounted for approximately 65 per cent of the total volume in fast-food restaurants, 40 per cent of the total in institutional settings and 44 per cent of the total in full-service restaurants. The investigators also estimated that 30–35 per cent of the waste generated could have been recycled.

In another study, McDonald's and the Environmental Defense Fund found that the waste at McDonalds' restaurants contained the following (by weight): 34 per cent food waste, 34 per cent corrugated shipping boxes, 15 per cent product packaging (7 per cent coated paper, 4 per cent uncoated paper, 4 per cent polystyrene), 11 per cent other and 6 per cent non-McDonald's waste (Ward and Richards, 1991).

School food service has been the setting for a number of waste studies investigating the composition of the waste stream and the effect that certain interventions can have. Waste hauliers have estimated that 0.5 pounds of solid waste per day is generated through school cafeterias for each student enrolled (Mann and Shanklin, 1990). Not all of this, however, ends up in landfills. Almanza, Hiemstra and Ghiselli (1993) found that, overall, school food service operations in Indiana were sending approximately 0.19 pounds of waste per day per student enrolled directly to landfills. The amount depended in part on the manner in which food service operations handled their service-related food waste. Specifically, schools that processed their plate waste in a garbage disposal were sending significantly less waste to landfills than those that did not use this waste management/waste reduction practice (Almanza, Hiemstra and Ghiselli, 1993).[4] In some areas composting was being used. Another factor that affected the total weight of waste was grade level (Almanza, Hiemstra and Ghiselli, 1993); one possible reason for the greater amounts of waste at higher grade levels was the large number of *a la carte* offerings – many of which were pre-portioned, pre-packaged products – used there.

Because they are a required component of the National School Lunch Programme, milk cartons have been an obvious target for school waste studies and waste reduction efforts. Researchers have found a significant decrease in the volume of solid waste generated by the milk component when polyethylene (PE) pouches are used instead of the traditional gable-top milk cartons (Hollingsworth, Shanklin, Gench and Hinson, 1990). In addition, there is a significant decrease in the weight of milk waste.

A number of studies have also focused on disposable service-ware. Most have found that the use of disposable service-ware is more cost-effective than using permanent service-ware. Labour costs were a significant factor when the cost of using permanentware was compared to the cost of reusing and recycling polystyrene trays (Schmicker, 1991). In this limited study, the use of polystyrene trays in school food service was found to be more cost-effective than using permanentware – even with the cost to recycle them included. At the time the cost to recycle was approximately \$0.0052 per meal served.

Similarly, two service-ware systems using either disposable polystyrene trays or permanent reusable trays were compared for volume of waste generated as well as for cost (Riley, Shanklin and Gench, 1991). As might be expected, the system using disposable polystyrene trays was found to generate significantly more volume of waste per participant than was the one using permanent (reusable) trays. Once all of the related costs were taken into consideration, however, the system using the disposable tray was found to cost less per meal than the system using the reusable tray. The cost per meal for the system using the disposable tray was \$0.07, whereas the cost per meal for the other system was \$.11. Dishwashing-related labour was cited as the reason for the higher meal cost associated with the use of permanent trays.

In another study of the costs associated with the choice of service-ware, the total cost of a service-ware mix (including replacement costs, dishwashing costs, waste-removal costs), tended to increase more with the use of permanentware than with disposable service-ware (Almanza, Hiemstra and Ghiselli, 1992). In the same study, the cost effectiveness of certain disposable service-ware products was examined. Generally, paper products were found to use landfill space more efficiently, but were not as cost-effective when the cost to dispose of and 'store' them in a landfill was included. This was due in part to the lower cost of other disposables, such as plastic and polystyrene, but also to the relatively low cost of landfill space in the place the study was conducted.

Using landfill densities and weight measurements, researchers estimated the effect of school food service waste on landfills (Ghiselli, Almanza and Hiemstra, 1995). In this procedure, the effect of the various waste components was determined and the success of waste reduction efforts estimated. They found that cardboard, metal waste products and milk cartons, could account for as much as 47 per cent of the space needed to store school food service waste in landfills. As in other studies, food waste was found to have a significant effect at the point of collection, but, because of its inherent density, its effect in the landfill was considerably less.

These studies have shown that the amount of waste generated and potentially sent to landfills, can be affected by the type of operation, the menu, the use of disposable service-ware, the products and packaging selected and the waste management practices used. The amount of food service waste that can be recovered through recycling, however, may be limited. Often, much of the waste is wet and/or contaminated with food and not suitable for recycling. Moreover, recycling has its costs (Almanza, Hiemstra and Ghiselli, 1992). Nevertheless, cardboard and metal waste products are quite prevalent and readily recyclable. In addition, less effort is required to prepare them for recycling (in comparison to some other waste products). Generally:

1) these two materials are typically cleaner and easier to clean than other waste materials;
2) they are generated and collected where management has better control, namely production (as compared to customer-related service waste);

3) fewer individuals are needed to process them; and

4) little training is required (Almanza, Hiemstra and Ghiselli, 1993).

CASE STUDIES

In this section some of the efforts that have been undertaken, or are currently being practised, by leaders in the hospitality field are explored. The activities and programmes that Disney, McDonald's, the Culinary Institute of America and school district U-46 in Elgin, Illinois have incorporated can serve as models that other hospitality companies can follow in their efforts and in developing an environmental strategy.

1. Disney World, Orlando, Florida

Disney World is recognized not only for its entertainment, but its hefty impact on the environment (Hayward, 1994). Disney operates thirteen hotels, leases the land for another five hotels, operates three theme parks, numerous restaurants and five golf courses. They have developed what they refer to as an experimental approach to environmental management and hope to become a recognized force over the next 25 years.

On a typical day, 143,000 people visit Disney World, generating 160 tons of rubbish and 300 tons of construction debris. The resort has instituted a recycling programme which recycles 30 tons of office paper, 17 tons of aluminium, steel and plastic, 40 tons of glass, 770–960 gallons of used oil and 85 tons of corrugated board a week. In addition, 210 cubic yards of food wastes and sludge are composted. Left-over food scraps are sold to nearby state-certified pig farmers.

Other products are reused. For example, paper products are shredded and then used in the gift shops for packing (estimated to save eight tons a year). Torn linens and towels are given to the workshop for return as rags.

Other reduction strategies include purchasing paper towels and toilet paper in jumbo rolls to minimize packaging (estimated to save 813,000 pounds a year), reducing the size of dispenser napkins by 25 per cent (a saving of 263,000 pounds a year) and setting copy machines to automatically make two-sided copies. Recycled good are purchased as often as possible, including lumber made from recycled plastics.

Four million gallons of waste water a day is also reclaimed for horticultural purposes, including watering of plants, hundreds of acres of lawn and its five golf courses. The 'gray water' as it is called, has been treated almost to the point fit for human consumption.

Disney is particularly proud of the resort's 28,000-square-foot Materials Recycling Facility (MRF). Completed in 1992, the plant processes 30 tons of trash a day. Materials are separated by workers and the recyclables are then marketed by Disney's broker in Jacksonville. Ultimately, Disney does not make a profit from its recycling programme. Corrugated board is the only recycled product that brings a profit. They are proud of the fact, however, that they are close to reducing their waste stream by 30 per cent. Disney's environmental philosophy is echoed in a quote from the late Walt Disney:

> If certain events continue, much of America's natural beauty will become nothing more than a memory. The natural beauty of America is a treasure found nowhere in the world. Our forests, waters, grasslands and wildlife must be wisely protected and used. I urge all citizens to join the effort to save America's natural beauty.

2. Culinary Institute of America, Hyde Park, New York

The Culinary Institute of America has instituted an extensive recycling programme at its Hyde Park, NY campus. In its 36 production and teaching kitchens and four restaurants, the students actively separate the waste into three colour-coded containers. In one container food waste is collected. In another mixed recyclables including glass, #1 and #2 plastics and metal waste products are gathered; these products are then removed by a waste haulier to a materials recovery facility for sorting. The third container is for other types of trash.

Since February 1994, food waste has been collected for composting. At the end of each class, food waste is removed and placed in a 20 cubic yard, open top container. Twice a week the waste is picked up by a local company for composting. An estimated 70–80 tons of food waste/month are processed in this manner, with annual savings to the school between $20,000–$30,000 in waste hauling expenses. To help control odours and insects in the warm months, the composting company provides cured compost to use as a layering agent.

Other efforts at the school include:

- In the centralized storage area, students collect and compact corrugated boxes before they are removed for recycling;
- Pallets, crates and baskets are collected and sent back to vendors for reuse.

3. McDonald's Restaurants

In November 1990, McDonald's decided to stop using polystyrene packaging and start using paper packaging (Liddle, 1990b). Even though McDonald's had been investigating the feasibility of recycling polystyrene, top management felt enough public pressure to change.

Although some scientific studies indicate that foam packaging is environmentally sound, our customers just don't feel good about it. So we're changing.

Ed Rensi, president of McDonald's (Liddle, 1990b, p. 1).

The Environmental Defense Fund supported the change and estimated that by switching to paper and paper-based products McDonald's would reduce its volume of waste by 70–90 per cent (Liddle, 1990a; McDonald's Corp. and Environmental Defense Fund, 1991). The support for the change came in spite of the fact that the new packaging materials could not be recycled.

Corporate McDonald's has been proactive since taking an active interest in the environment. This approach is expressed in its Corporate Environmental Policy:

> McDonald's believes it has a special responsibility to protect our environment for future generations. This responsibility is derived from our unique relationship with millions of consumers world-wide – whose quality of life tomorrow will be affected by our stewardship of the environment today. We share their belief that the right to exist in an environment of clean air, clean earth and clean water is fundamental and unwavering.

(McDonald's and The Environmental Defense Fund, 1991).

Among the numerous environmental efforts this industry leader has embarked on:

- In 1991 McDonald's adopted a Waste Reduction Action Plan (WRAP). This plan identified the activities that McDonald's would undertake to reduce its solid waste. Major accomplishments thus far include:
- Packaging changes have allowed McDonald's to reduce the amount of waste by close to 20 million pounds since 1991 (McDonald's Earth Effort Global Express, 6/6/94).
- 80 per cent of McDonald's restaurants are recycling their corrugated boxes (McDonald's WRAP Status Report, 1995).
- Through its 'McRecycle USA' programme, McDonald's has helped create markets for recycled products by using products containing recycled materials. McDonald's is the largest user of recycled paper in the industry; the products being used include carry-out bags, carry-out drink containers, corrugated boxes, napkins, toilet tissue, tray-liners, roll towels, Happy Meal® cartons and Happy Meal® bags (McRecycle USA, 1990; McDonald's Corp., 1992). Other products used by McDonald's that contain recycled materials include: in-store trays, pallets, trash receptacles, restaurant seats, patio tables and chairs and playland surfaces. Since 1990, McDonald's has purchased more than $1 billion worth of recycled products (Langert, 6/30/95).

- As a participant in the EPA's Green Light programme, McDonald's is replacing its indoor lighting to use less electricity. McDonald's is replacing T12 fluorescent lights with T8 fluorescent lights. The T12s have magnetic ballasts whereas the T8s have solid state electronic circuits. The expected savings are 7–8 cents per kilowatt hour (Lorenzini, 1994).

4. School District U-46, Elgin, Illinois

Since 1990 the food and nutrition services department at school district U-46 in Illinois has been recycling polystyrene waste materials generated through the district's food service operations. The programme began in response to concerns from students, administrators and others, in the community with the use of this material.

The school system has 44 sites and approximately 30,500 students. Thirty-three of the sites are elementary schools, all of which are satellites. Ten of the remaining eleven schools have on-site kitchens, but typically do little more than heat and serve. There are no dishwashers at any of the schools. Elgin High School is the site of the district's main production kitchen. Approximately 9,000 of the 11,400 regular lunches served daily are prepared there.

Polystyrene products are used extensively throughout the system. The products used include 9" ×7" cafeteria 'trays', eating utensils, bowls, cups, plates and salad containers. The polystyrene waste materials are separated and collected by the students in the normal course of operations. That is, each school has two waste receptacles in its cafeteria and, as they leave, the students have been trained to place the polystyrene waste materials in one bin after dumping all other waste products in the other.

The programme is operated in conjunction with a local polystyrene processor. During the 1994–1995 school year an estimated 23,000 pounds of polystyrene were recycled. The programme was estimated to cost the district between $13,000 – $14,000. However, these amounts do not take into account the savings that have accrued due to a reduction in the total amount of waste being collected by the district's traditional waste haulers. As a result of these (recycling) efforts smaller dumpsters are being used and fewer regular garbage pickups are needed. Greater cost savings may be in store as the school district has arranged with the local health departments to allow back-hauling of used polystyrene products as long as they are bagged and no food is on the trucks. This will allow the district to reduce the transportation cost of recycling.

Other waste reduction efforts by the food and nutrition services department include:

- Corrugated boxes are being baled and recycled – an estimated 20 bales each weighing 150 pounds are accumulated at the main production school each week;
- Collapsible milk cartons are being used;
- #10 cans are being rinsed and recycled;
- Aluminium soda cans are being recycled;

- Grease is sent back to the grease rehaulier.

ACCEPTING THE ENVIRONMENTAL CHALLENGE

Operational guidelines for the hospitality industry have been suggested to conserve energy, protect air quality, save water and reduce waste (Cook, Stewart and Repass, 1992). Although some of these guidelines may require short-term financing, the long-term benefits would have to be considered in light of the company's environmental policy. The payoffs of most solid waste programmes are not in the form of increased revenues (Cummings, 1992). While some make money (Lemonick, 1992), most simply seek to avoid costs, to offset costs and, to position for consumer demand (Frankel, 1992; Hemphill, 1991). Cost savings may result from scaled-down materials purchases, handling costs and disposal-related fees. Offset costs come with extended service lives of goods that may occur from good cleaning and maintenance programmes.

Energy Conservation

In the US, commercial buildings account for 27 per cent of electricity use (Cook, Stewart and Repass, 1992). The American Council for an Energy Efficient Economy estimates that computerized 'energy management and control systems' (EMCS) that automatically regulate heating, ventilation, air conditioning, lighting and other systems would save 10–20 per cent of energy.

Other measures include:

- The use of compact fluorescent light bulbs (while initially more expensive) which would use only about 1/4 of the energy that incandescents use and would last thirteen times longer (Cook, Stewart and Repass, 1992);
- The design of window exposures to maximize natural light whenever possible as well as retain heat and allow for natural ventilation for cooling;
- Energy audits to determine where caulking or insulation need to be added or replaced which could also result in energy savings (Cook, Stewart and Repass, 1992). These might also reveal when 'energy-hungry' activities might best be done (for example, during off-peak energy hours);
- The use of the by-products of some functions, such as the heat from compressor lines run through preheating tanks to heat the water (Lorenzini, 1994);
- The use of high efficiency gas fryers and grills (Liddle, 1991).

Handling Air Quality

To improve and protect air quality, companies have encouraged employee car pooling and alternative transportation use (Cook, Stewart and Repass, 1992). In the US, transportation is thought to be the single largest source of nitrogen oxides and carbon monoxide, which may pollute the air and cause acid rain. Careful selection and maintenance of energy-efficient cars, trucks and other vehicles would also decrease automotive emissions. Finally, careful maintenance or replacement of CFC-refrigerant based units would minimize impact on the ozone layer.

Water Resource Management

Hotels may wish to consider installing low-flow tap aerators and shower heads (Cook, Stewart and Repass, 1992). These would result in a 50 per cent reduction in water flow, although the streams appear stronger because air mixes into the water as it leaves the taps. Another possibility for hotels or food services would be to install displacement devices in toilets. Such devices would save 1–2 gallons of water per flush. Another more expensive alternative would be to install 'ultra-low' flush toilets, which empty the bowl with only ½ to 1½ gallons of water (compared to 5–7 gallons). Food service may also place a timer on garbage disposals to limit the time it runs and the amount of water it uses (Lorenzini, 1994)

The use of phosphate-free or low-phosphate detergents would prevent phosphate's entry into lakes and streams where they might encourage algae growth (Cook, Stewart and Repass, 1992). The use of latex paints instead of oil-based paints would decrease pollutant by-products during the manufacturing process.

Finally, landscaping with plants native to the region (xeriscape landscaping) may save as much as 54 per cent of the water that unsuited plants use (Cook, Stewart and Repass, 1992). Some plants are low-water-use plants. These include bougainvillaea, wisteria, jasmine, sweet alyssum and daffodils.

Waste Management

Throughout the next decade all food service operations will begin to feel some pressure to reduce the total volume and weight of their solid waste. Since the food service industry is a concentrated provider of meals and contributes to the solid waste stream associated with the consumer's desire to eat safely, conveniently and inexpensively, it is in the best position to implement cost effective and practical ways to reduce waste. The general public's overall uneasiness with incineration, coupled with the declining number of operating landfills will require all food service operations – either per force or through self-imposed industry initiative – to begin and/or continue reducing, reusing and recycling:

Actions that would decrease the amount of waste produced include:

- Using linen instead of paper;
- Using permanent service-ware – plates/trays, eating utensils, glassware;
- The implementation of company-wide recycling programmes for paper, glass, aluminium, plastic, corrugated board;
- Recycling food waste as mulch or compost;
- Encouraging recycling by purchasing recycled products such as napkins and

other paper supplies and/or other supplies that have been produced from post-consumer materials;

- Reducing the weight of packaging as found in bags for carryout, corrugated cardboard and buying in bulk sizes to reduce the amount of cardboard and the number of glass or metal containers;
- Encouraging the use of refillable containers. Germany, Switzerland and Ontario, Canada have pressured beverage industries to shift back to refillable containers (Cummings, 1992). In some cases, refillable containers are being encouraged even for non-food containers, such as detergents;
- Recycling of oil products (for example, food service grease) to decrease the amount of chemicals in the environment.

SUMMARY

One of the major forces impacting operational practices in the hospitality industry is environmentalism. Its influence is felt internationally in many hotel and food service management decisions. Many countries have responded by creating agencies and/or by passing laws and regulations to help protect the environment. Historically, the industry's environmental behaviour has been shaped largely by legislation, but today other factors have influenced operational decisions in many areas. Some of these include the cost of resources and the general public's environmental concerns.

The industry uses considerable amounts of both energy and water to bring its goods to market. Perhaps the greatest incentive to reduce or control the consumption of these two resources is their cost. Because the demand for these resources is sizeable in the hospitality industry, food service operations and lodging facilities will have to find ways to limit their use yet satisfy the needs and demands of their customers. This includes purchasing and using energy efficient equipment and installing equipment that uses water more efficiently. Also, computerized energy management and control systems may help to save energy and reduce costs. In some cases, it may be practical for large operations to process their waste water and re-utilize it elsewhere in the operation.

Air quality has also become an operational issue – both to customers and employees. The concern with second-hand smoke has prompted a number of states and local communities to limit or ban smoking in the workplace. Although not as readily perceptible, the effect of food service equipment on air quality has also been recognized. Most notably, the concern with ozone depleting chemicals has induced several countries, including the US and Canada, to phase out the use of CFC-based refrigerants.

Because of the uneasiness with current waste disposal methods, the largest environmental concern to date has been the quantity and type of waste generated by hospitality companies, in particular food service operations. Accordingly, managing solid waste has been *the* critical issue in the industry. For the most part, the industry and its suppliers have reacted responsibly. Many hospitality companies are recycling, purchasing reusable or recyclable products, purchasing recycled products, compacting or using products that need less space and composting.

Environmentalism is a critical issue for the hospitality industry and impacts many areas of operation. Because of its importance, changes in the way the industry has done business are imminent. Ultimately, the hospitality industry will be required to reduce/control the operational activities – in particular the by-products – that adversely affect the health or well being of others. Through their environmental efforts, industry leaders like Disney, McDonald's, the Culinary Institute of America and school district U-46 in Elgin, Illinois have laid the groundwork that will make it easier in the future for other hospitality companies to develop a responsible environmental strategy.

REFERENCES

Allen, R.L. (1994, November 7). Restaurateurs: OSHA's Air Tonic Too Tough to Swallow. *Nation's Restaurant News,* 28(44), 3+.

Allen, R.L. (1995, March 20). Maryland Restaurateurs fight to Snuff Smoking Bans. *Nation's Restaurant News,* 29(12), 3+.

Almanza, B.A., Hiemstra, S.J. and Ghiselli, R.F. (1992). *An Investigation of School Food Service Waste in Indiana.* Unpublished report submitted to the Indiana State Department of Education.

Almanza, B.A., Hiemstra, S.J. and Ghiselli, R.F. (1993). *An Investigation of School Food Service Waste in Indiana: Phase II.* Unpublished report submitted to the Indiana State Department of Education.

ASHRAE. (1987). *ASHRAE Handbook – HVAC Systems and Applications.* (Service Water Heating Ch. 54, p. 54.4). Atlanta: American Society of Heating, Refrigerating and Air-Conditioning Engineers, Inc.

Aulbach, R.E. (1988). *Energy and Resource Management* (2nd ed. p. 35–36). East Lansing: The Educational Institute of the American Hotel and Motel Association.

Byers, E. (1990, January). Now Entering the Age of Nimby? *Waste Age,* 21(1), 36–38.

Commoner, B. (1990). *Making Peace with the Planet.* New York: Pantheon Books.

Cook, S.D., Stewart, E., Repass, K. (1992). *Discover America, Tourism and the Environment.* Travel Industry Association of America, Washington, D.C.

Cummings, L.E. and Cummings, W.T. (1991). Foodservice and Solid Waste Policies: A View in Three Dimensions. *Hospitality Research Journal,* 14, 163–171.

Cummings, L.E. (1992). Hospitality solid waste minimization: a global frame. *Intl. J. of Hospitality Management,* 11(3), 255–267.

Frankel, C. (1992). Blueprint for green marketing. *American Demographics,* 14(4), 34–738.

Ghiselli, R.F., Almanza, B.A. and Hiemstra, S.J. (1995, August). The Effect of School Food Service Waste on Landfills. Paper presented at the Council on Hotel, Restaurant and Institutional Education, Nashville, TN.

Glenn, J. and Riggle, D. (1991a). The State of Garbage in America Part I. *Biocycle,* 32(4), 34–38.

Glenn, J. and Riggle, D. (1991b). The State of Garbage in America. *Biocycle,* 32(5), 30–35.

Glenn, J. (1992). The State of Garbage in America. *Biocycle,* 33(4), 46–55.

Goodno, J.B. (1994, June 20). Thai Hotels Maximize use of recycled water. *Hotel and Motel Management,* 209(11), 16.

Hasek, G. (1994, June 20). Hotel Chains Await Rollout of EPA's WAVE Program. *Hotel and Motel Management,* 209(11), 15.

Hayward, P. (1994, March). Disney Does the Environment. *Lodging*, 19(7), 46+.

Hemphill, T.A. (1991). Marketer's new motto: It's keen to be green. *Business and Society Review* 78, 39–44.

Hollingsworth, M.D., Shanklin, C.W., Gench, B. and Hinson, M. (1990). Effect of Type of Packaging on Acceptability and Volume of Solid Waste for the Milk Component in School Food Service Programs. *School Food Service Research Review*, 14(2), 86–89.

Langert, B./McDonald's Corp. (1995, June 30). Letter to the Environmental Community. McDonald's Corporation, Oak Brook, IL.

Landers, R. K. (1989, November 7). America Turns to Recycling. *Congressional Quarterly Editorial Research Reports*, 2(19), 650–662.

Lemonick, M.D. (1992). The big green payoff. *Time*, 139(22), 62–63.

Liddle, A. (1990a, November 19). McD's Switch to Paper Fuels Packaging Debate. *Nation's Restaurant News*, 24(46), 1+.

Liddle, A. (1990b, November 12). McDonalds Pulls Plastic Packaging. *Nation's Restaurant News*, 24(45), 1+.

Liddle, (1991, May 20). Restaurants rush to add ecology-friendly policies. *Nation's Restaurant News*, 25(20), 88+.

Lorenzini, B. (1994, May 1). The Green Restaurant. *Restaurants and Institutions*, 104(11), 124.

MacDonald, J. (1994, July 5). Burning Issue. *Hotel and Motel Management*, 209(12), 29.

Mann, N. and Shanklin, C.W. (1990). Solid Waste Management in School Food Service: A Critical Issue for the 1990s. *School Food Service Research Review*, 14(2), 83–85.

McDonald's WARP Status Report. (1995). McDonald's Corporation, Oak Brook, IL.

McDonald's Corp. (1994, June 6). *McDonald's Earth Effort Global Express*. Environmental Affairs Department, McDonald's Corporation, Oak Brook, IL.

McDonald's Corp. (1992). *The Planet We Share*. McDonald's Corporation, Oak Brook, IL.

McDonald's Corp. (1994). Facts and Resources in a small package. Environmental Affairs Department, McDonald's Corporation, Oak Brook, IL.

McDonald's and The Environmental Defense Fund. (1991). Waste Reduction Task Force Final Report. McDonald's Waste Reduction Policy, Appendix 1.

McRecycle USA. (1990). Environmental Affairs Department, McDonald's Corporation, Oak Brook, IL.

McLaughlin, J. (1995, Jan. 20). The Air is Clean but the Picture Isn't. *Restaurant Business*, 94(2), 14.

McLaughlin, J. (1995, Mar. 1). New Yorkers are Bracing for the Big Smoke-Out. *Restaurant Business*, 94(4), 14.

Mikkelsen, B.E. (1993). Foodservice and the Environment: A European Perspective. *Journal of Foodservice Systems*, 7(2), 93–104.

National Restaurant Association. (1994, December). 1995 Foodservice Industry Forecast. *Restaurants USA*, 14(11), 24.

National Restaurant Association. (1994, October). Restaurateurs as Conservationists. *Restaurants USA*, 14(9), 36–47.

National Restaurant Association and Deloitte and Touche. (1991). *Restaurant Industry Operations Report 1991*. Washington DC: National Restaurant Association.

National Restaurant Association and Deloitte and Touche. (1992). *Restaurant Industry Operations Report 1992*. Washington DC: National Restaurant Association.

National Restaurant Association and Deloitte and Touche. (1993). *Restaurant Industry Operations Report 1934*. Washington DC: National Restaurant Association.

National Restaurant Association and Deloitte and Touche. (1994). *Restaurant Industry Operations Report 1994*. Washington DC: National Restaurant Association.

National Restaurant Association and Deloitte and Touche LLP. (1995). *Restaurant Industry Operations Report 1995*. Washington DC: National Restaurant Association.

OECD. (1993). *Environmental Data Compendium 1993*. Paris. OECD/OCDE.

O'Leary, P. and Walsh, P. (1991a). Introduction to Solid Waste Landfills. *Waste Age*, 22(1), 42–50.

O'Leary, P. and Walsh, P. (1991b). Landfilling Principles. *Waste Age*, 22(4), 109–114.

Popkin, R. (1995). Good News for Waste Watchers. *EPA Journal*, 21(1), 18.

Rathje, W. L. (1991, May). Once and Future Landfills. *National Geographic*, 179(5), 111–134.

Riley, L. K., Shanklin, C. W. and Gench, B. (1991). Comparison of Volume of Waste Generated by and Cost of Two Types of Service-ware Systems. *School Food Service Research Review*, 15(2), 32–36.

Sanger, J. (1994, May–June). Hazardous Duty. *Club Management*, 73(3), 54+.

Scarpa, J. (1989, May 20). Trash Clash. *Restaurant Business*, 88(8), 143–154.

Scarpa, J. (1990, June 10). Trash Clash. *Restaurant Business*, 89(6), 138–146.

Schmicker, P. (1991). Recycling vs. Permanentware. Unpublished raw data.

Sellers, J. and Ward, B. (1991). The Environment and You: Part I. *Foodservice Equipment and Supplies Specialist*, 44(3), 28–32, 34, 36, 38.

Staff. (1994, Feb.). Lodging Trends. *Lodging*, 20(6), 15.

Thrasher, W.H. and DeWerth, P.E. (1994). New Hot-Water Use Data For Five Commercial Buildings (RP-600). *ASHRAE Transactions: Symposia*, 100(1), 935–943. NO–94–11–2.

Trager, S.M. (1994). Wet Windfall: Potential Savings for Clubs: Reclaimed Water Keeps Courses and Environment Green. *Club Management*, 73(5), 104–111.

US Bureau of the Census. *Statistical Abstract of the US 1994*. (114th edition). Washington DC, 1994. Tables 703, 931.

US Department of Commerce, Economics and Statistics Administration, Bureau of the Census. *Estimates of the Population of the United States to April 1, 1992*. Series P–25, No. 1087. Washington DC, June 1992.

US Department of Energy, Energy Information Administration. (1992). *Commercial Buildings Energy Consumption and Expenditures 1989* (DOE/EIA–031(89)), 5–20. Washington DC: US Government Printing Office.

US Environmental Protection Agency, Office of Solid Waste and Emergency Response. (1989). *The Solid Waste Dilemma: An Agenda for Action* (EPA/530–SW–89–019). Washington DC: US Government Printing Office.

US Environmental Protection Agency, Office of Solid Waste and Emergency Response. (1990). *Characterization of Municipal Solid Waste in the United States: 1990 Update* (EPA/530–SW–90–042). Washington DC: US Government Printing Office.

US Environmental Protection Agency. (1995). Creating a Healthier Environment. *EPA Journal*, 21(1) pp. 38 EPA/530–SW–90–069.

US Environmental Protection Agency. *The EPA Municipal Solid Waste Factbook*, version 1.2, May 27, 1994, Washington, DC.

Wall Street Journal/NBC News. (1990). In J. Miko and E. Weilant (Eds.), *Opinions '90* (p. 228). Detroit, MI: Gale Research Inc.

Ward, B.J. and Richards, G. (1991). The Solid Waste Crunch. *Foodservice Equipment and Supplies Specialist*, 44(4), 26–34.

1: This survey also found that 84% favoured banning foam containers altogether and that 74% favoured banning disposable diapers.
2: In this survey, conducted by the National League of Cities, education was cited as the most important problem facing government.
3: The EPA reports there were 5,276 landfills in 1992 (US EPA, 1994); in five US states the remaining landfill capacity (lifetime) is estimated at five or fewer years and 21 states have between five and ten years remaining lifetime (US EPA, 1994).
4: Moreover, since the water content of many foods is relatively high and since water is removed in the treatment that follows processing in disposals, processing in a disposal reduces considerably the amount of food waste and, in turn, the total amount of waste that ultimately ends up in landfills.

8

Financing and Investing in the Gaming Industry

Susan H. Ivancevich and Jannet Vreeland

OVERVIEW

The purpose of this chapter is to illustrate how competitive changes in the gaming industry have led firms participating in this industry to alter investing and financing activities. Specifically, this chapter will present these issues in terms of the Las Vegas gaming market, a market which has undergone rapid growth and significant market changes in recent years. In the first section of this chapter, we will discuss the history of gaming in Nevada, as well as provide a review of investing and financing trends in the gaming industry. Next, we will discuss the organizational development implications of these trends, providing examples from Mirage Resorts Incorporated, a major casino hotel corporation engaged in business in the Las Vegas market. Lastly, conclusions and recommendations for firms evaluating financing and expansion alternatives in the gaming industry will be presented.

BACKGROUND OF GAMING IN NEVADA

The Early Years of Legalization

Legalized gaming came to Nevada for the first time in 1869, only to become prohibited again by 1910. Over the next 21 years there would be various laws which would either liberalize or curtail legalized gambling; however, illegal gambling remained a flourishing business. During the 20–plus years that gambling was officially illegal, external environmental factors made legalized gambling more acceptable to the State. The 1920s saw a public shift in what was morally acceptable. The onset of the Great Depression forced governments to search for new sources of revenue. The legalization of gambling was promoted as a means to help the State recover from the depression and generate more revenues. Legalization was also perceived as an effort to curb the dissatisfaction over the lack of control of illegal gaming, especially in terms of capturing the economic benefits associated with such gaming. Finally, in 1931, the forces supporting legalized gambling prevailed and all forms of gambling, including bookmaking and sports betting, were legalized.

In the late 1930s and early 1940s, Reno gave gambling its first layer of respectability. The Smith family (Harold's Club) and William Harrah (Harrah's):

> . . . provided the foundations to legitimize the gaming industry. They treated gambling as any other legitimate business requiring marketing research and advertising (Skolnick, 1978, p. 109).

These gaming operators and others like them made the:

> Reno gambling industry itself not only a functioning part of Nevada's social and economic life, but an acceptable part as well. What had been a pariah industry was slowly evolving into a respected one as economic advantage transformed vice into virtue (Skolnick 1978, p. 109).

At the time Reno was laying the foundation to legitimize the industry, Las Vegas was undergoing a metamorphosis. The Boulder Canyon Project brought more than water and jobs to Southern Nevada. It brought a demand for an expansion of gaming in the southern part of the State. The dam workers were the first major impetus to the growth of gambling in Southern Nevada. They came to Las Vegas for entertainment. However, as the 1930s ended and the 1940s began, other factors would increase the demand for gambling throughout the State, but particularly in Southern Nevada. California's growing population would look to Nevada for entertainment. During World War II, the West Coast became a major embarkation point for troops and supplies. Since the majority of supplies and troops were transported by rail from the East to the West Coast, traffic through Nevada grew. In addition, the Federal Government established new military bases in Nevada. Military personnel looked to Nevada as the place to go for all forms of entertainment. All these events were stimuli to the legalized gambling industry.

In the early 1940s the industry responded to these external factors by changing the nature of the casinos. Gambling was still the number one priority, however the entertainment aspect of the business was expanded. To compensate for the expanding entertainment required of casinos, the physical nature of casinos began to change. Structures had to be large enough to provide space for floor shows and orchestras, as well as gambling. By the early 1940s the first developments by major hotel developers from around the country appeared on the outskirts of town, at a location now known as 'The Strip'. These new developments were designed to provide the full range of entertainment that the public wanted.

As the gaming industry began its expansion in the late 1930s and early 1940s, financing became an issue. While the industry was gaining respectability within Nevada, the rest of the country did not view gaming favourably. Outside of Nevada, the industry was not perceived as a valid investment opportunity because of the perceived immorality of gaming, therefore access to the stock and bond markets was closed. As a result, the majority of the casinos were privately owned.

The First Phase of the Modern Era

In 1946, an event took place which would have significant future consequences for all aspects of the gaming industry, but particularly in the areas of regulation, federal government intervention, investing activities and financing activities. This event was the construction in Las Vegas of the Flamingo Hotel by Benjamin 'Bugsy' Siegal. It was a *luxurious complex that offered gambling, recreation, entertainment and other services to the area's increasing tourist trade* (Skolnick 1978, p. 111). The Flamingo Hotel marked the beginning of Las Vegas' ascendance to the premier position in Nevada's gaming industry.

While the Flamingo set the standard for what the casino of the future would be in terms of physical investment (i.e., size, types of entertainment and other amenities), the financing for this entertainment complex would have even more far-reaching effects. Organized crime provided the financing for the Flamingo. It was organized crime's first venture into Nevada's legalized gaming industry; however, it was only the beginning. Over the next two decades, organized crime money would be an important source of financing for the gaming industry.

In the early 1950s, the gaming industry came under increased scrutiny from the federal government. The presence of organized crime had previously caused problems for Nevada and its unique industry with the federal government. In 1959, Nevada addressed these problems by creating the Nevada Gaming Commission. It replaced earlier regulatory efforts that had proved to be ineffective. The new commission was given the power

> to grant or deny any application for a gaming license. It could enact gaming regulations and act as the collection agency for all gaming taxes. The commission's regulatory and investigative powers were expanded to insure that criminal elements, mobs, or syndicates had neither interest in nor control of existing businesses' (Skolnick, 1978, p.120).

By 1966, the State of Nevada and its gaming industry were in a state of crisis. There were fears that the federal government would outlaw gaming, which would have had disastrous economic consequences for the State. A partial solution for the crisis was afforded by Howard Hughes' investment in the gaming industry and by the Corporate Gaming Act of 1969.

The Second Phase – Howard Hughes and the Corporate Gaming Act

In late 1966, Hughes took up residency at the Desert Inn, a Las Vegas hotel/casino. Within a year, he owned four casinos. Ultimately, he owned six casinos in Clark County and one in Reno. His investment gave the gaming industry two things it needed for future success: respectability and a broad capital base for expansion. Hughes gave the industry respectability by buying out some of the 'more questionable' owners. With their removal from the Nevada gaming scene, pressure from the federal government lessened substantially. Additionally, Hughes' investment provided a much needed measure of business respectability. Large hotel chains were now more willing to consider investing in Nevada casinos (Skolnick, 1978).

In 1969 Nevada enacted the Corporate Gaming Act, which allowed corporations to own casinos by limiting the number of people who must be licensed in gaming corporations. Prior to 1969, it was nearly impossible for a corporation to own a casino. While the 1931 Legalization Act had permitted ownership of gaming facilities by corporations, a 1955 provision required each stockholder to be a licensed gaming operator. This requirement effectively kept publicly traded corporations from owning casinos (Howard Hughes had made his purchases through the Hughes Tool Company of which he was sole proprietor). A 1966 study of the gaming industry commissioned by the Nevada legislature concluded that the major casinos had to enlarge or face severe financial problems. Few individuals had the money of Howard Hughes. Therefore, it was extremely unlikely that private individuals could finance the needed expansion.

The 1969 Act had broad support for several reasons:

> First, the availability of public money would 'speed up' the sale of problem casinos. Once again, the federal government was alleging criminal ownership of casinos was increasing. Second, it was hoped that SEC disclosure requirements and the involvement of federal laws would deter hidden control. Third, publicly traded companies would avoid negative publicity, fearing negative stock price reactions. Fourth, casinos owned by publicly traded corporations would tend to be larger, hotel-casino complexes. If they were caught cheating, they would stand to lose more. Fifth, large publicly traded corporations would have more accurate tax accounting systems, thus minimizing the possibility of revenues being diverted from the corporation (Skolnick 1978, pp. 142–144). Most importantly, the Corporate Gaming Act gave the industry access to the broader equity and bond markets, which lessened the temptation (or necessity) of relying on tainted financial sources (Lee, 1995).

The Corporate Gaming Act allowed major corporations, such as Holiday Inn and Hilton, to enter Nevada's gaming industry. These publicly traded corporations, which had established respectable reputations in other industries, helped to legitimize the gaming industry and provided the financing necessary for expansion.

THE SPREAD OF GAMBLING TO OTHER MARKETS

Legalization in New Jurisdictions

In 1976, Nevada's 45 year monopoly of legalized casino gambling came to an end. New Jersey in an effort to stimulate the distressed economy of Atlantic City legalized casino gambling (Bybee, 1995). The legalization of casino gaming in New Jersey was limited to the confines of Atlantic City and to this day casino gambling is prohibited in all other parts of the state. This spread of legalized casino gambling to Atlantic City signalled the beginning of the end of casino gambling's status as a pariah industry.

For thirteen years (until 1989) this two-state gaming market existed within the casino gaming industry. However external forces were at work that would make the expansion of casino gaming to other areas morally and socially acceptable. A driving force behind further expansion was the need for new revenue sources at the state and local government levels. As states searched for new revenues, lotteries became an acceptable source. New Hampshire enacted the first modern state lottery in 1964 and in the next 30 years, 36 other states and the District of Columbia would adopt lotteries (Vallen, 1995). The social acceptability of gambling in the form of state lotteries removed much of the immoral stigma attached to casino gambling.

The cause of legalized gaming was aided by the Federal Government in 1988 with the passage of the Indian Gaming Act. Finally, in 1989, South Dakota became the third State to legalize casino gambling. It was swiftly followed by several other states. By 1994, all but two states, Hawaii and Utah, had some form of legalized gaming. Table 8.1 shows the number of states with some type of legalized gaming.

The next two sections discuss investing issues and financing issues, respectively.

INVESTING ISSUES

In discussing investing alternatives and activities of any casino corporation in the 1990s, there are several factors that need to be considered. The first issue is whether to expand in an existing market, like Las Vegas, or expand in an emerging jurisdiction. After geographic location has been determined, the next

STATE	CASINO GAMING	CARD ROOMS	CHARITABLE GAMING	RIVERBOAT GAMING	HORSE RACING	DOG RACING	PARIMUTUEL GAMING	SLOTS/VIDEO	LOTTERY	INDIAN** GAMING	SPORTS POOLS/BETS
ALABAMA			X		X	X	X			X	
ALASKA			X							X	
ARIZONA	X		X		X	X	X	X	X	X	
ARKANSAS					X	X	X				
CALIFORNIA		X	X		X		X		X	X	
COLORADO	X	X	X		X	X	X	X	X	X	
CONNECTICUT	X		X		X	X	X	X	X	X	
DELAWARE			X		X		X		X		X
FLORIDA			X		X	X	X		X	X****	
GEORGIA			X					X			
HAWAII											
IDAHO			X		X	X	X		X	X	
ILLINIOS	X	X	X	X	X		X		X	X	
INDIANA	X		X	X	X		X		X	X	
IOWA	X	X	X	X	X	X	X	X	X	X	
KANSAS			X		X	X	X		X	X	
KENTUCKY			X		X		X		X		
LOUISIANA	X	X	X	X	X		X		X	X	
MAINE			X		X		X		X	X****	
MARYLAND		X	X		X		X	X	X		
MASSACHUSETTS			X		X	X	X		X		
MICHIGAN	X	X	X		X		X	X	X	X	
MINNESOTA	X	X	X		X		X	X	X	X	
MISSISSIPPI	X		X	X			X			X	
MISSOURI	X		X	X	X		X	X	X	X	
MONTANA	X	X	X		X		X	X	X	X	X
NEBRASKA	X		X		X		X		X	X	
NEVADA	X	X			X	X	X	X		X	X
NEW HAMPSHIRE			X		X	X	X		X		
NEW JERSEY	X	X	X		X		X	X	X		
NEW MEXICO	X		X		X		X			X	
NEW YORK	X		X		X		X		X	X	
NORTH CAROLINA			X							X	
NORTH DAKOTA	X	X	X		X		X		X	X	X
OHIO			X		X		X		X		
OKLAHOMA			X		X		X			X	
OREGON	X	X	X		X	X	X	X	X	X	X
PENNSYLVANIA			X		X		X		X		
RHODE ISLAND			X		X	X	X	X	X	X	
SOUTH CAROLINA			X					X			
SOUTH DAKOTA	X	X	X		X	X	X	X	X	X	
TENNESSEE					X		X				
TEXAS			X		X	X	X		X	X	
UTAH					X***						
VERMONT			X		X	X	X		X		
VIRGINIA			X		X		X		X		
WASHINGTON	X	X	X		X		X	X	X	X	X
WASHINGTON, D.C.			X						X		
WEST VIRGINIA			X		X	X	X	X	X		
WISCONSIN	X		X		X	X	X	X	X	X	
WYOMING							X			X****	

Sources of information used to compile this table:
Vallen, G. (1995) Legalization of gaming in the United States: A Past and Current Perspective. *The Bottomline* (January) p. 17.
North American Gaming Report 1995 (1 July, 1995) *International Gaming and Wagering Business* Supplement, pp. 1-82.
Ladenburg, Thalmann & Co. Inc. (29 March, 1994) *Investment Research Industry Report for the Gaming Industry* p. 5.
*   Includes Indian gaming operations.
**   Includes all types of Indian gaming (from bingo to casinos)
***   Horse racing is legal, but on and off-track betting on horse racing is not legal in Utah.
**** Indian gaming present, but not yet approved.

Table 8.1: Status of Legalized Gaming* by State

investing issue deals with the building. The issue is whether to construct a new building or renovate an existing structure. This decision has a major impact on the next investing issue, type of property. Casino owners need to determine what type of physical structure they want. This decision will drive not only the size of the gaming operations, but the size and nature of non-gaming attractions and entertainment.

All of the above investing issues need to be addressed by operators expanding in either existing markets or emerging markets. Further, entrants in emerging markets must weigh other factors when making a decision regarding investment in these areas. These factors include gaming expertise, entry fees and rates of returns and profit strategies. The investing issues concerning both existing and emerging markets are addressed next.

Investing in an Existing Market – Las Vegas

The Las Vegas market has undergone significant changes in the past six years. The growth of Las Vegas has been extensive and with this growth has come a large increase in the room capacity of Las Vegas. This increase in capacity may have impinged on previous expansion plans by firms considering expansion within Las Vegas. When the three mega-resorts (MGM, Luxor and Treasure Island) opened, many suggested that Las Vegas had become overbuilt. This prediction has not come true. Las Vegas hotels averaged about 90 per cent occupancy in 1994 (Lee, 1995). The Las Vegas Market can be thought of as *being one giant hotel and during the slow periods, you shut down a wing or the least desirable wing does not fill up* (Lee, 1995). While the increase in the number of available rooms in Las Vegas may not have caused a decline in the occupancy percentage of hotels on an overall basis, it may have caused a shift in occupancy from some hotels to others. This shift may cause some firms to re-evaluate expansion plans in an attempt to better utilize the market or re-evaluate due to declining revenues as a result of a dynamic market. Hence, firms will want to evaluate the expected future competitive climate of Las Vegas when considering investing plans in this area.

Buy Versus Build

Gaming companies have a choice, in both current and emerging markets, to convert existing buildings into casinos or build new buildings. In Atlantic City, two of the first casinos to open after gaming was legalized were situated in refurbished Boardwalk hotels that dated back to the early 20th century. While use of an existing building may hasten the opening day of a casino or be mandated by the licensing body, usually there are major difficulties in using existing structures for casino purposes. Frequently, such buildings are quite limiting in terms of allowable size or placement of a casino. Another potential problem of using existing structures for casinos is described below.

> ... casinos in refurbished buildings are often at a disadvantage – especially in comparison to purpose-built casinos – in the provision of various non-gaming amenities for visitors to the facility. Based on the size and configuration of the original structure, there may be significant limitations on space availability for restaurants, parking, entertainment venues, or other facilities that are complementary to a successful casino operation (Eadington, 1994).

Obviously, building a new structure will allow the gaming company to design a building which meets its specifications for both gaming and non-gaming activities.

Type of Property

Companies considering expansion must decide on the type of physical structure to create. There are two basic trends which have emerged in new casinos:

1) a theme is incorporated into the actual physical structure of the building, such as the Excalibur castle or the Luxor pyramid, or
2) the building is traditional in structure, such as Bally's or the MGM Grand.

Once the physical structure of the building is determined, there are several other issues in terms of physical investment that must be addressed. First, the type of design features which will be incorporated into the building must be decided upon. Second, the size of the structure must be determined, in terms of gaming space, hotel capacity and other facilities. The potential benefits of economies of scale also need to be considered. Further, the physical layout of the property, such as the placement of attractions and arcades in relation to the gaming area, needs to be considered.

Attractions

Another major investment decision facing casino resorts operating in the current Las Vegas market is whether or not to include attractions in their expansion plans. Traditionally, expansion plans within a given market have centred around whether or not to expand room capacity, or build a second location. Today, however, whether or not to build an attraction has become an increasingly important investment decision for many gaming firms.

In the early days of gaming, the majority of properties were solely gaming establishments without widespread entertainment. Over time, casinos began to offer entertainment in the form of musicians and shows to their patrons. Famous entertainers, such as Frank Sinatra and Sammy Davis Jr., became mainstays of Las Vegas entertainment.

The next step was for casinos to add structural entertainment. In 1966, Caesar's Palace opened the first themed resort in the Las Vegas market. In 1976, Circus Circus followed this with its own themed resort. Thirteen years later, in 1989, the opening of The Mirage, with its exploding volcano, white tigers and rain forest atrium, marked the true beginning of the 'attractions' era in Las Vegas. Following The Mirage, Excalibur, the Luxor, the MGM Grand and Treasure Island each opened with some type of major attraction.

The resorts slated for openings in the near future, such as New York-New York and Bellagio, have incorporated attractions into their designs. Further, older properties, such as Circus Circus, Bally's and the Las Vegas Hilton, have undertaken projects to introduce attractions to their properties. Hence, firms are now faced with decisions as to whether to expand their operations in traditional ways, like adding rooms, or to venture into the attractions arena by adding a major attraction. If a firm decides to add an attraction, the questions of where and how the attraction will be added must also be addressed. For instance, where will the attraction be located and will admission be charged?

Factors Affecting Investment Opportunities in New Jurisdictions

While expansion opportunities within existing markets have clearly provided investing opportunities in the 1990s, such opportunities have been nearly overshadowed by investing opportunities in new jurisdictions. Many Las Vegas gaming companies have decided to enter other gaming markets. Several factors must be considered when evaluating expansion opportunities into new jurisdictions. Some of the more important factors are discussed below.

Gaming Expertize

Gaming expertize can have a tremendous impact on the success or failure of a new gaming operation in an emerging gaming jurisdiction. According to Phil Satre, President of Promus Corporation, one of the distinguishing factors between who succeeds and who fails in a given market comes down to who has solid experience in the gaming area and which properties were built keeping in mind the competitive climate and demands of consumers in a particular market (Gros, 1994). The shakeout of the industry in Tunica, Mississippi illustrates the importance of gaming expertize.

> The Treasure Bay Casino is a casino built like a pirate ship in Tunica, an emerging jurisdiction. The guy who built it was not from the industry . . . and now they are bankrupt . . . Ironically, within a mile of Treasure Bay, the Boyd group built a property . . . called . . . Sam's Town. It is a hotel/casino with a western theme, just like the Sam's Town here (Las Vegas) . . .and it is well done. They didn't spend much more money than Treasure Bay. They are making tons of money, $30–$40 million per year. Treasure Bay is losing money. It is . . . interesting . . . because it was probably easier for Treasure Bay to get money out

because they had this nifty pirate ship . . ., but Boyd came in and replicated something that was a proven success before (Lee 1995).

Hence, gaming experience can be quite important when considering expansion alternatives.

Entry Fees And Rates Of Return

Another factor to consider when evaluating expansion plans into new jurisdictions is the entry fee (Gros, 1994). The costs to enter new markets have risen to quite high levels as gaming has spread across the country. When gaming first started to spread across the nation, the entry fees into new jurisdictions were quite low. At that time, the new jurisdictions were most interested in enticing gaming companies to invest in their market, so the jurisdictions could reap the tax benefits of gaming. Many of the firms which invested in the new jurisdictions in the early 1990s, were able to reap strong returns on their investment, particularly if the firm was the first entrant into a new market.

As time wore on and gaming continued to spread, gaming regulators began to raise the entry fees charged to firms wishing to invest in a particular market in order to capture some of the economic rents that had been accruing to the firms.

> The price of admission is going up. It's going to be much more difficult to get a reasonable rate of return on your investment in the future. Most of the deals we see out there we consider to be marginal, at best[1] (Gros, 1994).

Dan Lee concurs:

> Subsequent states that legalized gaming got smart and they started putting the licenses . . . up for auction so that the tax rates were higher and they started keeping more of the economic benefit for the State and City (rather) than allowing it to go to the casino, so the returns (on investment) came crashing down (Lee, 1995).

Hence, recovering the initial investment is much easier for a firm which was charged a relatively low rent, while earning a return on investment becomes more difficult as the entry fee increases.

While the higher entry fees into gaming markets have an obvious downside for future entrants into a particular market, they also have an upside for firms already operating within a market (Gros, 1994). Higher entry fees serve as a barrier to new entries into the market, thus protecting the investment of already existing firms. Gluk indicates that high entry fees into a specific market should make the properties already operating in the market more valuable (Gros, 1994). Further, the high costs of entry and the high taxes of certain markets, particularly many of the emerging markets where taxes can range as high as 25–33 per cent, make investments in markets such as Las Vegas (6 per cent tax) and Atlantic City (8 per cent) much more attractive, especially in the long run. A danger of these high taxes is that while high taxes may be overcome in the short run when a particular property has a monopoly in a market or a few groups of firms have oligopoly power, such high taxes make operating successfully in the long run much more difficult. As competition within a market increases, firms previously capable of earning an attractive rate of return on investment, find themselves adjusting to competitive pressures and facing a lowering rate of return (Gros, 1994).

Profit and Growth Strategies

The attractiveness of investment opportunities in new jurisdictions is also a function of profit strategy. Whether or not a company is publicly traded will influence its investing decisions in new jurisdictions. With publicly traded companies, share price is to some extent a function of the growth rate of earnings: the higher the growth rate, the higher the share price (Lee, 1995). Being a publicly traded company can affect investment decisions as follows:

> Let's suppose there is a riverboat out there for sale and that the next year's earnings would be $30 million, but because of additional competition coming in, the year after that it would be $20 million, the year after that it would be $10 million and the year after that zero. Also assume this riverboat is for sale for $40 million. Now, as an individual, that would be a great deal. You pay $40 million and in a year and a half you have your money back and you continue to make another $15–$20 million . . . As a corporation, for the next four years we would be explaining to people that our earnings growth rate would have been better if we had not had such a great deal buying this riverboat for $40 million that cash flowed 30–20–10. It becomes a component of negative growth in our portfolio of businesses because it is not an enduring business. That hurts our growth rate. Ironically, doing this great deal would hurt our share price. And frankly, that is the position that a lot of these riverboats are in because they are portfolios of individual businesses which are not enduring businesses. So let's say someone goes public with one boat that's making $50 million a year, but it is going to go 40–30–20, they have to find a second boat to replace the declining earnings from the one they got. But because lots of companies are looking for the second boat, the second boat is not going to be as profitable as the first one. So you need a third boat – you probably need two new boats to offset the decline in earnings that you had from your first one. But if you went public at a very high price because people were expecting you to grow and grow and grow, you don't need two new boats, you need three new boats so you have that growth. And you get into this hopeless situation and this cycle goes on (Lee, 1995).

Hence, for a publicly traded corporation, many of the opportunities in the emerging jurisdictions do not make sense.

Because of the risks associated with new jurisdictions, many gaming companies are re-evaluating their investment and expansion plans into new markets. The focus appears to be shifting away from 'taking the money and running' from new jurisdictions to a more long-term focus where long-run profitability is emphasized. Mark Grossman, Hilton Vice President of Communications, summarized his company's investment philosophy as follows:

> We look for economic viability and long-term potential . . . A lot of markets are successful now, but won't be in a few years. With our heritage and reputation, we must be in it for the long term (Gros, 1994).

Joint Ventures

Another trend that has recently developed in the gaming industry is the proliferation of joint ventures as a means of entering new jurisdictions. Gaming firms entering a new market can reduce their risk by teaming up with a partner from the locality of interest. Several benefits can accrue to a gaming firm in such a venture. By having a local partner, a gaming firm will have to share the profits, but it will also be able to cut its risks. It can also obtain a more realistic view of the market from the local partner, because when a local partner has to invest its own funds and face risks of loss, the local partner is more likely to divulge relevant, accurate information about the nature of the market than may be otherwise divulged were there no risk of loss to the local partner. Further, local politicians and regulators are more likely to pay serious attention to a gaming proposal if a local company with executives known by these parties is a part of any plan to establish gaming in the locale. Many industry experts agree that the best way into a new locale is with a local partner (Gros, 1994), because locals are more likely to listen to a 'grassroots effort' hoping to establish gaming than to a large gaming corporation from outside the area, proclaiming the benefits of gaming.

The benefits of a joint venture are not one-sided. Benefits accrue to the local partner, as well as to the gaming company. The local business gets a share of the profits and the opportunity to become involved with a leading gaming company in a project that will oftentimes reap substantial rewards, both for the local economy and the businesses involved. Not surprisingly, the local partner has an incentive to link up with a credible gaming company, with a strong financial position and a good reputation when evaluating joint venture opportunities. The local partners generally need to become involved with a company capable of raising large amounts of capital and with a clean reputation, for the project to have a reasonable chance of getting approved by local decision-makers (Gros, 1994).

FINANCING ISSUES

The ability of members of the gaming industry to take advantage of developing investment opportunities is dependent on their ability to finance the expansions. Capital financing has always been a critical issue in the gaming industry. As discussed previously, in the early days of Las Vegas, Valley Bank and the Bank of Las Vegas were the only sources of financing. Ironically, Valley Bank was known as a 'Mormon' bank with very close ties to the banks in Utah, but was willing to finance gaming. Committed to being in the financing business, the banks were willing to finance legal operations and casinos were legal (Lee, 1995).

In the 1950s, there came a need for greater sums of money and the underworld became a major source of financing for gaming operations. With the influx of organized crime came the Teamsters' Union Pension Fund. This fund was a major source of financing in the gaming industry from the 1950s into the late 1970s. In fiscal year 1973, the Teamsters' fund had outstanding loans to 20 out of 74 Class 1 licence holders in the State of Nevada. These properties included Binion's Horseshoe, the Sands, the Silver Slipper, Desert Inn, Caesar's, Dunes and the Primadonna, a Del Webb property.

> By 1974, under the management of Hoffa and his successors, the fund held 56.1 per cent of all loans to Clark County (Las Vegas) casinos, grossing annually more than $96 million. (By 1978, out of more than $1.5 billion in assets, the fund had more than $247 million invested In Nevada casinos) (Skolnick 1978, p. 298).

The financing environment changed in 1969 with the advent of public gaming companies, but it was still difficult for a pure gaming company to raise money. In the public's perception the industry was still associated with organized crime and shady business practices. Companies that had no other access to financing through non-gaming business activities were limited in terms of expansion.

Companies that invested in the gaming industry, that had other major business activities, were able to finance new gaming projects from capital raised in these other activities. Kirk Kerkorian could raise capital in the movie industry. Hilton raised capital from the hotel side of the business and used it to build its Las Vegas casino resorts. Del Webb raised capital from real estate businesses in Arizona. However, it remained difficult for a pure casino company to raise money in the capital markets because of the negative reputation associated with such a company (Lee 1995). Harrah's first public stock offering illustrates the difficulty.[2]

> When Mead Dixon, the lawyer who was Harrah's closest adviser, approached Dean Witter about underwriting a stock offering, the Wall Street firm turned him away. But one of Dean Witter's corporate finance executives called Jim

Lewis, a friend in Los Angeles who worked for a small, local securities firm. 'This is a company with a great record, great history, but its business is a might too gamy for us,' Lewis was told. Lewis put together a small stock offering, about $6 million and with Harrah's attorneys went to the Securities and Exchange Commission for approval. The government lawyers knew next to nothing about gambling as a business. Caesar's had already gone public, but through an existing publicly traded firm called Lum's. The Golden Nugget in downtown Las Vegas had stock, but it was state regulated with trading officially limited to Nevada, even though shares sold all over Southern California. The SEC staff's main concern was skimming[3] and they spent weeks soaking up all they could about the controls Harrah had developed to make sure no one skimmed his win. With the regulators satisfied, Harrah's prospectus went out in October 1971 and although no Wall Street firm would touch the deal, it was promptly oversubscribed. The buyers came mostly from Northern Nevada. Many investors were Harrah's players who hoped to get back a few of their losses and were attracted by the prospect of owning a piece of the best known gambling hall in Reno (Johnston, 1992, p. 41).

The 1980s was the junk bond era and the gaming industry was able to use this form of financing. Junk bonds by their definition were bonds that did not get an investment grade rating, had a high interest rate and a high level of risk. They tended to be for companies that were highly leveraged or in industries that were out of the mainstream. The casino industry met both of these criteria. Most of the gaming companies were highly leveraged because the huge demand for casinos, both in Las Vegas and in Atlantic City, created a tremendous need for capital.

> If a company is constantly building, it never has a strong balance sheet because it is busy raising the capital to build the next one (property). It is very difficult for a rapidly growing company not to have a fair amount of debt. In the case of the gaming industry, the entire industry was rapidly growing. Throughout the 1980s, most of the pure gaming companies were high-yield bond issuers. This is still the case today for the majority of the industry (Lee, 1995).

Today, there are three traditional ways to finance a building in the gaming industry:

1) start building hoping you will find the money;
2) borrow the money in advance and sit on the cash; or
3) have a bank line of credit (Lee, 1995).

Clearly, the first option is not a smart course of action:

> Like with so much of business, it comes down to negotiation. If you are a banker or an investment banker, first, you . . . are going to be very cautious lending to him (someone who started building without financing), but second

you . . . are going to charge him 20 per cent interest or some enormous amount. And he's stuck. He has no bargaining power and no one has an incentive to cut him a good deal because he is stuck. Not very many people attempt to do things that way but a few do and it is bad news (Lee, 1995).

The Dunes made the mistake of using this method of financing and ultimately ended up bankrupt.

The second alternative is also not optimal. With bonds, the company has to raise all its money upfront. Interest has to be paid on the full amount for the whole time even if the company does not need all the money up front, which is often the case with the construction of a building. Many of the construction costs are loaded at the rear end of the construction process (Lee, 1995; Bybee, 1995).

The third alternative, a bank line of credit, is the ideal financing mechanism for a new property (Lee, 1995; Bybee, 1995). This financing alternative allows the property to draw on the line as it is needed in the construction process. Other than a small commitment fee, the company pays a minimal amount until the money is used. Later if the company wants to repay the borrowed money early, there is no penalty for early repayment.

Unfortunately, lines of credit for financing expansion projects are not available to all gaming companies. A company must be able to demonstrate that it has been a successful participant in the gaming industry and has previously been successful in financing major expansions, before it can qualify for a line of credit that could be used to undertake another major expansion. It appears that in the current financing environment, only the top gaming companies, Harrah's, Caesar's, Hilton, Circus Circus and MRI, have this option available (Bybee, 1995).

A fourth method of financing, issuance of commercial paper, may become the preferred method of financing for the premier gaming companies. Commercial paper represents short-term notes, generally with maturities of 30–270 days, with a higher yield than Treasury Bills (Kieso and Weygandt, 1992). Generally only corporations with very strong credit ratings can successfully offer commercial paper. While this method of financing has not yet been utilized by gaming firms, Mirage Resorts Inc. is currently considering such a move (Lee, 1995).

A fifth method of financing is the issuance of equity, which is a source of capital for many gaming companies. However, equity financing is generally only available on favourable terms to proven managements and even then, only during narrow windows when equity markets are favourable (Lee, 1995).

A CASE STUDY OF MIRAGE RESORTS INCORPORATED[4]

The two previous sections have discussed some of the major financing and investing issues which casino operators must address when considering expansion. The following case study will examine each of the various investing and financing issues from the point of view of one major casino corporation, Mirage Resorts Incorporated.

Profile of Mirage Resorts Incorporated[5]

In the late 1980s, Steve Wynn owned Golden Nugget casino resorts in both Atlantic City and Las Vegas. He sold the Golden Nugget in Atlantic City to Bally's and earned a substantial profit on the transaction. Wynn then decided to concentrate his efforts on the Las Vegas market (Lalli, 1994). Wynn used the money from the sale of the Atlantic City Golden Nugget to purchase prime real estate on the Las Vegas strip, the land which now houses The Mirage. Wynn then developed the plans to build the $620 million Mirage on that property and financed the project through junk bonds. The Mirage project was the most expensive project undertaken in the history of Las Vegas at that time. When The Mirage was built, there were two types of resorts operating in the Las Vegas market: themed resorts like Circus Circus and simple, clean, modernistic resorts like the Las Vegas Hilton. In his resort, Wynn incorporated both of the resort types – The Mirage was clean, elegant and modernistic while at the same time offering themed attractions such as an erupting volcano, tropical rain-forest atrium and dolphins. From the day it opened, The Mirage was a wild success and set the trend for the 'new' Las Vegas identity.

In addition to The Mirage, Mirage Resorts Inc. (MRI) currently owns and operates three other casino hotels in Southern Nevada: Treasure Island, the Golden Nugget and the Golden Nugget – Laughlin. The Mirage originally opened in November 1989 and is located in the heart of the Las Vegas Strip. The Golden Nugget has been operating in downtown Las Vegas since 1946. In 1988, MRI purchased a small casino in Laughlin, Nevada that became the Golden Nugget – Laughlin. In October of 1993, the company opened the Treasure Island casino hotel on the property directly adjacent to The Mirage. During 1994, MRI opened a small international casino, Casino Iguazu, in Iguazu Falls, Argentina. MRI has a 50 per cent interest in this joint venture. The company also has plans to open a new luxury gaming resort, Bellagio and an economy casino resort, Monte Carlo, on the Las Vegas Strip. Bellagio will be wholly owned by MRI, while Monte Carlo is a joint venture project with Circus Circus. Both properties will be located on the property formerly housing the Dunes Resort, which was acquired by MRI in 1993. The combined cost of the two projects is expected to exceed $1.5 billion (Lee, 1995).

MRI has been a major operator in the Las Vegas gaming market for many years. The company has had steadily increasing earnings, cash flows and stock price over the past several years and is widely viewed as a market leader in the gaming industry. MRI's market leadership has carried over into its decisions concerning investing and financing activities. The company is generally at the forefront with progressive ideas for investing and financing opportunities and, as such, is the ideal subject for this case study. MRI's investing and financing philosophies, as they relate to the issues previously discussed in this chapter, will be addressed in the following pages.

Analysis of Investing Activities of The Mirage

Investment in Existing Markets

Since the opening of The Mirage, MRI's actual expansion in the United States has been exclusively in the Las Vegas area. While some have questioned whether the recent expansions in Las Vegas have saturated the market in terms of room availability, MRI doesn't appear to be concerned. This confidence in the Las Vegas market is evidenced by MRI's opening of the 3,000 room Treasure Island resort and plans for the opening of the 3,000 room Bellagio and the 3,039 room Monte Carlo. MRI's optimism about the future of Las Vegas can be explained as follows:

> There are two things that make Las Vegas unique to any place else in the world. One .. is the casinos themselves and the other is the size of the properties here. Because we have casino gaming and other tourism destinations do not, we have an inherent advantage over .. other places ... and a big inherent advantage at that. It is an advantage that other places cannot easily remedy, both because it is not easy to get legalization through and because even if they did get legalization through, just adding a casino to a resort that already exists does not make it a casino hotel. Las Vegas casino hotels are designed to surround and envelop the casino. Every place one goes, he or she must go through that casino. If a hotel in Hawaii converted its banquet rooms to a casino, it would probably be unprofitable. A casino is very expensive to operate. It must have high volumes for it to be profitable and that only occurs if it is surrounded and enveloped by other amenities. It is exceedingly difficult to retrofit such a design into an existing, non-casino resort. Hence, Las Vegas has had a competitive advantage and one that I don't see it losing ... The other advantage of operating in Las Vegas is size. This city has learned that you can go big and there are economies of scale in going big (Lee, 1995).

These two factors have led MRI to believe that Las Vegas is and will continue to be an attractive location for gaming operations and, at least in the near future, for expansion. While thus far, MRI has chosen to expand primarily in the Las Vegas area, its expansion activities have still enabled MRI to diversify its operations. Once Bellagio and Monte Carlo open, MRI will have properties that target all ends of the gaming market, from economy minded to upscale visitors.

Buy Versus Build

MRI's philosophy concerning the decision as to whether to buy or build, centres around the issue of how to build value. MRI wants the end result of each of its investment opportunities to be the creation of value. For example, The Mirage cost $620 million to build and has cash flows of over $200 million per year.[6]

When casinos are sold, the selling price is generally about eight times cash flow, so it is estimated that The Mirage would sell at approximately $1.6 billion.[7] It only cost $620 million to build, so the act of building The Mirage generated a billion dollars of value (Lee, 1995).

MRI believes that the creation of value from the purchase of a property can be difficult. For MRI to be interested in buying an existing property, it must be a property that can be substantially improved so that value can be added. The ideal acquisition for MRI is something that has a good location, but perhaps because of lack of capital or lack of management, the property has not done well. MRI will buy the property, put in the necessary capital, make sure the proper management is in place and get a positive earnings' effect. MRI did just that when it bought the property that is now the Golden Nugget-Laughlin. Clearly, the purchase fit MRI's criteria in terms of buying something that can be substantially expanded and improved to add significant value.

What is not in MRI's investment strategy is simply to buy someone else's cash flows:

> If we buy something, it is because we think it can be expanded and improved. We aren't going to buy something just to buy it. Think about it. There were a lot of rumours a few months ago that we wanted to buy Circus Circus. That's crazy. How do you expand or improve their properties? They do just fine. They run them well. If we bought Circus Circus, all we would be doing is doubling the size of our company, which just makes it more difficult to maintain the growth rate. So you double the size of the company and cut the growth rate in half and you have probably hurt the share price (Lee, 1995).

Hence, the critical issue for MRI is whether a particular investment, buying or building, provides the opportunity to add value.

In terms of what type of property to build, MRI's philosophy for its new properties is to build a normal building with a pretty facade that is customer friendly. The company believes that 3,000 rooms is the right size to capture economies of scale while maintaining a customer friendly environment. MRI spent a great deal of time and effort trying to figure out how to make The Mirage and Treasure Island big, but still have the personal touch – to give the customers the advantages of size, but not the disadvantages (Lee, 1995).

To minimize the negative effects of size, MRI has taken several steps. First, the company has chosen to build its structure in a Y shape (with three sides). Structure shapes common to casino resorts in Las Vegas are shown graphically in Figure 8.1.

MRI's rationale for choosing a Y shape rather than other possible structure shapes is described below:

> This type of structure minimizes the sum of the average distances of the guest rooms to the elevator . . . while still providing unimpeded views from all

rooms. If you go to a four winged design, rooms anywhere near the inside corner have impeded views. One looks out the window and has a wall and therefore doesn't have an expansive view. With ours, this doesn't happen, because the inside corners are more than 90 degrees. Otherwise we would have four or five or six wings, but by staying with three, our rooms don't have impeded views. Conversely, a building with only two wings will have long corridors. Excalibur compromised on this principle in order to capitalize on its unique castle design. As a result, its guest room corridors are very long. Ditto for Luxor. The front desk is often far from parking and far from the customer's room. With the Luxor, not all of the elevators go to every floor. A customer can easily end up in a room where he has to go to a far corner of the first floor to get an elevator that goes to his floor and then walk half the way around the square again to get to his room. The Luxor developers spent their money on the shape of their hotel. We spent our money on a shape that is customer friendly, but then put the glitz in the front door (Lee, 1995).

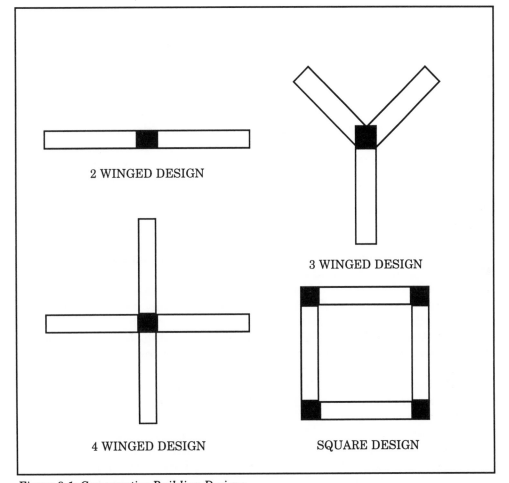

Figure 8.1: Comparative Building Designs

Second, MRI invested in other features which helps it deal with the size factor, while providing customers with efficient service. For instance, The Mirage has eighteen service elevators that on the ground floor are linked directly to room service kitchens. Parking is another area where MRI invested heavily in a non-revenue producing area in order to provide good customer service. A tunnel runs underneath the volcano, the entire length of a lake and connects to a parking garage that is between The Mirage and the Treasure Island. The tunnels provide fast, efficient parking. When a car is taken to the lot, another is brought back. The tunnels have no traffic lights or other impediments. Without this type of system, valet parking would take forever. The same type of tunnel system exists at Treasure Island.

MRI indicates that the economies of scale of large new hotels allow it to give better value than an older hotel casino, with an old 'plant' and fewer rooms. MRI can make good money with what it is doing for the customer, while the older, smaller place will simply break even with what they are doing for the customer. The outmoded plant cannot compete with the economies of scale of the newer, larger places.

Attractions

MRI also believes that entertainment, including attractions, are an integral part of its success (MRI, 1994). Its current philosophy is to heavily invest in one spectacular attraction rather than spreading out its resources on several ordinary attractions. The Mirage has the volcano and Treasure Island has the intricate pirate battle. MRI targets its attractions for adults rather than children. However, it realizes that children must still be accommodated (Lee, 1995).

MRI is constantly developing its philosophy concerning the design and placement of attractions. While MRI has developed several popular attractions, the company has adapted its strategy regarding its attractions over time, based on feedback from existing attractions. For instance, the volcano at The Mirage evolved from trying not to build a sign. MRI was attempting to distinguish itself from all the other places on the strip that had big neon signs. (Ultimately, The Mirage also added a sign like everyone else.) Instead of a sign, it would be recognizable from the volcano in front. The problem is that the best view of the volcano is from across the street. The volcano is practically not visible from The Mirage itself. There is no restaurant, bar or viewing area that looks at the volcano. A customer must leave the hotel and walk around the lake to get to a spot where he can see the volcano erupt, which is not ideal from the resort's standpoint.

With Treasure Island, MRI placed some revenue producing items near the Pirate Show and made the show readily accessible to the casino. There is a walkway right into the casino from the show. On the second floor a restaurant and bar are included as part of the facade. Most of the restaurant tables have a view of the pirate show and the bar is right in the middle of the battle.

Despite its successes, MRI has also learned important lessons from this attraction. For instance, the pirate show is in front of the main entrance to the resort, the arcade is located in the back and the casino is located in the middle. As a result, kids wishing to visit the arcade after seeing the pirate show often traverse through the casino to get to the arcade. This layout has the potential of discouraging gaming by serious gamers, who may feel uncomfortable gambling when minors are present. If the design could be reworked, the arcade would be moved to a more convenient location which would not encourage children to walk through the casino (Lee, 1995)

Another lesson learned by MRI with respect to this attraction is based on the popularity of the show. In fact, the show is so popular that people come looking for it. Hence, MRI now believes that the attraction did not have to be at the front of the property. Instead, the show could have been placed at the back of the property and an admission could have been charged (Lee, 1995).

Investment in Emerging Markets

MRI has considered expansion plans in both new and existing jurisdictions. Thus far, MRI has kept to existing jurisdictions in terms of actual projects started. The single most important criterion MRI considers in evaluating opportunities in new and existing jurisdictions is whether or not the investment is in an enduring business:

> The key is that it has to be an enduring business. It doesn't necessarily have to be large, it just has to be enduring. Let's say you had one of the big casinos outside of Chicago and legislation said there are only eight [allowed] – that is an enduring business and we don't have to build a hotel facility. If you are going into Tunica county, however, where there can be an unlimited number of casinos, you had better build something like Boyd did, because by . . . building the best hotel rooms and restaurants in the market, they have built an enduring business.

> So from our point of view, it has to be an enduring business. With a lot of these riverboat markets, it has been difficult to determine whether they are [enduring]. We would rather wait and see them stabilize. Ironically, Tunica county may now be right for us, because it has stabilized and every mistake that can be made has been made there somewhere. Now one knows what is going on; one can build something that maybe doesn't have a 200 per cent return the first year, but maybe it will have a 20 per cent return per year for 20 years (Lee, 1995).

MRI is currently looking at an opportunity to expand its operations back to Atlantic City. The company had been involved in Atlantic City prior to the building of The Mirage, but sold that property to help finance The Mirage. Now at the urging of Atlantic City officials – Atlantic City wants MRI to come in and help revitalize the economy and the area – MRI is considering returning to the area. Once again, the issue to address will be to determine if the opportunity will result in an enduring business. According to Lee,

> It is a lot easier to have a growth company if the businesses you have are solid. Look at the Golden Nugget, it has been around for 49 years and just had one of its best years ever.

Clearly, this concept of seeking out enduring businesses has proven successful for MRI.

MRI has also diversified its operations by expanding internationally. In 1994, the company made its first investment in an international casino. MRI used a joint venture to develop Casino Iguazu, in Iguazu Falls, Argentina. Each partner invested $4 million dollars in this venture. This property has 26 table games, 175 slot machines, but no hotel facilities (MRI, 1994).

Analysis of Financing Activities by MRI

MRI, formerly Golden Nugget Incorporated, has been a public company since the early 1950s. However, it was a small property and was not a factor in the industry until the mid–1970s. Even in the 1970s when more publicly traded companies entered the gaming industry, most of the traditional sources of funds were not available to pure gaming companies, including the Golden Nugget.

When casino gaming spread to Atlantic City, financing opened up for a while. Both the New Jersey Banks and Wall Street developed new attitudes towards financing casinos after the initial successes in Atlantic City (Bybee, 1995). This was the period when junk bond financing helped finance the growing casino industry. MRI used junk bond financing like the rest of the industry. However, in the late 1980s and early 1990s the favourable financing environment disappeared as bankruptcies started occurring in the industry (Bybee, 1995). Even MRI, which had successfully opened The Mirage, experienced financing difficulties:

> This company came pretty close to a potential problem five years ago [1990] when The Mirage had just opened. It was hugely successful and was showing big profits. But it built up huge accounts receivable. A good chunk of the revenues were generated on credit . . . so it really wasn't generating much cash for the first six months, until the credit began to be collected. Nevertheless, there were certain things that were not functional – we needed much more warehouse space etc. It's not that they were not designed properly, but we were not prepared for how much business this place would do. Everybody internally thought it would cash flow $120 million, maybe $130 million a year, which would have been a tremendous success on a $620 million investment. In fact, it cash flowed $200 million per year, which meant a much higher level of business. Therefore, we needed bigger warehouses, parking garages, better suites . . . and we began construction programmes to remedy this. Everybody believed the company was so profitable and it was. However, we were spending money expanding the place and it was not yet generating cash. It was clear that the cash flows would turn positive, when we started collecting the

accounts receivable, but there was a lag time of several months. Hence, the company needed money and went looking . . . Well, at the time, the bank market wasn't available and the bond market was also not available. The high yield market was in a real crunch, due to the collapse of Drexel Burnham Lambert, the default of Federated Department Stores and Federal rules mandating that savings and loans liquidate their high yield portfolios. There was literally a collapse for about six months in the high-yield market, which happened to be at the same time that The Mirage needed money to pay for the warehouse and all of the other stuff . . . The company was able to issue a secured first-mortgage bond (one of only a handful of successful high yield issues that year), but it had to pay 13¾ per cent interest to get the deal done. Now here was a perfectly fine hotel, making lots of money and it had to pay 13¾ per cent interest to get the deal done because it needed money at a time when the market just wasn't there (Lee, 1995).

In the last few years MRI has achieved the size and stability needed to allow the company to obtain financing from traditional sources (i.e., commercial banks and investment grade bonds). Today, MRI has the ability to issue investment grade bonds at less than 8 per cent interest with very few covenants and few restrictions. Investors are now comfortable that MRI has become a stable, large, honestly operated business in an industry now deemed acceptable and legitimate for investment (Lee, 1995).

MRI built The Mirage and Treasure Island with bonds. With Treasure Island the negative carry on the interest for the bonds used for construction offset 35 per cent of its earnings for two years because $300 million was borrowed at 9 and 7/8 per cent and invested short-term in US Treasury bonds at 3 per cent. MRI could not invest the money in anything risky because if it lost the money, the building could not be finished. With $300 million, paying interest at 10 per cent and earning 3 per cent results in a 7 per cent differential, or $21 million per year. It added approximately $30–40 million to the construction cost (Lee 1995).

Currently, MRI has a $1 billion line of credit available for funding operations and future expansions. With the bank line of credit, MRI pays 20 basis points to have a billion dollars of availability. In other words, MRI pays 0.2 per cent per year on the unused amount. For example, on the $300 million from the Treasure Island construction, 0.2 per cent per year is $600,000. When compared to the $21 million per year differential on the Treasure Island bonds, it is obvious that utilizing a bank line of credit is a much more attractive financing option than using bonds. In both cases there is absolute certainty that the money is available to build the building, but the cost of acquiring and using the money is much lower with the line of credit.

MRI believes that it is approaching the next step in terms of financing, which would be to issue commercial paper, like GM and ATT. Commercial paper is an even cheaper means of financing than bank lines of credit. In fact, banks borrow much of their money in the commercial paper market. By entering the commercial paper market itself, MRI may save as much as 50 basis points and actually gain a little flexibility, because the company can set its own maturities. MRI has already decided that whenever it issues commercial paper, the instruments will mature on Tuesdays, because Tuesday is the day that the company typically makes a large cash deposit from its weekend gaming revenue.

CONCLUSIONS

Based on the historical and contemporary financing and investing issues presented in this chapter, some conclusions can be drawn. First, it should be quite clear that financing and investing activities are closely related. Without adequate financing, investment and expansion plans may not reach fruition. Hence, these two activities will not be segregated in drawing conclusions regarding financing and investing issues.

At present there are five principal financing alternatives available to gaming firms. The most common method, but least attractive from the company's perspective, is high yield bonds. Even with the legitimization and expansion of the industry, most gaming firms still must rely on high yield bonds for financing. This method requires the company to secure all the financing for a project at the front end. Therefore, the company is forced to pay high interest rates for borrowed money that it may not need for several months.

The second method of financing is investment grade bonds. This alternative has all the disadvantages of high yield bonds, except the rate of interest is lower and they generally have fewer covenants. Only a select few of the major companies, like MRI, have been able to issue investment grade bonds.

The third method of financing capital projects which has evolved in the last few years is the bank line of credit. The advantage of a line of credit is that it allows the company to plan its investment in new projects, without having to worry about issuing bonds and incurring unnecessary interest costs. Companies that are able to arrange a line of credit have greater flexibility in planning their capital investments. Major lines of credit are only available to the premier gaming companies.

The fourth method of financing is the issuance of commercial paper. While this alternative has not yet been used by a gaming company, some major corporations have utilized this option. This option allows the company the greatest control and lowest costs when raising capital. It will be available only to the premier gaming companies which have proven track records in all aspects of their operations.

A fifth financing method which has been a source of capital for many gaming companies, the issuance of equity, is usually only available on attractive terms to proven companies during favourable market conditions.

Since the majority of gaming companies are presently limited to high yield bonds for major financing, these companies should benchmark companies like The Mirage to determine what measures can be undertaken to improve their own attractiveness in the capital markets. For example, smaller companies can attempt to diversify their operations. When a company operates a single property or a limited number of properties in one market, investment risk is higher than when a company spreads its operations across more than one jurisdiction or customer base. For instance, MRI is diversifying its operations in terms of customer base and jurisdictions. Within the Las Vegas market, MRI is diversifying into all levels of clientele with its existing and planned properties. Geographically, MRI has begun diversification with its joint venture casino in Argentina. Domestically, the company is seeking to re-enter Atlantic City and is exploring investment opportunities in other areas within the United States.

Smaller companies, which cannot obtain the financing to diversify into new areas or clientele levels, may find that mergers with other gaming firms which would complement their business and help diversify their operations may be beneficial. Another alternative would be to use joint ventures as a means to reduce risk for the individual partners, while obtaining the needed financing to expand into new areas.

If smaller companies can achieve better financing opportunities through mergers, joint ventures, or some other means, then these properties can concentrate on other investment and expansion issues. Chief among these issues are the location of the new property, the type of building, the inclusion of a hotel and the inclusion of attractions and other types of entertainment.

In evaluating any potential casino development, the company must consider the following:

1) Market: The company needs to determine what segment of the economy it is targeting – low, middle, or high-end. Also, is it targeting families or adults without children? Even if it is targeting childless adults, some concessions must be made to the 'child' factor;

2) Size: The company needs to determine what size property it can afford to build and maintain while still providing a base level of customer service. Some specific areas which should be considered are:

   a) Parking – How long does it take the customer to travel from the parking lot to the front desk;
   b) Room access – Is the physical layout of the building customer friendly? How convenient is elevator access to all rooms? How convenient is front desk access to all rooms?;
   c) Support services – Are services like valet parking and room service adequate? Is there adequate infrastructure to make these services customer friendly?

3) Attractions: Once a company decides that it wants to invest in attractions, then it needs to decide whether to make it free or a paid attraction. The location of the attraction must be studied for its impact on gaming and viewing. The attraction should be located so as to draw customers into the casino, regardless of whether or not admission is charged. Further, the best view of the attraction should be from the resort.

Another point which these companies should consider in evaluating investment opportunities is their commitment to the business. Are they investing for large, short-term profits, or are they building an enduring business which will provide a reasonable, long-term return? If publicly traded, companies need to think about the long term and the impact of their investments on stock price.

MRI has been successful because it has invested for long-term profitability. Other companies, particularly in the emerging locations, have opted for short-term profits without considering the position of the company in the long term. When the market matures and becomes more competitive, many of these short term oriented companies have failed. Gaming companies will be offered many new investment opportunities as the legalization and spread of gaming continues. The success of the individual companies will be largely driven by how they plan and operationalize their investing and financing activities. It is essential that gaming companies attempt to achieve the best possible financing options, because the financing terms will drive the investment decisions.

REFERENCES

Bybee, S. (January 1995) 'Gaming legalization efforts and activity in the US' *Speech to International Association of Hospitality Accountants: Casino Controllers Conference*, Imperial Palace Casino Hotel. Las Vegas, Nevada: pp 1–38.

Bybee, S. (April 7, 1995) *Interview.*

Conner, M. (June 4, 1994) 'Megaresort openings cause growth to slow in Laughlin' *Gaming and Wagering Business*, 16–17.

Eadington, W. (1994) 'The Emergence of Casino Gaming as a Major Factor in Tourism Markets: Policy Issues and Considerations' in *People, Places and Processes* edited by Richard Butler and Douglas Pearce, pp. 159–186. New York: Routledge.

Global Gaming Almanac 1995, pp. 1–559. New York: Smith Barney.

Gros, R. (July 1994) 'New frontiers: How the casino industry, "local partners", and politicians work together to advance gaming' *Casino Journal*, 38–40.

Johnston, D. (1992) *Temples of Chance*. New York: Doubleday.

Kieso, D. and Weygandt, J. (1992) *Intermediate Accounting*. Seventh Edition, New York: John Wiley & Sons Inc.

Ladenburg, Thalmann & Co. Inc. (March 29, 1995) *Investment Research Industry Report for the Gaming Industry*, p. 5.

Lalli, S. (July 1994) 'The Desert Inn's glorious, nefarious past.' *Casino Journal*, pp. 68–71.

Lee, D. (13 April, 1995) *Interview.*

Mirage Resorts Incorporated Annual Report (1993).

Mirage Resorts Incorporated Annual Report (1994).

Mirage Resorts, Inc. (February 1995) *Smith Barney Research Report*, pp. 1–7.

North American Gaming Report 1995 (1 July, 1995) *International Gaming & Wagering Business*, Supplement, pp. 1– 82.

Skolnick, J. (1978) *House of Cards The Legalization and Control of Casino Gambling*. Boston: Little, Brown and Company.

Spanier, D. (1992) *Welcome to the Pleasuredome*. Reno: University of Nevada Press.

Vallen, G. (January 1995) 'Legalization of gaming in the United States: A past and current perspective.' *The Bottomline: The Journal of the International Association of Hospitality Accountants*, Vol. 10, No. 1, pp. 14–19.

1: Statement made by Henry Gluk, Chairman of the Board of Caesar's World.

2: Bill Harrah was one of the pioneers of legalized gambling in northern Nevada. He opened a casino in Reno in the 1930s and was one of the first casino operators to employ marketing research and sound financial management to his casino operations.

3: Skimming is the practice of illegally taking a percentage of the cash which the casino has collected from slot machines and table games before it is officially counted. The effect is to reduce the amount of taxable income.

4: Information about Mirage Resorts Incorporated was obtained from research studies, annual reports, and from an interview with Dan Lee, Chief Financial Officer and Treasurer and Senior Vice President of Finance and Development for Mirage Resorts Incorporated on 13 April, 1995.

5: Mirage Resorts Incorporated was originally Golden Nugget Inc. In 1991 the name of the company was officially changed to Mirage Resorts Incorporated, reflecting the success of its flagship property

6: A cash flow of $200 million per year means that the Mirage nets a positive cash inflow of $200,000,000 after it has paid its operating expenses, jackpots, etc., but before capital costs, such as interest expense and income taxes.

7: When evaluating investing opportunities, one of the things a prospective buyer of a company analyses is the potential future cash flow of the target company. When a profitable casino is put up for sale, it is normally expected to sell for approximately eight times its annual cash flows.

9

Service Quality in the Hospitality Industry: The Process and Promise of Guest Satisfaction

Kye-Sung Chon, Martin Oppermann and Bonnie Farber Canziani

INTRODUCTION

Much has been written in recent years about quality service and guest satisfaction in the hospitality industry. As the industry becomes more competitive, the race for quality service and guest satisfaction seems to intensify at a faster rate. As one industry executive said, the race for quality service has no finish line – as the race progresses the finish line moves further away. Quality has become a critical value mentioned in many hospitality companies' business philosophies, the latter which subsequently drive strategic planning and functional area activities. This chapter discusses how the goal of quality has affected both marketing and service delivery systems and then describes various quality service and guest satisfaction programmes which have been successfully promoted and implemented in the hospitality industry. Industry examples in this chapter focus more on the 'ingredients' of quality service and guest satisfaction programmes which have been successfully carried out in the hospitality industry, rather than on explaining how companies created such programmes.

MARKETING STRATEGY AS A PRECURSOR TO SERVICE QUALITY

In order to provide a broader view of the impacts of a quality philosophy on the hospitality firm, a general overview of relevant marketing practices will be discussed in this first section, from the viewpoint of how they have been altered to help the hospitality firm achieve the goal of service quality. The marketing field has moved in many different directions, resulting in a plethora of co-existing theories and portfolios of marketing strategies. First, we will examine how quality is linked to the environmental scanning activities of the hospitality enterprise. This will be followed by a review of specific forces driving industry competition. Next, we will discuss the multiple quality related goal objects of market research activity: from customer description to customer satisfaction analysis. Lastly, the changing roles of promotion and advertising will be described, in order to clarify how these important activities help the customer to assess more accurately the value of quality in products and services. Overall, the primary emphasis with regard to these marketing practices will be to identify their significance in the maximization of service quality and customer satisfaction in the hospitality marketplace.

Marketing and Strategic Planning

Scanning the environment for quality management forces

The marketing concept is differentiated from the production or selling concepts specifically in the way it responds to forces from the external and industry environments in order to enhance customer satisfaction and long-run profitability of the firm. Each hospitality firm is challenged to scan its surrounding environments (see Figure 9.1) on a continuous basis in order to assess levels of change in external and industry forces: e.g., changes in consumer characteristics and behaviour; new technologies that might impact service design and delivery systems; and potential effects of impending legislation and regulatory practices.

Specifically, firms that have well developed marketing planning efforts (Buttle, 1992) can be more proactive in their quest for retention of customers and growth in market share, by foreseeing the quality management forces at work in both the external and industry environments and adopting a statement of quality within their business philosophy. Given the surge in interest in quality management and systems in the hospitality industry, hospitality firms are finding it necessary to operationalize this business philosophy in order to retain their current customer base. Firms desiring to be successful in this domain will accurately assess their marketing plan from multiple quality vantage points. First, as summarized by a Burger King executive, *The customer is the vital key to our success. We are now looking at our business through the customer's eyes and measuring our performance against their expectations, not ours* (Marketing News, 1990). Hospitality companies need to examine how salient the overall concept of quality is to their various target markets and also, how their myriad customers define quality in their own terms. Once firms are able to define quality in the words of the customer, they are well equipped to offer quality-driven products and services and create promotional devices using the quality motivation.

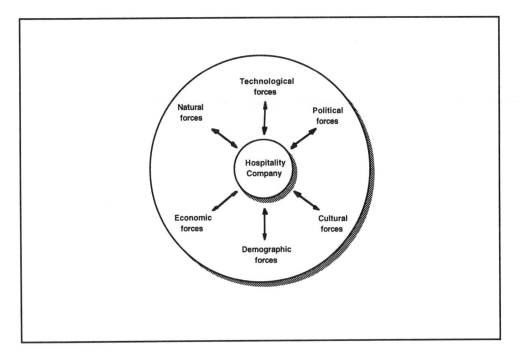

Figure 9.1: External Forces in the Macroenvironment

The second arena in which quality management plays a vital role is that of applied technology in the form of quality analysis and control systems. Quality management techniques emphasize the importance of continuously refining work processes so that a zero-defect service delivery may be provided. Reduction of operational and customer costs is an additional goal of the implementation of quality tools. For example, Marriott listened to customer complaints about check-in time waits and responded with a programme called *1st 10* that elicits key data during the reservation process, so that registration waits could be minimized. Future utilization of smart card technology is expected to further enhance this core service in the hotel. And as the members of the hospitality industry successfully differentiate themselves on the quality dimension, as did Ritz-Carlton by seeking the Malcolm Baldrige award, hospitality companies in general will need to self-monitor their service and products in accordance with external standards, or face loss of competitive advantage in a quality-driven marketplace.

Quality's link with forces driving industry competition

A review of the model of industry competition authored by Michael E. Porter (1980) provides a clear basis for understanding the impact the quality movement has on the hospitality firm of today. Figure 9.2 portrays the general forces driving competition within the hospitality industry.

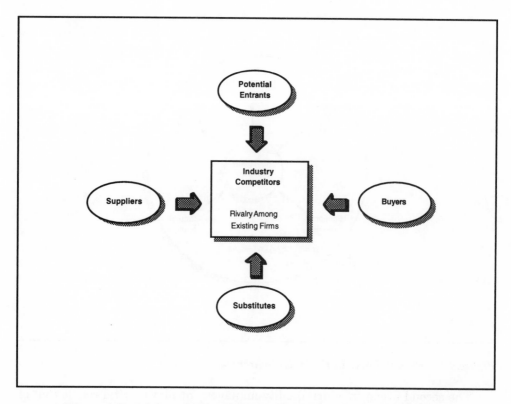

Source: Adapted from Porter, M. E. (1980) Competitive Strategy: Techniques for Analyzing Industries and Competitors, New York: The Free Press.

Figure 9.2: Forces Driving Industry Competition

With respect to the center of the diagram, rivalries that normally exist among firms within the same industry are affected in two meaningful ways by the quality movement. First, individual firms obviously view quality as an attribute of their service package upon which they can strive to differentiate themselves from other firms in their industry. Assuming Hospitality Firm A makes and promotes quality as a primary product/service attribute, then Firm A can cause its current customers to have a heightened sense of switching costs when they contemplate purchasing a competitor's (Firm B's) product or service, by persuading these customers that Firm B's product or service is potentially less defect free than that of Firm A.

The second effect the quality movement has on industry competition is to promote competition among rival firms by calling for the employment of benchmarking activities; as explained by Bob Camp (1989), this is the process of continually researching for new ideas and methods, practices and processes and either borrowing the practices, or adapting the best feature for one's own firm. Since benchmarking occurs at the industry level through coordinated efforts of hospitality and quality associations dedicated to research and norming of quality practices, it has the effect of reducing any one firm's ability to patent or protect quality as a tool for real differentiation of its service delivery system. However, benchmarking does not greatly hinder an individual firm's ability to promote and advertise using the quality motivation, so there is still potential for persuading customers to view one's firm as a leader in offering quality products or services.

At this point we examine the effects the quality movement has on the forces of buyers, suppliers, substitutes, or potential entrants into the industry. First, as consumers become increasingly educated about quality standards espoused by companies within or even external to the hospitality industry, they will demand more from companies they already patronize, or else switch to a company that offers higher quality goods or services. This scenario can unfold differently in the various price segments of hospitality subindustries. For example, quality may have more impact on the purchase decision of a buyer comparing higher-priced hotels or restaurants, than on a buyer seeking budget lodging or inexpensive food service, since the price attribute may overshadow the quality attribute. Also, playing competitors against each other on the quality attribute, when negotiating corporate contracts for lodging or contract food service, is an inevitable outcome of this quality movement. The role of consumer advocates is additionally supported by the quality philosophy and so this may well result in increased legal action, ultimately affecting industry standards, for such practices as overbooking and concomitant walking of guests. Hotels may need to respond by adopting less permissive overbooking strategies to avoid excessive walking of guests, or risk losing their image of being a quality-focused property and even potentially paying damages in a civil suit.

In the case of the bargaining power of suppliers, an amazing reversal of influences has been initiated by the just-in-time concept of supplier-company relationships. Instead of badgering suppliers for price discounts with threats of switching to competitor supply firms, hospitality companies are promising loyalty to chosen suppliers in return for high-grade goods and phenomenal response times for ordering and delivery. As mentioned by Zikmund and d'Mico (996, p. 108)

> whether it's sheets and linen, emergency fire exit signs, or cheesecake, Hyatt buyers comb the globe looking for the highest quality products. After Hyatt settles on a supplier, the company works hard at maintaining the relationship

Suppliers are forced, essentially, to compete on the quality attribute as well.

Threats of substitute products are even stronger in the quality environment. For example, if lodging companies make only half-hearted attempts at designing food and beverage services, that accommodate the modern hotel client on issues such as affordability, freshness and nutritional value, the clients will revolt by seeking alternative food sources such as restaurants, convenience stores and health food options in the surrounding locale. Hotels that do not guarantee the quality of the conference experience to their business clients may eventually be replaced by the ever more popular telecommunications industry – especially given the decline of business travel budgets and tax incentives for business travel.

Lastly, new entrants to the hospitality industry do not only increase capacity but often utilize newer technologies that have incurred them less capital expense than is incurred by existing firms attempting operational makeovers. This is particularly significant in the design of operational systems involving computer chip technologies, e.g., registration procedures using smart-card technology, or technologies designed to conserve natural resources, e.g., laundry equipment that reduces toxic chemical emissions and conserves energy. New entrants therefore may force existing companies to move from cash-flow objectives to reinvestment objectives in order to project a quality image.

Marketing Research Undergoes a Technological Revolution

The American Marketing Association (AMA) defines marketing research as follows:

> [Marketing research] links the consumer, customer and public to the marketer through information – information used to identify and define marketing opportunities and problems; generate, refine and evaluate marketing actions; monitor marketing performance; and improve understanding of marketing as a process. Marketing research specifies the information required to address these issues; designs the methods for collecting information; manages and implements the data collection process; analyses the results; and communicates the findings and their implications (Bennett, 1988).

Marketing research has been particularly affected by the adoption of quality goals within firms' business philosophies. New market research devices allow us to uncover more about what consumers want and how they behave and to make more powerful predictions about what products and services they will buy in the future and the channels of delivery that will be more profitable. It is very likely that market research departments and consultants will need to offer just-in-time market research studies on a continuous basis in order to market to an increasingly fragmented consumer base. Emphasis will be placed on internal sources of information and single source research using customer history databases, in order to build stable relationships among service firms and their customers.

This portends a plausible shift from dependence on secondary or sampling data on consumer geographics, demographics and psychographics to database marketing. This one-on-one marketing method fully promotes the achievement of the quality objective of responding to customers – in this case targeting individual needs and desires. Hospitality firms will then communicate with customers as individuals, often through direct marketing efforts, to bring them back, sell them new services, or even to recruit new customers. For example,

Sheraton Hotels gives points to its club members for every suggested name that results in a new member. Pizza-Hut take-out/delivery stores use a computer system that flags customers that haven't reordered within 30 days; management can opt to initiate a telephone campaign to call these individuals and check on the quality of the previous experience, as well as to offer a discount on the next purchase within a defined time period. (McGaw, 1990). Tourism Canada invented a novel approach for measuring arrivals from Americans to whom they sent mailed information packets. The packet contained a response card which offered the American target a gift or discount, but only if the card were mailed in Canada (Rapp and Collins, 1987).

Inroads have been made as well with respect to the content questions on studies of satisfaction with service delivery in hospitality firms. SERVQUAL, a multidimensional scale designed by Parasuraman, Zeithaml and Berry (1988) allows customers to evaluate a firm's service quality by comparing perceptions of service with their expectations of service. The scale captures five dimensions of service quality:

- responsiveness;
- reliability;
- assurance;
- empathy; and
- tangibles.

This instrument provides a fuller picture of service quality than do many customer feedback forms that over-rely on product-based attributes. Additional customer feedback mechanisms have been instituted in hospitality firms such as: critical incident collection, complaint solicitation studies and post-transaction surveys, e.g., Fairfield Inns asks hotel guests to answer several questions about their stay in the hotel using a computer terminal near the front desk. As noted, marketing research has a powerful role to play in the delivery of quality products and services and in achieving greater customer satisfaction.

Promotion and Advertising in a Quality World

According to Zeithaml and Bitner (1996) there are four critical uses of promotion and advertising related to service quality:

1) managing service promises;
2) modifying customer expectations;
3) educating the customer; and
4) promoting quality across in-house functional areas.

Hospitality firms today have to make promises they can keep and offer service guarantees that are appropriate for the services being promoted. Christopher Hart (1988) suggests that an effective service guarantee is easy to understand, meaningful to the customer, unconditional and easy to invoke and collect on.

With respect to modifying customer expectations, once hospitality companies analyse their operations and implement control systems, they will have a better idea of what they can deliver to the customer. Only then should they develop advertising schemes based on the quality motivation. Especially important is the use of advertising to justify prices set to specific quality levels and emphasize quality-added service components.

Educating both customers and in-house service employees to enact properly their individual roles in service delivery systems, is another objective of promotional and advertising campaigns. Using various promotional devices, hospitality firms can actually instruct customers to be better consumers of the hospitality product and thereby reduce related operational costs.

On line interactive information is the newest development to advertising media that historically comprise television, radio, magazines and newspapers. This method will further the goals of establishing relationships between customers and hospitality companies by facilitating one-on-one dialogues. This may well lead to electronic measurement of advertising results in the future, as well as enabling firms to continuously receive customer feedback via the Internet which will serve as a valuable resource for continuously improving service delivery systems. At this point in the chapter, we wish to offer specific examples of hospitality companies that are successfully promoting and implementing quality management programmes to underscore the importance of these initiatives in the hospitality industry.

QUALITY SERVICE AND GUEST SATISFACTION

There are two types of service quality that concern hospitality businesses. One type of service quality has to do with the product features that enhance customer satisfaction and the other type of service quality is related to freedom from deficiencies. It is the former type of quality service in which we are mainly interested, because of its potential to influence customer satisfaction. Guests perceive 'value' only when they believe that the benefits received are greater than the sacrifices made. So, the key to service quality enhancement is how one can generate the maximum perceived value in the eyes of the customer. The sacrifices of the guest include money spent at a hotel or a restaurant.

Re-engineering the Service Delivery System

In order to ensure the maximum customer value, there should be a service delivery system which meets or exceeds customer expectations. The service delivery system created will thus, in turn, create customer satisfaction. This means that hospitality operators must develop service delivery systems that create value for their target markets. Some of the economy lodging chains (e.g., La Quinta Inns and Hampton Inns) in the United States realized that clean and safe guest rooms and an efficient check-in and check-out, are the most important considerations for their target customers when choosing a hotel. They also realized that a majority of their clients are automobile travellers who spend the night and take off early the next morning for another day of journey. So, they created 'value' for their customers by providing clean and safe guest rooms plus a complimentary continental breakfast offered in the hotel lobby in the morning. The complimentary service in the hotel lobby allows the guest to continue his journey the next morning without consuming too much time for breakfast. This is how one can generate 'value'. The core product in most hotels in this class is the same or very similar. Therefore, the only way an hospitality firm can differentiate the product is by modifying the way it designs a service delivery system. In many cases, the delivery system does not have to be radically different or even innovative – it must help to solidify the firm's identity as a quality company with its target market. Differentiating one's product (or one's service) in the eyes of customers can add tangible and intangible value to one's business worth.

The 'value engineering' process involves the four steps of:

1) identifying the customer segments that give the most value to your hospitality company;
2) identifying what these target markets value;
3) developing a service delivery system that provides better customer value than the competition; and
4) listening to customers and modifying the service delivery system.

One Marriott hotel had been open for fifteen years before its management determined that two-thirds of all guest calls to housekeeping were to request ironing boards. This discovery prompted the idea of simply providing an iron and an ironing board in all guest rooms, an idea which would cost the hotel $20,000. The hotel's management reviewed the capital budget and saw that an equivalent amount was earmarked to replace black and white television sets in the bathrooms of the executive floor with colour sets. The management then inquired how many guests in the executive floor rooms requested a colour television set and found no one had made such a request. So the hotel decided to shift the budget for replacing televisions to providing irons and ironing boards in each guest room. By listening to the customer and seeking input from personnel that dealt with guest requests on a daily basis, management was able to change a service delivery system. It not only changed the system, but it did so in such a manner as to positively impact more customers. The programme was consequently implemented at Marriott hotels throughout the United States.

Listening to the customers and adapting services to customer tastes is critically important in this process. Ritz-Carlton Hotels make a considerable effort to make all employees a 'listening post'. Every employee is trained to listen to Ritz-Carlton guests (Partlow, 1993). Guests' comments, preferences, likes and dislikes are recorded and entered into a guest-history profile. Ritz-Carlton uses this information to develop a more 'personalized' service for the guest on subsequent visits. Additionally, the information is entered into a service-oriented data bank that is shared by all Ritz-Carlton hotels. Therefore, a guest whose favourite newspaper was *The Washington Post* would be thoroughly delighted to receive a copy of *The Washington Post* with his breakfast while staying at the Ritz-Carlton San Francisco. Since all he ever did was mention to a housekeeper that *The Washington Post* was his favourite newspaper, this unexpected response of the hotel improves his perceived value of staying with Ritz-Carlton even more. The customer information collected has been collectively utilized in modifying their product/service mix and also re-engineering their service delivery system.

Designing an effective service delivery system requires a shift of paradigm on the part of operators and managers who need to be open-minded about changes and the process of continuously adapting to the changes. Taco Bell is one such company which stands out for its efforts to change the paradigm in the fast food industry (Hammer, 1993). Taco Bell found in its research of fast food customers that there are three things which cause customers to perceive good value in the fast food experience. They are:

1) a lot of food for the money paid;
2) a clean and pleasant restaurant environment; and
3) accuracy in order taking and food delivery.

Based on its study, Taco Bell first made a change in its food cost. While in general the fast food industry considered that a good fast food operator would run the restaurant with 25 per cent food cost or less, Taco Bell decided to raise its food cost from 27 per cent to 35 per cent. In other words, the company committed to deliver 'a lot of food for the little money paid'. In an effort to deliver a clean and pleasant environment, Taco Bell redesigned its restaurant seating area and decor package. In doing so, the company changed its emphasis from being production oriented to being customer oriented. A typical Taco Bell went from being 70 per cent kitchen and 30 per cent customer area, to being 30 per cent kitchen and 70 per cent customer area! The company helped design its own technologically advanced point-of-sale systems to ensure the accuracy of order taking and food delivery. Imagine the impact on Taco Bell customers: more food for the same money, larger and more customer friendly dining areas and an accurate ordering and food delivery system. At the same time, Taco Bell looked at its internal customers. It found that employees disliked food production work and as a result, started the 'K-minus Programme', which was designed to eliminate the employees' kitchen work to the greatest extent possible. Taco Bell didn't stop there. It purchased a time-saving Management Information System which put the power of computer technology in the hands of its managers. Managers were freed from much of the drudgery of 'getting the management work' done and this gave the managers more time to spend with the customers. Customers were not the only ones to receive the additional benefits. The overall programme resulted in Taco Bell going from 1.6 billion US dollars annual revenue in 1988 to 3.3 billion US dollars in 1991 (Bowen, 1994).

Using Technology

Technology can be broadly defined as the process of transforming input into output. In addition to machine technology where you can adopt mechanical means (e.g., computers and automation), designing an efficient and effective service delivery system contributes to the creation of new technology. This was the case with Singapore Airlines (SIA), which has been consistently rated as the world's top airline in the poll of frequent flyers. In order to enhance quality service and passenger satisfaction, SIA re-engineered its service delivery system, by first drawing a sequential flow chart of all possible service incidents which could occur to a passenger. The service incidents were then grouped into the three areas of 'pre-flight service', 'on-flight service', and 'post-flight service'. Management then used creative brainstorming to imagine how they could ensure service quality and passenger satisfaction at each of these three phases. One idea which was generated as a result was the creation of 'city terminals' that allowed passengers to process their check in and also check their luggage at a city center (or a hotel) so that they will avoid waiting in long lines in the airport.

Recently, Southwest Airlines began utilizing 'ticketless' travel. Customers may now purchase tickets over the telephone or using the Internet. There are numerous benefits for both the airlines and the customers: fewer waiting lines, reduced 'redundant' personnel, one less piece of paper to keep up with, streamlined electronic record keeping and an improved customer identification database. If Ritz-Carlton has 240,000 repeat customers in its data base (Partlow, 1993), imagine the possibilities for an airline that services that many people over a time period of a few days. In summation, as customers' needs change, the hospitality organization must continually anticipate and respond by upgrading its service delivery systems and embracing new support technologies.

Organizational Culture

Successful quality service delivery systems would not be possible without creating a customer oriented culture. An organization's culture is a deposit of values, beliefs, ideals and rituals of the organization. Developing an organizational culture that focuses on serving the customer is essential in providing quality customer service. Socializing employees to an organization's culture begins during the interviewing process (Schneider, 1994). Prospective employees observe the visible cues of the organization. They make judgements and assumptions at the subconscious level. They rely on their instincts to help them through the hiring process. Anyone who has been through the interviewing and hiring process can probably remember certain 'quarks or blimps' from the interview: seeing a certain smile (or frown), identifying (or not identifying) with the pictures or objects in an office, or having that 'certain feeling' about how the interview went. Once hired, new employees are like sponges, absorbing everything (good and bad) that they encounter. The first few days are critical to a new-hire for the organization.

What information do you give them? Why/why not? How? It is imperative that the organization have a definitive position on who it is and what it wants to be. The Ritz-Carlton Hotels have the 'Ritz-Carlton Credo', which reads:

> The Ritz-Carlton is a place where the genuine care and comfort of our guests is our highest mission. We pledge to provide the best service and facilities for our guests who will always enjoy a warm, relaxed yet refined ambience. The Ritz-Carlton experience enlivens the senses, instills well-being and fulfils even the unexpressed wishes and needs of our guests.

Based on this credo, Ritz-Carlton Hotels came up with the 'Gold Standards' which they use as their yardsticks for service quality within each property and managers spend a considerable amount of time working on those standards. One such 'Gold Standard' specifies that all telephone calls must be answered within three rings and with a 'smile'. Another 'Gold Standard' states: *Smile. We are on stage. Always maintain positive eye contact. Use the proper vocabulary with our guests. (Use words like: 'good morning', 'certainly', 'I'll be happy to', and 'my pleasure')* These become more than 'catchy phrases' or slogans as employees move through the organization's culturalization process, during which they see that everyone in the organization from the top-down practises the same rituals. Employees begin to live the creed. This not only helps to reinforce their own beliefs and practices, but it also serves to reinforce the behaviours of those around them. In essence, an organization can help to prolong its own success, the success and development of its employees and future employees, by establishing a strong corporate culture. In the case of the Ritz-Carlton Hotels, they practice rituals like daily 'line ups', frequent employee recognition ceremonies and employee performance appraisals based on parameters clearly outlined during the employee orientation phase (Partlow, 1993).

Organizations that take the time to formulate a plan and develop a specific quality minded culture can achieve additional benefits from their employees. Line, staff, or management workers who are adequately meshed into the values and beliefs of the organization feel a greater sense of belonging. They are more likely to remain on the job longer which reduces turnover costs. They tend to contribute more ideas and input. They are less likely to resist change and can help to innovate and make the organization more viable in tough times. Organizations that have a strong corporate culture are able to compete in all situations and eliminate the service gap between what is promised to the customer and what is actually delivered.

Members of these strong culture organizations respond in unison. They have eliminated many of the barriers which divide more traditional organizations. The Ritz-Carlton, for example, exhorts its staff to 'own' a problem, to feel empowered, to do whatever it takes to resolve a guest's problem or complaint and not to be afraid to take risks when solving guest problems. The organization has formal support systems built into its guest satisfaction and retention programmes, but it is the informal cultural support system that the employee draws from the most. When the corporate culture supports the employee, making the right customer service decisions becomes instinctive: it just 'feels' right . . .

Internal Marketing

The internal marketing concept states that the internal market of employees is the best motivator for service-mindness and customer-oriented performance. Internal marketing uses a marketing perspective to manage the firm's employees. The employee becomes the target market within the organization. The organization is challenged to provide the resources to motivate the employee to respond to customer needs in the most effective manner, during routine or unusual circumstances. The internal marketing concept is operationalized via a four step process of:

1) Establishing service culture;
2) Developing a marketing approach to human resources management, from hiring to employee development programmes;
3) Disseminating marketing information to employees;
4) Implementing a reward and recognition system.

According to W. Edwards Deming (Walton, 1986), the man credited with starting the current Total Quality Management (TQM) programmes, an organization must institute leadership. In the case of Ritz-Carlton, top management determined that quality service was to be the cornerstone of their operations. They instituted this in a top-down fashion; however, top management reinforced this directive by example and by continually striving for higher levels of customer satisfaction. Even though the company is less than fifteen years old, it has already been recognized for its commitment to service excellence. In 1992 the Ritz-Carlton Hotels became the second service organization in the United States to be awarded the Malcolm Baldrige National Quality Award. Remarkably, the top executives at Ritz-Carlton Hotels are quick to point out that their customer service goals have not been met fully. *We weren't stopping at the Baldrige, we wanted the highest level of quality* (Partlow, 1993).

What is the highest level of quality? Obviously, quality is perceived differently among organizations, employees and guests. Within the organization employees need to be 'schooled' to recognize service opportunities. Employees that know what is expected of them are better equipped to respond positively at 'the moment of truth' (Kotler, Bowen and Makens, 1996). A moment of truth occurs when an employee is faced with a customer interaction. After proper orientation, training and indoctrination into the corporate culture, an employee should feel 'empowered' to make decisions regarding customer problems or requests. In a liberal, service oriented culture employees should view guests' problems and complaints as opportunities to surprise and delight the guest (Wagner, 1993). Customer-contact employees establish the invisible bonds of brand loyalty on an incident by incident basis. Those organizations that become adept in supporting their employees' 'service contracts' with their guests will become successful in marketing their entire operations.

It is not surprising that employees would rather work in fun, exciting environments. Walt Disney Enterprises recognizes this fact and uses it to its advantage. Employees are provided with their own on premises recreational facilities, dining rooms and library. The message that Disney sends to its employees and prospective employees is:

1) we care about you as an individual;
2) your health and well-being are important to us;
3) we want you to grow and develop as an individual; and
4) we want you to be happy here, stay, relax and enjoy.

This is a message that has helped Disney remain a leader in the hospitality industry for four decades. They understand who they are and where they want to be. Disney employs a fifth 'p' in their marketing plan: product, pricing, place, promotion and people (Pope, 1979). They understand that their employees are in constant contact with their guests. To insure that their people perform at the guests' level of expectations, Disney takes extra steps to train and socialize their employees. They want every employee to become part of 'the Disney Family'. Everyone in the organization from the CEO to the most-recent-hire is on a first-name-only basis. Doing away with titles may seem trivial, but not when you are the new-hire that is working on the same theme ride with a corporate president or vice-president during his annual 'cross-utilization' week. Team work takes on a new dimension when you support or are supported by someone who could have had a greater mechanistic control over you under different circumstances.

How an organization disseminates information to its employees is also important to the internal marketing of an organization. The concept of the medium is the message' is commonly accepted today. However, organizations often forget this valuable idea when training their employees. Sometimes 'telling' or 'showing' is not sufficient. Westin Hotels include visits to their restaurants, clubs, recreation areas and other guest service facilities for front desk and reservations specialists. Lunches, dinners, overnight stays which require the new-hires to use room service, in-room movies, valet parking, video check-out and other regular guest services help to immerse these employees into the guests' world. Employees are regularly provided discounts in the restaurants and clubs in an effort to expose them to what the Westin has to offer its guests. The more that key customer-contact employees know about available guest amenities, the more they will be able to recommend these truthfully. As more chains begin to 'follow the leader' and provide like services or products, it becomes more imperative that your employees know what the benefits of these products are. A motivated, knowledgeable employee becomes an effective marketing tool when facing an inquiring guest. The typical hospitality organization should recognize that not only does everyone 'sell', but that it must engage its employees on several psychological levels to achieve the greatest results. Using state of the art videos, music, 'tasting parties', incentive programmes and other types of interactive media to grab employees' attentions, are some other recent ideas on how to engage and reach younger employees.

Instituting a positive reward and recognition system for employees is not a recent idea. Many organizations have had reward programmes in place for a number of years. What is new is that there is a recent movement to direct the focus of the reward from being associated with 'control' items (e.g., cost controls, labour controls, maintenance/repair controls) to customer oriented, service parameters. The true leaders in customer service organizations recognize and reward employees for delivering outstanding customer satisfaction (Schneider, 1994). Plaques, prizes and trophies are awarded to those employees that go above and beyond the regular service standards to ensure that their guests receive excellent service. Often times, recipients of these awards have been faced with making difficult decisions regarding customer service. Should they have responded by doing what was best or 'right' for the guest? Or, should they have responded by staying within the confines of their organizational guidelines? Employees who respond by delivering extraordinary service in unusual situations win more than guest satisfaction and approval.

Highly satisfied guests are motivated to speak volumes of praise about the organization and its employees. Sometimes outstanding service is reported in the news media. Whole public relations campaigns are founded on one supposedly small act. News commentator Paul Harvey still relates his favourite customer service story every so often over ten years of his news broadcast. It involves then Soviet President Mikel Gorbachov, a Cincinnati Hotel, a bellman, Mr. Gorbachov's only pair of pants (in need of a pressing) and a dinner-speaking engagement within the hour. As time quickly slipped away, the bellman who had taken President Gorbachov's pants to housekeeping for the pressing realized that Mr. Gorbachov had to leave immediately in order to make his important speaking engagement. The bellman noted that they were about the same height and size. Without hesitating, he offered his own pants to Mr. Gorbachov. Mr. Gorbachov gladly accepted, went on to make his speech and later personally thanked the bellman. Of course, when the story hit the media everyone thought that it was a perfect solution and a brilliant political move. The bellman received recognition from the hotel, but it was minimal compared to the amount of praise and respect that the bellman received from the many agencies and people who responded with calls, cards and letters of appreciation. The reward system in organizations sometimes does not match the level of sacrifice from the employee. But sometimes the intrinsic rewards are immeasurable and fit the act better. Of course, one must remember that without extraordinary service there cannot be extraordinary rewards.

SUMMARY

The purpose of this chapter was to clarify the roles of marketing and service delivery systems within the quality framework and to highlight the components of quality service and guest satisfaction programmes which have been successfully implemented in the hospitality industry. As evidenced, marketing strategy today mandates a focus on the customer. Yet without a good service delivery system, a hospitality company cannot hope to promote itself as differentiated on the service quality attribute.

Developing and implementing a good delivery system requires a great deal of commitment, effort and creative endeavour, from management and top leadership. Management first needs to develop an eye for examining the product and service offerings from the customer's point of view. Then management needs to create the maximum value in the eyes of the customer for the service that they are offering. The 'value engineering' process takes much devotion and creativity, but, when successfully employed, it will allow the hospitality operator to enhance service quality and guest satisfaction. It is important for management to constantly listen to the customer through just-in-time market research and customer feedback systems and, to make the necessary adjustments in their service delivery systems, before promoting on the basis of quality. Ideally, management needs to be open-minded in their thought processes, as illustrated by the case study examples of Taco Bell and Ritz-Carlton. When necessary, management needs to make adjustments and shift the paradigm of thinking to embrace new concepts and ideas from the quality framework. Employing appropriate technology, whether that be hardware or software, is the next most important step in developing a successful service delivery system. Finally, a service quality enhancement programme requires the creation of a service oriented culture within the organization that is upheld with good internal marketing practices.

REFERENCES

Bennett, P.D. (1988) *Dictionary of Marketing Terms*. Chicago, Ill.: American Marketing Association, p. 114.

Bowen, J. (1994). *Achieving Service Quality through Customer Satisfaction*, an unpublished monograph.

Burger King Opens Customer Hot Line (1990) *Marketing News*, May 28. p. 7.

Buttle, F. (1992). The marketing strategy worksheet: A practical tool, *Cornell Hotel and Restaurant Administration Quarterly*, 33, no. 3 , pp. 55–67.

Camp, R. C., (1989), *Benchmarking,* Milwaukee: Quality Press.

Great Expectations – Hotel Company of the Year (1994). *Hospitality Design*, 16 (11), December, pp. 18–23.

Hammer, M. and Chappy, J. (1993). *Reengineering the Corporation*. New York: Harper Business, Division of Harper Collins, pp. 171–181.

Hart, C.W.L. (1988) The power of unconditional service guarantees, *Harvard Business Review*, July-August, pp. 54–62.

Kotler, P., Bowen, J. and Makens, J. (1996). *Marketing for Hospitality and Tourism*, Englewood Cliffs, New Jersey: Prentice-Hall, pp. 315–339.

McGaw, R. (1990) Pizza Hut's Plan. *News-Journal*, Nov. 17, Section B, 5.

Partlow, C. (1993) How Ritz-Carlton Applies TQM, *Cornell Hotel and Restaurant Administration Quarterly*, August, pp. 16–21.

Parasuraman, A., Zeithaml, V.A. and Berry, L.L. (1988) SERVQUAL: A Multiple-Item Scale for Measuring Consumer Perceptions of Service Quality, *Journal of Retailing*, 64, 1 (Spring).

Pope, N.W. (1979) Mickey Mouse Marketing, *American Banker*, July 25.

Pope, N.W. (1979) More Mickey Mouse Marketing, *American Banker*, September 12.

Porter, M. E. (1980).*Competitive Strategy: Techniques for Analyzing Industries and Competitors*, New York: The Free Press, pp. 7–29.

Rapp, S. and Collins, T.L. (1987) *MaxiMarketing*. New York: McGraw-Hill, p. 49.

Schneider, B., Gunnarson, S. K. and Niles-Jolly, K. (1994) Creating the Climate and Culture of Success, *Organizational Dynamics*, 23 (1), pp. 17–29.

Walton, M. (1986).*The Deming Management Method*, New York: The Putnam Publishing Company, pp. 70–71.

Wagner, G. (1994) Satisfaction Guaranteed, *Lodging Hospitality*, 50 (6), June, pp. 46–47.

Zeithaml, V.A. and Bitner, M.J. (1996). *Services Marketing*, New York: McGraw-Hill, p. 457.

Zikmund, W.G. and d'Amico, M. (1996), *Marketing,* St. Paul, MN: West Publishing Company, p. 108.

10

Information Systems Planning

Daniel J. Connolly and Michael D. Olsen

There is nothing more difficult to take in hand, more perilous to conduct, or more uncertain in its success, than to take the lead in the introduction of a new order of things.

Niccolò Machiavelli, The Prince

INTRODUCTION

Today's environment is increasing in complexity and is constantly changing with the introduction of new information systems and computer-based technology. Technology, in one form or another, has crept into almost all facets of everyday life. The use of technology in homes, education and the workplace has grown exponentially over the past decade, often altering the way society behaves and impacting many of the services and amenities that travellers have grown to expect in hotels. Today, personal computers, cellular telephones, fax machines and Internet access are part of the standard cadre of tools for a large percentage of the population, both within and outside of the workplace. It is technologies like these, coupled with advances in telecommunications, that make the world a smaller place to live and do business.

By taking advantage of technology, hotels can access new markets, develop new services, or enhance existing services. The increased power of the personal computer, the creativity of software developers and the declining costs of computers and technology, have made it possible to automate business processes and services within hotels and restaurants that were never before considered. To a large extent, these advances are now redefining how business is being conducted throughout the world. The opportunities to apply computerization in the hospitality industry (or any industry for that matter) is limited only by one's imagination – and a good information systems plan.

For the hospitality industry, the application of computers and information systems are important as a competitive method, for they play a crucial role in service delivery, product differentiation and organizational economics. To be effective as a competitive method, these computer-based systems must be built upon a comprehensive information systems architecture. Up to now, the hospitality industry has not embraced information systems planning. Information systems planning is a methodical process that looks at an organization's goals and objectives, studies the business plan and develops a strategy to apply information technology or computer-based systems to support the organization in executing its business plan. Information systems planning involves researching and experimenting with new technologies and applications and helping the organization prepare for their implementation (McFarlan *et al.*, 1983). It is basically an exercise in predicting and planning for the future so that the proper people and financial resources can be allocated and so that the organization can quickly and easily adapt to a changing environment, while minimizing any adverse impacts to the organization. The purpose of this chapter is to explain the process of information systems planning and how it relates to business planning, so that hotel companies can maximize the benefits received from their information systems, achieve competitive advantage and survive in dynamic, uncertain times. After reading this chapter, you should have a clear understanding of the information systems planning process, the significance of such an effort, the steps involved and how to conduct a systems planning effort.

The hospitality industry, like most other industries, has grown to depend upon information technology in order to carry out the day-to-day operations of the business. Through sophisticated reservation systems, hotel operators have been able to reach larger markets, collect better guest information and deliver more personalized and more consistent service. Property management systems have streamlined the check-in and check-out processes, improved the accuracy of guest records and improved the collection of revenue. Marketing information systems have enhanced guest tracking, guest recognition and guest loyalty, while revenue (yield) management systems have strengthened hotel profits through the development of better controls on room inventory and more formalized selling strategies. Throughout the hotel industry, there are many examples like those cited above, where computers and information-based systems are essential in supporting the daily operations and delivery of guest services. These applications have become fairly commonplace and are very essential in this business. However, the degree of integration of these applications (or information sharing) is limited, thus reducing their overall effectiveness in providing benefits to the hotel operation. The reason for this shortcoming is due in part to the lack of a common information systems architecture focusing on the needs of the customer.

Information systems are complex in nature and as such, they must be carefully thought-out if they are to be successful in serving guest needs. They cannot be implemented haphazardly. Organizations that implement technology without rhyme or reason will find themselves with more problems than solutions. Their information systems will be incomplete and unable to share important information from one process to another (e.g., reservations and check-in). Today, disparate systems or 'islands of information' are all too common throughout the hotel industry and they create a void in the service delivery process that is easily detected by guests. With a good information systems plan, organizations can take a much more methodical approach to their investment in information systems. In return, they will find more seamless integration between applications and better flow between processes. The net effect will be better and more consistent guest service.

A HISTORICAL PERSPECTIVE OF THE USE OF INFORMATION SYSTEMS IN THE HOSPITALITY INDUSTRY

The first real computer-based applications were introduced to the business world in the early 1960s on very large, expensive mainframe computers. Initial applications were accounting-related and involved highly repetitive tasks such as payroll processing, accounts payable and general ledger. The main focus was on control, improved accuracy through machine calculations rather than by people and cost savings through labour reductions. However, the cost of computer technology (both hardware and software) limited its use to only large organizations that could leverage the cost over multiple divisions. It was not until the 1970s and early 1980s that companies began to apply technology with a more operational and strategic focus. Also around this time, the price of technology began declining with the introduction of mid-range systems and personal computers, making it more affordable for use in smaller organizations. During the 1980s and 1990s, personal computers proliferated throughout the business world (and home market) and connectivity through modems, local area networks and wide area networks set the wheels in motion for the 'information age' that describes the present-day use of computers in society.

Use of technology in the hospitality industry followed a similar life cycle as illustrated in Figure 10.1; however, even to this day, it tends to lag behind other industries – sometimes by ten years or more. For example, automated reservation systems became popular in the airline industry in the late 1960s and early 1970s with the introduction of American Airlines' SABRE system and United Airline's Apollo system. It was not until the mid-1980s that computer-based reservation systems were introduced in the hospitality industry, with many of the large chains like Holiday Inns, Sheraton and Marriott. At the time, only the large chains could afford the high cost of reservation systems and the mainframe computers required to run this application.

Yield management is another example. Airlines began using sophisticated information systems to allocate seat inventory and discounted rates based on supply and demand patterns during the late 1970s. It was not until the early 1990s that this type of application was introduced to the world of hotels. Bar coding, voice mail, satellite communications and decision support systems, are just a few other examples of technologies that found their way to the hospitality industry long after being used by other industries. Figure 10.1 depicts the evolution of technology in the hospitality industry. It further illustrates the pattern of technology applications and how they initially focused on repetitive, clerical functions to improve financial controls and accuracy. Over time, the focus changed to more of a strategic focus, as the cost of computerization declined, as users became more comfortable with using computers, and as managers began to recognize the role of technology as a tool that could enable them to work more efficiently and make better, more informed decisions.

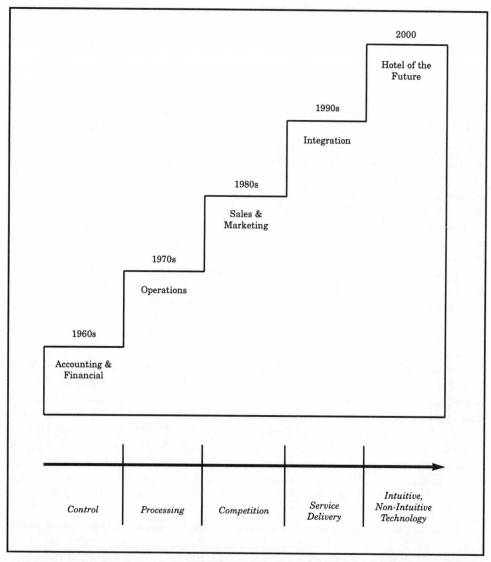

Source: *Looking Forward: A Management Perspective of Technology in the Lodging Industry,* Andersen Consulting and AH&MA, 1989.

Figure 10.1: Evolution of Technology in the Hospitality Industry

Based on the types of software applications and computer technologies available in the marketplace today, however, the use of computers and information systems within the hospitality industry is not as sophisticated as it could be. As previously stated, the application of technology within the hospitality industry has typically followed other industries. The reasons for this are many, but perhaps the most significant is how information systems were first introduced to the hospitality industry. Since the introduction of computer-based applications was piecemeal, hotel organizations found themselves somewhat constrained in terms the ability of their core applications to share information. There was no all encompassing plan or grand scheme as to how the different systems tied together. Little thought had been given to the entire guest life cycle and the services required to fulfil each stage of the life cycle. Furthermore, the applications were not entirely guest focused. They were traditionally centred around supporting or expediting processes or transactions that were handled manually. As a hotel's investment in technology grew with the implementation of more information systems, the problem of dissimilar systems became more pronounced. Meanwhile, executives grew to expect more from these new systems because of the large sums of money invested. Needless to say, they were often disenchanted in the benefits achieved by the organization, because many of the systems implemented were incompatible and required duplicate data entry. Moreover, recent technology failures in the industry by well-known companies (e.g., the CONFIRM project, a partnership between AMR, Hilton Hotels, Marriott and Budget Rent-A-Car) prolonged scepticism and cautious attitudes towards technology, when considering the value versus the risks and high costs. As a result of such frustration, executives were somewhat reluctant to invest further in technology or new applications until they could see a more definite payback. Because of the cautious attitude held by many hotel executives, the advancement of information systems in the hotel industry was repressed until a particular technology or application was observed and proven in other industries.

The adaptation of computers in the hospitality industry was slowed further by a certain stigma traditionally associated with them: impersonalization. It was often thought that the use of computers in hotels would depersonalize the service provided to guests, because of the loss of eye contact and because computers typically index information by a unique record number rather than a guest's name. Hoteliers had great difficulty in conceptualizing how a computer could 'think' as well as an individual, particularly in an environment where each guest encounter is unique. Because of these factors, the progress in hotel technology has been incremental rather than revolutionary. But now, the rapid pace of technological developments in both the business and home markets and the declining costs of computer hardware, are changing how computers are perceived in the hotel industry and the role they can play in enhancing service delivery. Service providers are now recognizing technology as a tool and an enabler in providing personalized, consistent service delivery in an environment that is plagued by high employee turnover, increasing labour costs and more requests from the guests during their hotel visits and as such, they are trying to play 'catch-up' with the technologies available in today's marketplace.

Today, the trend toward using automation in the hospitality industry is finally reversing. As Figure 10.2 illustrates, there are many environmental events that are creating a need to rethink the role information technology can play in the hospitality industry. The scarcity of resources (both people and capital), the increased industry competition and the more sophisticated traveller, make it essential for hotel operators to seek new avenues to provide better, faster and cheaper services and accommodations. With increased global competition, hoteliers must look for new methods to attract and retain guests. Information systems is one approach that offers great promise, particularly as the US lodging industry spends millions of dollars each year on information systems and technology to find ways to enhance the guest stay and to reduce overheads (Quek, 1995). Such investments in technology indicates a significant commitment and a belief in the power information systems has to transform the hospitality industry. It also underscores the need for information systems planning within hospitality organizations.

WHY PLAN?

To paraphrase Lewis Carroll in his book *Alice in Wonderland*, if you do not know where you are going, any road will get you there. As a corollary, if you do not know where you are going, you will not know when you get there. It is important for an organization to have a good sense of vision that outlines the future direction of the company and its information systems. This advice holds true with any type of planning effort and emphasizes the need for a good plan – whether it be a business plan, information systems plan, or marketing plan. To support this notion, Gary Hamel and C. K. Prahalad (1994) suggest that if senior managers are not spending the majority of their time focusing on the future, they are not doing their jobs and their companies will be unable to sustain market leadership. Goldberg and Sifonis (1994), Theobald (1994) and Tombazian (1994) suggest that strategic/visionary planning is critical to an organization's ability to manage change and grow in the future. Bates (1985) and West and Olsen (1988) note that organizations taking the time to scan the environment and plan strategies tend to outperform those who are less structured in their planning efforts.

With technology and the capabilities of computers changing so quickly, it is critical for organizations of any kind, regardless of the particular industry in which it competes, to develop an information systems plan or road map that allows them to chart a course of action for the implementation of future business applications and information systems. These applications and information systems should support the mission of the business and can, in many cases, drive the business to new heights or assist in establishing the business strategy. Companies need a unified strategy that details their investments in technology, ensures systems integration and aligns technology spending and development with the organization's goals, objectives and strategies. It is important that organizations work to avoid creating 'islands of information' and implementing technologies that will limit the organization's growth potential or ability to quickly adjust to dynamic business conditions.

Technology is ever-changing and becomes obsolete so quickly. Therefore, when selecting and implementing information systems and computer hardware, organizations must consider flexibility, support/maintainability, stability, impact on the organization and its staff, integration to existing systems, migration paths to newer technologies and return on investment. Paramount to all of these

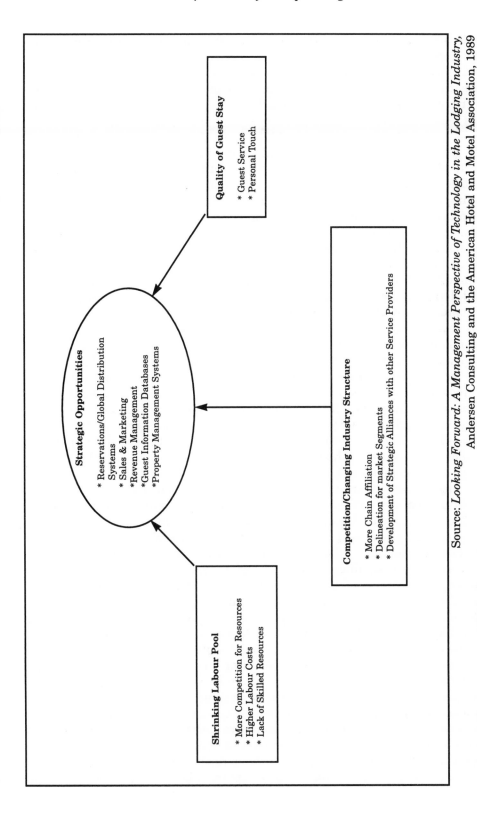

Source: *Looking Forward: A Management Perspective of Technology in the Lodging Industry,*
Andersen Consulting and the American Hotel and Motel Association, 1989

Figure 10.2: Forces Driving Technology Investment

considerations is the needs of the customer. After all, that is why a company is in business.

The need for information systems planning has long been recognized by information systems professionals and academicians alike. In fact, it is frequently cited in surveys, research articles and trade journals as one of the top issues facing information systems professionals (Sprague and McNurlin, 1986; Lederer and Sethi, 1988; Spewak, 1993; Liao, 1994; Laberis, 1994; Dreyfuss, 1995). Research by Pyburn (1983) and Raghunathan and King (1988), as cited in Liao (1994), suggests that the changing role of information systems has heightened the awareness and importance of information systems planning and that planning is considered to be one of the most significant factors impacting information systems performance within organizations. Business environments are becoming more complex, global in nature and fiercely competitive. With computer hardware becoming faster, cheaper, more reliable and portable and software applications becoming more capable, flexible, user friendly and more widely available (off-the-shelf), end users are demanding more from their organizations' information resources. Data is now recognized as a corporate asset and the user community wants more and faster access to this data. In addition, technology is more likely to support critical points of customer contact (Mills, 1986; Caldwell and DePompa, 1995).

Hagmann (1994) suggests that effective information systems planning can assist organizations in exploiting opportunities created by technological change and innovations while reducing the likelihood of any problems or threats resulting from new technologies. McFarlan *et al.* (1983) identified four primary events driving information systems planning in organizations. First, are the rapid advances being observed with the technology itself. With the speed in which new technologies (software and hardware) are introduced, it is difficult at best to stay current. Organizations risk technical obsolescence. Gone are the days of the legacy mainframe systems that had useful lives of fifteen or more years. Today, the useful life of most PC-based technologies and applications is three years or less. The second factor driving information systems planning is the scarcity of resources, both people and capital. With recent downsizing and the financial hardships experienced by the hotel industry in 1990 and 1991, hotel organizations have suffered significant cutbacks and are constantly being challenged to do more with less – to squeeze more productivity out of their budgets. Information systems are playing a key role in filling this void.

A third factor is the need for better integrated systems. As noted previously in this chapter, the degree of disparate or incompatible systems in the hospitality industry is problematic and, become more acute, as departments implement information systems, without first consulting the company's information systems department. Information systems are infiltrating all levels and aspects of the organization. As computers becomes cheaper and as users become more knowledgeable about their use, the technology purchase decisions are often being made by end users rather than members of the organization's information systems staff. In fact, the cost of personal computers and software today has dropped enough such that many hotel general managers and perhaps some department managers, can authorize computer-related purchases from their own budgets without the capital expenditure approvals that were traditionally required. Consequently, the purchase decision is based mostly on price and the resulting product may or may not be consistent with the organization's information systems plan. As a result, support costs tend to increase and compatibility issues arise, thereby creating complex challenges for an organization's management information systems department. However, as organizations become more dependent upon technology applications to run their operations and to communicate with their employees and customers, this behaviour must be minimized, so that the organization can truly leverage its information systems resources. To that end, organizations need technical direction and guidance. Hence, information systems planning is going to be essential. Last but not least is the importance of linking information systems strategies and directions to those of the corporation. Organizations are looking at how to grow, expand into new markets, cut costs and preserve and protect their existing assets – including their technology assets.

While absence of information systems planning may not necessarily lead an organization to total chaos, it can create many organizational difficulties and costly challenges that could otherwise be avoided. At the very least, there is likely to be unlike hardware and software applications that will be unable to communicate with one another, creating frustration throughout the organization, thereby limiting its ability to operate or implement chain-wide programmes. In essence, it is likely that companies will not be able to take full advantage of their information systems due to incompatible technologies and their inability to implement common strategies throughout the entire company.

In the hospitality industry, this concept can best be illustrated by looking at the lodging concepts under Marriott International's umbrella. Standardization of information systems has afforded the company opportunities to establish consistent services, amenities and marketing promotions, with relative ease compared to other chains. For example, because Marriott had a standardized property management system in all of its full-service hotels, the company could quickly implement video check-out in all of its hotels throughout the world, while other companies struggled to develop interfaces to multiple property management systems. The company could also share guest information between properties to enhance guest recognition and reward frequent travellers with special upgrades. Conversely, Holiday Inn had difficulty in implementing new selling strategies for guest rooms and checking availability at many of the properties in its portfolio, because of the heterogeneity of its property management systems. As a result, the corporate office financed the rollout of a standard property management system that enabled the company to implement chain-wide programmes and improve consistency throughout its organization. The project was costly, but the lesson observed is extremely valuable in underscoring the criticality of information systems planning.

In summary, the real thrust of information systems planning, as summarized in Figure 10.3, is:

* to provide competitive methods that will enhance guest service and strengthen guest loyalty by creating more personalized service or higher switching costs;

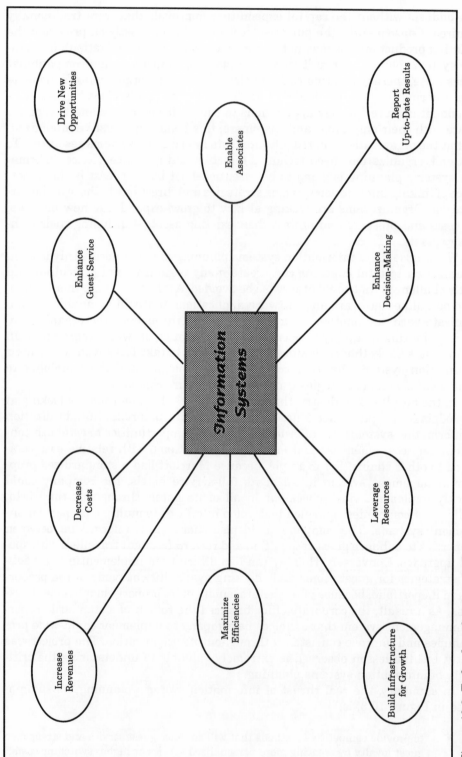

Figure 10.3: Technology Serving the Business

- establish consistency and integration so that resources can be leveraged throughout the organization;
- drive revenue through new business opportunities;
- decrease operating expenses to improve the overall cost structure of the firm through economies-of-scale or product synergies;
- provide employees and decision-makers with the tools needed to effectively and efficiently carry out their responsibilities; and
- support the organization's corporate mission.

The underlying theme is that information systems are the foundation on which all other activity of the organization stems. Information systems are so widespread throughout organizations that a key dependency has been formed. No longer can information systems be separated from the business decisions and day-to-day operations of the business. There is an interdependent relationship (Henderson and Thomas, 1992) that must be recognized if an organization is to take full advantage of its information systems when charting its future course. As Gorry and Morton (1989) so eloquently point out, if there is no framework to direct managers and systems planners, the information systems direction of the organization is likely to follow the direction of those who scream the loudest. The result is nothing but one crisis after another.

WHAT IS INFORMATION SYSTEMS PLANNING?

Before going further, it is important to note what information systems planning is not. It is *not* business re-engineering. The two are frequently used interchangeably and mistaken to mean the same thing. While information systems planning can play an important role in business re-engineering, the concepts and goals are very different from those found in information systems planning. Business re-engineering, as defined by Hammer and Champy (1993) is the process of starting over. It is the ***fundamental*** rethinking and ***radical*** redesign *of business **processes** to achieve **dramatic** improvements in critical, contemporary measures of performance, such as cost, quality, service and speed.* This distinction is mentioned here in passing so as to avoid any confusion when trying to develop an information systems plan, or misunderstanding as to the impact or expected results from the information systems planning effort.

In looking at the definition of information systems planning, it is helpful to first understand the concept of strategic planning. The body of literature reveals that there is a lack of agreement as to the precise definitions for strategic planning and information systems planning. In fact, there is not even agreement as to what these processes should be called. In simplest terms, strategic planning can be defined *as the process of determining the long-term vision and goals of an enterprise and how to fulfil them* (Bean, 1993). Similarly, Gorry and Morton (1989) define strategic planning as the process of setting broad goals and policies for a firm. Liao (1994) describes planning as a complex, multidimensional concept which varies based on the time horizon, the level in the organization where the planning takes place and the objectives of management. McFarlan,

McKenney and Pyburn (1983) add that the type and degree of planning depend on the sophistication of an organization, the knowledge level and experience of its employees (particularly those performing the planning function), the scope of the planning effort and business factors such as size of the organization, nature of its business, organizational complexity, etc. In defining information systems planning, Liao calls upon a definition established by Lederer and Sethi (1988):

> Information systems planning is the process of identifying a portfolio of computer-based applications that will assist an organization in executing its business plans and realizing its business goals.

Hagmann (1994) defines information systems planning as the process of defining a vision for the role of information systems within an organization and any potential opportunities to apply information systems and technology to support business strategies. According to Henderson and Thomas (1992), there is general agreement among academicians that business and information systems strategies should be linked, since they are interdependent and since the role of information systems has emerged as a significant ingredient in defining and executing the business strategy. Moreover, it recognized that planning is an ongoing process that requires constant monitoring, validation and fine-tuning.

The desired outcome of information systems planning is a better use of information systems and computerization throughout the organization and the key to effective information systems planning, is to understand the business environment and the impact of information systems at the task level. Successful planners anticipate new trends so that an appropriate strategy can be formulated and implemented in a timely fashion. To do this, they develop multiple, 'what-if' scenarios for each environmental event and the probabilities of each event occurring, so as to have multiple courses of action to prevent getting trapped in an undesirable situation (Dill, 1958; Child, 1972; Duncan, 1972; Parsons, 1983; Slattery and Olsen, 1984; Bates, 1985; Jackson and Dutton, 1988).

STRUCTURED INFORMATION SYSTEMS PLANNING METHODOLOGIES

There is no shortage of formal systems planning methodologies in the literature. In fact, research by Hagmann (1994) suggests that there are well over 40 different methodologies widely recognized throughout the literature. Figure 10.4 lists twenty of the more commonly recognized approaches to information systems planning. Hagmann's research, however, shows that most organizations use either their own methodology or no formal methodology at all. She suggests that the reasons for this are due to management's unfamiliarity or limited understanding of these planning approaches, the inability for these methodologies to address an organization's needs and management's lack of responsiveness or unawareness to the needs of aligning its systems applications with the organization itself. Spewak (1993) advises anyone preparing to undertake a planning effort to first review the different methodologies and determine what approach or approaches would best serve his/her particular organization. Perhaps the real conclusion to Hagmann's study is that most firms create their own systems planning methodology based on what they perceive to be the best of each methodology, thereby creating a hybrid of activities suggested by each approach.

Methodology	Author(s)
* Business Systems Planning	* IBM
* Critical Success Factors	* Rockart
* Strategy Set Transformation	* King
* Business Information Analysis and Integration Techniques	* Burnstein and Carlson
* Ends/Means Analysis	* Wetherbe and Davis
* Strategic Data Planning	* Martin
* Information Engineering	* Martin, Finkelstein and Others
* Strategic Systems Planning and Tactical Systems Planning	* Holland
* Systems Architecture and Investment Strategy	* Nolan and Norton
* Master Planning	* Atkinson
* Strategic Value Analysis	* Curtice
* Information Systems Architecture	* Inmon
* Enterprise Information Management	* Parker
* Method/1	* Andersen Consulting
* Value Chain Analysis	* Porter
* Enterprise Architecture Planning	* Spewak
* Information Quality Analysis	* Vacca
* Business Information Characterization Study	* Kerner
* Portfolio Management	* McFarlan

Source: Lederer and Sethi (1988) and Spewak (1993)

Figure 10.4: Common Systems Planning Methodologies

To illustrate the types of practices typically found in formal information systems planning methodologies, three of the more well-known approaches are outlined below. These three methodologies are fairly representative of those used in business practice today. By providing a sampling of the different approaches, one can get a flavour of the different techniques and have an opportunity to select what he/she sees as 'best practices' for his/her organization. When looking at each method, one will note several similarities when conducting an information systems planning process. There are also significant differences in the methodologies which stem largely from the creator's philosophy as to the importance of data versus business processes. Within information systems planning, there are basically two schools of thought. One approach suggests that data is the most important component of the plan and as such, an organization's need for data or information should drive the planning process and the subsequent information systems. An alternative perspective is that business processes should define the information systems used by an organization. By understanding the steps involved in each of the many processes that are required by an organization, one can define and implement information systems that serve the activities of the business. There is no right or wrong answer as to which approach one should use. The decision should be based largely on the value the organization places on data and business processes. Both approaches have merits and deficiencies. What seems to be lacking, however, in both approaches is a true focus on the customer and ways to add value to an organization's customers. This topic will be revisited later in this chapter because it has far-reaching implications within the service industry.

Business Systems Planning (BSP)

Business systems planning was the first structured information systems planning methodology developed by IBM during the 1960s (Davenport, 1994). It was developed during the age of the mainframe, long before the personal computer was even conceptualized and has its underpinnings in a manufacturing environment. Today, however, it is perhaps the most widely used and recognized approach to information systems planning, even in the service industry. In fact, this methodology is generally the basis from which all other methodologies were developed. BSP involves a top-down planning approach with a bottom-up implementation. The founding principle behind this methodology is that data is a corporate resource and should be managed from an overall corporate perspective if it is to best serve the company (IBM, 1984). The intent is to establish a stable, enterprise-wide information structure, that will support all aspects of the business. This methodology attempts to link the information systems planning process with the business planning process in a unidirectional mode, as illustrated in Figure 10.5, by having the information systems planning team fully understand the organization's business plan as part of the process of defining the information systems plan.

When following this method, a company looks at its corporate mission, objectives and functions, to determine its business processes. Data requirements to support these processes are then assessed and grouped into data classes or entities. Finally, the information architecture (in essence a series of entity-relationship diagrams that illustrate the data required to support each process of the business) is defined and a corresponding implementation plan is established for developing information systems that will support the needs of the business. In total, there are 13 steps to the BSP approach. These steps are outlined in Figure 10.6.

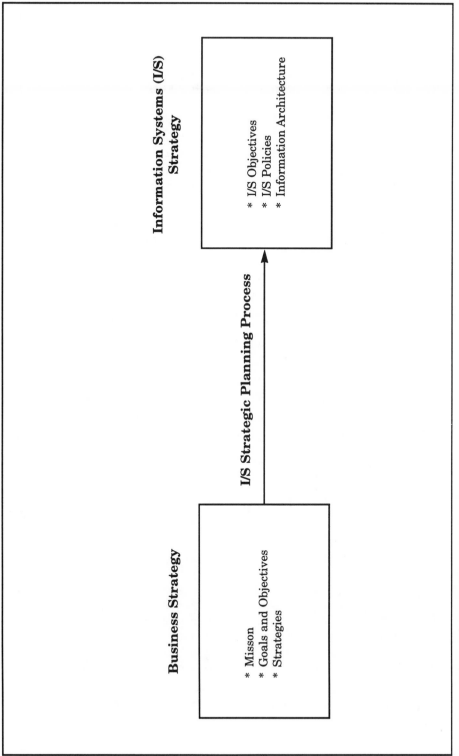

Figure 10.5: IBMs BSP Methodology Linking Business Strategies and Information Systems Strategies

(1) **Gaining commitment:** The success of BSP, or any planning methodology for that matter, requires commitment and sponsorship form all levels of the organization, particularly senior management.

(2) **Preparing for the Planning Effort:** This step of the process is important for laying the initial groundwork to kick-off the plan. It involves staffing and scheduling, the establishment of the project scope and planning horizon and the development of the project work plan.

(3) **Commencing the Study:** Typically, an initial kick-off meeting is scheduled with the project team and sponsors to introduce the planning effort, purpose and goals of the effort, the scope of the project, major milestones, the methods to be used in completing the study and the critical success factors of the project.

(4) **Defining the Business Process:** The project team identifies all of the business processes supported by the organization such as accounting, marketing, reservations, purchasing, guest registration, etc. This is typically done by studying organizational charts and creating a functional decomposition of the organization. This step is critical in the overall process as it serves as the foundation of the executive interviews, the information architecture, the date analysis and other follow-on activities.

(5) **Defining Business Data:** Once the business processes or applications needs are identified, the project team begins the define all of the data required to support these processes. After the data has been defined, it is grouped into logical groupings called classes or entities. These entities serve to show relationships between data used throughout the organization and will become the basis for any future database design work. The focus in this step is to ensure that all data needs have been identified, to understand what parts of the organization need what data and to reduce any duplication in data.

(6) **Defining the Information Architecture:** In this step, the relationship between data classes, processes and the organization are defined. During this stage in the process, the fucus is on data sharing. This step also helps to set priorities for the implementation of the proposed architecture.

Figure 10.6(A): IBMs Business Systems Planning Methodology

Source: IBM, 1984

(7) **Analysing Current Systems Support:** During this step, the current and planned systems are analyzed to illustrate how well they are supporting the business processes identified in step four above.

(8) **Interviewing Executives:** The company's senior management is interviewed to verify any organizational assumptions made during the planning process and to validate the business processes and data classes defined in steps five and six above. In addition, the executives are asked for their insight and perspectives on future directions of the company and the information they need to do their jobs. This step also helps in gaining executive support by involving them in the actual planning process.

(9) **Defining Findings and Conclusions:** This step in the process involves the synthesis and analysis of all the information collected in the previous steps. The focus is on recognizing any problems that surfaced, their route causes and viable solutions to correct or eliminate them. At this point in the process, the project team begins to formulate strategies and recommendations.

(10) **Establishing Architecture Priorities:** As part of the recommendations identified in the prior step, a list of projects and initiatives is developed. These projects must be rank ordered based on, a needs assessment, benefits, impact to the organization, cost, time to development/implement and available funding.

(11) **Reviewing Information Resource Management:** During this phase of the process, the organization's policies and procedures with respect to information systems are reviewed and revised to support the new architectural directions developed.

(12) **Developing Recommendations:** The recommendations from the planning effort are finalized and an implementation plan is established. This implementation plan addresses the next steps and in particular, how to go about implementing the newly defined plan.

(13) **Reporting Results:** Once the final recommendations and implementation plans are prepared, they need to be presented to senior management and the project sponsor(s) for their review and approval. The results of the planning effort should be presented in the form of a written report and an oral presentation summarizing the project team's findings and recommendations.

Figure 10.6(B): IBMs Business Systems Planning Methodology

Source: IBM, 1984

Enterprise Architecture Planning (EAP)

Spewak (1993) defines enterprise architecture as 'the process of defining architectures for the use of information in support of the business and the plan for implementing those architectures.' The main focus of enterprise architecture planning is the development of three models to describe an organization's data, applications and technology needs. The scope of this effort is generally the entire organization and the primary goal is to provide quality data to those who need it. This seven-step approach outlined in Figure 10.7 assesses an organization's current state, its desired state and the effort required to transition the organization to where it wants to be.

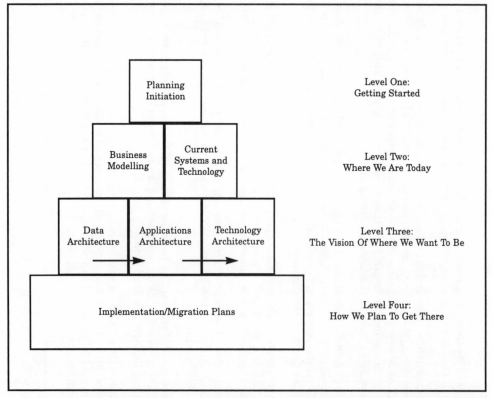

Source: Spewak, 1993

Figure 10.7: Seven Steps to Enterprise Architecture Planning

Enterprise architecture planning borrows extensively from traditional systems planning methodologies such as IBM's Business Systems Planning and the Zachman Framework (Zachman, 1987). The Zachman Framework is a six-level model used for defining architectures based on different analytical views. To explain this framework, Zachman uses an analogy of building a house. The design and construction of a house involves a multi-step process involving several different players and each player (e.g., owner, architect, builder, etc.) brings a particular perspective to the table. With each perspective comes the need for different levels of detail. In this house example, the level of detail required by an owner is far less than that required by the builder. In the Zachman Framework, these different perspectives are each given a name indicative of the level of detail required. These perspectives include the ballpark view (the scope and description), the owner's view (the model of the business), the designer's view (the model of the information systems), the builder's view (the technology model), the out-of-context view (the detailed description) and the actual system. The second item of significance in the Zachman Framework is the distinction of the three architectures that make up EAP: data, process (application) and network (technology). EAP uses the first two levels of the Zachman model (the ballpark view and the owner's view) to establish a conceptual framework. The third level of his model goes beyond the scope of EAP since it gets more involved with systems design and away from the planning aspects.

Where EAP differs from other planning methodologies is that it tends to concentrate more heavily on data and the business versus processes and technology. Spewak highlights four major differences between EAP versus more traditional planning methodologies:

1) A functional business model is the premise of EAP, for it is the knowledge base of the organization. The focus in preparing this model is to understand what the business is and what information is essential to support or run it. It is less concerned with what systems executives would like to see and what the organization's critical success factors are because, in Spewak's estimation, these tend to create a short-term focus rather than a more long-term vision;

2) Data is defined before the applications. This is the antithesis of more traditional systems planning methodologies. They tend to define the applications needed by the organization first and then the data necessary to support these applications. In EAP, the data architecture model is defined first for all aspects of the organization. The applications architecture is then defined. The goal is to create cross-functional systems that allow sharing of data across departmental boundaries rather than 'stovepipe' systems;

3) Data dependencies define the implementation plan. Project priorities are established by the data needed by the organization. The basic premise behind this approach is to develop applications that create the data before developing applications that need to use the data;

4) Both short-term operational needs and long-term strategies are considered.

The final product is a long-term plan that describes the implementation of the architectures defined. In essence, the developed model or set of models becomes a blueprint or set of instructions which must be followed when carrying out the plan.

Critical Success Factors

Understanding the information requirements of any organization is critical in any information systems planning project. One of the frustrations of executives is that they receive too much information yet not enough to assess the health of the organization (Rockart, 1979). To best define the information needs within an organization, Rockart suggests a method called critical success factors. He calls upon the works of D. Ronald Daniels (1961) to support his approach, citing that a company's information system must be 'discriminating and selective' to eliminate distractions so that managers can quickly focus on the key measurements of the organization. Rockart defines critical success factors as *the few key areas where things must go right for the business to flourish*. As such, company management should constantly monitor these factors to determine performance of the organization. To define these critical success factors, a series of meetings is held with different levels of management within the organization. During these meetings, management goals (the results an organization hopes to achieve) and critical success factors (areas in which high-level performance is required if the goals are to be achieved) are defined by focusing on four main sources:

- structure of the industry;
- competitive strategy, industry position and geographic location;
- environmental factors; and
- temporal or internal factors.

For the hospitality industry, critical success factors may include location, fast and friendly service, guest recognition and a powerful, global distribution system.

THE INFORMATION SYSTEMS PLANNING PROCESS FOR THE HOSPITALITY INDUSTRY

As hinted at earlier in this chapter, the information systems planning models presented above were initially developed for manufacturing environments, where the focus was mostly on process and machine technology. Because of this, these frameworks do not adequately address all of the needs of service organizations like hotels. While these methodologies can be adapted to the hospitality industry, there are some inherent weaknesses. The focus of manufacturing is centred almost exclusively on an assembly line where the process is very repetitive and predictable. Mills (1986) points out that technology is critical in the production of goods and services and the type of technology required is dependent upon the degree of interaction with the consumer. He relies on Emery and Trist's (1965) input-output model to illustrate how raw materials are transformed by technology into a final product. A manufacturing environment involves no involvement with the consumer and the raw materials are the ingredients used to manufacture a product. Mills considers this environment very predictable and a prime candidate for machine-based technology. In the hospitality industry (and other service industries), the consumer is involved in the production of the service and the raw material that must be transformed into the delivered products (services) is information about the customer. This 'social' encounter, as Mills terms it, involves a greater degree of unpredictability and is more complex due to concurrent production and consumption and the personalities involved. Schostack (1984) adds that to the customer, people are an essential part of the service delivery process and because of this, there is a greater risk associated in delivering consistent quality. The content and quality of the service delivered will be largely based upon the individuals giving and receiving the services, the time of day and their emotional state. Because each service encounter is truly unique, it is harder to predict each situation and every customer need. As such, Mills suggests that the type of technology needed here is more knowledge-based. By employing knowledge-based systems, an organization can programme routine transactions and scenarios so as to broaden the service employee's repertoire of service skills and techniques (Barrington and Olsen, 1987). Schostack suggests as part of her service blueprint methodology, that during the design stage, one must consider every possible encounter between the consumer and the service provider. This is a very overwhelming task at best, but certainly, many of the more common scenarios can be anticipated.

As indicated earlier, information systems planning processes fall short in the hospitality industry because, the guest is not the focal point of the design. While one could argue that by focusing on an organization's data requirements or business processes, the information systems planning process is inherently addressing the guests' needs. However, one cannot be so certain to make this assumption. There are many business processes that are performed by organizations that support the internal workings of the organization and have nothing at all to do with serving or satisfying the customer. Perhaps these processes add little value to an organization and should be considered for elimination or restructuring. According to a basic finance principle, the goal of an organization is to maximize wealth or increase shareholder value. The best way to do this is to focus on the customer and identify better ways to serve his/her needs.

Other than the need to be customer-driven and how the technology is implemented, the hospitality industry is not all that uncommon when it comes to its need to plan the use of information technologies. The types of applications, the way in which technology is used within the industry and the current state of technology, may be more unique than in other industries, but this is irrespective of the planning process. Characterized by a short-term, operational focus, most hotel organizations lack resources who know how to create a strategic, long-range plan, much less an information systems plan. Plagued by mixed results when it comes to developing and implementing information systems, the industry could benefit from structured information systems planning.

GUIDELINES FOR CONDUCTING AN INFORMATION SYSTEMS PLANNING EFFORT

In the strategy literature, three planning windows are frequently mentioned: strategic, operational and tactical. From an information systems planning perspective, all three apply. At the very least, organizations should maintain a strategic information systems plan and a tactical systems plan. The former is the long-range vision; the latter focuses on the short-term and the actual implementation. By its very nature, a tactical plan is at a much lower, more detailed level than the strategic plan. Its time span is generally one year or less. A strategic information systems plan typically forecasts an organization's needs for three, five, or ten years. The general tendency, however, is to stay within three years because of the difficulties in predicting technology advancements beyond that period. The important thing to consider which is often overlooked is that the planning function is an on-going function. It is not just a snapshot in time. Since the business environment and technology change so quickly, it is important to continually review, validate and modify, the plans so that they are current and useful to the organization. These plans should serve as road maps, outlining future directions to all employees within the company.

In his book *Future Shock*, Alvin Toffler quoted a Chinese proverb, *To prophesy is extremely difficult – especially with respect to the future*. However, the planning process does not have to be perceived as difficult when one uses a very logical approach. It should be noted, however, that the planning process is as much an art as it is a science. The planning method (for business planning or system planning) should address five basic questions based on who, what, when, where and how. These questions are typically incorporated in all types of planning models and are generic to all industries. The questions are the following:

- Where is the organization currently?
- Where does the organization want to be?
- How can the organization get from where it is today to where it wants to be?
- What is the overall cost and timeframe?
- How can technology help?

By exploring each of these questions in more detail, a better understanding of the planning process can be had. The first question looks at a number of key ingredients noted in other planning methodologies. First, there is the notion of understanding the organization, its mission and objectives, its strategic domain and its product offerings more clearly. Knowing the core businesses and the critical success factors for these businesses, is essential when trying to identify information systems needs for an organization. It also essential to understand the company's current information systems and applications portfolio as well as the company's information (data) requirements. Second, this question addresses how the organization fits into its external environment. This involves a complete understanding of any competitor activity taking place, Porter's five forces (Porter, 1980), the remote environment, the task environment and the functional environment (Dill, 1958; Duncan, 1972; Bates, 1985; Mills, 1986; DeNoble and Olsen, 1986). In addition, attention must be given to technology (hardware and software) trends that are happening throughout the business world, not just within the industry itself. Third, this question addresses the organization's strengths and weaknesses, the threats imposed upon the organization, the competitive advantages the firm enjoys and the opportunities for new systems applications or enhancements to current applications.

The second question addresses the organization's future. Based on everything learned in question one, the organization should be able to develop a long-range view of where it should be. Factored into this decision should be organizational needs, industry trends, technology trends and the organization's attitude towards risk. This latter point is of particular importance when considering the role of information technology and specifically what types of technology the firm should implement. Technology has a life cycle (see Figure 10.8) just as consumer products have life cycles from a marketing perspective. The firm's attitude towards risk will determine where the organization wants to be positioned with respect to new, innovative technology or more stable, mature technology. This is true for both hardware and software. To some extent, this touches upon the Miles and Snow framework (1978) of prospectors, defenders, analysers and reactors and how an organization chooses to position itself.

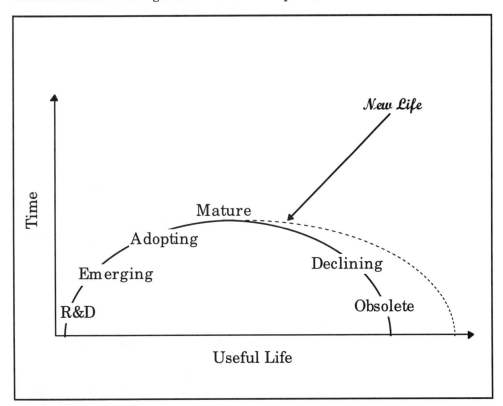

Figure 10.8: Technology Life Cycle

The third question outlines the implementation process or the action plan that will transform the firm from its current position to its desired state. This step, however, is not as easy as it first looks. It involves careful consideration of the resources (people, equipment, office space) required, the timing of events, the project priorities and the impact to the organization. Many firms often underestimate the notion of 'organizational readiness.' Since it is common knowledge that people generally resist change, planners must consider the impact their plans will have on the organization, its workers and its customers. Whether it is generally accepted or not, technology is changing the way people work and interact with one another and to some, this creates anxiety. If an organization wants its plan to be successfully implemented, it must address this issue. After all, a great plan is worthless if it never gets implemented.

The question regarding cost is necessary to satisfy the accountants and senior management. Before any plan can be approved, it is necessary to have a good understanding as to what the overall costs will be and when the expenses will be incurred. What many executives often fail to realize with information planning, is that technology is an asset to the organization and what they are doing is investing in a corporate asset. Traditional executives, especially in the lodging industry, have viewed technology more as an expense. However, technology, like any other asset (land, buildings, equipment, etc.) requires maintenance and continued investment in order to extend its useful life to the organization.

The final question focuses specifically on technology and how it can assist organizations in achieving their objectives. The basic thrust behind this question is that the business planning process and the systems planning process should no longer be done separately, as is typically the case. Management should look to technology to create opportunity, generate new business, or contain costs. It is no longer enough to have technology assume only a supporting role within the organization. Many of the information systems planning methodologies and the research on information systems recognize that there should be some link between the technology plan and the business plan of an organization. However, none go so far as to suggest that the two planning processes should be done in tandem. Itami and Numagami (1992), for example, suggest that the interaction between business strategy and technology strategy has not been enough. They argue that technology is typically considered a constraining factor in determining opportunities for a firm. As an alternative, they suggest three types of relationships between these two processes:

1) The relationship between current business strategy and current technology;
2) The relationship between current business strategy and future technology;
3) The relationship between future business strategy and current technology.

While these three relationships are very important and essential to consider, it could be argued that Itami and Numagami should go one step further to understand the relationship between future business strategy and future technology strategy. It is important to align these two strategies within the same timeframe so that one can actually see how future technologies can impact future business strategies and events. In fact, the model should be taken one step further as Hagmann suggests to include organizational strategic planning in addition to the business systems planning. In summation, since technology, the business and the organization are so interdependent, the strategy processes for each should be interwoven as illustrated in Figure 10.9. Information systems and technology represent the foundation for all aspects of the business. It is impossible to separate the technology from the organization's business processes and just as in any building, if the foundation is weak, the structure built upon it will collapse.

DEFINING AN INFORMATION TECHNOLOGY ARCHITECTURE

The term information technology architecture is becoming more widely used in reference to systems planning. This architecture can be defined as a set of principles, guidelines, or rules used by a company to direct the process of acquiring, building, modifying and interfacing information technology resources (hardware, software, programming environments, communications protocols, operating systems, user interface, database engines, etc.) throughout the organization (Rosser, 1992). When followed, these architectural principles will ensure systems compatibility with the overall systems plan, thereby simplifying systems implementation, integration and support. The significance of architectural principles has become more apparent within the hospitality industry as lodging companies attempt to integrate unlike or heterogeneous systems throughout the company. This problem is further compounded within the lodging industry due to franchizing. In the past, hotel companies have found it particularly challenging to implement programmes chain-wide due the inconsistencies and incompatibilities of hardware and software throughout all of their hotels. As case in point, Holiday Inn Worldwide realized this difficulty when trying to implement new marketing programmes and when trying to establish a two-way interface between its central reservation system and the property management system. The company could not effectively compete with other, more standardized hotel organizations in terms of service levels and consistency. After standardizing its hardware and software platform, Holiday Inn Worldwide was able to develop (and now supports) a single interface to its central reservation system and each property can now take advantage of the company's HIRO yield management system. This standardization also benefits the customer because all hotels can now offer the same pricing structure, room availability information and marketing programmes.

The challenge with systems or technology planning is to select architectures (hardware and software) and programming environments that are flexible, stable, easy to modify, have a long life expectancy and offer a migration path to some other platform or operating environment. Because the speed in which technology changes and the lead time to develop new applications are so great, it is difficult to select technology architectures that will withstand the test of time.

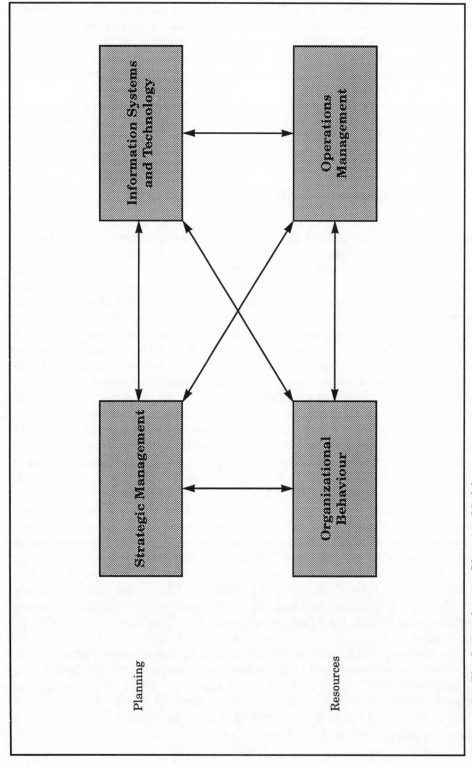

Planning

Resources

Figure 10.9: The Comprehensive Planning Model

For example, Marriott first embarked on the development effort for its new hotel property management, known as its 'Next Generation System' nearly seven years ago. Today, the company is still developing many of the core modules; however, most of the key technologies used to build this system are now obsolete. In fact the entire programming paradigm has changed, making the system less functional. Fortunately for Marriott, there is some flexibility within the systems architecture to allow the company to benefit from some newer products like faster hardware or newer database engines. However, because the project is so far along, the company is committed to and constrained by some of the older technologies.

To offer another perspective of how a company addresses issues such as this, one could turn to Hyatt. In an effort to avoid technical obsolescence before a product reaches market, Hyatt consciously tries to keep all of its systems development efforts to under a year's timeframe. With technology, perhaps the most feared (and frustrating) situation for a company, is to find itself unable to implement a new strategy or react to a competitor's strategy because its technology infrastructure cannot support the change. Perhaps one of the best examples to illustrate this was the industry's inability to quickly respond to Marriott's 21-day advance purchase marketing promotion, offering non-refundable discounted room rates to those willing to commit to a purchase decision at least 21 days in advance (similar to the airlines). Because of the way most hotel reservation systems maintained room inventory, they were unable to allocate and unallocate rooms to the special discounted rates without extensive manual involvement. As a result, Marriott enjoyed a competitive advantage until the rest of the industry was able to modify their central reservation systems to accommodate this functionality.

To avoid the situations cited above, it is important for companies to develop a good information technology architecture. As a guideline for defining and standardizing upon an information technology architecture, ten architectural principles are defined below:

1) To employ open systems and mainstream technologies (i.e., proven or established with a healthy product life cycle), that provide avenues for growth and migration and that are scaleable to handle small, medium and large communities and the home office computing needs in an affordable manner;
2) To create a strong, lasting technical infrastructure on which to build future applications;
3) To create an environment of highly-integrated, seamless applications that support all aspects and needs of the business;
4) To support computer processing and data entry in the locations that make the most economic or business sense (e.g., centralized at the home office, decentralized at the hotels, regionalized or shared between several hotels, or any combination thereof);
5) To create a paperless environment driven by on-line applications, electronic mail, electronic forms transmission, electronic data transfer, electronic data interchange (EDI) and electronic funds transfer (EFT);
6) To support fast data access anywhere and anytime by anyone who needs and is granted access to the data within the organization;

7) To implement systems and applications that are easy to learn and easy to use;
8) To select systems and applications that are high in reliability, low in maintenance, flexible and easy to modify to support changing business needs;
9) To adhere to industry standard programming conventions and communications protocols;
10) To ensure systems and applications integrity through advanced security techniques and internal control mechanisms.

PITFALLS IN PLANNING

There are many pitfalls that information systems planners can stumble upon during the planning process. Experience suggests a few in particular about which one should be cautioned before commencing an information systems planning process. All too often planning projects fail because of the lack of management commitment, inadequate resources, unrealistic expectations and the project team's inability to stay focused. There is typically a tendency to attempt tackling all aspects of the organization in a single pass or the desire to computerize everything an organization does, regardless as to whether or not there is good financial reasoning. To avoid these traps, information systems planners should consider setting the goals and objectives of the planning process up-front at the onset of the project, having a well-defined scope for the planning effort, assembling a team of well-qualified individuals to carry out the planning process and the analysis involved, having access to the 'right' tools and resources to complete the planning effort, understanding the chosen systems planning methodology and the products (deliverables) that will be produced as a result of following that methodology, establishing executive commitment, avoiding getting distracted in the details and maintaining a long-term, enterprise-wide focus. It is important to understand that the planning process is only as good as an organization's commitment, the quality of the effort and the accuracy of the information used to formulate the plan. Information systems planning is a complex and time-consuming task. For that reason, organizations should plan to invest the right resources (including time, personnel and funding) to successfully complete the project according to the goals and objectives of the organization. There is no magic in the planning process and at the end of the process, the organization will not be miraculously transformed to the desired state. The old adage 'garbage in, garbage out' still applies, but if done correctly, an organization will have a good set of plans, a road map and a vision for transitioning the organization to the desired state.

CONCLUDING COMMENTS

The common themes over the past decade and for the foreseeable future are change and opportunity. The hotel industry is ever changing, as is the world around it. Today is very different from yesterday and it is certain that tomorrow will be unlike today. As such, the opportunities are abundant for those who possess creativity, embrace change and aggressively seek new ways of approaching traditional situations. The key, however, is to methodically plan for these new technologies and applications. Those who can develop a good understanding of their environment and a vision for the future are likely to be the more successful organizations that will drive and shape the rest of the industry.

REFERENCES

Andersen Consulting and the American Hotel and Motel Association (1989). *Looking forward: A management perspective of technology in the lodging industry*. Washington, DC.

Barrington, Melvin N. and Olsen, Michael D. (1987). Concept of service in the hospitality industry. *International Journal of Hospitality Management*, 6 (3), pp. 131–138.

Bates, Constance S. (1985). Mapping the environment: An operational environmental analysis model. *Long Range Planning*, 18 (5), pp. 97–107.

Bean, William C. (1993). *Strategic planning that makes things happen*. Amherst, MA: Human Resource Development Press, Inc.

Caldwell, Bruce and DePompa, Barbara (1995, May 8). CEO's click on IT: Business executives are learning more about information technology. Is that good news for technology managers? *InformationWeek*, 29.

Child, John (1972). Organizational structure, environment and performance: The role of strategic choice. *Sociology*, 6, pp. 1–22.

Davenport, Thomas H. (1994, March-April). Saving IT's soul: Human-centred information management. *Harvard Business Review*, 72 (2), pp. 119–131.

DeNoble, Alex F. and Olsen, Michael D. (1986). The food service industry environment: Market volatility analysis. *F.I.U. Hospitality Review*, 4 (2), pp. 89–100.

Dill, William R. (1958). Environment as an influence on managerial autonomy. *Administrative Science_Quarterly*, 2, pp. 409–443.

Dreyfuss, Joel (1995, January 30). Rethinking the customer. *InformationWeek*, 28.

Duncan, Robert B. (1972). Characteristics of organizational environments and perceived environmental uncertainty. *Administrative Science Quarterly*, 17, pp. 313–327.

Emery, F. E. and Trist, E. L. (1965). The casual texture of organizational environments. *Human Relations*, 18, pp. 21–32.

Gartner Group IS Research Note. (1992, 22 January). What do you mean by 'IT architecture'? (Key Issues Brief No. K-140-869). Stamford, CT: B. Rosser.

Goldberg, Beverly and Sifonis, John G. (1994 July–August). Keep on keepin' on. *Journal of Business Strategy*, 15 (4), pp. 23–25.

Gorry, G. Anthony and Morton, Michael S. Scott (1989, Spring). A framework for management information systems. *Sloan Management Review*, 30 (3), pp. 49–61.

Hagmann, Constanza (1994). Strategic information systems planning: Does practice follow theory? *Proceedings of the Decision Sciences Institute*, USA, 2, pp. 1061–1063.

Hamel, Gary and Prahalad, C. K. (1994, July–August). Competing for the future; what drives your company's agenda: Your competitor's view of the future or your own? *Harvard Business Review*, 72 (4), pp. 122–128.

Hammer, Michael and Champy, James (1993). *Reengineering the corporation: A manifesto for business revolution*. New York: Harper Business.

Henderson, John C. and Thomas, James B. (1992, Spring). Aligning business and information technology domains: Strategic planning in hospitals. *Hospital & Health Services Administration*, 37 (1), pp. 71–87.

IBM (1994, July). *Business systems planning: Information systems planning guide* (4th ed.). (No. GE20-0527-4). Atlanta, GA.

Itami, Hiroyuki and Numagami, Tsuyoshi (1992). Dynamic interaction between strategy and technology. *Strategic Management Journal*, 13, pp. 119–135.

Jackson, Susan E. And Dutton, J. E. (1988). Discerning threats and opportunities. *Administrative Science Quarterly*, 33 (3), pp. 370–387.

Laberis, Bill (1994, October 17). Impossible dream: Linking information systems with corporate goals and the evolution of the chief information officer position. *Computerworld*, 28 (45), p. 34.

Lederer, Albert L. and Sethi, Vijay (1988, September). The implementation of strategic information systems planning methodologies. *MIS Quarterly*, pp. 445–461.

Liao, Jianwen (1994). A theoretical model of IS planning and business strategy. *Proceedings of the Decision Sciences Institute*, USA, 2, pp. 858–860.

McFarlan, F. Warren, McKenney, James I. and Pyburn, Philip (1983, January–February). The information archipelago – plotting a course. *Harvard Business Review*, 61, pp. 145–156.

Miles, R. E., Snow, C. C. and Coleman, H. J. (1978, July). Organizational strategy, structure and process. *Academy of Management Review*, pp. 546–562.

Mills, Peter K. (1986). *Managing service industries: Organizational practices in a postindustrial economy*. Cambridge, MA: Ballinger Publishing Company.

Parsons, Gregory L. (1983, Spring). Information technology: A new competitive weapon. *Sloan Management Review*, 13 (3), pp. 3–14.

Porter, Michael E. (1980). *Competitive strategy: Techniques for analyzing industries and competitors*. New York: The Free Press.

Quek, Patrick (1995, March). Hotel technology: Current user opinions and investment trends. *Lodging*, pp. 19–20.

Rockart, John F. (1979, March-April). Chief executives define their own data needs. *Harvard Business Review*, 57 (2), pp. 81–93.

Schostack, G. Lynn (1984, January–February). Designing services that deliver. *Harvard Business Review*, pp. 133–139.

Slattery, Paul and Olsen, Michael D. (1984). Hospitality organizations and their environment. *International Journal of Hospitality Management*, 3 (3), pp. 55–61.

Spewak, Steven H. (1993*). Enterprise architecture planning: Developing a blueprint for data, applications and technology*. Boston: QED Publishing Group.

Sprague, Ralph H., Jr. and McNurlin, Barbara C. (Eds.). (1986). *Information systems management in practice*. Englewood Cliffs: Prentice-Hall.

Theobald, Robert (1994, September–October). Visionary planning for a compassionate era. *Planning Review,* 22 (5), pp. 12–15.

Tombazian, Charles M. (1994, September). Looking to your future: Managing change through strategic planning. *Managers Magazine*, 69 (9), pp. 16–22.

West, Joseph J. And Olsen, Michael D. (1988). Environmental scanning and its effect upon firm performance: An exploratory study of the foodservice industry. *Hospitality Education and Research Journal*, 12 (2), pp. 127–136.

Zachman, J. A. (1987). A framework for information systems architecture. *IBM Systems Journal*, 26, (3), pp. 276–292.

PART THREE
REGIONAL DEVELOPMENT

Graham Brown

INTRODUCTION AND OVERVIEW

Tourism academics and researchers in Australia may feel they have been in the right place at the right time for the 1990s have seen a dramatic increase in the importance accorded to tourism. International tourist numbers have increased dramatically as Australia has benefited from visits generated in the buoyant economies of Asia. The figure of 1.26 million international tourists in 1985–86 had risen to over three million in 1993–94. According to the Federal Government's Tourism Forecasting Council, the number is expected to increase by an average of 10 per cent a year to 7.6 million by 2003, with visitor expenditure climbing from $6 billion to $14.7 billion (McCathie and Thomas, 1996).

The growth in tourism has created greater recognition of its economic importance and the role it plays in the social and cultural life of the country. This has been reflected in a heightened political profile. In December 1991, the Government established a separate Ministry for Tourism with Cabinet status. The Department of Tourism (Figure 1), which was established shortly afterwards, has sought to encourage:

- the development of an economic environment in which tourism can optimize its contribution to Australia's economy;
- responsible planning and management practices which promote environmentally sustainable tourism development; and
- positive social outcomes of tourism (Commonwealth Department of Tourism, 1992).

The way the Department has attempted to achieve these objectives can be illustrated by the allocation of resources in the most recent Federal budget which awarded:

- $80 million to the Australian Tourist Commission for overseas marketing activities;
- $5.2 million for the Regional Tourism Development Programme;
- $3.4 million for the National Tourism Ecotourism Programme and the Forest Ecotourism Programme;
- $2.6 million to stimulate the development of special interest tourism markets including rural tourism, the backpacker market and cruise shipping;
- $1.3 million for the Bureau of Tourism Research for the ongoing development of the statistical research base of the industry.

(Commonwealth Department of Tourism, 1995).

Despite concern that there is a 'perceived lack of commitment to research at both the industry and government levels' (Faulkner *et al.*, 1995: 3), the number of tourism academics has increased and their activities have become more organized in recent years. There were only three tourism and hospitality degree programmes in 1984 but this had risen to 26 undergraduate programmes offered by 22 universities in 1994. In 1992, the universities established the Council for

Australian University Tourism and Hospitality Education (CAUTHE) to represent their interests. One of the council's main activities is to organize the annual Australian Tourism and Hospitality Research Conference. Over 150 papers were presented at the conference in 1996 which was hosted by Southern Cross University (Prosser, 1996).

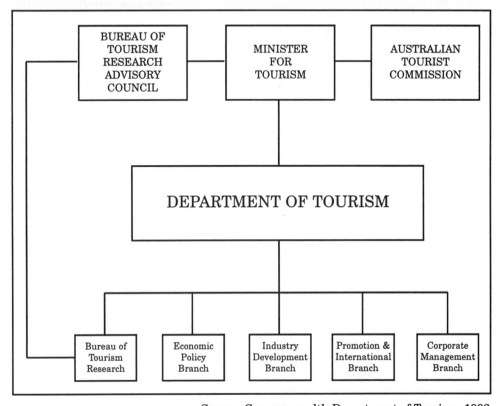

Source: Commonwealth Department of Tourism, 1992
Figure 1: Commonwealth Department of Tourism Portfolio

The chapters included in this book provide further evidence of the growing contribution made by tourism academics in Australia. Each of the authors has played an important role in guiding the development of major education programmes and have been prominent members of CAUTHE. Brian King and Bob McKercher report research conducted as part of their doctoral programmes whereas the chapter by Gary Prosser reflects a growing body of work he has prepared about the 'destination life-cycle' concept.

In chapter 11 Prosser uses the 'destination life-cycle' concept to provide a framework for the description and analysis of two Australian tourist destinations. A thorough literature review is provided which traces the debate about the utility of the concept and describes the range of locations where it has been employed. This is followed by a detailed examination of tourism on the Gold Coast and at Coffs Harbour. It is explained that although both destinations have passed through similar developmental stages, the structural outcomes are very different. A need to understand more about 'the dynamics of growth' is advocated.

Due to the scale and impact of tourism on the Gold Coast and at Coffs Harbour, both areas are sometimes cited as examples of inappropriate forms of tourism development. This is particularly the case for the Gold Coast where a highly developed infrastructure has created a 'user-friendly' environment for tourists, who generate $1.3 billion of revenue and create 14,000 jobs (Queensland Tourist and Travel Corporation, 1994). It has been suggested that the Gold Coast:

> has attained a size and critical mass which has an internal momentum for growth. The ever-growing resident population is an important market for many tourism enterprises – for the restaurants and shops and the theme parks which target this market outside the peak season, when locals are told 'the Coast is clear' to visit Movie World. (Brown and Raedler, 1994: 23–24).

In view of the important relationship between tourism and the host community, it is interesting to note that a recent study found that:

> Despite the advanced stage of tourism development that has been reached on the Gold Coast and the manifestations of mass tourism that are associated with this, residents of the area are generally positively disposed towards tourism (Faulkner and Tideswell, 1996: 32).

One variable which influences resident attitudes toward tourism is the seasonal pattern of tourist activity. Communities are provided with an opportunity to 'return to normal' in the off-peak periods and predictability in terms of the timing and duration of the peak periods has been found to enhance the ability of residents to cope (Brown and Giles, 1994). Seasonality affects ski resorts, such as those examined in chapter 12 by Bob McKercher, more than most other types of destination. Although the benefits must be gained in a more condensed time frame, the economic impact can be significant with skiers in Victoria spending $270 million in the alpine villages (CSAES, 1993). Tension between a competitive instinct and the need to co-operate is a recurrent theme in this chapter which discusses practical challenges faced by an organization with regional planning and administrative responsibilities. It examines the role played by the Alpine Resorts Commission in shaping the development and profitability of three ski resorts.

The final chapter, by Brian King, evaluates the extent to which progress has been made toward achieving a coordinated approach to marketing in the Whitsunday region of Queensland. An analytical framework is used which incorporates a number of dimensions. They include the relationship between the social and natural environments, tourism development, a geographic dimension, which considers the criteria for regional boundaries and the spatial relationship between regional centres or gateways and the remainder of the region. A political dimension includes an assessment of the exercise of power by tourism enterprises and by the host community. A planning dimension makes reference to the extent to which initiatives should be formalized into a regional planning strategy and a marketing dimension is used to assess whether the region has sufficient distinctive features to justify co-operative regional marketing using a single image.

Despite acknowledging difficulties associated with the identification of appropriate boundaries and with gaining constituent support, the benefits of adopting a strategic approach to regional planning are clearly demonstrated in both the Victorian Alps and the Whitsundays. Co-operation is presented as a key ingredient in each case as illustrated by King's comment that:

> Most operators expressed the view that the scale of active collaboration between operators within the region had grown significantly after a period of considerable division. The improved commonality of interest was viewed as indicative of a stronger commitment by major operators towards the Whitsundays as the key destination, rather than to the properties themselves.

In combination, the three chapters provide representative coverage of geographically diverse tourism environments in Australia including major 'urban' coastal destinations, an Alpine region and island resorts. More importantly, they provide alternative perspectives of issues which have considerable theoretical and practical relevance. Each contribution reinforces that it is important to learn from the past by, as McKercher observes, *addressing the historical issues that have driven past development at the destination.* In addition, although the scale and form of tourism may vary in the different locations, a desire to establish appropriate forms of management and to achieve sustainability are consistent objectives.

The contributions indicate that tourism has reached a high level of maturity as a field of academic endeavour. The wealth of literature that is devoted to topics such as destination development and regional planning has made it possible for the authors to provide evidence from a wide range of settings, gathered over an extended period of time. This kind of evidence must be made as readily available to tourism managers as it is to tourism academics. As Gary Prosser insists:

> To effectively analyse and respond to their external environment, managers must first be prepared to recognize it as an important part of their responsibilities, along with provision of quality service, staffing and productivity issues, balance sheet ratios and other traditional areas of concern. This attitudinal shift must be matched with appropriate knowledge and skills.

The three Australian chapters represent valuable additions to a growing base of 'appropriate knowledge'.

REFERENCES

Brown, G. (1992). Politics and policies: a review of recent changes affecting the tourism industry, *Australian Journal of Leisure and Recreation*, 2, 2, pp. 31–33.

Brown, G. and Giles, R. (1994) Coping with tourism: an examination of resident responses to the social impact of tourism. In A.V. Seaton (Ed.), *Tourism the State of the Art*, pp. 755–764. Chichester, John Wiley & Sons.

Brown, G. and Raedler, S. (1994) Gold Coast hotels: examining the prospects for growth, *International Journal of Contemporary Hospitality Management*, 6, 4, pp. 16–24.

CSAES (1993) *The Economic Significance of Alpine Resorts*, Centre for South Australian Economic Studies, Adelaide.

Commonwealth Department of Tourism (1992). The Department of Tourism, *Tourism Facts*, 1,1, Commonwealth Department of Tourism.

Commonwealth Department of Tourism (1995). 1995–96 Federal Budget. Tourism Industry Overview, *Tourism Facts*, Commonwealth Department of Tourism.

Faulkner, B., Pearce, P., Shaw, R. and Weiler, B. (1995). Tourism research in Australia: Confronting the challenges of the 1990s and beyond. In *Tourism Research and Education in Australia*, Proceedings from the Tourism Educators Conference, Gold Coast, Bureau of Tourism Research, pp. 3–25.

Faulkner, B. and Tideswell, C. (1996). Gold Coast resident attitudes toward tourism: the influence of involvement in tourism, residential proximity and period of residency. In G. Prosser (Ed.) *Tourism and Hospitality Research. Australian and International Perspectives*, Proceedings from the Australian Tourism and Hospitality Research Conference, 1996, Bureau of Tourism Research, pp. 19–35.

McCathie, A. and Thomas, I. (1996). Shore thing: Tourism on track for record feat, *Australian Financial Review*, March 15, pp. 1,8.

Prosser, G. (1996). Graduate hosts create a leading attraction, *The Australian*, January 17, p. 28.

Queensland Tourist and Travel Corporation. (1994) Queensland Visitors Survey 1993–94.

11

The Development of Tourist Destinations in Australia: A Comparative Analysis of the Gold Coast and Coffs Harbour

Gary Prosser

INTRODUCTION

The challenge of anticipating and managing change in tourist destination areas has practical implications for tourism industries and local communities. Attempts by researchers to model the process of tourism development, particularly in coastal areas, have been a long standing feature of the tourism literature. Perhaps the most famous attempt to model the tourism development process, Butler's (1980) tourist area cycle of evolution, formalizes an idea that can be traced back through the tourism literature over a period of more than thirty years (Choy, 1992). During that time, a large body of research has been published seeking to describe, explain and predict the dynamics of growth and change in tourist destination areas.

The main purpose of this chapter is to gain a better understanding of factors influencing the evolution of tourist destinations by comparing aspects of the social and economic development of two Australian coastal resort areas – the Gold Coast and Coffs Harbour. The comparison is based on the history of tourism development in each location, their population growth rates, economic and employment structures, visitor numbers and characteristics, amount and type of tourism development and resident population numbers. From the analysis, it is possible to identify practical implications for tourism planners and managers in destination areas and topics for future research.

EVOLUTION OF TOURIST DESTINATIONS: LITERATURE REVIEW

One of the first descriptions of a cyclical process of tourist destination evolution was made by Plog (1973), who observed that destination areas carry with them the potential seeds of their own destruction and lose their qualities which originally attracted tourists. Doxey (1975) used similar principles to develop an *index of tourist irritation* to describe the increasing level of irritation and antagonism between hosts and guests, as the number of tourists and the threat they posed to resident lifestyles, increased. Butler (1980) further developed these ideas and proposed a staged model of the tourist destination life cycle, beginning with the *exploration* of a new destination by adventurous travellers. Following this exploratory stage, some members of the host community would start to provide low key services and facilities to cater for the needs of tourists, so entering the *involvement* stage. Increasing numbers of tourists would require more formal and larger scale *development*, probably with the investment of capital from external sources. After a period of rapid growth, the destination would enter the *consolidation* phase with reducing rates of growth, followed by *stagnation*. At this point the resort area may either *decline* in popularity or enter a *rejuvenation* phase with the addition of new attractions (see Figure 11.1).

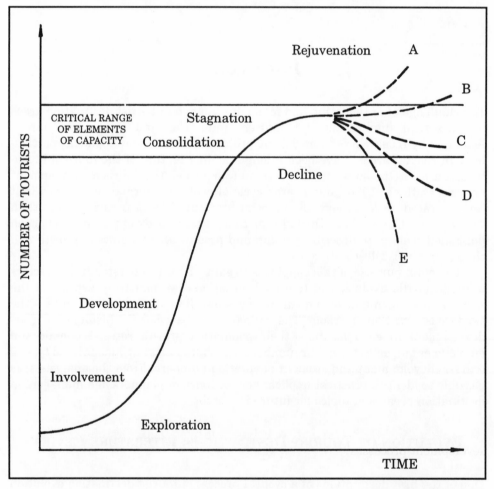

Source: Butler, 1980: 7

Figure 11.1: Hypothetical Evolution of a Tourist Area

Butler's simple model is *based upon a combination of two widely utilized but fundamentally different principles* (Butler, 1991: 203). The first is the *product life cycle* derived from the marketing literature. The other principle is that of *carrying capacity*, originally borrowed from the literature on agricultural science, although since applied to a range of environmental settings, as well as recreation and tourism (see Martin and Uysal, 1990). The notion of development life cycles is not unique to tourist destination areas, having been applied extensively to the evolution of cities and neighbourhoods since the late 1950s (Roberts, 1991).

The large body of literature which has developed around Butler's model of the destination life cycle is testimony to its significant impact on the study of tourism development processes. At least three main factors have contributed to the enduring attraction of the destination life cycle concept. First, the model offers an easily comprehended conceptual framework in a field where relatively few such frameworks are available. Second, it has sufficient descriptive power to provide intuitive appeal to researchers. For example, reporting his research on the evolution of beach resorts in Thailand, Smith explains his research motives by reference to informal observations over a number of years *that contemporary beach resort development, especially in the Asian Pacific area, apparently starts well but ends with excessive undesirable features and impacts* (Smith, 1992: 305).

The third factor contributing to the enduring attraction of the destination life cycle is that research completed in a range of different tourist areas has provided (qualified) empirical support for the model. For example, Weaver (1988; 1990) found that tourism developments on both Antigua and Grand Cayman Island in the Caribbean *do conform in many critical respects with Butler's model* (1990: 15). In the case of Grand Cayman Island, Weaver found evidence to support the model

> particularly with respect to the institutionalization of tourism, the extensive physical modification of the landscape, the dominance of large-scale accommodations, increased accessibility, the emergence of a well defined, seasonal market, the appearance of 'man-made' events and attractions and the implementation of a development plan to regulate growth (1990: 14).

The only qualification of the model was that in contrast to Butler, Weaver found that local ownership and control of tourism increased rather than decreased during the 'development' stage which he suggests may account for reduced levels of social impact.

These three factors may explain the attraction of Butler's model for researchers, but what contribution has it made to our understanding of tourism development processes?

Testing the Life Cycle Model

The destination life cycle model has been evaluated in a range of different locations, including Pennsylvania (Hovinen, 1981; 1982), Malta (Oglethorpe, 1984), Louisiana (Meyer-Arendt, 1985), Galveston (Richardson, 1986), Canada's North West Territories (Keller, 1987), the Isle of Man (Cooper and Jackson, 1989), the Caribbean (Weaver, 1988; 1990), Majorca (Morgan, 1991), Cyprus (Ioannides, 1992), Pacific island destinations (Choy, 1992), Niagara Falls (Getz, 1992), Pattaya, Thailand (Smith, 1992), Minorca (Spain), (Williams, 1993). It has also provided the conceptual framework for investigations of second homes (Strapp, 1988) and the impact of 'alternative' tourism (Jarviluoma, 1992). Butler's model has been used also as a framework for evaluating how the evolution of a tourist destination influences the development of local entrepreneurship (Din, 1992) and formal and informal sectors of local economies (Kermath and Thomas, 1992). Others have used the model as a framework for assessing how a destination is influenced by corporate strategy (Debbage, 1990), external events (di Benedetto and Bojanic, 1993) and the interaction of national institutions and transnational firms (Ioannides, 1992).

A number of these empirical studies have led to refinements or embellishments of the model to account for the evolution of a specific destination, or the particular focus of interest of the researcher. Some authors have modified the number of stages in the cycle, or the shape of the cycle itself. For example, Smith (1992) proposes an eight phase model of contemporary (post World War II) beach resort development. The model emphasizes resort morphology but also makes reference to tourist characteristics, resident attitudes, industry and investment characteristics, environmental impact and governmental involvement. di Benedetto and Bojanic (1993: 561) move away from the conventional S-shaped curve depiction of the tourism life cycle and utilize a step-logarithmic function which 'can represent sequentially periods of development, stagnation, rapid revitalization and stagnation at a higher level'. Williams (1993) expands Butler's model by incorporating major elements of dependency – external control theory. This expanded model has four descriptive stages and four predictive stages to account for both historical growth and future changes based on two alternative tourism policies.

Other authors have not changed the form or sequence of the cycle but have sought to enhance its descriptive and explanatory power by incorporating additional variables with those originally proposed by Butler. Examples of this approach include Keller (1984) who expands the model with reference to the increasing complexity of decision making processes and investment at different stages of tourism development. Local control of development authority and input of capital and infrastructure in the early stages of tourism development gives way to regional control and input before finally succumbing to national and international forces.

In a similar vein, Kermath and Thomas (1992) have used Butler's work as the framework for a model of development of formal and informal economic sectors in resort areas. Their model attempts to explain structural and spatial differences between these two economic sectors and incorporates development of the informal sector with Butler's representation of the formal tourism sector. Debbage includes analysis of the competitive strategies of firms within the resort life cycle framework which *extends the theoretical context by more fully considering the broader industrial environment that facilitates the flow of visitors from origin to destination* (1992: 357). Weaver (1988) proposes a modified resort cycle to account for the special circumstances of Third World economies.

As would be expected, a conceptual framework which has been adopted in such a wide range of empirical research has also attracted the attention of critics.

Limitations of the Destination Life Cycle

Criticism has been directed at the destination life cycle on both conceptual and empirical grounds. The critical arguments can be broadly classified into five areas:

- scepticism about the feasibility of a single model of tourism development;
- conceptual limitations of carrying capacity and the product life cycle;
- conceptual limitations of the life cycle model as it has been applied to tourist destination areas;
- a lack of empirical support for the destination life cycle concept; and
- the limited practical utility of the life cycle concept in tourism planning.

Each of these arguments is considered briefly below.

An early rejection of the notion of a single model of tourism development was provided by Cohen who argued that *rather than search for the model of transformation of tourist destination areas, one should try to discover different types of basic dynamics* (1979: 24). Bianchi (1994) extends this idea and suggests that attempts to formulate a single model of tourist development simplify complex processes and fail to account for the range and diversity of tourist developments. In his view, more attention must be paid to the context of development because:

> the essentially unilinear conceptions of tourist-area evolution prevalent in the literature disregard the principal conditioning components of development by virtue of assimilating a diversity of components and interlocking subsystems into convenient homogenous categories for the purposes of explanation (Bianchi 1994: 186).

Empirical support for this position is provided by Choy (1992) who argues that variations in growth patterns of tourist destinations defy any attempt to generalize.

The second area of criticism of the resort life cycle is based on limitations of the product life cycle and carrying capacity concepts, its twin conceptual foundations. The general S-shaped product life cycle curve has been challenged on the basis of empirical evidence of alternative growth patterns for many products. For example, Kotler (1988) identifies three alternative product life cycles based on *growth-decline-maturity, primary cycle-recycle* and *scalloped growth.* Hart, Casserly and Lawless (1984) demonstrated eight product life cycles in the hospitality industry which do not conform to the conventional S curve. In the context of the evolution of cities and neighbourhoods it has been argued

> ... that the city life cycle idea is inadequate from both the instrumentalist and realist positions (it is neither a useful classificatory device nor a 'truthful' statement about real processes) and . . . has been allowed to become transformed into a myth (Roberts 1991: 444).

A number of critics argue that the notion of a generic product life cycle has limited utility because the fate of any individual product is shaped by the strategic actions of competing firms (Day 1986), or destinations in the case of tourist resorts. In fact, Gordon, Calantone and di Benedetto (1991) have argued that American business strategy has too often managed products for short term profitability, assuming they had matured or were in decline, when a better strategy may have been to revitalize the product and aim for sustained growth.

The other main conceptual element of the resort life cycle model is the notion that as carrying capacity thresholds are reached, visitation levels will stabilize and even decline as the quality of the destination deteriorates. Arguments rejecting the idea of there being fixed, inherent limits on growth are well documented (see, for example, Prosser 1985; Prosser and Cullen 1987). In a single location, different capacity limits may be imposed by physical, natural, social or economic factors. Further, individual perceptions of the carrying capacity of a destination may vary between different tourists and for the same tourist in different locations and even for the same tourist in the same location at different times. Perceptions may also vary between tourists and residents, tourism operators and conservationists. Differences may also occur among residents and so on. Getz (1983) identifies six methods of determining carrying capacity, while Martin and Uysal (1990) argue that different capacity thresholds requiring specific policy responses will apply at each stage of the destination life cycle. In this context, it can be seen why the resort life cycle's reliance on the concept of carrying capacity is described by Getz (1992) as *controversial.*

The conceptual limitations of the *product life cycle* and *carrying capacity* lead to specific criticisms of their application to tourist destination areas. Haywood (1986; 1992), a prominent critic of the destination life cycle concept, argues that the model cannot account for *gradual, continuous change* and fails to reflect:

- competition between resort areas;
- corporate and host community strategies;

- conditions that *trigger shakeouts* – too rapid growth destroying the industry and environment;
- environmental context; and
- the impact of uncertainty in emerging resort areas about customer acceptance of the destination and eventual market size.

A number of other authors have since expanded on these points (see, for example, di Benedetto and Bojanic, 1993; Kermath and Thomas, 1992; Debbage ,1992).

Choy (1992) also identifies a conceptual limitation of the destination life cycle arising from fundamental differences between tourist destinations and manufactured products. The characteristics of conventional products are fixed and do not change with increases in volume of sales. If there is a substantial change in the characteristics of a product, a new life cycle would commence. On the other hand, an increase in number of visitors (volume of sales) for a tourist destination (product) inevitably changes the nature and characteristics of the product. Choy identifies three types of changes that may occur in a destination as a travel product. First, expansion and modernization of existing facilities to accommodate increasing numbers of visitors. Second, introduction of new and different attractions which modify the destination and its appeal to different market segments. Third, repositioning existing facilities to appeal to new markets as a strategy for rejuvenation of the destination. The first and third types of change may be regarded as extensions of the existing product life cycle but the second type of change results in a new travel product with a new life cycle. As Choy points out,

> Butler's description of the stages of a destination does not clearly distinguish the types of 'product' changes, but this distinction is necessary to determine whether a new life cycle curve is applicable or the changes relate to the extension of an existing life cycle' (1992: 31).

Similarly, attention has been drawn to other limitations of the Butler model, including *poor demarcation between the stages* (Pearce, Moscardo and Ross, 1991). Progression from one stage to the next is more easily recognized in retrospect than in prospect, according to Cooper and Jackson (1989). Shaw and Williams (1994: 165) note criticism of the *exact shape of the Butler curve* and the *notion that all resorts have to pass sequentially through the six different stages of the life cycle*. In regard to the latter point Pearce, Moscardo and Ross (1991) ask whether progression from one stage to the next necessarily precludes on-going evidence of the previous stage. They also question whether development impacts are merely a reflection of life cycle stage or whether there might not be other variables which influence the impact of development, such as the rate of change. Bianchi (1994) also doubts the linkages between impacts and progression through the stages of growth, describing it as an 'arbitrary correlation' and 'tantamount to a crude determinism'. Another limitation of the Butler model is its presumed universality. There are likely to be a range of factors on both the demand and supply side which will influence the characteristics of the cycle in specific situations. Even in one destination at one time, there are likely to be discrete sectors of the market behaving in different ways and diverse attitudes to tourism among different sectors of the host community.

The fourth main area of criticism of the destination life cycle concept is its lack of empirical support and the methodological limitations of some of the studies which have purported to evaluate the model. The numerous attempts to refine or embellish the life cycle concept, reviewed above, bear testimony to the limitations of the original model in different settings. Empirical support for the model is generally qualified, as in the case of Pattaya where 'the underlying theory that today's beach resorts undergo deterioration of quality with increasing urbanization does find some support in the analyses' (Smith, 1992: 318). However, in other situations the conclusions point to little or no predictive capability: 'the destination life cycle model as proposed by Butler is not applicable to all destinations and, in fact, can be misleading in the case of Pacific island destinations' (Choy, 1992: 32). An important limitation of some of the studies which have attempted to test empirically the destination life cycle is their overly simplistic research design, based on little more than descriptive analysis of patterns in visitor arrivals for whatever period data happen to be available (see Williams, 1993).

Finally, the fifth criticism is the limited practical utility of the life cycle concept in tourism planning. A number of authors have drawn attention to the difficulties involved in operationalizing the life cycle model. For example, Haywood (1986) identifies six major issues to be resolved:

- the area of analysis (site, town, region);
- relevant market segments (which may exhibit different cycles);
- the shape of the curve;
- identifying the destinations stage in the life cycle;
- unit of measurement (visitor numbers, bed nights, expenditure levels, profitability etc); and,
- determining the relevant time frame for analysis (which often seems to be driven by available data sets).

Getz (1992), found that all six issues were important in his attempt to apply the model in Niagara Falls.

The extensive criticism levelled at the resort life cycle concept shows no sign of dissuading researchers from adopting the model as a framework for their research. What, then, are the prospects for further refinement of the model and opportunities for future research?

Implications for Future Research

Despite the large number of studies undertaken utilizing the conceptual model developed by Butler (1980) and the criticism it has received, the original model survives largely intact and, according to some, offers the prospect of further development. For example, Getz has described the concept as having the:

> potential to advance the theory and practice of tourism planning, particularly as a conceptual framework within which long-term changes can be forecast and strategies for land use, economic development and marketing can be harmonized (1992: 752).

Others do not share this optimism. For example, Choy has argued that 'the factors which determine the shape of a specific life cycle are often unique to that particular situation' (1992: 31). This may be true, but tourism impact studies have been criticised as being largely descriptive and hence inadequate as a base for anticipating the kinds of impacts that tourism will have in other locations and at other times (Dann, Nash and Pearce, 1988; Jafari, 1987). The inadequacy of tourism research is often reflected in the poorly developed conceptual foundations of planning practice (Getz, 1986). In this context, the destination life cycle stands out as a notable attempt to provide a research framework that will enable knowledge of tourism development processes to be translated from one location to another at other times.

The relative simplicity of the model has exposed it to criticism. However, one suspects this simplicity may have been an important factor contributing to its widespread adoption by scholars in different parts of the world. Simplicity has not diminished its value as a framework for empirical studies of different types of destinations. Those empirical studies also have the potential to contribute to greater conceptual sophistication of the model and enhance its explanatory and predictive power. Overall, the main potential of the destination life cycle is as a framework for description and analysis of tourism development processes (see Cooper and Jackson 1989), rather than as a forecasting tool. On-going examination of the variables on which the framework is based could lead to refinements which enhance its value for analysis and evaluation of tourist destinations.

Even Haywood, who has described the model as 'misleading' (1986) and suffering from conceptual 'problems' (1992), has endorsed the analysis of 'tourist-area evolution'. In contrast to Butler, Haywood suggests 'the ultimate success of any tourist area and hence its evolution' (1986: 164) is determined by seven 'major economic and social forces', including:

- rivalry among existing tourist areas;
- developers and development of new tourist areas;
- substitutes for the tourism/travel experience;
- groups opposed to tourism or tourism development;
- the bargaining power of tourism industry operators;
- the needs and expectations of tourists; and
- governmental intervention.

More recently, Haywood (1992) has suggested that the resort cycle model needs to be 'dynamic and open-ended', focusing on competition between corporate entities and resort locations. He argues that the resort life cycle concept needs to

take better account of the range and complexity of factors influencing the supply side of tourism systems, particularly at the level of individual firms. This is
consistent with Bianchi who suggests that to adequately understand the evolution of tourist destinations requires a more systems-oriented approach to
account for the *differential growth dynamics of individual resorts within the
structural context of the international tourism system* (1994: 190).

The approach advocated by Haywood and Bianchi reflects current interest in
tourism's industrial organization and impact and the extent to which it is 'a
"new" form of "post-fordist" industrial organization, emphasising economics of
scope over economics of scale and a multiplicity of sub-contracted arrangements
with a wide array of suppliers and distributors' (Debbage, 1992: 358).
Alternatively, is it merely 'the incipient stages of mass tourism characteristic of
the early stages of the resort cycle' (Debbage, 1992: 358) which will evolve into
more traditional economic structures as a destination matures? These issues are
attracting increasing interest in developed economies, including Australia (see
Warde, 1990). For example, Mullins (1990; 1992a) describes the development of
new urban forms, or tourist cities, which result from a process of tourism urbanization, 'an urbanisation formed from the rapid expansion of resort areas'
(Mullins, 1993: 187). According to Mullins, tourist cities are distinguished by

> rapid population and labour force growth, a 'flexible' labour market, a different
> class structure, a different household and residential organization, somewhat
> more limited state intervention and the large number of tourists who flock into
> these cities for fun (1991: 340).

The process of tourism urbanization described by Mullins, is based on the
evolution of coastal resort areas and assumptions about the factors which influence the nature and extent of change in the social and economic characteristics
of tourist destination areas. These factors have important implications for all
sectors of the tourism industry and local communities and offer a range of
research opportunities. The destination life cycle provides a useful framework
for both conceptual and empirical research to enhance our understanding of
tourism development processes and their implications. Conceptually, there is the
lure of formulating more powerful and sophisticated models of tourism development. For example, Bianchi calls for a move away from reductionist models,
such as the destination life cycle, to 'a sociological framework that can conceive
of the dynamics of tourism development at differentiated levels of society' (1994:
190-191). This is consistent with the thrust of Mullins' work in Australia, but
Bianchi provides little direction on how such a framework might be developed.
One way to progress is to improve our empirical understanding of change
processes in tourist destination areas, particularly by focusing on the main
agents and indicators of change.

Aspects of the social and economic development of two Australian coastal
resort areas – the Gold Coast and Coffs Harbour – have been compared to gain
a better understanding of factors influencing the evolution of tourist

destinations. The comparison is based on the history of tourism development in each location, their population growth rates, economic and employment structures, visitor numbers and characteristics, amount and type of tourism development and resident population numbers. From an analysis of similarities and differences in evolution of the two destinations, it may be possible to identify the main agents of change and draw practical implications for tourism planners and managers in destination areas.

EVOLUTION OF TOURIST DESTINATIONS: THE GOLD COAST AND COFFS HARBOUR

The Gold Coast and Coffs Harbour are popular tourist destinations on Australia's east coast (see Figure 11.2). Located only 400 kilometres apart, between Sydney, the capital of New South Wales and Brisbane, the capital of Queensland, the destinations share attractive sub-tropical climates and similar physical settings with popular surf beaches and access to outstanding natural environments in their hinterlands. Each has been attracting holiday makers for more than 100 years and there are striking similarities in the evolution of the two tourist destinations, in the rapid population growth rates they have experienced over the last forty years and in their economic and employment structures.

Similar Histories

Southport, at the northern end of the 50 kilometre coastal strip now known as the Gold Coast, started to receive tourists in significant numbers when it was connected to Brisbane by rail in 1889. By 1903, the railway line had been extended to Tweed Heads at the southern end of the Gold Coast. The 'South Coast', as it was known at the time, became a popular weekend retreat for the residents of Brisbane, 75 kilometres to the north. In 1917 a real estate development called 'Surfers Paradise' went on to the market near the beach at East Southport. The name caught on, with development of a sixteen bedroom 'Surfers Paradise Hotel' in 1925, although it was not until 1933 that Surfers Paradise became the official name of what was to become the tourist centre of the Gold Coast.

During the 1950s, the Gold Coast started to attract interstate visitors. The rapid growth of domestic tourism was influenced by the increasing affluence and mobility of Australians in the post war period and the aggressive actions of Gold Coast political leaders and entrepreneurs. Rapid expansion of tourist accommodation, attractions and infrastructure to service increasing domestic visitor numbers continued for the next three decades, before starting to falter in the early 1980s. In 1982, according to the Survey of Tourist Accommodation conducted by the Australian Bureau of Statistics (ABS), there was a decline of 4 per cent in the number of guest nights spent in Gold Coast hotels/motels. However, a new phase of tourism development was about to commence, heralded by the dramatic growth in international visitors to Australia during the 1980s. New international standard hotels and resorts, golf courses and theme parks were developed to cater for this rapidly expanding and big spending sector of the market. An indication of the extent of change during this period is provided by figures on growth in the number of hotel beds. Between 1983 and 1985 there was an increase of only 4 per cent in the number of Gold Coast hotel beds but this was followed by four years of frenetic activity between 1986 and 1989 when bed numbers increased by 56 per cent (ABS). Development activity then stalled again with a 2 per cent increase in rooms between 1989 and 1994. With hotel room occupancy rates back up to around 72 per cent in 1994, the next round of construction activity may not be far away.

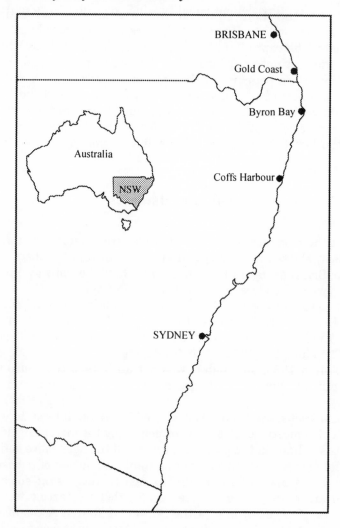

Figure 11.2: Location Map

Coffs Harbour also received its first tourists in the 1880s. Within 20 years, organized tour groups were arriving by ship from Sydney. By 1910 there were five hotels and guest houses and a camping reserve, catering for 'travellers and families taking a seaside holiday' (Yeates, 1990). Soon after, day tours were being arranged for fishing and sightseeing in other parts of the region. The advent of a rail line in 1915 and increasing car ownership during the 1920s further boosted tourist numbers, with the assistance of a motoring guide for 'The Magic North Coast' distributed by the Royal Automobile Club of Australia. In 1925, a developer was 'convinced of the area's potential as a holiday resort' (Yeates, 1990: 149) and sold land for holiday shacks and other tourism-related purposes including a hotel, a boarding house and a hostel for 'country women needing a seaside holiday'.

The increasing affluence and mobility which contributed to tourism growth on the Gold Coast during the 1950s also had an impact on Coffs Harbour. A shortage of accommodation led to a development 'boom' with seven motels constructed between 1958 and 1962, all catering to the increased traffic on the Pacific Highway linking Sydney with Brisbane. From the 1950s to the early 1980s Coffs Harbour catered to increasing numbers of family groups from Sydney and rural areas of New South Wales seeking a 'no frills' summer holiday by the beach, with caravan parks the principal form of tourist accommodation (see Figure 11.3). However, growth had stalled by the early 1980s, illustrated by a decline in guest nights in Coffs Harbour hotels/motels between 1983 and 1985. Then, a dramatic change took place. In the mid 1980s, six new tourist 'resorts' were developed and, at the same time, an increasing proportion of caravan park sites were being taken over by permanent residents.

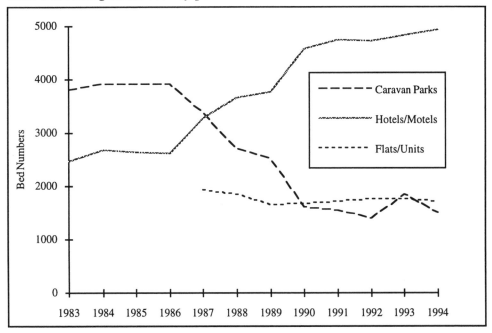

Figure 11.3: Coffs Harbour Accommodation Supply

The growth in hotel bed numbers in Coffs Harbour at this time follows a very similar pattern to the Gold Coast. A flat period between 1983 and 1986 when bed numbers increased by 6 per cent was followed by a 74 per cent increase in the number of hotel beds over the next four years (ABS). Bed numbers then increased by only 8 per cent between 1990 and 1994. Rapid hotel development combined with a loss of caravan sites for tourists changed the ratio of caravan park capacity to hotel beds from 1.5:1 in June 1986 to 0.3:1 in June 1992. In the space of five years in the late 1980s, the supply of tourist accommodation in Coffs Harbour was transformed, tourism became a controversial issue in the local community and there was a change in the character of Coffs Harbour as a holiday destination.

Both the Gold Coast and Coffs Harbour have evolved through distinct phases of development which are remarkably similar and bear a close resemblance to the stages in Butler's life cycle model. The exploration stage in each location commenced in the 1880s and lasted until about the 1920s, when local developers started to realize the potential gains to be made from holiday makers and the destinations entered the *involvement* stage. This lasted until the 1950s when a combination of external and internal factors led to an increase in visitor numbers requiring more formal and larger scale *development*. After a period of rapid growth, both destinations entered the *consolidation* phase with reducing rates of growth, followed by *stagnation* in the early 1980s. At this point both destinations entered a *rejuvenation* phase with the addition of new facilities and attractions and the pursuit of new markets. Not only have the Gold Coast and Coffs Harbour evolved through similar phases of tourism development, they have also become significant urban centres in their own right.

Similar Rapid Population Growth Rates

Since the end of World War II both the Gold Coast and Coffs Harbour have undergone a period of rapid and sustained urban growth. Each grew from a small population base. In the late 1940s the Gold Coast had a population of about 13,000 people (Mullins, 1990) and Coffs Harbour around 5,000. Coffs Harbour's population increased between three and fourfold between the late 1940s and 1971, while the population of the Gold Coast region has doubled every ten years since the late 1940s (Mullins, 1990).

Population growth remained strong at Coffs Harbour during the 1970s with an increase of more than 28 per cent between 1971 and 1976 and growth was boosted even further in the late 1970s with resident numbers increasing by 44 per cent between 1976 and 1981. Rapid population growth during the 1970s slowed somewhat during the 1980s but remained at a relatively high 22 per cent between 1981 and 1986 and 20 per cent between 1986 and 1991. These growth rates are significantly higher than those experienced in most parts of Australia during the same period.

The rate of increase of the Gold Coast population was even higher, increasing by 37 per cent between 1971 and 1976 and 33 per cent from 1976 to 1981, before peaking at 42 per cent between 1981 and 1986 and reverting to 32 per cent from 1986 to 1991 (see Table 11.1).

	1986-91	1981-91	1976-91	1971-91
Coffs Harbour	19.8	46.5	110.3	169.7
Gold Coast	32.1	87.5	149.6	242.8
Australia	8.0	15.6	24.4	32.1

Source: Australian Bureau of Statistics

Table 11.1: Cumulative Population Change – Coffs Harbour (LGA) and Gold Coast (SD) (per cent)

Table 11.1 shows that the rate of population growth for the Gold Coast was more than seven times the national figure over the twenty year period from 1971–1991 and growth at Coffs Harbour was over five times the national increase.

Rapid population growth in popular tourist destination areas is not unique to Australia and has occurred in a number of countries overseas (see for example Champion, 1989). This trend has been explained partly by retirement migration to sunnier and cheaper areas, but also as an outcome of a broader structural shift in national economies – the rustbelt/sunbelt phenomenon – with the older cities based on manufacturing being unable to satisfactorily accommodate the shift towards tertiary and quaternary employment (see Weinstein *et al*, 1985; Sawers and Tabb, 1984; Dean, 1988). Both these factors seem to have been important at Coffs Harbour and the Gold Coast and are reflected in the demographic and economic and employment structures that characterize the two locations.

Similar Economic and Employment Structures

The importance of tourism in the Gold Coast and Coffs Harbour economies is demonstrated in Table 11.2 which presents employment figures in the 'Recreation, Personal and Other Services' sector, including many of the jobs in tourism. At least since 1976, tourism related employment has consistently played a much more important role in the economies of Coffs Harbour and the Gold Coast than it has in the national economy. In 1991, the Recreation, Personal and Other Services sector accounted for 12 per cent of total employment at Coffs Harbour and 16 per cent on the Gold Coast, but only 7 per cent nationally. As well as accounting for a greater proportion of employment at Coffs Harbour and the Gold Coast, the rate of growth in tourism employment is also greater in these economies with a 150 per cent increase in the number of tourism jobs at Coffs Harbour between 1976 and 1991. During the same period tourism jobs increased by 157 per cent on the Gold Coast compared with 76 per cent across the nation.

	1991		1986		1981		1976	
	No	%	No	%	No	%	No	%
Coffs Harbour (LGA)	2,147	12.0	1,318	9.3	1,078	8.5	858	9.9
Gold Coast (SD)	9,333	15.6	7,171	15.6	4,859	11.3	3,638	11.7
Australia	496,172	7.0	394,238	6.1	329,109	5.2	282,122	4.9

Source: Australian Bureau of Statistics

Table 11.2: Employment in 'Recreation, Personal and Other Services', 1976–91

Despite the relative significance and strong growth of tourism employment over the fifteen year period from 1976–1991, the pattern of growth fluctuated at both Coffs Harbour and the Gold Coast, even though the national trend was fairly consistent over the same period. For example, between 1976 and 1981 employment in Recreation, Personal and Other Services on the Gold Coast increased by 34 per cent but accounted for a smaller proportion of Gold Coast jobs in 1981 (11.3 per cent) than it did in 1976 (11.7 per cent). It is interesting to note that employment in Recreation, Personal and Other Services in Coffs Harbour increased sharply by 63 per cent between 1986 and 1991, a period when the number of hotel/motel beds rose by 81 per cent from 2,624 to 4,760 (ABS). The volatility in employment growth patterns can probably be attributed to cyclical and other fluctuations in employment composition in rapidly expanding centres. Also, the figures provide a snapshot based on census data collected on a specific date (30 June) at five yearly intervals and do not offer any insight to the pattern of job creation during intervening periods.

Tourism also generates employment in other sectors of the economy such as 'Wholesale and Retail Trade'. Coffs Harbour and the Gold Coast have experienced impressive growth in total labour force numbers between 1976 and 1991 (129 per cent and 107 per cent respectively), especially when compared with the national figure (33 per cent). Construction services and related areas of economic activity, such as 'Finance, Property and Business Services', are other important sources of employment in rapidly expanding centres such as Coffs Harbour and the Gold Coast.

Despite sustained growth in the size of their labour force in recent years, both the Gold Coast and Coffs Harbour experience very high levels of unemployment compared to the rest of the country (see Table 11.3). Mullins (1990; 1992b) explains the high rate of unemployment in tourist cities as a function of a number of factors. These include: the seasonal nature of some tourism employment; the cyclical nature of employment in construction and related industries which are also important sources of employment in these centres; and, the large number of small operators in these industries whose enterprises are characterized by instability and very high failure rates.

The Table clearly demonstrates the high levels of unemployment in these tourist destinations. Unemployment rates on the Gold Coast have been at least

33 per cent and up to 82 per cent higher than the national average at each census since 1976. Unemployment at Coffs Harbour has been even worse, ranging from 80 per cent to 113 per cent above the national figure. High levels of unemployment in these regions are not necessarily the result of large influxes of young unemployed sun-seekers, as popular mythology suggests. In fact more unemployed young people leave than arrive in these regions (Bell, 1992 and Flood *et al*, 1991). If unemployed people are moving in they are more likely to be families seeking a cheaper, healthier life than that which the larger cities offer (Prosser and Lang, 1994).

	1991	1986	1981	1976
Coffs Harbour	18.7	19.6	10.6	8.9
Gold Coast	15.4	16.0	9.2	8.0
Australia	11.6	9.2	5.9	4.4

Source: Australian Bureau of Statistics

Table 11.3: Unemployment – Coffs Harbour (LGA) and Gold Coast (SD)
(per cent Labour Force)

Further similarities in the labour force characteristics of Coffs Harbour and the Gold Coast are evident in the proportion of the workforce who are either employers or self-employed. In 1991, more than 26 per cent of the Coffs Harbour labour force and 24 per cent of the Gold Coast labour force were either employers or self-employed, compared with 15 per cent across the nation as a whole. These figures provide further evidence of the relative importance of small enterprises in the economies of these tourist cities, an important source of volatility in employment patterns.

Despite the similar cycles of development in their evolution as tourist destinations and the similarities in the process of tourism urbanization they have experienced over the last fifty years, there remain important points of difference between the two destinations. These differences include the number and type of visitors they attract, the level and character of tourism development that has taken place and the size of resident population growth.

Different Visitor Numbers and Characteristics

The Gold Coast attracted over three million visits by domestic Australian and international tourists during 1993 (Bureau of Tourism Research). While the Gold Coast is widely promoted as an 'international' destination, its roots remain firmly in the domestic market with 76 per cent of overnight visits in 1993 being made by Australians and more than half these being made by other residents of Queensland. The largest proportion of domestic visitors (24 per cent) who stay in commercial accommodation are drawn from Brisbane, located 75 kilometres to the north. The last decade has seen spectacular growth in the number of international visitors to the Gold Coast, up from 70,700 in 1984 to 713,500 in 1993

(Bureau of Tourism Research). The most important source of overseas visitors was Japan (44 per cent). New Zealand and other Asian countries are also important source markets. In 1993 the international sector of the market accounted for 26 per cent of total visitor nights spent on the Gold Coast, up from about 5 per cent ten years earlier. Growth in the international sector of the market has overshadowed a sustained period of little or no growth in the domestic market, which seemed to peak in the mid 1980s. According to the Domestic Tourism Monitor conducted by the Bureau of Tourism Research, there were fewer domestic visitor nights spent on the Gold Coast in 1993–94 than there were during 1985–86.

In 1993–94 Coffs Harbour attracted an estimated 911,000 visitors. It is difficult to estimate accurately the proportion of international tourists, but it is almost certainly less than 5 per cent of total visitor numbers. Most visitors are drawn from Sydney, 800 kilometres to the south and regional areas of New South Wales. Visitor numbers to Coffs Harbour are less than one third of the Gold Coast figure and, with a shorter length of stay, visitor nights at Coffs Harbour (3,156,000 in 1993/94) are less than 30 per cent of domestic nights spent on the Gold Coast and around 25 per cent of total (domestic and international) nights on the Gold Coast. On a more positive note for Coffs Harbour, domestic visitor nights continue to grow strongly, from an estimated 2,278,000 in 1985–86 to 3,156,000 in 1993–94, a 39 per cent increase during a period when domestic nights on the Gold Coast actually declined (Bureau of Tourism Research).

These data indicate that, compared with the Gold Coast, Coffs Harbour attracts fewer visitors who stay fewer nights on average. At the Gold Coast, the domestic market is stagnant with strong growth in the international sector of the market. Coffs Harbour, on the other hand, is still experiencing solid growth in the domestic market, signifying increased market share among competing domestic destinations, but has not been able to establish a significant presence in the international sector.

Different Level and Character of Tourist Development

The Gold Coast is an aggregation of once distinct coastal villages which span a 50 kilometre stretch of coastline. At the tourist 'heart' of the Gold Coast is Surfers Paradise, dominated by high rise apartment buildings which now overshadow the famous beaches for much of the afternoon. Visible from a distance of many kilometres, the high rise buildings of Surfers Paradise serve to create a powerful symbol of unrestrained tourist development for pleasure seeking holiday makers and for communities in other locations wanting to pursue different models of tourism development. In 1994, the Gold Coast had 31,700 beds in holiday flats and units and a further 22,400 beds in hotels and motels. The total supply of beds had increased by 16 per cent from 46,600 in 1987 to 54,100 in 1994. Most of this growth was in hotel/motel beds which grew by 62 per cent between 1984 and 1994, from 13,800 to 22,400 (Australian Bureau of Statistics).

Over the same period, the construction of larger and more sophisticated resort properties targeting the international market increased the average number of beds per hotel property from 109 to 218. In the last quarter of 1994, according to the ABS Survey of Tourist Accommodation, accommodation takings were $49 per guest night and $101 per occupied room in Gold Coast hotels and motels. Takings in holiday units and flats were $67 per occupied unit per day.

The substantial stock of tourist accommodation on the Gold Coast is complemented by a range of theme parks and built attractions, some of which date back four decades. For example, Sea World is a popular theme park which evolved with the growth of tourism from humble origins as a water ski spectacular in the 1950s. In the last decade, it has been joined by two other major theme parks – Dreamworld and, most recently, Movie World a $120 million development opened in 1991. Other attractions include over 30 golf courses, a casino, restaurants, speciality retail developments and the range of visitor services seasoned travellers would expect to find in an established international resort destination.

With the exception of one beachfront apartment building of fourteen storeys, approved in the early 1980s, Coffs Harbour has largely avoided the high rise development which characterizes the Gold Coast. Despite the absence of high rise buildings, tourism development has still been a controversial issue in the Coffs Harbour region, particularly since the late 1980s when the composition of tourist accommodation changed dramatically. Development of six resort hotels between 1984 and 1989 introduced a new form of tourist accommodation to a destination previously dominated by highway motels and caravan parks. Some of this new resort development occupied prominent sites and changed the previous activity patterns of local residents. Controversial issues included restrictions on public access to beach areas, shortfalls in infrastructure provision and corruption of local government elected representatives.

Holiday units are a less important form of accommodation at Coffs Harbour, comprising about 26 per cent of commercial beds, compared with 59 per cent at the Gold Coast. In 1994, Coffs Harbour had 1,700 beds in holiday flats and units and a further 4,900 beds in hotels and motels. The total supply of beds had increased by 18 per cent from 5,600 in 1987 to 6,600 in 1994. Hotel/motel beds grew by 85 per cent between 1984 and 1994, from 2,600 to 4,900. Even despite this growth, Coffs Harbour has only 12 per cent of the total beds offered by the Gold Coast in hotels and holiday units (ABS). Between 1984 and 1994, the average number of beds per hotel/motel increased from 60 to 93 in Coffs Harbour, reflecting much smaller properties than the Gold Coast average of 218 beds per establishment. In the last quarter of 1994, according to the ABS Survey of Tourist Accommodation, accommodation takings were $33 per guest night and $77 per occupied room in Coffs Harbour hotels and motels. These returns are significantly lower than comparable figures for the Gold Coast and are reflected also in lower takings from holiday units and flats at $53 per occupied unit per day.

Tourism at Coffs Harbour has relied heavily on its natural attractions – there are few built attractions of any size or significance. The only attempt at a major theme park development failed in the late 1980s. This failed development was based on the 'Big Banana' – one of Australia's first famous roadside attractions, established in 1964. Coffs Harbour is located about half way between the major population centres of Brisbane and Sydney, on the main road link between the two – the Pacific Highway. Situated just a couple of kilometres from the centre of town, the Big Banana is well placed to capture passing highway traffic and quickly became a regular refreshment stop for travellers and particularly holiday makers. With minimal capital investment, the Big Banana became a highly successful tourist 'attraction'. Seeking to cash in on its prime location and established reputation, a group of investors purchased the site in the mid 1980s and spent approximately $30 million in an attempt to create a major horticultural theme park. However, the redevelopment was beset by bad luck and worse planning and soon failed. The Big Banana has since changed hands again and the current owner has returned to the previously successful format – a modest highway stop for travellers.

Tourism development on the Gold Coast is dominated by high rise apartment buildings which still provide the majority of tourist accommodation, despite the recent establishment of large hotel properties. Coffs Harbour is a low rise destination with accommodation dominated by caravan parks until the rapid construction of new hotels in the late 1980s. Theme parks are an important part of the contemporary Gold Coast tourist product while Coffs Harbour continues to rely primarily on its natural attractions.

Different Resident Population Numbers

Since the late 1940s, the population of the Gold Coast region has doubled every ten years. Despite rapid development of Gold Coast City land during the 1960s and 1970s, the population continued to increase as the construction of high rise condominiums created one of the most densely populated parts of Australia. At the same time, suburban and rural residential development sprawled into the hinterland. By 1991 it had become Australia's eighth largest urban centre (Mullins, 1992a) with a population of nearly 290,000 (see Table 11.4). Population expansion ignored administrative boundaries, extending into adjacent local government areas and across the State border into New South Wales. In March 1995, two Queensland local government areas – Gold Coast City and Albert Shire – were amalgamated to cover an area of 1,370 square kilometres with an estimated resident population of 317,500 people (in 1994).

	1991	1986	1981	1976	1971
Coffs Harbour	51,510	43,010	35,170	24,498	19,100
Gold Coast	290,000	219,458	154,706	116,168	84,586

Source: Australian Bureau of Statistics

Table 11.4: Population – Coffs Harbour (LGA) and Gold Coast (SD)

Population growth at Coffs Harbour, although relatively high in a national context, has been consistently outstripped by the Gold Coast. In 1991, the resident population on the Gold Coast (290,000) was 5.5 times that of Coffs Harbour (51,510).

DISCUSSION: UNDERSTANDING THE EVOLUTION OF TOURIST DESTINATIONS

While Coffs Harbour and the Gold Coast appear to have evolved through similar cycles of tourism development over the last hundred years, the outcome is different in important respects at each location. Indeed, given the similarities, the extent of their current differences is surprising. For example, the Gold Coast receives three times as many visitors who stay for four times as many nights and has a resident population more than five times that of Coffs Harbour. There are at least four possible explanations for this phenomenon. First, it may be that the destination life cycle is the same at each location but Coffs Harbour is developing at a slower rate and is currently at a different point of the cycle. In this case, as described above, the Gold Coast would be at the mature stage showing signs of stagnation and rejuvenation. Coffs Harbour, on the other hand, would be still progressing through the development stage. What appeared to be a stagnation and rejuvenation during the 1980s would be explained as a variation in the rate of development rather than a major shift to a different stage in the cycle.

A second explanation for the lack of 'fit' between Coffs Harbour, the Gold Coast and the destination life cycle, is that the basic 'S' shape of the cycle is the same at both locations, but location specific factors determine the level at which destinations 'mature'. That is, different destinations will peak with different tourist volumes and resident populations because of the impact of local factors. With this scenario, both destinations may have matured and prospects for future growth will depend on successful implementation of rejuvenation strategies.

Third, it may be misleading to think in terms of a single life cycle for a destination when each destination could have a number of different cycles simultaneously for different elements of its tourism product. As Choy (1992) has suggested, if a substantial change occurs in the characteristics of a destination, a new life cycle will commence. This is inevitable because the nature and characteristics of a destination change with the number and type of visitors it receives. In the case of the Gold Coast there are clearly distinct life cycles for the domestic and international sectors of the market and the introduction of new attractions such as theme parks and the Indy Grand Prix may also have introduced new life cycle curves. At Coffs Harbour, there may be a life cycle curve for the caravan park sector which has matured and is in decline while the new resort style developments have introduced another life cycle curve which is still in the early 'development' stage of the cycle. A final explanation for the different outcomes in each location is that the destination life cycle may have no descriptive, explanatory or predictive value. The life cycle concept may simply be a distraction from the specific factors influencing the rate and nature of tourism development in any given location.

A thorough evaluation of these alternatives will require further research into a range of variables that may be relevant to a fuller understanding of how and why these locations have changed over the last hundred years or so. For example, one of Butler's (1980) key indicators of the evolutionary cycle was the impact of tourism on residents and its consequences for the attitudes of local residents to tourists. This is an issue which has received some attention at Coffs Harbour (Pigram, 1987) but warrants detailed comparative investigation utilizing a consistent methodology. Other factors which warrant further research include the role of local and State government in supporting and encouraging tourism development, the role of individual entrepreneurs in the tourism development process and the relationship between tourism, retirement and urban growth. Even then, it may be the geographic proximity of the Gold Coast to the major population centre of Brisbane, with its major international airport, that sets it apart from the more remote Coffs Harbour, 600 kilometres from a major metropolitan centre. Residents of Brisbane still accounted for 24 per cent of the Gold Coast's domestic overnight market in 1993–94 and the figure would have been even higher during the 1950s, 1960s and 1970s.

The availability of alternative explanations for the development of tourist destinations over a period of one hundred years or more is hardly surprising given the diverse range of social, ecological, economic, political and technological factors which may influence growth in different locations. It is unrealistic to expect unqualified explanatory power from what remains a relatively simple conceptual framework. Yet despite its simplicity, the destination life cycle continues to provide a useful reference point for formulating the kinds of research questions that will assist in improving our understanding of the dynamic processes influencing the evolution of tourist destination areas. Continuing attention to issues such as the area of analysis, relevant market segments, the shape of the curve, identifying stages in the life cycle, units of measurement and relevant time frames (Haywood, 1986) and factors influencing the magnitude and/or importance of tourism's impact on a destination will further improve its utility.

Further research into the evolution of tourist destinations is warranted because of its potential importance to a range of interest groups, including local decision makers. For example, following local government elections in 1995, the mayor of Byron Bay – another popular tourist destination located between Coffs Harbour and the Gold Coast – was quoted as saying that his electors 'don't want another Gold Coast or a Coffs Harbour' (*Coffs Harbour Advocate*, 14 September: 3). He went on to criticize the rate of development at Coffs Harbour and the infrastructure shortfalls it had caused, commenting: 'Coffs Harbour having been there and done it provides us with a lesson in the pitfalls to avoid'. It seems clear that the Mayor of Byron Bay takes an interest in the destination life cycle and its potential implications for the physical scale and character of an area, impacts on the natural environment and the social and cultural life of host communities. Similar issues will be relevant to local, regional and national tourism industry bodies with responsibility for policy, marketing and product development strategies.

The destination life cycle also has important implications for private sector operators concerned with the profitability of existing tourism businesses, future investment opportunities and business strategy. Effective management of tourism enterprises demands attention to strategic issues both internal and external to the firm, as well as those day-to-day operational issues which can easily overwhelm other, seemingly less immediate concerns. Destination growth and decline trends may threaten established strategies or create new strategic opportunities. Strategic business decisions, such as whether to target short-term profitability with existing resources and infrastructure or to revitalize a product and aim for sustained growth in the longer term, may be crucial to profitability and corporate survival. In this context issues such as the life cycles of specific market segments are likely to be of central interest.

As Andrews (1991:49) has pointed out, corporate executives must have a *keen interest in what is going on outside their companies. More than that, a practical means of tracking developments promising good or ill and profit or loss, needs to be devised* . . . This requirement for an 'environmental scanning' capability has implications for the knowledge, skills and attitudes needed by tourism and hospitality managers. To effectively analyse and respond to their external environment, managers must first be prepared to recognize it as an important part of their responsibilities, along with provision of quality service, staffing and productivity issues, balance sheet ratios and other traditional areas of concern. This attitudinal shift must be matched with appropriate knowledge and skills. Managers need systems in place to monitor and analyse the implications of trends in their external environment in order to identify early signs of structural change in tourism demand and supply patterns. For these reasons, understanding more about the dynamics of growth and change in tourist destination areas will continue to be important to managers of hotels and resorts, attraction and tour operators, small businesses proprietors and property developers and investors, as well as a range of other interest groups.

CONCLUSION

The Gold Coast and Coffs Harbour have a similar sub-tropical climate, are located in relatively close proximity, have had an enduring attraction for holiday makers, share similar natural attractions, operate in the same cultural context and have evolved through similar phases of development. The two destinations have also become rapidly growing urban centres with similar population and labour force growth rates and economies dominated by tourism and service industries. Yet despite the similarities, there are important differences between the destinations, not the least of them being the volume of tourists they attract. They also differ in the amount and type of tourist development that has taken place, the level of population growth that has occurred and the physical form of development.

The destination life cycle has potentially important implications for those with an interest in the evolution of tourist destinations and tourism and hospitality managers who are under increasing pressure to monitor changes in their external environment. In its most basic form, the notion of a destination life cycle has attracted legitimate criticism because of its conceptual limitations and inconclusive empirical support. Some of this criticism has been based on unrealistic expectations of the model's explanatory and predictive capability and a concern to emphasize factors which are specific to development of an individual destination, rather than those factors which are shared with other places. However, a generalized framework for understanding tourism development offers the prospect of moving beyond isolated empirical studies undertaken with no common conceptual base. In this context, the destination life cycle continues to provide a useful framework for research seeking to enhance our understanding of tourism development processes and their implications.

REFERENCES

Andrews, K.R. (1991). The concept of corporate strategy, in Mintzberg, H. and J.B. Quinn (eds.), *The Strategy Process: Concepts, Contexts and Cases*, 2nd Ed, Prentice Hall, Englewood Cliffs, N.J.

Ap, J. (1990). Residents' perceptions research on the social impacts of tourism, *Annals of Tourism Research*, 17 (4), pp. 610–616.

Australian Bureau of Statistics (various). *Census of Population and Housing*, ABS, Canberra

Australian Bureau of Statistics (various). *Tourist Accommodation, New South Wales*, Cat. No. 8635.1, ABS, Canberra.

Bell, M. (1992). *Internal Migration in Australia, 1981–1986*, Australian Government Publishing Service, Canberra.

Bianchi, R. (1994). Tourism development and resort dynamics: an alternative approach, in Cooper, C. P. and A. Lockwood (eds.), *Progress in Tourism, Recreation and Hospitality Management*, Vol 5, John Wiley and Sons, Chichester.

Bureau of Tourism Research (various). *Domestic Tourism Monitor*, BTR, Canberra.

Bureau of Tourism Research (various). *International Visitor Survey*, BTR, Canberra.

Butler, R. W. (1980). The concept of a tourist area cycle of evolution and implications for management, *The Canadian Geographer*, 24, pp. 5–12.

Butler, R. W. (1991). Tourism, environment and sustainable development, *Environmental Conservation*, 18 (3), pp. 201–209.

Champion, A.G. (1989). Counterurbanisation in Europe. 1. Counterurbanisation in Britain *The Geographical Journal*, 155 (1), March, pp. 52–59.

Choy, D. J. L. (1992). Life cycle models for Pacific island destinations, *Journal of Travel Research*, 30 (3), pp. 26–31.

Coffs Harbour Advocate, Byron mayor out of line – Sullivan, Thursday September 14, p. 3.

Cohen, E. (1979). Rethinking the sociology of tourism, *Annals of Tourism Research*, 6 (1), pp. 18–35.

Cooper, C. and S. Jackson (1989). Destination life cycle: The Isle of Man case study, *Annals of Tourism Research*, 16 (3), pp. 377–398.

Dann, G., D. Nash and P. Pearce (1988). Methodology in tourism research, *Annals of Tourism Research*, 15 (1), pp. 1–28.

Day, G. S. (1986). *Analysis for Strategic Market Decisions*, West, St Paul.

Dean, K.G. (1988). Inter-regional flows of economically active persons in France, 1975–1982, *Demography*, 25 (1), February.

Debbage, K. G. (1990). Oligopoly and the resort cycle in the Bahamas, *Annals of Tourism Research* 17, pp. 513–527.

Debbage, K. G. (1992). Tourism oligopoly is at work, *Annals of Tourism Research*, 19 (2), pp. 355–359.

di Benedetto, C. A. and D. C. Bojanic (1993). Tourism area life cycle extensions, *Annals of Tourism Research*, 20, pp. 557–570.

Din, K. H. (1992). The 'involvement stage' in the evolution of a tourist destination, *Tourism Recreation Research*, 17 (1), pp. 10–20.

Dogan, H. Z. (1989). Forms of adjustment: sociocultural impacts of tourism, *Annals of Tourism Research*, 16 (2), pp. 216–236.

Doxey, G. V. (1975). A causation theory of visitor-resident irritants: methodology and research inferences, *Proceedings of the Travel Research Association*, 6th Annual Conference, San Diego, California, pp. 195–198.

Flood, J., C. Maher, P. Newton and J. Roy (1991). *The Determinants of Internal Migration in Australia*, CSIRO Division of Building, Construction and Engineering, Melbourne.

Getz, D. (1983). Capacity to absorb tourism: concepts and implications for strategic planning, *Annals of Tourism Research*, 10, pp. 239–263.

Getz, D. (1986). Models in tourism planning: towards integration of theory and practice, *Tourism Management*, 7 (1), pp. 21–32.

Getz, D. (1992). Tourism planning and the destination life cycle, *Annals of Tourism Research*, 19 (4), pp. 752–770.

Gordon, G. L., R. J. Calantone and C. A. di Benedetto (1991). Mature markets and revitalization strategies: an American fable, *Business Horizons*, 34 (3), pp. 39–49.

Hart, C. W., G. Casserly and M. J. Lawless (1984). The product life cycle: how useful?, *Cornell Hotel and Restaurant Administration Quarterly*, 25 (3), pp. 54–63.

Haywood, K. M. (1986). Can the tourist-area life cycle be made operational, *Tourism Management*, 7, pp. 154–167.

Haywood, K. M. (1992). Revisiting resort cycle, *Annals of Tourism Research*, 19 (2), pp. 351–354.

Hovinen, G.R. (1981). A tourist cycle in Lancaster County, Pennsylvania, *Canadian Geographer*, 15 (3), pp. 283–286.

Hovinen, G. R. (1982). Visitor cycles: outlook in tourism in Lancaster County, *Annals of Tourism Research*, 9, pp. 565–583.

Ioannides, D. (1992). Tourism development agents: the Cypriot resort cycle, *Annals of Tourism Research*, 19 (4), pp. 711–721.

Jafari, J. (1987). Tourism models: the sociocultural aspects, *Tourism Management*, 8 (2), pp. 151–159.

Jarviluoma, J. (1992). Alternative tourism and the evolution of tourist areas, *Tourism Management*, 13, pp. 118–120.

Keller, C. P. (1987). Stages of peripheral tourism development – Canada's North West Territories, *Tourism Management*, 8, pp. 20–32.

Kermath, B. M. and R. N. Thomas (1992). Spatial dynamics of resorts: Sosua, Dominican Republic, *Annals of Tourism Research*, 19, pp. 173–190.

Kotler, P. (1988). *Marketing Management: Analysis, Planning, Implementation and Control*, 6th ed., Prentice Hall, Englewood Cliffs.

Long, P. and J. Nuckolls (1992). Economic, Social and Environmental Impacts of Tourism Development: A Review of the Literature, Unpublished working paper, Hunter Valley Research Foundation, Newcastle.

Martin, B. S. and M. Uysal (1990). An examination of the relationship between carrying capacity and the tourism life cycle: management and policy implications, *Journal of Environmental Management*, 31, pp. 327–333.

Mathieson, A. and Wall, G. (1982). *Tourism: economic, physical and social impacts*, Longman.

Meyer-Arendt, K. J. (1985). The Grand Isle, Louisiana resort cycle, *Annals of Tourism Research*, 12 (3), pp. 449–465.

Morgan, M. (1991). Dressing up to survive: marketing Majorca anew, *Tourism Management*, 12 (1), pp. 15–20.

Mullins, P. (1990). Tourist Cities as New Cities: Australia's Gold Coast and Sunshine Coast, *Australian Planner*, 28, pp. 37–41.

Mullins, P. (1991). Tourism Urbanization, *International Journal of Urban and Regional Research*, 15 (3), pp. 326–342.

Mullins, P. (1992a). Cities for pleasure: the emergence of tourism urbanization in Australia, *Built Environment*, 18 (3), pp. 187–198.

Mullins, P. (1992b). Do industrial cities have the highest rates of urban unemployment?, *Urban Policy and Research*, 10 (1), pp. 24–32.

Mullins, P. (1993). Decline of the Old, Rise of the New: Late Twentieth Century Australian Urbanization in Najman, J.M. and Western, J.S. (eds.), *A Sociology of Australian Society*, Macmillan, Melbourne.

Oglethorpe, M. (1984). Tourism in Malta, *Leisure Studies*, 3, pp. 147–162.

Pearce, P.L., Moscardo, G. and Ross, G.F. (1991). Tourism impact and community perception: an equity-social representational perspective, *Australian Psychologist*, 26 (3), pp. 147–152.

Peck, J.G. and Lepie, A.S. (1989). Tourism and development in three North Carolina coastal towns, in Smith, V.L. (ed.), *Hosts and Guests: The Anthropology of Tourism*, 2nd Ed, University of Pennsylvania Press, Philadelphia.

Pigram, J.J. (1987). Tourism in Coffs Harbour: Attitudes, Perceptions and Implications, Unpublished Paper, University of New England, Armidale.

Plog, S.G. (1973). Why destination areas rise and fall in popularity, *Cornell Hotel and Restaurant Administration Quarterly*, 12 (1), pp. 13–16.

Prosser, G.M. (1985). The limits of acceptable change: an introduction to a framework for natural area planning, *Australian Parks and Recreation*, 22 (2), pp. 5–10.

Prosser, G.M. and P. Cullen (1987). Planning natural areas for sustainable tourism development, in *Metropolitan Prospectives in Parks and Recreation*, Royal Australian Institute of Parks and Recreation, Canberra.

Prosser, G.M. and J. Lang (1984). Post-modern regional economies: tourism and economic development, in Faulkner, B.W. *et al.*, *National Tourism Research Conference*, Bureau of Tourism Research Occasional Paper, Canberra.

Richardson, S. L. (1986). A product life-cycle approach to urban waterfronts: the revitalization of Galveston, *Coastal Zone Management Journal*, 14, pp. 21–46.

Roberts, S. (1991). A critical evaluation of the city life cycle idea, *Urban Geography*, 12 (5), pp. 431–449.

Sawers, L. and W.K. Tabb (1984). *Sunbelt / Snowbelt. Urban Development and Regional Restructuring*, Oxford University Press, New York.

Shaw, G. and A. M. Williams (1994). *Critical Issues in Tourism: A Geographical Perspective*, Blackwell, Oxford.

Smith, R. A. (1992). Beach resort evolution: implications for planning, *Annals of Tourism Research*, 19, pp. 304–322.

Strapp, J. D. (1988). The resort cycle and second homes, *Annals of Tourism Research*, 15 (4), pp. 504–516.

Urry, J. (1990). *The Tourist Gaze Leisure and Travel in Contemporary Societies*, Sage, London.

Warde, A. (1990). Production, consumption and social change, *International Journal of Urban and Regional Research*, 14 (2), pp. 228–248.

Weaver, D. (1988). The evolution of a 'Plantation' tourism landscape on the Caribbean island of Antigua, *Tijdschrift voor Economische en Sociale Geografie*, 79, pp. 319–331.

Weaver, D. B. (1990). Grand Cayman Island and the resort cycle concept, *Journal of Travel Research*, 29 (2), pp. 9–15.

Wernstein, B.L., H.T. Gross and J. Rees (1985). *Regional Growth and Decline in the United States*, Praeger, New York.

Williams, M. T. (1993). An expansion of the tourist site cycle model: the case of Minorca (Spain), *Journal of Tourism Studies*, 4 (2), pp. 24–32.

Yeates, N. (1990). *Coffs Harbour Vol I: Pre-1880 to 1945*, Bananacoast Printers, Coffs Harbour.

12

Developing a Strategic Approach to Skiing in Victoria

Bob McKercher

INTRODUCTION

Skiing is a little recognized, but highly significant activity in Australia where snowfields, covering 5200 km², extend over a greater area than in the European Alps. During the ski season which operates from early June to late September, up to 2.5 million people take part in downhill skiing with hundreds of thousands more visiting the adjacent national parks for cross country skiing. Victoria alone has ten ski areas however, until 1983, the ski industry in the state was disjointed and poorly coordinated. The major resort villages were managed by different arms of government that had little expertize and less interest in tourism, with each agency becoming involved in the ski industry as a result of historical accidents. The lack of central planning resulted in the duplication of some services and the non-provision of others. The servicing and marketing of the resorts was felt to be sub-optimal (CSAES, 1993), resulting in low profitability for the ski industry. The industry itself was fragmented and infighting occurred. As well, because of the lack of cohesion, environmental concerns were often ignored (CSAES, 1993). In 1983, the Victorian government established the Alpine Resorts Commission (ARC) in an attempt to redress these deficiencies.

This chapter discusses issues which have affected the development of alpine tourism in Victoria and examines the challenges faced when trying to impose a planning structure on a tourism region that has developed in a spontaneous, ad hoc and unplanned manner. It focuses on the three major resort villages that are managed by the Alpine Resorts Commission, Falls Creek, Mount Hotham and Mount Buller and analyses the roles played by the private and public sectors in their development.

STRATEGIC REGIONAL PLANNING: LITERATURE REVIEW

The strategic tourism planning challenge varies depending on the scale and focus of the organization involved in the activity. State and regional public sector agencies are often most interested in optimizing the benefits of tourism, while minimizing the social, cultural and environmental costs of this activity. To a large extent, public sector tourism planning is an attempt to control tourism by imposing a structure over an industry that has developed in a spontaneous manner. Consequently, many plans adopt a remedial focus (de Kadt, 1979). In a similar manner, public sector agencies involved in tourism activities in or near protected areas, are striving to develop sustainable tourism plans that permit tourism activities, while protecting important natural values (Elliott, 1987; McIntyre, 1993; CFL, 1990). Many of these plans also tend to be reactive in nature.

Local government agencies face somewhat different strategic planning challenges. In many instances, demand-driven tourism activity has simply overwhelmed the community's ability to cope with both large numbers of tourists and intense development pressures. The development of mass tourism is essentially similar to the urbanization process and from a local government perspective, involves the provision of a vast array of urban services (Smith, 1992; Singh *et al.* 1989). In such instances, the ideal of proactive strategic planning, leading to a supply led tourism industry becomes no more than a dream. In reality, too many communities have been forced into a reactive approach to strategic planning, striving first to provide suitable infrastructure for the existing tourism plant and then to limit further growth (Painton, 1990). It is only once these tasks have been achieved that community leaders can then begin to develop means by which the future development of the tourism industry can occur in an ordered manner (Getz, 1986).

The needs of the tourism industry at specific tourist precincts are different again. Operators' needs tend to be focused more closely on private sector issues relating to economic returns and the desire to renew or extend a destination's life cycle. As such, a stronger marketing and/or product development orientation is often adopted. Cooper (1990), for example, has identified four strategies to revitalize English resort areas in decline. His turnaround strategy suggests a concerted effort to reverse falling visitor numbers by investing in development, planning and substantial promotional efforts. His incremental growth strategy focuses on test marketing new products and phased development of new projects as the resort seeks new markets. Alternatively, a resort area may choose to focus only on specific niche markets that capitalize on the resort area's strengths.

Finally, tourism marketing agencies, including many Australian state tourism departments, have adopted a pure marketing approach to strategic planning. The goals of such strategic plans are to identify and capitalize on the Sustainable Competitive Advantages (SCAs) of a destination area. If SCAs are not evident, a parallel goal is to create them (Aaker, 1992). The recently completed Tourism Victoria Strategic Plan is a prime example of such an approach (TV, 1993). This document adopts a product focus that proposes a range of strategies to capitalize on or develop new SCAs for the State. Little attention is given, however, to such issues as the adverse social and environmental consequences of tourism; an omission that has created disquiet among the conservation movement.

Regardless of the scale of the organization involved in the process, the ultimate goal of strategic planning is to formulate longer term objectives and strategies for the entire business or business unit by matching its resources with its opportunities (Brown, 1992). Brown (1992:2) further states that *its purpose is to help a business to set and reach realistic objectives and to achieve a desired competitive position within a defined time.* From the perspective of different tourism organizations, the business or business unit can be defined along spatial terms according to the organization's influence. Thus the 'businesses' for a state tourism agency would be its entire tourism sector.

Planning is complicated further by the potentially different objectives of strategic and long range planning. The World Tourism Organization (1994) identified long range plans as the preferable planning option. Such plans, which are developed for periods of twenty years or more, should aim to create an ordered development of a destination area that will facilitate the achievement of broader goals, such as sustainability. The WTO feels that strategic plans, on the other hand, tend to adopt a shorter time frame, focusing on the identification and resolution of immediate issues. If applied without the benefit of a long term plan, strategic planning can be less comprehensive in its approach and may only be able to address immediate issues. A succession of strategic plans, without a longer term vision may deviate from the achievement of long term objectives.

At its heart, strategic planning, regardless of the level at which it is imposed, strives to ensure the long term viability of a tourism destination. Butler (1980), adopting a marketing approach, Plog (1976) using consumer behaviour theory and others illustrate that tourism destinations, like any other consumer product have defined life cycles. The roots of the decline can often be traced to an earlier lack of planning at the destination. This lack of planning is manifested in inadequate infrastructure development, lack of development controls and inappropriate developments that changed the fundamental character of the destination (Pearce, 1989), leading to a loss of appeal to visitors.

The sustainable tourism challenge for existing destination areas that have developed without strong planning guidelines becomes one of trying to impose a structure over an industry that has developed without one. In essence, this type of remedial planning strives to impose order over chaos. Unfortunately, this is where practice and theory diverge. A variety of *how to* planning guidelines for local, state and national tourism organizations have been developed (WTO, 1994; McIntyre, 1993; NSWTC, 1990; WATC, 1989) that strive to illustrate how tourism development can be planned. The weakness of these planning manuals is that they focus on future tourism development activities, often without addressing the historical issues that have driven past development at the destination. As such, they fail to account for the considerable amount of inertia that drives the ongoing development of many destinations. For these and other reasons, most tourism plans are either not implemented or do not achieve their objectives (Pearce, 1989).

Foster (1985) described various typologies of tourism development. Spontaneous development is most likely to occur in a region that has attractive scenery and climate, few large towns and little or no other commercial or industrial activity. Rapid development will occur if the place appeals to the mass market, if capital is available and if there is little or no control of development by a central or local government. The conditions for catalytic development are similar, except here, the actions of a single developer trigger complementary tourism developments. On the other hand, planned, localized development follows the careful analysis of relevant points, including the assessment of potential markets and the tourism capacity of the region. If properly planned, there should be few adverse effects. Development or expansion decisions are made based on the desire to optimize the benefits of tourism, while minimizing its costs.

In describing the types of tourism development, Foster also discusses the factors that influence their occurrence. Table 12.1 lists some key factors and describes the conditions in the Victorian Alps at the time the ski industry evolved. Clearly, the conditions were ideal for spontaneous development. Few, if any, development controls existed during the early years of skiing. Because the alpine villages were sited in non-populated areas above the snow line, the impact on local residents was negligible. Development was spawned initially by clubs, which meant that little finance was needed to build lodges and lifts. Tourism was seen as a positive activity by local residents and was regarded as an important adjunct to the local economy.

Both the public and private sectors have roles to play in developing and implementing effective strategic plans. Middleton (1986) suggests that it is appropriate to consider the public sector's role in resort development as being supply oriented, while the private sector's role is market oriented. He demonstrates that the public sector can play an important role in influencing the supply of tourism product through such actions as:

1) land use planning and the release of development land;
2) exercising influence over building types and styles, controlling the infrastructure;
3) influencing the development of facilities and services; and
4) influencing investment opportunities.

The public sector can also exert some influence over demand by controlling licensing of facilities, visitor flows, placing physical restrictions on parking and by influencing pricing policies.

The private sector can achieve its objectives through the judicious application of a number of initiatives designed to manage the market. Aaker (1992) discusses a range of strategies available to businesses to identify and capitalize on their competitive strengths, to overcome their competitive weaknesses, to exploit competitors' weaknesses or to nullify competitors' strengths. Essentially, Aaker argues that organizations have two major strategic options: low cost and differentiation. Skiing in Victoria enjoys no real cost advantages over skiing elsewhere, and so operators must strive to differentiate their product from other destinations to make it appealing. Alternative strategies include focusing on a small number of market segments or developing actions that preempt competitors. As discussed in the second half of this chapter, the Victoria ski resorts have differentiated their product and adopted both focus and pre-emptive strategies.

Factors Influencing Tourism Development	Conditions in the Victorian Alps
Size and extent of existing population	* Non-populated area
Diversity and vitality of existing activities prior to the introduction of tourism	* Limited activities, hydro-electric development at Falls Creek, tourism pioneering activity at Mount Hotham and Mt. Buller
Extensive or localized nature of the area	* Extensive, undeveloped alpine region
Whether facilities were planned or grew spontaneously because of some natural or man-made attraction	* Initial spontaneous development at Falls Creek, Mt. Buller and Mt. Hotham driven by clubs and only later by commercial tourism interests
Availability of land and finance	* Land readily available, little finance needed in initial stages
Impact on the local community	* No local community, regional centres saw skiing as a beneficial activity
Relationship of local traditions and attitudes of local residents to the tourism project	* Positive
Magnitude and speed of development	* Development slow until after WWII, rapid development in the 1950s and 1960s
State of the local economy and the possibilities of other forms of development	* Rural area with limited economic diversity
Presence or absence of development controls	* Few if any controls, lands managed by government agencies with other agendas
Size, dynamic nature of the local community and its facilities	* Non-existent in ski villages
The characteristics of the site and the financial and technical possibilities for development	* Attractive alpine sites offering excellent downhill skiing potential and reliable snow

(Source Foster, 1985)

Table 12.1: Factors Influencing Tourism Development

Brown (1992) discusses a range of marketing options available for organizations that are in a variety of competitive situations. He discusses three common forms of offensive strategy; *head on* strategy, *innovation* and *flanking*, that can be used in joint dominance situations like those found in the Victorian snow fields. He also discusses a range of strategies to assist lesser players position themselves against the leaders. Falls Creek, was able to adopt a head on strategy to compete against Mount Buller, once it identified it had greater snow making potential. Mount Hotham, on the other hand, being a smaller resort has had to position itself in a way that it can compete with the larger resorts. Reis and Trout (1986) in their seminal work on positioning, similarly, discuss a number of strategies available to enable a product or, by extension, a tourism destination to remain commercially viable. Positioning strategies have been used effectively in the Victorian Alps. Mount Buller has traditionally positioned itself as the leader of Victorian skiing, with all others as followers. In the last few years, however, Falls Creek has been able to create an attractive market position by promoting its ski guarantee. It has been able to re-position its main competitor, Mount Buller, as being a less attractive destination. Mount Hotham has effectively positioned itself in three niche markets, the rural Victorian club market, the expert skier's market and recently through the Dinner Plain residential development, as a four season alpine destination.

The dominant skiers' market for Victoria is the State's capital Melbourne. Market access, therefore, becomes a key factor in influencing the development and promotion of the region. Pearce (1989) defines market access as a relative term that is measured by travel time, cost, distance or effort required to travel to a destination. While physical access relates to the access infrastructure, market access relates to the relative proximity of competing destinations to their major markets. The basic premise of market access is that the destination that is closer to the market will generally enjoy higher use levels than a destination offering similar products that is located further away. Moreover, the nearer destination will generate greater short break or weekend visits than the further destination. Market access builds on the concept of the distance decay function (Bull, 1991). A relationship exists between time availability and willingness to travel longer distances to consume a tourism product. The greater the distance involved, the less willing the visitor will be to travel, unless the product is unique. As well, the preferred distance one is willing to travel is related to time availability and the total intended stay away from home. People travelling for longer periods of time are more willing to travel further than those travelling for shorter periods.

THE MANAGEMENT OF SKIING IN VICTORIA

Historical Development

Downhill skiing in Victoria is confined to the highest peaks of North-eastern Victoria's Great Dividing Range (Figure 12.1). As previously mentioned, the three most important resorts are Mount Buller, Falls Creek and Mount Hotham. They, along with Mount Stirling, Lake Mountain, Mount Baw Baw and, former-ly, Mount Donna Buang are managed by the Alpine Resorts Commission (ARC), a specialist government agency with broad environmental, planning and devel-opment powers (Keage and Fetterplace, 1993). Falls Creek and Mount Hotham are surrounded by the Alpine National Park, while the remaining resorts are either bounded by national park land, reserved forest or unreserved crown land.

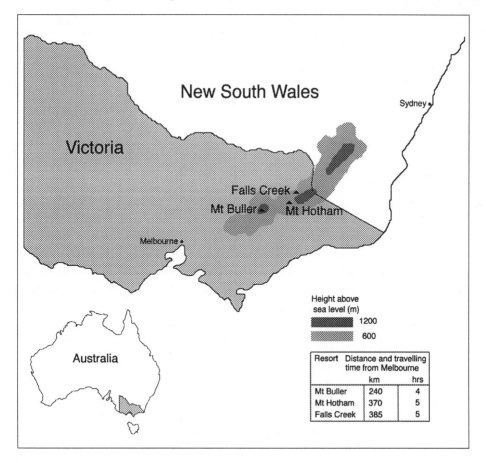

Figure 12.1: Victorian Alpine Resorts

Figure 12.1 summarizes key features of the three major resorts. Mount Buller is the largest resort in terms of skiable area, lift capacity and accommodation and is also the closest major resort to Melbourne. It has 26 lifts and over 160 hectares of skiable snow and offers 6,200 beds for visitors. Because of its proximity to Melbourne, it has had to develop a huge lift capacity to cater for peak weekend crowds. The resort, however, suffers from a capacity oversupply during the week. Falls Creek is the second largest ski area, offering 145 hectares of skiable snow, serviced by 22 lifts and 4,100 beds. It has the largest snow making area in the state and has effectively marketed its snow guarantee to gain market share from Mount Buller. Mount Hotham is the smallest of the major resorts, with nine runs servicing 52 hectares of skifields. It has about 3,400 beds available for club and commercial guests. Both Mount Hotham and Falls Creek are located more than five hours from Melbourne.

	Mount Buller	Falls Creek	Mount Hotham
Distance from Melbourne	240 km	385 km	370 km
Resort area (ha)	2,300	1,510	3,030
Elevation (m)	1,805	1,842	1,845
Skiable area (ha)	162	145	52
Number of lifts	26	22	9
Lift capacity (skiers/hr)	41,500	25,400	13,600
Snow making (ha)*	40	65	
Number of beds	6,300	4,100	3,430
Car parking capacity	2,000	1,700	1,020
Visitor days (1994)**	317,000	326,000	219,000
Commercial site holders	24	38	13
Non-commercial site holders	127	50	66

| * | Snow making has been extended at both Mount Buller and Falls Creek |
| ** | 1994 was a low snowfall year |

Source: Russell and Teller 1994, ARC 1995

Table 12.2: Key Features of Victoria's Major Alpine Resort Areas

Recreational clubs played a vital role in the early development of skiing. Their impact is still evident at Mount Buller and Mount Hotham where over 80 per cent of all sites are occupied by club lodges. Falls Creek, on the other hand, developed later than the other resorts and adopted a commercial focus earlier. As such, it has relatively fewer club sites. The preponderance of clubs has been cited as one of the reasons why the ski resort sector was slow to realize its potential. Alpine Resorts Commission staff feel that most sites occupied by clubs at

Mount Buller are not being used at their optimal levels. Many of the clubs built 'huts' with 10–25 beds, when the sites could and should cater to 40 or more beds. As well, some of the clubs are under-capitalized, which has meant that improvements and upgrading of facilities has not occurred. The ARC has initiated a policy of ensuring the clubs bring their facilities up to minimum standards by the turn of the Century or risk forfeiting their leases.

Australia and Victoria have played a key role in the development of skiing throughout the world. The world's first ski club was established in the NSW goldfields town of Kiandra. Mount Buffalo in Victoria was the second destination in the world to install a motorized ski lift when a rudimentary rope tow was installed in 1935 (Waters, 1967). It was the development of Mount Buller, however, that is recognized as signalling the beginning of downhill skiing as a mass tourism experience in this state (Waters, 1965). Development of Mount Buller was delayed by poor access, which was not rectified until 1939 when a road was completed as a Depression era labour relief programme. The first 'modern' chalet was built in 1929, housing up to 30 people. By 1934, Mount Buller was attracting international ski events. In 1948, the ski village site for Mount Buller was gazetted and the first leases for seven lodges were allotted. In 1949, the first ski tow was built. By the mid 1960s, 130 lodge sites had been allocated and developed and nine different types of tows had evolved to serve the varied needs of skiers (Waters, 1965).

Falls Creek began in 1940 when the Bogong Ski Club was formed by a group of workers from the Kiewa Valley Hydro Electric Development scheme. Falls Creek also enjoyed a period of rapid expansion after the War, thanks to the straightening and sealing of the Kiewa Valley Highway to better serve the needs of the hydro development. The identification of the Falls Creek village site by the State Electricity Commission in 1947 and subsequent development of ski lodges accelerated in the 1950s and 1960s with the development of ski lifts and commercial accommodation facilities.

Mount Hotham began life as an offshoot of Mount Buffalo. Seeking better quality skiing than that offered at Mount Buffalo, hardy skiers began exploring the nearby Alps in the 1920s. The first hospice for skiers was built in the 1920s and the area enjoyed a brief period of popularity in the 1930s. The fires of 1939, the advent of the Second World War, poor access and the development of Falls Creek, however, meant that Mount Hotham would never regain its ascendancy as a major ski resort.

Economic Importance

The Victorian skifields rank as one of the top five domestic tourism destinations in Australia (CSAES, 1993). In 1991, it is estimated that alpine tourism generated $269 million in expenditure in and around the alpine resorts and created the equivalent of 5,700 full time jobs. These activities also generate in excess of $15 million in tax revenue and fees for the State of Victoria (CSAES, 1993). In a good ski season, up to one million people will visit the resort areas and spend up to 1.5 million visitor days skiing. As well, it is estimated that upwards of 200,000 people visit the resort communities in the summer. The Victorian Alpine villages attract a predominantly domestic, Victorian market, with Melbourne alone accounting for 76 per cent of all visitors in 1991 (CSAES, 1993). Visitor figures for the year ending 31 December, 1994 show that 92 per cent of the 210,000 visitors to Mount Buller live in Victoria, while 84 per cent of the 109,000 visitors to Mount Hotham and 69 per cent of the visitors to Falls Creek were also Victorians (TV, 1995).

The viability of the ski industry has been affected by highly variable snow-falls in the last six years. The industry was very profitable during high snowfall years in 1990, 1991 and 1995, but suffered through low snow years in 1992, 1993 and 1994. The 1993 season was especially poor, being described as the winter of no snow. One low altitude resort, Mount Buffalo, operated for only three days throughout the entire winter, while all other resorts recorded significantly reduced visitation levels. Operators plan on an eight week optimal ski season. If this figure is achieved or exceeded, the businesses will remain profitable. If poor snow conditions reduce the ski season to six weeks or less, operators will record losses. Efforts made to extend the season through artificial snow making are discussed elsewhere in this chapter.

Administration

Until the mid 1980s, ski resorts in Victoria developed in an uncoordinated and spontaneous manner, due mainly to the lack of an over-riding coordinating management structure. Importantly, each ski area was managed by a number of State Government agencies (Russell and Teller, 1994), often with little interest or expertise in tourism management. The three largest resorts areas, Mount Buller, Falls Creek and Mount Hotham, for example, were managed by the Forests Commission, the State Electricity Commission of Victoria and the Lands Department, respectively. The State Electricity Commission became involved in the ski industry at Falls Creek because a ski village developed around its construction site for the Kiewa Valley Hydro Electric project. As a result, few effective means were available to control the industry. Complicating the issue was the fact that each resort village was administered by development-oriented Committees of Management.

The resulting fragmented approach to the down hill ski industry restricted its ability to achieve its recreational or economic potential. The lack of a common administrative body led to the duplication of facilities, fierce competition between resort areas and uncoordinated approach to skiing. Moreover, necessary capital investment and infrastructure development did not occur. As a result, rather than co-operatively working together to build a viable Victorian ski industry and to position it effectively against the NSW industry, the individual resorts competed inefficiently among themselves.

Even the ski industry itself recognized that the existing management structure was ineffective. In 1950, a Parliamentary State Development Committee was created to investigate the issue of alpine development. Their recommendations led, eight years later, to the creation of the Tourist Development Authority and, in 1961, to the formation of the Alpine Resorts Development Advisory Committee (ARDAC). As an advisory committee, ARDAC served its purpose well. It succeeded in raising the quality of the standards of accommodation in the alpine villages and in improving the infrastructure. As a regulatory body, however, it proved to be almost totally ineffective. As Johnson noted (1974: 89) ARDAC *proved to be little more than a forum and a means by which official recommendations for tourist funds could be made. Because no department felt challenged in the continued control of its traditional areas, they all co-operated freely.*

The Report of the Ski Industry of Victoria Working Party in 1980 acknowledged that ARDAC and other existing management structures were badly in need of change. It recommended the formation of a Ski Resorts Council by an Act of Parliament to *co-ordinate the planning, development, standards and financing of ski resorts* (SIVWP, 1980). Among the key responsibilities of the proposed Ski Resorts Council was the development of a broad strategic plan for all ski resorts as a group and the initiation of a coordinated approach to the planning, establishment development and public funding of ski resorts. The council would further ensure that ski resorts are viable business undertaking and that the Council would prevent any undesirable exploitation of the features or facilities of ski resorts (SIVWP, 1980).

This report was the catalyst for the creation of the Alpine Resorts Commission through the enactment of the Alpine Resorts Act of 1983. The Alpine Resorts Commission Act (1983) stipulates that its role is:

- to plan the proper establishment, development, promotion and use of alpine resorts, having regard to environmental ecological and safety considerations . . . ;
- to undertake the orderly establishment, continuation and development of alpine resorts, a range of tourist accommodation . . . and facilities and services;
- to control and manage alpine resorts and their use; and
- to carry out the functions of a planning authority and a responsible authority for alpine resorts.

(Part 1, Sect 8, ARC Act, 1983)

The ARC is a self funding agency which derives its revenue from entry fees, lease payments and a 'rating' system. It receives no funding from the State government. Any surplus is injected back into the resorts. The operations of the Commission and the day-to-day management of the resorts have been devolved largely to the individual resort areas. As outlined in Figure 12.2, the ARC has a lean management structure. The Commission itself is governed by an overall management committee and has separate planning and financial/administration branches. Each resort also has a committee of management that advises the ARC on corporate issues, vets development proposals and comments on all plans affecting the resort. The Committee of Management for Falls Creek, for example, is composed of ten individuals, including representatives from the lift company, the chamber of commerce, skiers' groups, Victorian Roads Corporation, management staff from the adjacent national park and a local government representative.

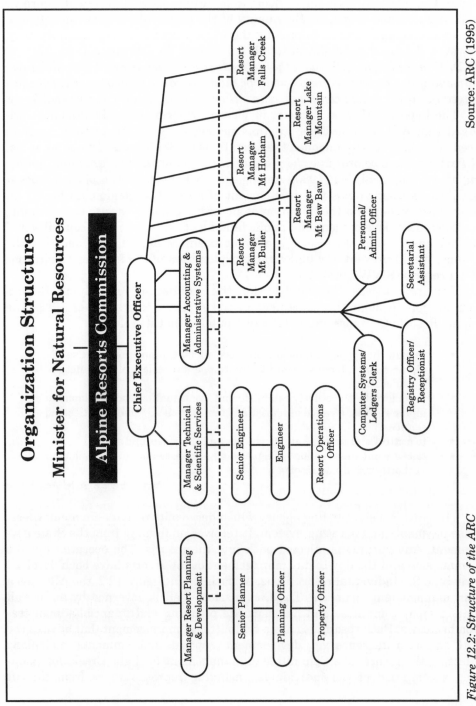

Figure 12.2: Structure of the ARC

Source: ARC (1995)

Section 9 of the Act, gives the Commission virtually the same powers as a municipal council. As all land within the resorts is Crown land, the ARC acts as the landlord on behalf of the State government. The ARC, therefore, is responsible for all leases of occupation, the approval of development proposals, the provision of urban services of sewage, water, garbage collection and electricity, manages the road network and invests in capital projects that are felt to be in the common good of the community.

The other important stakeholder is the lift company, which is also the largest investor at the resort. These operators hold the lease over the ski slopes and lifts and may also be the leaseholders for some commercial sites. The Falls Creek Ski Lifts Pty Ltd, for example, is responsible for the 145 hectares of skiable snow in the resort, the 22 lifts, the ski school and also runs some hospitality services. The lift company employs over 300 people during the peak ski season. It has invested in excess of $15 million on new ski lifts and snow making facilities in the last seven years. At present, Victoria has not adopted the approach used in New South Wales of offering the lift company the head lease over the entire resort.

Management Issues: the role of the Alpine Resorts Commission

The transition from an *ad hoc* approach to ski development to a planned, centrally controlled and integrated Victorian ski industry has not been easy for the ARC, the ski industry, conservationists or the Victorian Government. The early years of the organization were typified by rising expenses and public disquiet about the performance of the Commission. As Russell and Teller (1994) report, the period from 1984–1990 saw the activities of the ARC expand along with its operating losses and the level of government subsidy. As well, during this time *the ARC approach* [to managing the resorts] *created significant conflict and alienation with the* [tourism] *industry participants* which led to *a public image of widespread discontent with its performance* (Russell and Telle,r 1994: 4, 5). Among the complaints were that the ARC did not consult relevant players on planning and development issues, that it assumed roles that were not relevant to its role, that it failed to pay adequate attention to environmental issues and that it added costs to the operation of the ski industry (Russell and Teller, 1994).

In 1990, a number of apparently successful steps were taken to reform the ARC. Its budget was controlled and its operations were streamlined. In the next four years, it succeeded in turning an operating deficit of almost $6 million into a net surplus. Staff numbers have been cut in half from a peak of 134 in 1989 to 67 by 1993. It has altered its promotional strategy from one of initiation to facilitation. It has aggressively promoted the resorts as four season destinations. Importantly, it has striven to create a greater sense of confidence among ski industry operators. As Russell and Teller (1994) illustrate, a number of ongoing issues still remain, including environmental concerns, better industry consultation and the provision of a State-wide ski industry strategy. The conservation movement has also documented the ARC's environmental shortcomings (Ensor, 1989; Pittock, 1990).

A complete review of the ARC was commissioned by the Victorian Government in mid 1994, as the result of public outcry over proposed plans to develop Mount Stirling as Victoria's next downhill ski resort. Its report was submitted to the government in mid 1994. At the time of writing, final actions from the Victorian Government were still pending, although in early 1995, it announced that the contracts of all five Commissioners would not be renewed (Elias, 1995). Many people involved in the ski industry view the report as a political document with an unwritten agenda of providing a means of extracting the State Liberal/National Government from an unpopular development proposal and in doing so, to rid it of the last vestiges of the previous government. The document can be criticized as it identifies and then chooses to ignore the underlying structural challenges facing the ARC in developing a strategic vision for Victorian skiing.

The document recognizes, for example, that when the ARC was formed, it inherited an arrangement of *ad hoc* planning procedures, leasing arrangements and financial practices where a variety of work practices and policies had been used. It also acknowledges that its task has been made harder by the arbitrary nature of the establishment of the individual resort boundaries, which were established without much regard for management requirements, optimal planning and environmental protection. Lastly, it recognizes that the ARC is in the process of developing draft planning strategies for all resorts, but condemns the organization for failing, as yet, to have these plans reach the stage of Ministry approval. The Alpine Resorts Commission Review Panel acknowledges, however, that it has significantly improved its performance since 1990 and that it has begun to achieve its goals of a coordinated and planned approach to the development and promotion of the alpine resorts (Russell and Teller, 1994). The findings of the review panel describe a destination that is still in transition from unplanned to planned development.

In spite of these obstacles, the Alpine Resorts Commission has managed to address many of the issues restricting the development of skiing in Victoria. As mentioned earlier, the management of the ski industry had been previously vested in a variety of government agencies that had no formal mandate in tourism. Moreover, each agency had discharged its duties in a different way, resulting in some resorts being advantaged over others. The ARC, by being able to impose a central management structure, has been able to overcome many of these inequities resulting from different organizational attitudes and cultures. It has initiated a planning and approval process in a consistent manner across the state. It also managed to standardize the leasehold arrangements across all resorts, which has provided a degree of security for investors that did not exist previously. In a similar manner, it has set up development guidelines and is pursuing the creation of design advisory bodies, to encourage developments of a scale and form that are suitable for each property and consistent with the broader goals of the resort. Prior to its formation, large developments that changed the character of the resorts had been constructed at both Mount Buller and Mount Hotham.

The greatest strength of the ARC lies in its abilities to adopt a state-wide perspective on the needs of the ski industry and to initiate major infrastructure programmes for the benefit of the entire sector. Such projects have included a $2 million investment to connect Mount Hotham to the State Electricity grid (ARC ,1995). Prior to 1994, Mount Hotham generated its own electricity; a costly and potentially environmentally hazardous exercise that limited the resort's capacity. The ARC has also invested in upgrading the water and sewage systems at the resorts. While work still needs to be done at other properties, Falls Creek's sewage outflow meets Environmental Protection Authority guidelines (ARC, 1994). The ARC has also invested in the development of visitor centres and day-use shelters, notably at Falls Creek and Mount Buller. In addition, since all resort facilities are on Crown land, the ARC has become an effective landlord on behalf of the state for the release of new land for development. It has the ability, therefore, to approve development projects and to ensure that the type, nature and timing of new projects achieves the optimal use of the resort area.

The ARC has been criticized for failing to develop a state-wide master plan for the orderly development of the ski industry (Russell and Teller, 1994). It concedes that there is an ongoing question of who leads the development of skiing in Victoria, the ski industry or the ARC. A series of draft strategic plans were developed for each resort area between 1989 and 1991. As well, 'Ski Plan Victoria' was written in 1992 to provide guidelines for the development of the ski industry over the next fifteen years. To date, none of these documents has been formally adopted by the minister responsible for the ARC. In addition, staff readily admit that there has been no attempt to integrate the individual draft plans into a state-wide strategy. As such, vital issues relating to the optimum size of the state's ski industry have not been addressed. The completion, acceptance and implementation of these plans has been identified as a priority objective for the organization.

Achieving this level of integration has proved difficult for a number of reasons. Skiing in Victoria has become highly politicized. A change of government in 1992 meant that the planning process had to be halted until the new government set its agenda and became familiar with the issues. The process received another setback when a complete review of the ARC was commissioned by the Victorian Government in mid 1994, as the result of public outcry over proposed plans to develop Mount Stirling. The ski industry also resisted efforts to impose an overall plan for Victoria. It has been difficult to get both the ARC field staff and the individual resorts to see the benefits of a master plan. The resorts are geographically diverse and have not traditionally had a lot to do with each other. The issue is complicated by the historic management of the resorts by different government agencies, resulting in different operational and philosophical cultures emerging. Finally, the alpine villages are fiercely competitive with each other.

The co-ordination challenge is complicated by the rapidly changing business environment affecting skiing and the perceived lack of flexibility of the plans that were developed. The draft development plans which were written in 1989 and called for up to $650 million of investment and the virtual doubling of the ski industry in Victoria, are now outdated. In the early 1990s, Australia suffered its worst recession since the Great Depression and the demand for skiing declined. Moreover, the plans were developed based on historic annual growth rates of 8 per cent to 10 per cent registered in the 1970s. The background growth rates in the last 15 years, however, has been less than 3.0 per cent (Keage and Fetterplace, 1993). In fact, the low snow years of 1992–1994, coupled with the recession have resulted in a real decline in interest in skiing. Additionally, many ski operators felt that the proposed development plans were inflexible statements of how the resorts would be developed rather than guidelines to be considered for future developments. As a result, they generated a level of antipathy from the operators. As Ian Grant from the Falls Creek Ski Lift Pty Ltd suggests, the best plans are dynamic in nature and able to evolve to changing market conditions. They should provide a broad visionary statement and propose planning guidelines, but they should not be inflexible. Falls Creek has adopted the intent of the 1989 master plan and consults it when debating future development proposals.

Whether the Alps need a comprehensive master plan is open to debate. Submissions to the ARC review process revealed a range of opinions. Conservation groups and anti-skiing organizations see the need for a master plan, primarily to bring the ski industry under control. The industry, however, sees the need for a general planning strategy for each resort which is flexible, sets standards and has a vision (FCMC, 1994). It does not see the need, however, for a state-wide plan.

Management Issues: Market Access and Resort Development

As illustrated in Table 12.3, market access plays a critical role in the use of Victoria's ski fields. Mount Buller, the closest resort to Melbourne, attracts over 75 per cent of its visitors from the metropolitan region. On the other hand, Falls Creek and Mount Hotham, which are located five or more hours from Melbourne attract a relatively smaller percentage of their total clients from the city. While Melbourne remains the largest single market for both resorts, in 1992, Mount Hotham generated 34 per cent of its business from country Victoria, whereas Falls Creek generated 31.4 per cent of all visitations from inter-state. Mount Hotham is the nearest resort to the major population centres of central Victoria and Gippsland. Falls Creek, which enjoys strong highway access from Albury, is the closest resort to Queensland, New South Wales and South Australia.

Table 12.3 also illustrates two other important features resulting from the different market access enjoyed by the resorts. Mount Buller has the greatest number of day visitors and the greatest proportion of day visitor-days of any of the three resorts. Further, the mountain recorded the lowest average length of stay of overnight visitors, signifying its appeal as a short break or weekend ski destination. Peak weekend visitor flows have meant that Mount Buller has had to develop the greatest lift capacity, the largest number of car and bus parking spaces and the largest amount of accommodation to cope with the demand. Its capacity has been designed for the six or seven most popular weekends on the year, leaving the resort with a major over-capacity problem in non-peak periods. The ski season at Mount Buller is typified by large crowds on the weekends and low occupancy levels during the week. To overcome this weekly cycle, resort marketers have tried to attract Japanese inbound skiers who arrive Sunday evening and leave Friday night. This scheme, however, has not been successful, partly because of the poor snow seasons recorded in 1993 and 1994. The ARC has developed plans to reduce Mount Buller's lift capacity to a more sustainable level.

	Mt. Buller	Mount Hotham	Falls Creek
Proximity to Melbourne.	3 hrs	5 hrs	5+ hrs
% of visitors from Melbourne (1994 ski season)	75.8	42.8	42.0
Total Visitors (1992)	308,424	106,147	155,841
Total Visitor days	452,470	233,391	347,487
Number of Day Visitors	226,323	61,442	97,327
Number of overnight visitors	82,101	44,705	58,514
% Day Visitors	73.4	57.9	62.5
% of Vis/days attributed to day visitors	50.0	26.3	28.0
Number of overnight visitor-days	226,139	171,949	250,160
% of Vis/days attributes to overnight visitors	50.0	73.7	72.0
Average length of stay all visitors (nights)	1.47	2.20	2.23
Average L.O.S of overnight visitors (nights)	2.75	3.85	4.28

Source: ARC Visitor Statistics, 1993, 1994

Table 12.3: The Impact of Market Access on Skifield Visitation in Victoria (1992)

Falls Creek and Mount Hotham are classic examples of destinations that have identified and capitalized on an opportunity created by relatively poorer market access. Poorer market access does not necessarily mean that the destination is disadvantaged. It simply means that it has to position itself in a manner that accounts for the relatively greater time or effort involved in getting to that destination. Falls Creek and Mount Hotham have positioned themselves as Victoria's destination resorts for longer ski holidays and have more aggressively sought non-metropolitan markets. As evidenced by Table 12.3, day visitors accounted for only about one-quarter of all visitor days spent at the resorts in 1992. At the same time, while these resorts had fewer overnight visitors than Mount Buller, they tended to stay almost twice as long. Mount Hotham and Falls Creek attract both weekend and week-long skiers. The result is that demand is spread more evenly through the ski week, reducing the need for greater lift capacity, accommodation and parking as found at Mount Buller.

The longer lengths of stay create the demand for more varied skiing at Falls and Hotham. Responding to consumer demand, Falls Creek constructed the Maze, a series of expert runs cut through the snow gum forest at the north end of the resort. To service the demand for this run, the lift company invested $1.6 million to build a new quad chairlift on its Summit run. Mount Hotham has also developed new black diamond runs in the area initially skied in the 1930s but long abandoned. As well, a snow bridge was constructed over the main access highway to develop a longer run and built 'the Australia Drift' chairlift to access a new intermediate ski area. The bridge was funded largely by the ARC.

Management Issues: the Role of the Private Sector and Resort Positioning

The private sector has adopted a strategic marketing approach to ensure the long term viability of each of the resort areas. Each has positioned itself differently in the marketplace based on its market access opportunities, its historic evolution, its terrain and its proximity to the Alpine National Park. Further, each is planning its future development to capitalize on opportunities or to overcome perceived weaknesses. Competition between the resorts is intense and has been described by one operator as 'cut throat'. Mount Buller is being positioned as the up-market day or weekend destination for Melburnians and as Victoria's high quality, prestige resort. Mount Hotham is capitalizing on its reputation as a 'skiers' mountain, having the steepest terrain in Victoria and the largest number of black diamond runs. As well, the development of the nearby Dinner Plain condominium village has enabled Hotham to become a popular summer destination. Falls Creek is positioned as a mid market, family ski destination with the most reliable snow in Victoria. Capitalizing on its European village feel, it is promoting itself as *Switzerland with gum trees*.

Private sector development of Falls Creek has been market driven, with the community's largest business, the Falls Creek Ski Lift Pty Ltd leading the development. Significant changes in the strategic direction of Falls Creek began in

1990 with the appointment of a new general manager of the lift company. Prior to that time, Falls Creek, like most moderately successful destinations, was content to continue to offer the products that had led to its initial success. There was little innovation in the product offering and a lack of a strategic vision in the future development of the resort.

Since 1990, however, its development, marketing and promotional strategies have been market driven. To begin, it conducted extensive market research to examine its own strengths and weaknesses in comparison with other ski resorts. The research revealed that Falls Creek had a unique, but previously unrecognized sustainable competitive advantage that no other resort in Australia could match. This asset was the State Electricity Commission's Rocky Valley Dam, a water catchment dam for the Kiewa Valley Hydro-electric scheme. The dam created the potential for virtually unlimited snow making. As a result, Falls Creek embarked on a massive expansion of its snow making area. This $4.0 million investment paid immediate dividends during the record low snow year of 1993. Total visitor days fell by 70 per cent at Mount Buller and by more than one third at Mount Hotham between 1992 and 1993, while Falls Creek's visitation levels fell by only 23 per cent (ARC, 1995).

Building on the reputation it earned in 1993, Falls Creek initiated a snow guarantee for 1994. The snow guarantee promised to refund the full cost of accommodation and lift tickets if there was insufficient snow. No other resort was able to match the guarantee. This proved fortuitous for 1994 was also a low snow year. Falls Creek is now firmly positioned in the consumers' mind as offering the most reliable skiing in the State. The ability to identify and capitalize on this opportunity through the use of strategic planning principles has enabled Falls Creek to reach its target of attracting 40 per cent of the Victorian ski market. Interestingly, Mount Buller, which had previously invested in extending its car parking facilities embarked on an ambitious snow making programme of its own in 1994. It too now offers a snow guarantee, but has been pre-empted in the marketplace by Falls Creek.

Each resort conducts ongoing market research to gain a better understanding of the consumer impressions of their ski destination. The research at Falls Creek revealed that it was seen as a lovely resort that offered good quality intermediate skiing. It was seen to lack steep terrain and the type of expert skiing available at either Mount Hotham or Mount Buller. It was also seen to lack modern lift facilities. With the co-operation of the ARC, the lift company set about to correct this perceived deficiency by developing the Maze ski area which offers the longest, steepest and tightest runs at the resort. As well, the lift company embarked on an ambitious multi-million dollar scheme to replace older T bars with new high speed detachable triple and quad chair lifts.

The research also revealed that there was a lack of comprehensive and well coordinated marketing of the resort. To overcome this weakness Falls Creek Inc. was established in 1993–94. As outlined in the annual report for the resort:

this initiative which was approved by the [ARC] Management Committee following a request from the Falls Creek Chamber of Commerce, was aimed at generic marketing of Falls Creek to complement the existing Chamber and Lift Company programmes. The marketing programme was based on a funding allocation of $A 85,036 derived from a 7 per cent levy on service charges. (ARC 1994: 22).

Falls Creek Inc. has been able to achieve a greater level of marketing activity than was attainable previously. In doing so, all businesses at the resort have benefited. The programme was so successful that it has been introduced to mount Buller for the 1994–95 ski season.

CONCLUSIONS

This chapter has illustrated some of the practical challenges involved in attempting to convert a destination region that has evolved in an unplanned manner into an integrated, destination managed under the auspices of an umbrella government agency. It examined the varying approaches to strategic planning and discussed some of the pragmatic factors inhibiting the effective co-ordination of tourism in a regional area. The chapter highlighted two major strategic issues that must be considered by regional tourism destinations. The first is the need, role and purpose of an over-arching public sector body. The second addresses some of the strategic planning challenges the private sector must consider.

The need to create a State-wide management body responsible for the entire Victorian downhill ski industry was recognized by all parties involved in skiing in Victoria in the 1960s. Yet, in spite of this, it took nearly another 25 years to create the Alpine Resorts Commission. Once operational, it took a further seven years before the agency clarified its role and began to do the job the ski industry felt it should. To a very real extent, even though the ARC had been operational for twelve years, it is still a very new organization that is striving to clarify its role.

The experiences of the Alpine Resorts Commission highlight some of the advantages and disadvantages of creating a state-wide tourism body with wide ranging powers to manage a specific tourism sector. Its greatest benefits have been the imposition of consistent land use and regulatory management regimes to areas that had been managed previously by different government departments with highly variable management structures. The lack of consistent rules for each destination area had disadvantaged many of the destinations, hindering their growth and ultimately their long term viability. As a result, with each destination operating under the same management and legislative structure, they are now able to compete in a more balanced manner.

As well, organizations such as the ARC can play a vital role in the creation of a state-wide vision for an industry sector and in enabling smaller players to overcome some of their infrastructural weaknesses. The ARC has begun to develop a strategic vision for skiing in Victoria and has also begun to remove some of the planning activities away from individual resorts. It would have been impossible for Mount Hotham to be connected to the State Electricity Grid, for example, without the creation of the ARC. In a similar manner, the development of non-revenue generating day use facilities and investments in upgrading of urban infrastructure at each destination has been facilitated by the ARC.

But, the experience of the ARC also highlights a major challenge of trying to impose an outside organization to force the integration of geographically isolated destination areas that have traditionally viewed each other as fierce competitors. While a greater level of integration between industry and the ARC and among the resorts themselves has been achieved, to a large extent, the resorts still see themselves as independent entities that are competing for a share of the same domestic market. Each sees itself as a discrete community with a unique personality and history; each is located in a geographically dispersed area; and each is driven by market factors. Perhaps it is naive to assume that any government agency could integrate completely the activities of ten discrete destination areas. If the umbrella state organization succeeds in developing a strategic vision for each resort, ensures that suitable infrastructure is provided to reduce environmental costs and to optimize tourism opportunities and succeeds in imposing a consistent management, regulatory and licensing structure across all resorts, it has done its job. The resorts themselves can then compete effectively and fairly within this framework.

The second key lesson from this chapter relates to the strategies that can be developed by the private sector to enable destination areas to be competitive in a small marketplace. The paper highlighted the importance of market access and illustrated how it should influence the strategic development of destination areas. Mount Buller, with strong market access to Melbourne has become a day and weekend destination. It has had to develop the largest lift infrastructure and the greatest amount of car parking to accommodate weekend peaks. Falls Creek and Mount Hotham, on the other hand, enjoy relatively poorer market access. Rather than regarding this as a strategic weakness, however, these ski areas have positioned themselves as destination resorts and have developed their facilities accordingly.

As well, the chapter highlights the need for a market driven approach to positioning a destination. Falls Creek was able to re-invigorate its life cycle in the early 1990s by the judicious application of a strategic marketing plan. The initial analytical phase identified its water supply as a strategic competitive advantage held by no other ski area, enabling it to introduce the state's first snow guarantee. This proved fortuitous as the following two winters recorded low snow. Further, by conducting market research, it was able to develop an understanding of the consumers' perception of the resort and of its product strengths and weaknesses. As a result, Falls Creek developed new expert ski slopes and upgraded its lift system. Mount Hotham and Mount Buller also embarked on similar programmes.

The result of the public and private sector initiatives to develop a more strategic approach to skiing in Victoria has been the revitalization of the ski industry. At present, the ARC and the ski industry seem to be working well together, although the question of leadership needs to be resolved. The roles played by each sector are consistent with those identified by Middleton (1986), with the public sector influencing the supply of tourist facilities and the private sector influencing demand for these facilities. The situation should continue to function well into the near future, providing that each player recognizes and respects the role of the other. Certainly the Victorian ski industry is in a far more favourable position than it was at the beginning of the 1980s. The risk of this approach, however, is that without a comprehensive state-wide vision, the potential exists for each resort to embark on an unsustainable development programme designed not to expand the market, but to steal market share from other resorts. As Victoria's ski industry matures, the need may become greater for a more influential umbrella organization.

REFERENCES

Aaker, D. (1992) *Strategic Market Management* 3rd Ed. Brisbane: John Wiley and Sons.

ARC (1994) *Falls Creek Alpine Resort: Annual Report Operations and Services 1993/94*, Alpine Resorts Commission, Melbourne.

ARC (1995) *Annual Report 1993–94*, Alpine Resorts Commission, Melbourne

Brown, L. (1992) *Competitive Marketing Strategy*. Melbourne: Nelson.

Buckley, R., Pannell, J (1990) Environmental Impacts of Tourism and recreation in National Parks and Conservation Reserves *The Journal of Tourism Studies*, Vol 1, No. 1, May, pp. 24–32.

Bull A (1991) *The Economics of Travel and Tourism*, Pitman, Melbourne.

Butler R.W. (1980) The Concept of Tourist Area Cycle Evolution; implications for the management of resources, *Canadian Geographer*, 24(1) pp. 5–12.

CFL (1990) *Presenting Victoria, CFL's Tourism Policy*, Victorian Department of Conservation Forest and Lands, Melbourne.

Cooper C (1990) Resorts in Decline – the management response, *Tourism Management* March, pp. 63–67.

CSAES (1993) *The Economic Significance of Alpine Resorts*, Centre for South Australian Economic Studies, Adelaide

de Kadt E. (1979) *Tourism: Passport to Development*, Oxford University Press, New York.

Elias, D. (1995) Government Dumps all Five Alpine Commissioners, *The Age*, Mar 30, 1995, pp. 1, 2.

Elliott, J. (1987) Government management of Tourism – a Thai Case, *Tourism Management*, Vol 8 (3), pp. 223–232.

Ensor, J. (1989) Victoria's Alps: Still at the Cross-roads, *Parkwatch*, March, pp. 5–8.

FCMC (1994) *Falls Creek Management Committee Submission to the Alpine Resorts Commission Review Panel*, Falls Creek Management Committee, Falls Creek, Vic.

Fetterplace, D. (1994) Alpine Resort Management in Victoria, paper presented at the Sixth Australasian Regional Seminar on National Parks and Wildlife Management.

Foster, D. (1985) *Travel and Tourism Management*, Macmillan, London.

Getz, D. (1986) Models in Tourism Planning: Towards Integration of theory and practice, *Tourism Management*, March, pp. 21–32.

Johnson, D. (1974) *The Alps at the Crossroads*, Victorian National Parks Association, Melbourne.

Keage, P., Fetterplace, D. (1993) Ecologically Sustainable Development and Victoria's Alpine Resorts, paper presented at the East Asia Pacific Mountain Association, Canterbury, NZ.

McIntyre, G. (1993) *Sustainable Tourism Development: Guide for Local Planners*, World Tourism Organization, Madrid.

Mercer, D. (1991) *A Question of Balance: Natural Resource Conflict Issues in Australia*, The Federation Press, Leichardt, NSW.

Middleton, V. (1986) Public Sector/Private Sector Resort development; conflict or co-operation, in Hollingshead, K. (ed.) *National Conference on Tourist Resort Development: Markets, Plans and Impacts,* the Centre for Leisure and Tourism Studies, Kuring-gai College of Advanced Education, Sydney.

NSWTC (1990) *New South Wales Tourism Development Strategy: A Plan for the Future*, Sydney.

Painton, P. (1991) Fantasy's reality, *Time Magazine*, 27 May, pp. 44–51.

Pearce, D. (1989) *Tourist Development, 2nd Edition*, Longman Scientific, Harlow.

Pittock, J. (1990) Alpine Resorts: Issues of Expansion, *Parkwatch*, September, pp. 22–24.

Plog, S. (1973) Why Destination Areas Rise and Fall in Popularity, *Cornell Hotel and Restaurant Administration Quarterly,* November, pp. 13–16.

Reis, A. and Trout, J. (1986) *Positioning: The battle for your mind*, Warner Books, New York.

Russell, B., Teller, L. (1994) *Alpine Resorts Commission Review Panel Report*, prepared for the Minister for Natural Resources, Melbourne.

Singh, T.V., Theuns, H.L., Go, F.M. (Eds) (1989) *Towards Appropriate Tourism: The Case of Developing Countries*, European University Studies, Peter Lang, Frankfurt.

SIVWP (1980) Report of the Ski Industry of Victoria Working Party, Ski Industry Association, Melbourne.

Smith, R. (1992) Beach Resort Evolution: Implications for Planning, *Annals of Tourism Research,* Vol. 19, pp. 304–322.

TV (1993) *Tourism Victoria Strategic Business Plan*, Tourism Victoria, Melbourne.

TV (1995) *Visitors to Victoria's Attractions: Year Ending 31 December 1994*, Tourism Victoria, Melbourne.

Waters, W.F. (1965) Mount Buller Victoria's Alpine Village – A Brief History of the Mountain – its discovery and development, *Melbourne Walker*, Vol. 36, pp. 8–18.

Waters, W.F. (1967) The Buffalo Mountains – A Brief History, *Melbourne Walker*, Vol. 38, pp. 17–33.

WATC, EPA (1989) *The Eco Ethics of Tourism Development.* Western Australia Tourism Commission and the Environmental Protection Authority, Perth.

WTO (1994) *National and Regional Tourism Planning: Methodologies and Case Studies*, Routledge, London.

13

Developing a Regional Concept for a Resort Destination: Challenges and Opportunities in the Whitsundays

Brian King

INTRODUCTION

This chapter outlines the attempt by one of Australia's prime resort destinations to develop a coherent regional marketing concept. It charts the historical development of tourism in the Whitsundays, a chain of continental islands off the north Queensland coast between Mackay and Bowen (Figure 13.1). Although the Whitsundays are within the area administered by the Great Barrier Reef Marine Park Authority (GBRMPA), they are located some 40 kilometres from the Reef itself at the closest point (GBRMPA, 1993a).

Market trends are outlined to highlight the types of consumer attracted to the mainland and to the islands, two of which – Hayman and Hamilton resorts – are the subject of more detailed examination. Each is relevant to the emerging redefinition of regional tourism, since during their early development, both were promoted as being set apart from and superior to, both their competition and the region itself. More recently, both have embraced the regional Whitsundays concept as a better way of establishing consumer recognition in key source markets. Finally some conclusions are drawn to show that resorts need to acknowledge the regional environment within which they operate as an integral part of their marketing. Co-operation within a regional tourism structure is an important element in a strategy to recognize that island resorts are not self-sufficient, but rely on the appeal of the region in which they are located.

The research is based on a review of secondary data and on a series of semi-structured personal interviews with the general managers of each of the Whitsunday island resorts, with the chairman of the regional tourism bureau and with representatives of the Queensland Government and the State tourism authorities.

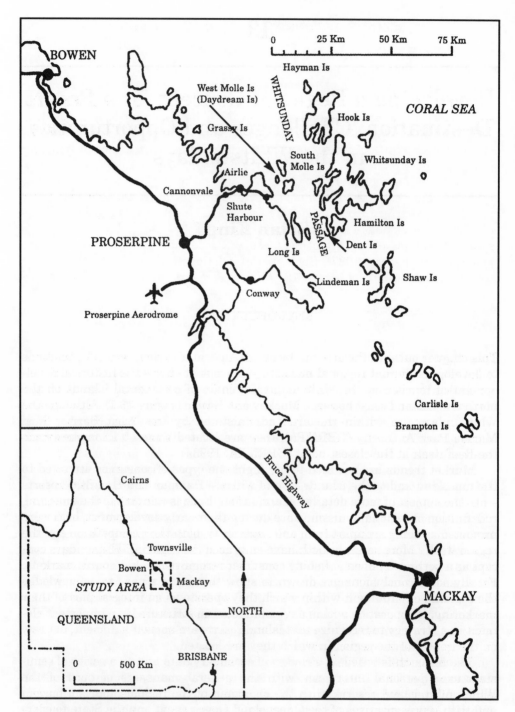

Figure 13.1: The Whitsunday Islands

REGIONAL TOURISM: LITERATURE REVIEW

Regional tourism is an eclectic field of research and a loosely defined one (Piperoglou, 1967). Whilst a tourism region may be defined by a national plan, in other cases the initiative may come from the region (Pearce, 1989). Some general theories of regional planning have taken some account of tourism (Hall, 1970) and Heeley applied these and related planning theories to tourism specifically (1981). White (1981) examined the role played by tourism in 'structure plans' in the UK and the work undertaken by Innskeep (1993) for the World Tourism Organization has made a useful contribution in exploring the relations between tourism plans at regional and at national level, though most of his examples are drawn from developing countries. Pearce (1988) applied concepts of tourism development within the context of various European regions with the spatial functions of regions being a central issue addressed by many tourism geographers (Pearce, 1987). Such spatial relations have included the issue of core-periphery relations (Seers, 1979) and Pearce has discussed the emergence of a structural hierarchy within regions, typically with a major centre featuring higher level facilities and acting as a gateway (1987). Such a hierarchy is clearly evident in the Whitsundays with the airports of Mackay and Whitsunday (previously Proserpine) acting as mainland gateways and Hamilton Island performing the same function for the islands.

Tourism within the Whitsundays has been subjected to little academic analysis, though more general consumer studies on Queensland (Brian Sweeney and Associates, 1991) have provided insights into consumer perceptions of individual resorts and of the regions. Barr (1990) examined the historical development of tourism and emphasized the increasing dependence on externally generated capital. Hundloe *et al.* (1989), undertook a comprehensive study of tourism in the Great Barrier Reef region. The study paid particular attention to the documentation of visitor flows and activities and to their interactions with the environment. It also provided some insights into individual resorts and to the emergence of the Whitsundays as the major centre for water-based tourism in Queensland. Craik's *Resorting to Tourism* (1991), incorporates a useful critical analysis of tourism development in Queensland with a major component focusing on development in the islands. Her critique expressed dissatisfaction at what she claimed has been insufficient recognition of the social and cultural dimensions of tourism in Queensland. She called for greater account to be taken for the types of development goals and priorities identified by locals and for a more inclusive concept of regional tourism in Queensland.

The literature on tourist resorts has approached the subject from various angles (King, 1993). These include resort development (Dean and Judd, 1985; Stiles and See-Tho, 1991), planning, (Smith, 1992), the assessment of local attitudes (Witter, 1985), marketing (King and Whitelaw, 1992), the resort life cycle (Butler, 1980), resorts as communities (Stettner, 1993), architecture (England ,1980) and landscaping (Ayala, 1991). Budowski (1976) developed a typology to classify three alternative relationships between resorts and the environment – conflict, co-existence or symbiosis. Some of this literature has depicted resorts as 'enclave' developments, separated from the reality of daily life in adjacent areas or regions (Freitag, 1994). This is relevant to this examination of the links between resorts and emerging tourism regions.

Social scientists have shown an interest in resorts. Krippendorf (1987), for example describes resorts as therapy zones for the masses. He refers to self-sufficient holiday complexes, designed and run on the basis of careful motivation studies as enclaves for holiday-makers. Total experience and relaxation. Fenced off and sterilized (pp. 70–71). Resorts are a particular target for his acerbic analysis of contemporary tourism. He does not regard typical resorts as complementing the regions in which they are located.

For the purposes of the current research, the definition of an island resort used is as follows:

> A complex of tourism facilities incorporating accommodation, food and beverage and recreational provision located on an island. The destination offers a sufficient range of activities and attractions to lend itself to an extended stay.

TOURISM IN THE WHITSUNDAYS

According to Colfelt (1985) the generic term *Whitsundays* has emerged as the popular name for the whole group of islands described as the Cumberland Islands by Captain James Cook. Aborigines of the Gia and Ngaro clans resided in the region prior to Cook's arrival (Tindale, 1974) with 300 estimated to have lived on the islands (Barker, 1992). In the twenty years following initial European settlement in the 1860s virtually the entire indigenous population of the Whitsundays was wiped out, though there are some descendants of the original inhabitants of the region resident in the mainland Whitsundays (Office of the Coordinator General, 1994).

The Whitsunday local government area incorporates the Whitsunday islands as well as the towns of Airlie Beach, Proserpine, Cannonvale and Shute Harbour. The population was recorded as 11,429 in 1991 with 14,830 projected for the year 2000 (Australian Bureau of Statistics, 1992; QDHLG, 1991). The adjoining local government areas of Mackay, Pioneer and Bowen are considered integral to the Whitsunday region for State Government planning purposes, though these are not considered as a part of the Whitsundays tourism region. The population for the four shires is projected to increase from 87,083 in 1991 to 117,629 by the year 2000. Apart from tourism and construction, the main regional industries are commercial fishing and sugar production.

The introductory phase of tourism in the Whitsundays occurred in the 1930s, with the construction of rudimentary visitor accommodation on several of the islands. During the 1950s problems with jetty facilities and with the state of Proserpine Airport caused the Queensland Government Travel Bureau (QGTB) to give preferential publicity to Mackay as the gateway to the Whitsundays. According to Barr (1990:30) *Mackay's dominance was confirmed in 1956 when the QGTB launched a major package holiday promotion of an eight day tour through Mackay and the Whitsundays.* Barr quoted the QGTB as writing that 'Mackay is the take-off point for the islands of the Barrier Reef on which there is a suitable standard of accommodation for overseas visitors' (Barr, 1990: 30). An upgrading of facilities within Proserpine during the later 1950s did enable it to recover some of its position. The ebb and flow of Mackay and Proserpine as gateways, however, clearly indicates that historical practice has not been over-concerned by strict geographical definitions of the Whitsundays. Practical and political issues seem to have been the major deciding factors. The tide is, how-ever, unlikely to shift back to Mackay Airport again. Proserpine Airport is now more commonly named Whitsunday Airport, indicating the facility's regional gateway status.

In common with other remote resort regions in Australia, the Whitsundays have experienced a variety of growing pains linked to the development of tourism in the country as a whole. Access to the region was interrupted for an extended period during the so-called pilots' dispute of late 1989 and early 1990. The impact of the dispute was exacerbated because it occurred at the end of a decade characterized by development excesses when resorts had expanded at a rapid rate on the coast and islands of Queensland, especially at the four and five star level.

Today, there are nine Whitsunday island resorts (Table 13.1), catering for a variety of markets, including the exclusive (e.g. Hayman Island), the 'middle' market (e.g. Daydream Island) and the 'budget' market (Hook Island). Daydream is located three kilometres from Shute Harbour and has been twice demolished, once for redevelopment in 1952 and then by Cyclone Ada in 1970. Adjacent South Molle Island resort was, until recently, owned by Ansett Airlines, but in 1994 the lease was taken over by the hotel management company, the Jewel Group. Of the remaining islands, Hamilton Island claims to be the largest resort in the South Pacific. It has a large marina, but is not dependent on boats because of the airport located on the island. In 1985, Hayman was closed, demol-ished and rebuilt *as the premier international resort in Australia.* What is now the Club Crocodile resort on Long Island was established as Happy Bay Resort and began operation in 1934 and nearby Palm Bay was also established in the 1980s.

Resort	Room Capacity
Brampton	108
Club Med	200
Daydream	305
Hamilton	667
Hayman	225
Hook	12
Palm Bay	14
Radisson	140
South Molle	202
TOTAL	1,873

Source: Accommodation Australia. Melbourne. RACV.

Table 13.1 Resort Room Capacity in the Whitsundays

Four of the Whitsunday islands have attracted investment in excess of 100 million dollars (Hamilton, Daydream, Hayman and Lindeman Islands) and epitomize the development excesses of the 1980s. Nevertheless, the location of the Whitsunday Group within the Great Barrier Reef Marine Park and the designation of most of the islands as national parks, has acted as a constraining influence and has ensured that developments have been spatially confined, despite the common perception that Hamilton Island Resort is intrusive (King, 1995).

All of the resorts are located within the Central Zone of the Great Barrier Reef Marine Park and all are classed as Marine National Park 'A' Category (a small part of Hook Island is 'B' Category) which aims to achieve *protection of the resources of the park while allowing recreational activities and approved research* (Green and Lal, 1991: 23). The juxtaposition of National and Marine parks, with resort development has, unsurprisingly prompted some conflict between developers and conservation interests. However, Hundloe, Neumann and Halliburton (1989), who examined the evolution of tourism to the Great Barrier Reef, regard the watershed for management of the region as the formation of the GBRMPA in 1975, which allowed the resolution of disputes over the extent of Commonwealth versus State jurisdiction. All of the development has taken place without the involvement of the indigenous population and this absence of an Aboriginal presence or even representation, may have acted as a barrier to the emergence of a genuine concept of regional tourism based on historical continuity.

Because of the relative remoteness of the islands, visitation to the Whitsundays lags far behind that of the Gold and Sunshine Coasts, both of which are a close driving distance from Brisbane. The Cairns region offers more direct competition, because of its tropical climate, rapidly growing international airport, easy accessibility to the Great Barrier Reef islands and highly developed mainland tourism infrastructure and superstructure. Competition from Cairns may have prompted the individual Whitsunday operators to take the more co-operative approach to marketing evident over the past three or four years. Faced with the larger accommodation and airline capacity of Cairns, individual Whitsunday operators appear to have accepted that a combined regional strategy is needed to allow individual Whitsunday operators to take market share from their competitors in Cairns. This issue of an emerging regional identity in the face of growing competition from other destinations is a key issue in this chapter.

Tourism Supply and Demand Factors

According to Claringbould, Deakin and Foster (1984), arrivals in the Whitsunday region grew from 28,000 in 1962, to 69,000 in 1969 and finally 182,000 in 1979. Visitor arrivals grew strongly by 41 per cent and visitor nights by 59 per cent between 1989–90 and 1992–93 (Table 2). International visitation also grew, though at a slower rate. The average length of stay was 5.1 nights and average visitor expenditure was $186.78, higher than for any other Queensland region and reflecting the higher cost of accommodation and related services in the islands. Average daily expenditure by international visitors was about $270. Seventy-five per cent of visitors arrived by air and 21 per cent by private vehicle (and then launch). Figures for the June quarter of 1993 (Australian Bureau of Statistics, 1993) indicated that the Whitsunday Shire offered a total of 2,417 rooms in the category *licensed hotels, motels etc. with facilities*, with two thirds of this total located on the islands.

	1989/90	**1990/91**	**1991/92**	**1992/93**
Visitors	103,700	115,300	134,100	146,700
Visitor Nights	467,000	579,900	672,600	740,900

Source: Queensland Visitor Survey

Table 13.2: Visitor Numbers and Nights in the Whitsunday Islands (Mackay Area 69)

Table 13.3 points to an improving performance by the Whitsunday islands relative to the Whitsunday mainland. The reason for this may be partly explained by the Product Development Manager of Sunlover Holidays who stated that *there's not enough product in the mainland* (S.Brewster pers. comm.). By this he meant that many of the mainland operators did not offer *product* which could be included within air-inclusive tour packages for reasons of either structure or quality. It is noteworthy that the islands attract half of the total Whitsundays interstate total, but just over one third of all domestic visitors including Queenslanders. These figures point to the relatively higher island dependence on the interstate air-inclusive market, the higher mainland dependence on Queenslanders travelling by car and to the different tourism roles played by the mainland and island areas. The reliance on different market bases is probably a strength for the region. The mainland, for example, showed greater resilience during the pilots' dispute, because of its greater accessibility to car-based travellers.

Visitor Origin	Visitor Destination			Year		SHARE %
		1989/90	1990/91	1991/92	1992	1991/92
Total	Mainland	238.9	182.5	182.1	187.8	48.1%
Visitors	Islands	103.6	115.3	134.1	134.9	35.5%
	Marine	34.0	44.0	62.0	n/a	16.4%

Source: Queensland Visitor Survey (QTTC)

Table 13.3: Number of Visitors (X 1000) using Commercial Accommodation

In 1992, the mainland Whitsundays accounted for marginally more visitor nights than the islands (725,000 versus 670,000). Ninety-six per cent of all visitors using commercial accommodation in the Whitsunday islands for the year 1991–92 were on holiday.

The two regional airports are at Hamilton Island and Proserpine (Whitsunday Airport) with Mackay Airport located just outside the region to the South. One of Australia's two major airlines, Ansett Australia has sole access to Hamilton and dominates flight capacity into the Whitsundays region as a whole. The Ansett strategy spanned both the mainland and the islands (Reg Ansett made major improvements to Hayman Island in the 1940s, but also developed Proserpine Airport and accommodation at Airlie Beach). The airline is currently owner of Whitsunday Connections which provides inter-island launch services and sightseeing trips to the Barrier Reef and to other sites of interest. Ansett executives have consistently argued that the risk taking and investment in Whitsunday tourism development by the airline in the post-war period justifies its monopoly of Hamilton Island Airport. Without mentioning the airline by name, current Ansett Managing Director Graeme MacMahon referred to *other airlines which simply piggy-back risk taken by others* (*Travel Reporter*, 1992: 10).

Australia's other major airline, Qantas does have rights to operate from Whitsunday Airport, along with Ansett, though the latter are joint leaseholders of the airport with the Aqua del Rey corporation and the airport handles substantially fewer arrivals than Hamilton Island. By 1991–92, Hamilton Island Airport dominated air arrivals into the region with 224,500 passengers with Whitsunday receiving less than a quarter of that figure with 50,300. This contrasted with the figures for a decade earlier (1981–82) prior to the construction of Hamilton Island Airport when the (then) Proserpine Airport accounted for 126,800 arrivals.

In addition to the attractions of its island resorts, the Whitsundays are a centre for marine recreational activities. Hundloe *et al.* (1989) claim that the Whitsundays account for 37 per cent of all boat passengers in the Barrier Reef area and for 36.5 per cent of the total Barrier Reef fleet (the ports of Whitsunday, Mackay, Bowen and Mackay are included in this total). According to the authors *only the Whitsunday area offers the tourist as large a number and variety of sailing trips* (1989: 40). Scheduled day trips account for 60 per cent of all passenger movements. The prominence of marine activity is an opportunity for regional integration, with the coast and the islands being integral to sailing and other boating activities. Despite other obvious contrasts between mainland and island activities, the boating relationship creates obvious synergies.

Because of the fairly long distance separating most resorts from the Great Barrier Reef, the introduction of the first fast and large catamaran in 1980 was particularly significant in extending the range of tourism options within the island group. This has helped overcome a common consumer perception that the resorts are inaccessible, particularly in poor weather conditions (King, 1995). Boating technology has also prompted a fusion of islands and reef into a regional concept by making the Great Barrier Reef more easily accessible. This fusion is very evident in the Whitsunday Visitors Bureau (WVB) logo which depicts images of both elements.

The Administrative Dimension – the Organization of Regional Tourism

The Whitsundays form one of Queensland's sixteen tourism regions, coordinated by the Regional Tourism Department of the Queensland Tourist and Travel Corporation (QTTC). The sixteen RTA's received grant funds of $1.710 million during 1992–93, supplemented by funds for participating in co-operative advertising activities.

- The QTTC Corporate Plan (QTTC 1993), set out key regional strategies including:
  1) Improved regional business plans;
  2) The development of a *zonal marketing concept* across the State;
  3) To create co-operative marketing initiatives; and
  4) To improve industry quality and professionalism, product development and marketing.

Since its establishment in 1979, the QTTC has been the most *entrepreneurial* of the various Australian State and Territory Tourism Commissions through its active involvement in major tourism development projects, its development of the Sunlover package holiday brand and its computer reservations and information initiative, ATLAS.

The QTTC funds a brochure covering each region in the State including the most developed to the least developed, using a standard presentation. The QTTC determines its financial support for regional tourism organizations through an efficiency measurement mechanism. Individual operators work through the regional tourism associations to secure QTTC funding for co-operative promotions.

In practice more developed tourism regions attract greater QTTC funds because the large operators represented in such places are able to raise their own funds and attract dollar-for-dollar funding. Those of the Whitsunday islands which are managed by international hotel companies are major beneficiaries, since they can justify the more costly television advertising. Such advertisements usually begin with an overall Whitsundays promotion followed by a focus on a particular property. Smaller operators can only afford less costly promotional media such as radio and print. The fact that the Whitsundays span a highly developed area (the islands with their large promotional budgets) and an area perceived as lacking in tourism product (the mainland), allows it to use diverse media for its promotions. In contrast to regions such as the Sunshine Coast which are regarded as suffering from a lack of local co-operation (*Travel Reporter* 1993a: 2), the Whitsundays with their improving display of co-operative activity are seen as a sort of advertisement for the QTTC's attempt to strengthen the tourism regions. Whilst there may be some mainland concern that island images dominate the television medium, there is widespread agreement that promotion of the Whitsundays name benefits all operators in the region.

Local tourism administration is organized by the Whitsunday Visitor Bureau, a membership based organization which aims: *to facilitate and co-ordinate the collective interests and efforts of the Bureau's members* (WVB 1993: 2). Called the Whitsunday Tourism Association until 1992, the organization's previous role was confined to destination marketing but has subsequently incorporated the regional development responsibilities of the former Whitsunday Development Bureau. The WVB's activities include encouraging investors and financiers, enhancing infrastructure and increasing community awareness of the importance of tourism as well as marketing related roles such as research dissemination and promoting increasing visitor expenditures. Four WVB Board committees deal with marketing, regional development, membership services and finance and audit issues. The Bureau is funded by QTTC, by the Whitsunday Shire and by members.

The range of responsibilities allocated to the WVB is wide and the ability of the WVB to implement its far-reaching objectives is debatable in view of its limited staffing. The organization's Business Plan (WVB, 1993) acknowledges the increased importance for consumers of product presentation, the natural environment and visitor service. It makes no commitment to tangible environmental initiatives. The Bureau does appear to enjoy the support of the membership and produces regular strategic planning documents. These indicate that Whitsunday residents and operators have an opportunity to debate regional tourism issues through a formal process, albeit one committed to an expansion of tourism activity.

In discussion with the author, the WVB and a number of individual resort island managers all acknowledged that commitment to regional co-operation within the region began only in 1991–92. Most resort general managers perceived benefits in the regional approach for their own property as well as expressing more altruistic ambitions for the region. One outlined the competitive environment in the following terms:

> destination marketing will benefit Daydream more than any other resort. First they (consumers) choose the Whitsundays, then they can choose between Hamilton – high rise –, Hayman – too expensive –, South Molle – too old –, Club Med – don't know what it is . . . and it is more expensive – and Laguna Quays – golf resort – We fit best.

Convincing managers that self–interest and collective interest can co-exist is probably the best recipe for effective regional marketing.

Balancing Competing Interests – the Islands and the Mainland

The politics of Whitsundays tourism is complicated by the existence of the mainland with its predominantly smaller operations and backpacker style facilities and the islands with their image of exclusivity and the prevalence of international hotel brands. Almost all of the residential population is on the mainland

and makes up the electorates of the councils of Pioneer and Whitsundays which are in turn members of the WVB. According to one state government tourism official, councils seek to influence regional tourism development throughout Queensland, often arguing that their case has the backing of thousands of electors. He indicated that the Whitsundays is no exception. The strength of the mainland is its electoral and administrative base, whilst the island resorts are notable for their large marketing budgets.

The range of current and projected developments is indicative of the increasing tourism significance of the mainland (Table 13.4). With the exception of the (currently stalled) project for Dent Island associated with Hamilton Island, there are no significant island resort developments underway or projected. In contrast, major development is proposed for the mainland. Laguna Quays Resort, developed by Japanese owned Aqua del Rey on an 1850 hectare parcel of land on the coast of Repulse Bay south of Proserpine, involves a fifteen year grand plan of staged building programme. Laguna Quays was granted Integrated Tourism Resort status by the Queensland Government in September 1992 and consists of a:

- 5-star 'boutique' style hotel;
- 109 condominiums and villas;
- an 18 hole golf course;
- a 15 hectare enclosed filtered lagoon; and
- a marina.

The property went into receivership in July 1995. Acqua del Rey together with Ansett, have commenced work on the upgrading of Whitsunday Airport and its terminal with a view to accepting increased domestic traffic and international flights in late 1995 (*The Travel Reporter,* 1992). A $1 billion resort development is proposed for Woodwark Bay, near Airlie Beach. Work has also re-commenced on the construction of the previously aborted Qintex Group's Sailport marina-hotel project at Airlie Beach.

Project Description
Ansett Whitsunday Harbour Project (Shingley Beach, Cannonvale)
Sailport Boathaven Marina (Airlie Beach, developer FAI)
Various redevelopment plans for Shute Harbour
A golf resort associated with Hamilton Island on nearby Dent Island
Further redevelopment of Abel Point Marina, Airlie Beach

Source: Whitsunday National and Marine Parks Draft Management Plan. Oct. 1993

Table 13.4: Whitsunday Projects Currently Proposed

From a commercial and political point of view, the predominance of main-land development is symptomatic of a likely shift in the balance of power with-in the region away from the islands and towards the mainland. The shift in emphasize has posed challenges for Laguna Quays. According to a spokesman for the resort; *The perception of the Whitsundays is of an island destination and that has been perhaps the hardest problem for us to become associated with* (*The Travel Reporter* 1994: 19). In the same way that promotions by Brampton Island Resort have attempted to capitalize on the island's location immediately adja-cent to the Whitsundays, so Laguna Quays has sought to share the positive dimensions of the islands. As already observed, consumers perceive the Whitsunday islands as exclusive and up-market, two labels readily applied to the Laguna Quays complex (King, 1995). In its promotion, Laguna Quays has undertaken joint initiatives with Hamilton and Hayman Islands and has emphasized its outlook over the islands. Less emphasise is placed on its main-land location, perhaps to avoid association with the more down-market elements of the Whitsundays mainland, particularly the backpacker association of Airlie Beach.

Compromise does not necessarily lead to beneficial planning outcomes, but in the case of the Whitsundays, the different interests are harnessed through the Whitsunday Tourism Strategy (still in draft form at the time of writing). According to the Tourism Policy Unit within the Department of Tourism, Sport and Racing (DTSR), co-ordination through the Premier's Office gives the strate-gy greater impetus amongst government departments at the implementation stage. Involvement of industry (through the WVB) and local government (through the Pioneer and Whitsunday Shire Councils) as the main participants in the process along with the State Government encourages a co-operative approach to the resolution of competing sectoral interests.

The image development for the Whitsundays proposed in the Draft Strategy consists of three elements, namely an island/Reef/marine theme for the offshore area; a coastal theme emphasizing the land/sea interface for the Whitsundays coast and a rural theme for the Proserpine hinterland (Office of the Coordinator General 1994: 27). The absence of resort development opportunities in the islands due to environmental constraints, may shift the regional balance towards the coast and reduce any residual bi-polarization.

The incorporation of the mainland and the islands within a regional approach can assist the islands to develop a stronger sense of place. Currently they draw heavily on the proximity of the Great Barrier Reef and on the classic imagery of the *tropical island paradise*. Greater emphasize on regional concepts, however, can provide the destination *with a stronger sense of integrity and authenticity. The Draft Strategy has encouraged links between resorts and main-land to improve the use of complementary services and shopping opportunities to include local products for the emerging local arts and crafts industry, the facili-tation of multi-resort visits* and the encouragement of links *between resorts and national parks regarding visitor use and support* (1994: 32).

The strategic approach to tourism development can help integrate tourism marketing with physical and local government planning. This is particularly important in the Whitsundays with two local government strategic planning schemes, as well as the large number of national and marine parks included within the Great Barrier Reef World Heritage Area.

Industry Views

A surprisingly high level of agreement about the priorities for tourism in Whitsundays was evident from discussions between the author and industry operators (as listed at the end of the chapter). Most operators expressed the view that the scale of active collaboration between operators within the region had grown significantly after a period of considerable division. The improved commonality of interest was viewed as indicative of a stronger commitment by major operators towards the Whitsundays as the key destination, rather than to the properties themselves. This was seen primarily as a function of the entry into the region by transnational corporations such as Southern Pacific Hotels Corporation, Holiday Inn and Club Med. The changing emphasise of Hamilton and Hayman towards a stronger regional identity and the emergence of mainland properties were also cited as likely agents for change. In the latter category, the establishment of the five-star Laguna Quays was viewed as significant because of its potential as a complement to island-based properties. Such complementarity is expected to increase as further large-scale mainland properties are completed.

Minor tensions were evident between the priorities of the mainland and the island operators. It was claimed by the managers of one small island resort, that property rates off-shore are excessive, because the rating structure is seen as skewed in favour of the mainland sugar farmers. It was also claimed that the (typically smaller) mainland properties were not in a position to benefit from the type of co-operative advertising undertaken by the region due to the smaller marketing budgets available to such properties.

Despite such concerns, co-operative endeavours were clearly growing in relative importance. The state tourism authorities indicated that the co-operative marketing campaign offers the option of a variety of cheaper media, more suited to the smaller, less well resourced operators. It was suggested that the stronger presence of island operators on the Board of the WVB than previously, was a sign of commitment. It was also regarded as an indication that the bigger marketing resources of the island resorts could ultimately benefit operators throughout the region. The hosting of periodic Council and WVB meetings on the islands was seen as symbolic of closer integration between the island and mainland interests. There was an acknowledgment by the WVB Chairman (himself a mainland-based operator), that the islands are the primary attraction within the region. At the same time, island resort operators appeared to support the emergence of stronger mainland facilities as a reinforcement of the overall competitiveness of the region.

The discussions indicated that involvement from the largest operators is vital to the health of a regional tourism organization. Once the major players acknowledge the strength of competition from other regions and acknowledge the value of collective action, then the results improve. One interesting dimension is the exclusion of one island resort – Brampton – from the deliberations of the WVB. Whilst geography may play some part in indicating the island's marginality to the Whitsundays group, the actual reason for its exclusion are clearly political. Brampton is operated by Qantas whilst the Whitsundays islands are predominantly served by Ansett through Hamilton Island Airport.

Entrepreneurs and their Visions

Two resorts have been selected as case studies to provide an insight into the, at times, uneasy relationship between island properties and the Whitsunday region as a whole. Hayman Island Resort and Hamilton Island are resort concepts which were driven by the 'vision' of particular individuals, respectively Sir Peter Abeles of Ansett Transport Industries and Keith Williams. The original objectives of these two resorts was to be better than anything offered elsewhere in Australia. In pursuing this objective (also pursued by other now bankrupt Australian entrepreneurs), the resorts removed themselves from the day-to-day activities of regional tourism. Whilst both properties sought to identify themselves with the Great Barrier reef, both kept at arms' length from co-operative initiatives under the regional banner. The ultimate failure of this approach and acceptance by the management of the two resorts – albeit at a later date – that they can benefit from a regional identification – may provide some lessons for 'exclusive' properties in other parts of the world.

Hayman Island Resort was first built in 1927 and was purchased in 1947 by Sir Reg Ansett, founder of Ansett Airlines who renamed the property Royal Hayman Resort. In the mid 1980s the owners of Ansett, TNT-News Corp, spent in excess of $200 million to transform the property into an international five star resort, with the objective of being one of the top five in the world. Ansett have not revealed the exact investment though estimates have ranged from $200 million to as high as $350 million (Rennie, 1994). Sir Peter Abeles' vision was to create a European style concept in Australia. In contrast to Hayman's efforts to attract a predominantly international clientele, Hamilton set out to satisfy the Australian market. As Williams has stated *we wanted to have them holiday in their own country* (quoted in Hyde and King 1989: 207).

In a sense, both Hayman and Hamilton are monuments to the development excesses of the 1980s. In 1988, it was reported that Hayman island was losing in excess of $20 million per year (Sandilands, 1991). The resort can never offer a return on the original investment to its owner and developer Ansett Transport Industries. If one relates the redevelopment cost of $250 million to the 225 rooms, the development cost works out at $1.1 million per room. Other estimates have ranged to as high as $1.3 million. This is far in excess of any other major hotel or resort development in Australia. Asked if Hayman really needed to charge $1,000 a night per room to break even on the basis of a $1 million investment per room, then Ansett Executive Director Alan Notley responded that *this is typical of the shallowness of so-called analysts who work on the rule of thumb* *that for every $100,000 a room costs to build, you have to charge $100 a night. It doesn't work that way* (quoted in Sandilands, 1991: 103). Nevertheless the doubts remain. An analysis of Hayman estimated occupancy rates in 1991 of 45–48 per cent including non-revenue guests, a figure much higher than the travel industry generally accepts – and this is roughly a cash break-even situation where the takings pay for the daily running costs but not the servicing of the debt. If that is true the real losses on the resort would be running at between $30 million and $40 million per annum (Sandilands, 1991: 103).

In 1991, the resort opened up to travel retailers for the first time, offering 50 per cent discount to bona fide travel agents (*Inside Tourism*, 1991). This remedial policy points to the abandonment of the initial view that clients would pay rates substantially higher than at any equivalent destination and that the resort would avoid the need to pay commissions, overrides and substantial tour operator margins. Hayman now advertises through wholesalers and engages in deep discounting, just as its competitors have done. The failure of its earlier strategy calls into question the research and policy capability of a major Australian tourism operator. Whilst Hayman's rates are the highest in the Whitsundays, the price differential has become increasingly smaller.

Despite the profligacy of Hayman, a positive outcome of the Abeles' vision was Ansett's consolidation of its dominant position in the Whitsunday islands. The leasing of the $16 million South Molle Island at the middle range of the market ensured that Ansett's Whitsunday focus was not too narrow. By concentrating its resort leases in the Whitsunday area, Ansett is better able to tie its fortunes to a particular region. When rival Qantas promotes its Queensland island resorts, it is promoting the Queensland islands as a whole, including properties owned or leased by Ansett. In Ansett's case, its Whitsunday promotions can emphasize that the Whitsunday islands *are* Ansett.

Hamilton Island offers almost three times the number of rooms found in any of the other resorts. It is the only resort island in Australia with its own jet airport and was Australia's first resort, designated as fully integrated when it was initially developed in 1984 (Millar, 1992). This involved the private development of large scale infrastructure and the provision of local services normally provided by local government. Controversy dogged Hamilton Island from the start. The subsequent resort owner and developer Keith Williams had acquired the 750 hectare island as a grazing lease (Williams, 1988). However, the lease expressly forbade the development of tourism, raising questions as to how Williams managed to secure development rights for much of the island (Dickinson, 1982: 39). Questions were also raised about the small lease payments and the secrecy with which Cabinet had changed the conditions of the lease. Questions were also raised about the preparation of an Environmental Impact Statement (EIS) requested by Proserpine Shire Council and received in May 1981. The strident rhetoric of Williams' dealings with both government and environmental issues contrasts with the more diplomatic tone which prevails in the 1990s in the Whitsundays.

The Williams philosophy was very different to the types of values espoused in the Current Draft Whitsundays Tourism Strategy. Whilst the Strategy espouses effective environmental protection, Williams bitterly opposed the inclusion of Hamilton Island in the Great Barrier Reef Marine Park (Marshman, 1992). He also opposed the involvement of international hotel management in the operation of resorts. International chains became increasingly keen to gain a foothold in the Whitsundays. Holiday Inn's acquisition of the management rights to Hamilton Island subsequent to the placing of Williams' venture in receivership, has been described as *almost deferential* with a *performance based contract emphasizing the shift towards strict performance criteria and increased owners' involvement.* (Colliers Jardine, 1994: 3). Payment by Holiday Inn is now linked directly to the owners' overall financial return.

In practice international chains are now prominent in the Whitsundays though overseas-based corporations cannot own Whitsunday islands outright. The presence of international hotel management companies was welcomed by all of the resort managers interviewed for the present research. Williams' insistence that Qantas not be granted operating rights at Hamilton Island Airport, put him at odds with the WVB and with most of the other resort managers (apart from those directly associated with Ansett of course). Finally Williams withdrew from the WVB because of Council's opposition to the expansion of Hamilton Island resort and airport because it might damage Proserpine. He also argued that Hamilton was the hub of the Whitsundays and consequently did not need the WVB. In practice the relationship between Hamilton and the Bureau became increasingly cordial as Williams' influence waned. The softening of the Hamilton Island stance towards the WVB was important because of the huge capacity of the property.

The incoming Holiday Inn management were highly critical of the management systems put in place prior to their arrival (Dowling, 1994). On the other hand Williams' development of a rapid and efficient transport enabled him to *reduce building costs on the island to approximately 30 per cent above comparable mainland prices. 100 per cent had been the previous norm* (Williams,1988: 198). This type of investment helped bring about a change in perceptions about how business could operate on islands. The construction of the airport was also visionary in that it was an astute investment (it cost approximately $18 million). Though environmental concerns persist about the way in which the airport was developed, Williams' vision has undoubtedly enabled the Whitsunday islands to compete with otherwise more easily accessible mainland destinations such as Cairns.

Daydream is another major Whitsunday resort which did not provide its developers or investors with a return on their investments. In December 1994 its owner, the Jennings Group, launched a formal campaign to sell the resort. According to Smith (1994) the selling price will be approximately $30 million. *The island was the subject of a $100 million rebuilding programme in the late 1980s* (1994: 1). Smith has estimated that if the resort is sold for $30 million and on the current profit estimate of $2 million a year, the yield on the resort will be 6.5 per cent well below the 10 per cent yield that institutional investors expect from their investments. In view of the major losses sustained by developers in the 1980s, it is perhaps not surprising that little resort development is currently underway or proposed for the islands.

Environmental and Cultural Factors

The respective environmental roles of the Commonwealth and State governments have been the subject of heated debate during the 1980s and 1990s. The Bjelke-Peterson led Queensland Nationalist government sought to exempt Queensland from what it portrayed as excessive bureaucratic interference by Canberra. State intervention in tourism and other development projects was ironically a hallmark of the Bjelke-Peterson's years and the Premier's enthusiasm for Keith Williams' Hamilton Island development was typical of this.

The GBRMPA was established through the *Great Barrier Reef Marine Park Authority Act 1975* (Cwlth). An important strategic objective of GBRMPA as outlined in its 25 year strategy was the enhancement of Aboriginal involvement in park management (GBRMPA, 1993b). This involvement could have significant repercussions on the Whitsundays. A report by Bergin (1993) which proposed an increase in Aboriginal participation regarded the lack of Aboriginal involvement as a management deficiency, particularly relative to the World Heritage listed Kakadu and Uluru National Parks where Aboriginal involvement includes management, operational and interpretative roles.

Though Aborigines and more particularly, Torres Strait Islanders, played a part in Whitsunday tourism in the interwar years acting as entertainers and musicians, they have been nowhere to be seen in recent imagery or activities of the island resorts. Some resurgence may be occurring. Bergin (1993) had pointed to the likelihood that native title claims would arise. One was lodged by a group of 172 direct descendants of the Dagaman people covering land between Bowen and Proserpine including the Whitsunday islands (*The Sunday Age*, 1994: 2). The absence of a permanent Aboriginal population in the Whitsunday islands, means that any indigenous involvement in Park management is likely to be low key and the type of community liaison proposed by Bergin as appropriate for areas with permanent populations is less likely in the Whitsundays. Nevertheless, there is undoubtedly a prospect of increased Aboriginal involvement as park rangers, as participants in research projects to identify significant sites and in overall park management. Bergin (1993) points out that the Boards of Management in Kakadu and in Uluru are empowered to approve or disapprove the relevant management plan and have a majority of Aboriginals. Given that Club Med relies on National Parks and Wildlife Service rangers to show resort guests around Lindeman Island, it is likely that visitors will come into contact with Aborigines occupying such roles in future.

The physical environment has always played an important part in Whitsundays tourism, but has further potential as an aspect of regional integration. A number of issues referred to in the Queensland Government's Draft Ecotourism Strategy are of relevance to the Whitsundays (DTSR, 1994). The Great Barrier Reef and the Central Mackay Coast were identified as bio-geographic regions offering outstanding potential. The strategy proposes a *combination of physical, biological, social and managerial conditions that give value to a place* as being the foundation of ecotourism potential (DTSR, 1994: 16).

The Draft Strategy classes a number of activities as ecotourism, including some readily applied to the Whitsundays. These include:

- A boat trip to the Great Barrier Reef which presents and interprets marine and reef ecosystems;
- A forest walk with an Aboriginal guide explaining the Aboriginal culture of the local area, traditional food and medicine, resources, native plants and animals;
- Bird watching in a natural environment;
- Participating in studies with scientific or environmental research groups;
- A guided bushwalk through a local area of remnant forest; and
- Staying at accommodation designed to integrate and educate visitors in the natural environment and minimize impacts through sewerage, waste disposal, power generation use, landscaping, design and appropriate hardening of tracks (1994: 12).

If the island resorts respond positively to the initiative, it may lessen the barriers between the *enclave* resorts and the more integrated mainland properties and attractions. The Draft Strategy also considers the involvement of local people in tourism as an integral part of ecotourism and states that *The relationship of indigenous people with many of Queensland's protected areas and other natural resource areas should be incorporated into planning and management of natural resource* (1994: 19).

In contrast to the anti-environmental and government planning rhetoric of the earlier National Party Government, the Whitsundays have recently been the subject of a plethora of planning and environmental studies, many of them instigated by the State Government. The Draft Whitsunday Tourism Strategy, the Draft Management Plan for the Whitsunday National and Marine Parks and the Draft Queensland Ecotourism Strategy are symptomatic of a convergence of marketing, environment and planning into a coherent whole. In light of the diversity of the Whitsundays with its contrasting islands, coastline and hinterland, some formal mechanism was clearly required to draw together the various relevant parties. One can readily appreciate the likelihood that internecine quarrels would emerge over a contentious issue such as tourism where different organizations driven by very different philosophies (e.g. environmental, entrepreneurial, bureaucratic) and representing contrasting constituencies came into contact with one another.

A number of the relevant tourism plans and strategies are still in draft form at the time of writing and changes may be made to the proposals of these documents following the consultation processes entailed for each document. Implementation of the various proposals will face a number of hurdles. The diversity of the region is an advantage in marketing terms, but what if accommodation and other facilities fail to deliver the type of service standards expected by visitors? The Whitsundays area as a whole could be sullied by substandard product. Will a Whitsunday tourism style emerge? The *Draft Whitsunday Tourism Strategy* (Office of the Coordinator General, 1994) expressed a desire for the application of regional design criteria to new resort and building development. It is of course difficult to persuade private developers to build in a certain way if they are not coerced or encouraged with hard-to-justify taxpayer subsidies. The question remains as to whether a distinctive Whitsunday style will prove to be more than rhetoric. Even allowing for such difficulties, the strategic and management planning approach will allow problem areas to be addressed in a systematic fashion. The Whitsundays are well placed to take advantage of prospective tourism growth with the necessary structures in place to resolve potential disputes along the way.

CONCLUSION

The Whitsundays example indicates that whilst significant differences between sub-regions (in this case the mainland and the islands) can undermine the unity of a destination, that the diversity can be a source of strength. The use of a collective image based on reef, islands and coast demonstrates how various elements can be brought together in a cohesive and effective way. The example of Brampton Island indicates that political factors are often as potent as marketing ones in determining which tourism products should or should not be included within a region. Whilst major corporations may be able to exert excessive influence within a region, the presence of several significant companies can certainly benefit the overall collective effort.

Island resorts need to look outwards to the region in which they are located, even if only to exploit the resource for the *benefit* of their guests. In contrasting inward versus outward looking resorts, we should consider how the resort owners and operators interpret the value of the surrounding environment. The author agrees with Ayala (1991a), that resorts will ultimately make the best contribution to the locality and the region in which they are located, by actively investing in local institutions and in socio-cultural and environmental concepts, such as marine reserves and heritage trails. This will provide local populations with a sense (real or manufactured) of ownership and will enable the resort to move beyond a pure consumer fantasy product, to one which can offer visitors a sense of context. The Whitsundays provide an example of how island resorts elsewhere can benefit from an *inclusive* approach to both environment and region.

Individual operators in the region have shown themselves willing to invest in facilities such as coral viewing platforms on public land or water, along with the public sector, thereby providing a stable institutional framework, taking responsibility for overall land and sea management and for regulatory activity. Ayala's suggestion (1991b) that resorts *adopt* an adjoining natural attraction and then contribute to its maintenance is a sound one, though one which individual operators will be unlikely to undertake without cooperation amongst competitors and the provision of outside funding.

Resorts have often been depicted as the epitome of the meaningless experience (Krippendorf, 1987). In attempting to assess the best prospects for destination regions, it has been shown that island resorts can play a constructive and central role. The view that island resorts represent no more than a stereotyped blend of sun, sea and sand is outdated. Sensitively managed resorts can complement the landscape. They also offer their guests the prospect of a shared community experience alongside elements of secluded tranquillity. The emergence of the Whitsundays as a coherent tourism region has entailed co-operation between island resorts and mainland operators, as well as government and community. The obvious differences between the mainland and island have been overcome to create a viable tourism destination region. The entrepreneurship and individualism characteristic of the 1980s has been replaced by a more cooperative approach which recognizes the importance of environmental, cultural, marketing and institutional integration. Aspects of the Whitsundays experience may serve as a model for other regions of Australia facing the challenge of contrasting sub-regions.

It has been shown that the Whitsundays have advanced significantly towards an integrated regional tourism concept with tourism acknowledged as the key economic activity in the islands. The region is clearly defined with the exception of Brampton Island. All of the Whitsunday resorts appear committed to the regional concept, even those which have had little involvement in the WVB. The Whitsundays enjoys a solid and strengthening regional structure backed strongly by resources from the QTTC. WVB marketing has been successful to date, providing it with the impetus to extend its involvement in tourism from promotional activities into product development and quality assurance. The incorporation of the mainland *and* the islands within the region was previously a source of conflict. Whilst competing interests are still in evidence, the complementarity of the well developed island resorts and the smaller mainland properties has emerged as a key strength. At last enjoying high occupancies, the Whitsunday Islands with their constrained capacity can emphasize their *exclusivity* as the bulk of regional expansion takes place on the mainland. The mainland connection is also a potential strength as the islands attempt to develop closer economic and theme-based linkages with their hinterland.

The minimal contact with mainland residents and particularly with indigenous population that once inhabited the region is a limitation. The environmental context provided by the resorts has focused exclusively on the physical realm. Closer linkages with the mainland offer the prospect of stronger social and political integration. Aborigines could be employed as park rangers and guides, in both the interpretation of sites of Aboriginal significance and in overall environmental management. Local arts and crafts from the Whitsunday mainland could be given greater prominence. Building this social and cultural dimension will strengthen the region. Ratification of the Draft Whitsundays Tourism Strategy which offers strong Government backing should accelerate the pace of change. Not all resorts need to pursue an ideal of *authenticity* based on some interpretation of *tradition*. The absence of current Aboriginal settlement in the Whitsundays deprives any depiction of authenticity based on a contemporary human involvement. Nevertheless, an acknowledgment of Aboriginal involvement in the historical shaping of the region and recognition of contemporary Aboriginal issues in Queensland could add an additional dimension.

The presence of internationally managed larger resort properties has provided the region with substantial bed capacity and with access to management and marketing expertise. Though the larger corporations are skilled at managing *relaxation*, their resorts exhibit an element of institutionalization. Only the two smallest resorts with a collective room capacity of about 26, appear to offer an alternative style. Shifting too far towards an *international* style could threaten the uniqueness of the region unless regional linkages are reinforced. Nonetheless the quality facilities of the largest island resorts are a major asset for the region.

Developers and financiers from outside the Whitsundays lost money on the development of several of the resorts, but the area itself is the beneficiary of their legacy of high quality resort amenities. The initial over-capitalization will only be a problem if the current operators and owners are unable to maintain the facilities at an appropriate level. This is unlikely to happen as long as international hotel management companies are queuing up for the privilege of managing a property in the Whitsunday islands.

The location of the Whitsundays offers the prospect of developing tourism in tandem with sustainable environment concepts. With easy accessibility to a World Heritage listed natural icon, the Great Barrier Reef, large scale resort-based tourism is perpetuated (Craik, 1987). Hopefully the scale of this involvement will continue to benefit the regional tourism concept.

The Whitsunday example offers useful lessons for significant resort operators in other relatively remote regions. A co-operative approach to marketing and an involvement in regional tourism can be good for business. Setting one's property above the region in which it is located is a way of ignoring the key symbolic relationship between destination regions and individual properties.

This chapter has explained the relationship between resorts and tourism regions, and is an issue worthy of further research. There are undoubtedly examples of resorts which have successfully marketed themselves as destinations in their own right. Some such *success* stories would be worthy of examination, though as has been suggested in the present study, the assessment criterion should include political, social and environmental factors as well as business operations considerations.

REFERENCES

Aboriginal & Torres Strait Islander Commission (1994) *Draft National Aboriginal and Torres Strait Islander Tourism Strategy* Canberra, AGPS.

Australian Bureau of Statistics (1992) *Short-Term Overseas Departures by Australian Residents* Canberra, AGPS.

Australian Bureau of Statistics (1993) *Queensland Pocket Year Book* Brisbane, ABS Queensland Office.

Ayala, H. (1991a) Resort Hotel Landscape as an International Megatrend. *Annals of Tourism Research* 18.4 pp. 568–587.

Ayala, H. (1991b) Resort Landscape Systems. A Design Management Solution. *Tourism Management* December pp. 280–290.

Barker, B.C. (1992) *An Assessment of the Cultural Heritage Values on the Mainland Coast of the Whitsunday Region Extending from George Point to Repulse Bay* Published report to Queensland Department of Environment and Heritage.

Barr, T. (1990) *No Swank Here? The Development of the Whitsundays as a Tourist Destination to the Early 1970's* (Studies in North Queensland History, No. 15). Townsville, James Cook University.

Bergin, A. (1993) *Aboriginal and Torres Strait Islander Interests in the Great Barrier Reef Marine Park* Townsville, GBRMPA.

Budowski, G. (1976) Tourism and Conservation: Conflict, Coexistence or Symbiosis? *Environmental Conservation* 3 (1) pp. 27–31.

Butler, R. (1980) The Concept of a Tourist Resort Life Cycle of Evolution: Implication of Management of Resources. *Canadian Geographer*, 34(1), pp. 5–12.

Carruthers, F. & Cant, S. (1994) Commonwealth Hits States on Park Management Deals. *The Weekend Australian* Oct 29–30 p. 12.

Colfelt, D. (1985) *100 Magic Miles of the Great Barrier Reef. The Whitsunday Islands* 2nd Ed. Sydney, David Colfelt and Windward Publications.

Colliers Jardine (1994) *Australian Hotel and Tourism Property Market Report* Melbourne, Colliers Jardine.

Craik, J. (1987) A Crown of Thorns in Paradise: Tourism on Queensland's Great Barrier Reef. In *Who From their Labours Rest? Conflict and Practice in Rural Tourism* eds. Bouquet, M & Winter, M. Avebury. Aldershot. pp. 135–158.

Craik, J. (1991) *Resorting to Tourism. Cultural Policies for Tourist Development in Australia* Sydney, Allen and Unwin.

Dean, J. and Judd, B. (eds) (1985) *Tourism Developments in Australia* Red Hill, Royal Australian Institute of Architects Education Division.

Department of Tourism, Sport and Racing (1994) *Queensland Ecotourism Strategy Discussion Paper* Brisbane, QGPS.

Dickinson, (1982) The Three Billion Boom in Holiday Resorts. *National Times* June 13–19. p. 39.

Dowling, J. (1994) Hamilton Island Looking for New Markets. *Australian Financial Review* 20th April p. 40.

England, R. (1980) Architecture for Tourists. *International Social Science Journal* 32 (1) pp. 44–45.

Fitzgerald, R. (1982) *From the Dreaming to 1915. A History of Queensland* Brisbane, Queensland University Press.

Freitag, T.G. (1994) Enclave Tourism Development. For Whom the Benefits Roll? *Annals of Tourism Research* 21 (3) pp. 538–554.

Great Barrier Reef Marine Park Authority (1993a) *Annual Report 1992–93* Townsville, GBRMPA.

Great Barrier Reef Marine Park Authority and the Queensland Department of Environment and Heritage (1993b) *A 25 Year Strategy Plan for the Great Barrier Reef World Heritage Area* Townsville, GBRMPA.

Green, G. and Lal, P. (1991) *Charging Users of the Great Barrier Reef Marine Park* Townsville, GBRMPA.

Hall, P. (1970) *Theory and Practice of Regional Planning* Pemberton Books, London.

Heeley, J. (1981) Planning for Tourism in Britain *Town Planning Review* 52, pp. 61–79.

Hundloe, T., Neumann, R. and Halliburton, M. (1989) *Great Barrier Reef Tourism* Brisbane, Institute of Applied Environmental Research, Griffith University.

Innskeep, E. (1993) *National and Regional Tourism Planning. Cases and Methodologies* Routledge, London.

Inside Tourism (1991b) Hayman Turns to Agents to Fill Space. 12 Aug. p. 6.

King, B.E.M. (1994) Research on Resorts. A Review. In Cooper, C. and Lockwood, A. (eds.) *Progress in Tourism, Hospitality and Recreation Management* pp. 165–180 Wiley, London.

King, B.E.M. (1994) Australian Attitudes to Island Resorts. A Comparison of Queensland and Fiji. In Seaton, A. *et al.* (eds) *Tourism: the State of the Art* pp. 347–358. London, Wiley & Sons.

King, B.E.M. (1995) *Creating Island Resorts. Tourism in the Whitsundays and the Mamanucas* PhD Thesis, Monash University.

King, B.E.M. and Hyde, G. (1989) Resorts. In *Tourism Marketing in Australia* pp. 197–227. Melbourne, Hospitality Press.

King, B.E.M. and Whitelaw, P. (1992) Resorts in Australian Tourism. A Recipe for Confusion? *Journal of Tourism Studies* Vol. 4, No. 1.

Krippendorf, J. (1987) *The Holidaymakers. Understanding the Impact of Leisure and Travel* trans. V. Andrassy, Oxford, Heinemann.

Marshman, I. (1992) Hamilton Island Show is Not Over Until the Fat Lady Sings – Williams. *Traveltrade* 3rd June p. 10.

Millar, M. (1992) Business as Usual While Hamilton Looks for Buyer. *Travelweek* 27th May p. 12.

Office of the Co-ordinator General (1994) *Draft Whitsundays Tourism Strategy* Brisbane, Government Printer.

Pearce, D.G. (1987) *Tourism Today: a Geographical Analysis* Longman, Harlow and Wiley, New York.

Pearce, D.G. (1988) Tourism and Regional Development in the European Community *Tourism Management* 9(1) pp. 13–22

Pearce, D.G. (1989) *Tourist Development* Longman, Harlow.

Piperoglou, J. (1967) Identification and Definition of Regions in Greek Tourist Planning *Papers, Regional Science Association* pp. 169–176

Queensland Government Department of Housing and Local Government (1991) *Population Projections* Brisbane, Government Printer.

Queensland Tourist and Travel Corporation (1993b) *Corporate Plan* Brisbane, Government Printer.

Rennie, P. (1994) Buying a Slice of Tropical Paradise. *Business Review Weekly* 9 May, p. 72.

Sandilands, B. (1991b) How Hayman Island is Gnawing into TNT. *Bulletin* 6 Aug., pp. 102–103.

Smith, F. (1994) Daydream Sale Tests Interest in Tourism. *The Weekend Australian Property* Dec., 10–11 p. 1.

Smith, R.A. (1992) Beach Resort Evolution. Implications for Planning. *Annals of Tourism Research* Vol. 19 pp. 304–322.

Stettner, A.C. (1993) Commodity or Community? Sustainable Development in Mountain Resorts. *Tourism Recreation Research* Vol. 18 (1). pp. 3–10.

Stiles, R.B. and See–Tho, W. (1991) Integrated Resort Development in the Asia Pacific Region. *Travel and Tourism Analyst* 3, pp. 22–37.

Sunday Age (1994) Native Title Claim on Whitsundays. 4 Sept., p. 2.

Sweeney, B and Associates (1991) *Domestic Tourism Segmentation Study Report on the Islands*. Brisbane, Queensland Tourist and Travel Corporation.

Tindale, N. (1974) *Aboriginal Tribes of Australia*. University of California Press.

Travel Reporter (1992b) Airlines Squabble Over Hamilton Island. 14 Dec., p. 10

Travel Reporter (1993a) Comment: Too much Influence. 18 Aug., p. 2

Travel Reporter (1993b) Government Operates in a 'Policy Vacuum'. 23 July, p. 4

Travel Reporter (1994b) Laguna Quays Changing Trade Perceptions. 19 July, p. 19

White, J. (1981) *A Review of Tourism in Structure Plans* Occasional Paper No. 1, Centre for Urban and regional Studies, University of Birmingham, Birmingham.

Whitsunday Visitors Bureau (1993) *Business Plan 1993 to 1996* Whitsunday, WVB.

Williams, K. (1988) Establishing an International Resort – a Case Study. In Blackwell, J. (ed.) *The Tourism and Hospitality Industry: 1988–89 Edition* pp. 189–200. Chatswood, Australian-International Magazine Services.

Witter, B.S. (1985) Attitudes about a Resort Area: A Comparison of Tourists and Local Retailers. *Journal of Travel Research*, Summer 1985, pp. 14–19.

LIST OF INDIVIDUALS CONSULTED AND/OR INTERVIEWED

*(i) Structured Personal Interviews (where taped, marked **)*

- Brewster, S. Product Development Manager, Sunlover Holidays. 9th February 1994**
- Cogar, S. General Manager, Hamilton Island Resort, 10th November 1993**
- Collins, K. General Manager, South Molle Resort. 6th November 1993**
- Giampaolo, B. Chef de Village, Club Med Lindeman Island. 4th November 1993**
- Gregg, S. General Manager, Marketing, Queensland Tourist and Travel Corporation. 9th February 1994**
- Harrold, N. Marketing Manager, Group Sales Australia, Qantas Airways. March 1992.
- Hutchen, D. Chairman, Whitsunday Visitors and Promotions Bureau and Chief Executive, Fantasea Cruises. 1st November 1993**
- Kelly, N. General Manager, Radisson Long Island Resort 3rd November 1993**
- Klein, T. General Manager, Hayman Island Resort, 5th November 1993**
- Lindsay, R. Marketing Manager, Page McGeary Resorts (including Palm Bay Hideaway)
- Maloney, J. Joint Resident Manager, Palm Bay Hideaway. 2nd November 1993**
- Maloney, C. Joint Resident Manager, Palm Bay Hideaway. 2nd November 1993**
- Mahony, G. General Manager, Brampton Island Resort, 8th November 1993**
- Robertson, G. Manager, Ansett Holidays, March 1992
- Tall, C. Resort Manager, Hook Island Wilderness Lodge, 6th November 1993**
- Vincent, W.L. General Manager, Daydream Island Travelodge Resort, 9th November 1993**
- Wallace, B. Regional Tourism Co–ordinator, Queensland Tourist and Travel Corporation, 9th February 1994**

(ii) Informal Discussions and / or Interviews about the Research were Conducted with the Following Individuals:

- Bennetts, R. General Manager, Coral Sea Resort. 5th November 1993
- Court, G. Manager, Market Research, Planning and Administration, Ansett Australia. September 1994
- Davie, R. Office of the Co-ordinator General, Government of Queensland, 20th November 1994
- Diamond, B. Guest Relations Manager, Hamilton Island Resort, 10th November 1993
- Kelly, N. Guest Relations Manager, Hayman Island Resort, 5th November 1993
- McKinnon, M. Director, Hambleton Ruff Advertizing, September 1993
- Wall, S. Tourism Development Co-ordinator, Tourism Policy Unit, Queensland

INDEX OF AUTHORS CITED

Note Works with several authors are indexed substantively under the first-named, with cross-references from all co-authors (including those covered by *et al* in the text).

SUBJECT INDEX